CONTROVERSIES IN THE COMMON LAW

Tracing the Contributions of Chief Justice Beverley McLachlin

Controversies in the Common Law

Tracing the Contributions of Chief Justice Beverley McLachlin

EDITED BY VANESSA GRUBEN,
GRAHAM MAYEDA, AND OWEN REES

UNIVERSITY OF TORONTO PRESS
Toronto Buffalo London

Toronto Buffalo London
utorontopress.com

ISBN 978-1-4875-4072-2 (cloth)
ISBN 978-1-4875-4074-6 (EPUB)
ISBN 978-1-4875-4073-9 (PDF)

Library and Archives Canada Cataloguing in Publication

Title: Controversies in the common law : tracing the contributions of Chief Justice Beverley McLachlin / Vanessa Gruben, Graham Mayeda, and Owen Rees.
Names: Gruben, Vanessa, editor. | Mayeda, Graham, editor. | Rees, Owen (Senior general counsel), editor.
Description: Includes index.
Identifiers: Canadiana (print) 20220253056 | Canadiana (ebook) 20220253501 | ISBN 9781487540722 (hardcover) | ISBN 9781487540746 (EPUB) | ISBN 9781487540739 (PDF)
Subjects: LCSH: McLachlin, Beverley, 1943– | LCSH: Law – Canada. | LCSH: Common law – Canada.
Classification: LCC KE444 .C66 2022 | LCC KF385.ZA2 C66 2022 kfmod | DDC 349.71 – dc23

We wish to acknowledge the land on which the University of Toronto Press operates. This land is the traditional territory of the Wendat, the Anishnaabeg, the Haudenosaunee, the Métis, and the Mississaugas of the Credit First Nation.

University of Toronto Press acknowledges the financial support of the Government of Canada, the Canada Council for the Arts, and the Ontario Arts Council, an agency of the Government of Ontario, for its publishing activities.

Canada Council for the Arts
Conseil des Arts du Canada

Funded by the Government of Canada
Financé par le gouvernement du Canada

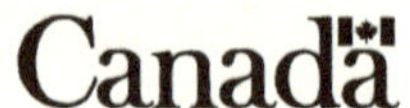

Contents

Part Two: Controversies in Public Law

Acknowledgments

This volume comprises polished versions of texts originally presented at a conference held on 10 and 11 April 2018 at the University of Ottawa to honour the career of Chief Justice Beverley McLachlin, who retired from the Supreme Court of Canada at the end of 2017. The conference was organized by Vanessa Gruben, Vanessa MacDonnell, and Owen Rees. It was supported by an advisory group consisting of His Excellency the Right Honourable David Johnston, Governor General of Canada; Lady Brenda Hale, President of the Supreme Court of the United Kingdom; the Honourable Justice Robert Sharpe, judge of the Court of Appeal for Ontario; Jacques Frémont, President of the University of Ottawa; and Catherine Dauvergne, Dean of the Allard School of Law, University of British Columbia. The editors are grateful to the organizers and to the members of the advisory group for their contributions to the conference.

We also wish to thank the Social Science and Humanities Research Council of Canada for supporting the conference by means of a Connection Grant.

Research assistants Nick Fleming, Raphael Ribeiro, and Sumaya Sherif were invaluable in preparing the chapters for publication. We thank Barbara Tessman for copyediting the volume. Finally, we wish to thank Daniel Quinlan, acquisitions editor at the University of Toronto Press, for guiding us through the publication process.

Vanessa Gruben
Graham Mayeda
Owen Rees
Ottawa, September 2021

CONTROVERSIES IN THE COMMON LAW

Tracing the Contributions of Chief Justice Beverley McLachlin

1 Controversies in the Common Law: Innovative Solutions and Future Challenges at the Supreme Court of Canada

VANESSA GRUBEN, GRAHAM MAYEDA, AND OWEN REES

When Chief Justice Beverley McLachlin retired from the Supreme Court of Canada at the end of 2017, she closed a chapter in her career as one of the most influential Canadian jurists, as well as an important chapter in the history of the Court. During her twenty-eight years on the Court, seventeen of which she spent as its first woman chief justice, Justice McLachlin heard cases of national importance that raised novel issues in every area of the law. She also defended the Court against threats to its legitimacy, such as challenges of judicial activism,[1] insinuations by the Prime Minister about her impartiality,[2] and controversial decisions in areas such as assisted suicide[3] and prostitution.[4] This book

1 In the late 1990s and early part of this century, criticisms of the Supreme Court of Canada for being overly "activist" multiplied. Jeffrey Simpson wrote in response to the SCC's decision in *Sauvé v Canada (Chief Electoral Officer)*, 2002 SCC 68, [2002] 3 SCR 519 [*Sauvé*], which struck down section 51(e) of the *Canada Elections Act*, RSC 1985, c E-2, that denied the vote to prisoners serving a sentence of two years or more: "That decision was one of the most aggressive in asserting judicial supremacy over Parliament. It dismissed parliamentary debates on the issue as having offered 'more fulmination than illumination' ... So much for the vaunted but rather tattered notion of the Supreme Court and Parliament engaged in a 'dialogue.' It's more like diktat from the court" (Jeffe, "The Court of No Resort," *Globe and Mail* (22 November 2002) A25, cited in WJ Waluchow, *A Common Law Theory of Judicial Review: The Living Tree* (Cambridge: Cambridge University Press, 2007) at 6.

2 Sean Fine, "Harper Alleges Supreme Court Chief Justice Broke Key Rule with Phone Call" *Globe and Mail* (1 May 2014), online: <https://www.theglobeandmail.com/news/politics/harper-alleges-supreme-court-chief-justice-broke-key-rule-with-phone-call/article18382971/>; Tonda MacCharles, "Stephen Harper Lashes out at Top Judge on Supreme Court" *Toronto Star* (2 May 2014), online: <https://www.thestar.com/news/canada/2014/05/02/stephen_harper_lashes_out_at_top_judge_on_supreme_court.html>.

3 *Carter v Canada (AG)*, 2015 SCC 5 [*Carter*].

4 *Canada (AG) v Bedford*, 2013 SCC 72 [*Bedford*].

documents some of these challenges, as reflected in its title, *Controversies in the Common Law.*

One of the purposes of this book is to describe specific common law controversies – i.e., key developments in areas of both private and public law in which judges rather than legislators advanced the law. More specifically, each contributor to this volume addresses a legal principle or rule that had been uncertain and whose resolution in decisions in which Beverley McLachlin participated significantly transformed an area of law.

The chapters also explain the role of the common law tradition in Canadian law. It will not be a surprise to read that the controversies each of the contributors addresses in relation to specific areas of law are not fully resolved: there remains a tremendous amount of "unfinished business" at the Supreme Court of Canada. This fact serves to illustrate a key feature of the common law itself – its open-ended and iterative nature. The common law is open-ended because judges are always engaged in revising the law to conform to social circumstances; it is iterative because these circumstances are in constant flux.[5]

But while the Supreme Court's jurisprudence conforms to this traditional iterative and incremental model of the common law, it also challenges it. The chapters reveal that the "common law" is neither easily defined nor confined to its historical boundaries. For instance, contributors challenge the orthodox juxtaposition of common law and statute. They also provide examples of the application of the common law beyond the boundaries of its traditional territory – private law – thus demonstrating that the common law method of reasoning is today applied in areas of public law, including constitutional law, administrative law, and criminal law.

It is important to document the breadth of the common law in terms of both its definition and its boundaries, because lawyers and law teachers still tend to think of it as confined to a particular silo. Ask any first-year law student about the relationship between common law and statutes, and they will give the same answer that Justice Benjamin Cardozo did in his lectures published in the 1940s as *The Nature of the*

5 Waluchow describes the common law method as "bottom-up," by which he means that "judges ... decide the unforeseeable issues of constitutional morality ... in ways that allow for incremental changes and improvements in the moral blueprint" (Waluchow, *supra* note 1 at 235, 261). On the incremental nature of the common law, see *Winnipeg Child and Family Services (Northwest Area) v G (DF)*, [1997] 3 SCR 925 [*Winnipeg*]; see also Cass R Sunstein, *One Case at a Time: Judicial Minimalism and the Supreme Court* (Cambridge, MA: Harvard University Press, 1999).

Judicial Process, where he writes, "The constitution overrides a statute, but a statute, if consistent with the constitution, overrides the law of judges."[6] The chapters in this book demonstrate that the real picture is more complicated. Indeed, Justice Cardozo immediately complicates the picture by asking what the role of the judge is when the meaning of the statute or its relationship to common law rules regarding the same subject are unclear. Cardozo cites the German legal theorist Lorenz Brütt, who described the complex role of the judge in such cases as follows: "One weighty task of the system of the application of law consists . . . in this, to make more profound the discovery of the latent meaning of positive law. Much more important, however, is the second task which the system serves, namely the filling of the gaps which are found in every positive law in greater or less measure."[7] What kinds of gaps need to be filled? How do courts know what to fill them with? A number of the chapters in this book deal explicitly and implicitly with such questions about the interplay of the common law and statutes such as the *Canadian Charter of Rights and Freedoms* or the *Criminal Code*. They question the simplistic dichotomy between common law and statute, and, in so doing, help develop our understanding of what the common law is.

A final theme that emerges from the chapters in this volume is a description of the style of judgment that Chief Justice Beverley McLachlin adopted during her tenure on the Supreme Court of Canada. As we will see, her approach was based on the common law model of incremental change, although with a philosophical penchant for discovering consistent principles in it. Through each contributor's description of the Chief Justice's contributions to the various areas of the law, a picture emerges of a thoughtful judge who sought to identify principles that unified the areas of law in which she initiated or oversaw change and modernization. Rather than stating principles abstractly, she preferred to tease them out of the fabric of the common law itself. No

6 Benjamin N Cardozo, *The Nature of the Judicial Process* (New Haven, CT: Yale University Press, 1949) at 14.

7 Lorenz Brütt, *Die Kunst der Rechtsanwendung. Zugleich ein Beitrag zur Methodenlehre der Geisteswissenschaften* (Berlin: J Guttentag, 1907) at 72, quoted and translated by Cardozo in *The Nature of the Judicial Process, supra* note 6 at 15–16. The original text reads: "Die eine wichtige Aufgabe des Systems für die Rechtsanwendung besteht also darin, die Auffindung des latenten Inhalts des positiven Rechts zu vertiefen. Viel bedeutender ist aber die zweite Aufgabe, der das System dient, nämlich die Ausfüllung der Lücken, welche sich in jedem positiven Rechte in größerem oder geringerem Maße finden."

doubt this approach was in part attributable to the fact that the Chief Justice favoured incremental change rather than cutting out new rules from whole cloth. To be faithful to this incremental view, she sought the principles that were buried within the common law patchwork of cases in areas such as tort law, equity, unjust enrichment, and criminal law and then applied these to new situations. In the area of constitutional law, she also promoted principles, such as the rule of law and judicial independence, that are traditionally considered part of the unwritten common law constitution.[8] This is consistent with her common law approach to the judicial role.

Before turning to an overview of the chapters, it is useful to point out one glaring omission from this book: Chief Justice McLachlin's contribution to Aboriginal law. Throughout her tenure as Chief Justice, she underlined the importance of reconciliation between Indigenous and non-Indigenous peoples in Canada. In a speech in 2013,[9] she marked the Supreme Court of Canada's decision in *R v Van der Peet* as a seminal moment in the recognition of the Court's role in promoting reconciliation.[10] Her reasons in *Haida Nation v British Columbia (Minister of Forests)* established one of the most importance legal tools for facilitating reconciliation: the duty to consult.[11] She further developed this duty in *Rio Tinto Alcan Inc v Carrier Sekani Tribal Council*, and applied it in *Tsilhqot'in Nation v British Columbia*.[12] Despite her undeniable role in establishing the legal framework in this area, many have criticized the Supreme Court's approach to the topic. John Borrows has pointed out the problems inherent in the Court's insistence that, to garner the protection of section 35 of the *Constitution Act, 1982*, the practices of Indigenous communities must have an origin prior to contact with Europeans.[13] He

8 *Trial Lawyers Association of British Columbia v British Columbia (AG)*, 2014 SCC 59 (re rule of law); *Reference re Remuneration of Judges of the Provincial Court of Prince Edward Island*, [1997] 3 SCR 3 (re judicial independence).

9 Beverley McLachlin, "Defining Moments: The Canadian Constitution" (Remarks delivered at the Canadian Club of Ottawa, 5 February 2013), online: <https://www.scc-csc.ca/judges-juges/spe-dis/bm-2013-02-05-eng.aspx>.

10 *R v Van Der Peet*, [1996] 2 SCR 507 [*Van der Peet*].

11 *Haida Nation v British Columbia (Minister of Forests)*, 2004 SCC 73. On the importance of this contribution, see Peter W Hogg, "The Duty to Consult and Accommodate Aboriginal Peoples" in Daniel Jutras & Marcus Moore, eds, *Canada's Chief Justice: Beverley McLachlin's Legacy of Law and Leadership* (Toronto: LexisNexis Canada, 2018).

12 *Rio Tinto Alcan Inc v Carrier Sekani Tribal Council*, 2010 SCC 43; *Tsilqot'in Nation v British Columbia*, 2014 SCC 44.

13 John Borrows, "Challenging Historical Frameworks: Aboriginal Rights, The Trickster, and Originalism" (2017) 98:1 Can Historical Rev 114.

explains that this makes "colonialism ... the 'all or nothing moment for establishing Aboriginal rights.'"[14] Larry Chartrand goes a step further, writing that "reliance on section 35 in the courts is largely illusory, as the claims must be characterized to fit within an excessively narrow colonial construct."[15] Given critiques of the Supreme Court of Canada's approach to section 35, assessing the Chief Justice's legacy in this area requires more in-depth study than is possible in this volume.

I. The Contributions of the Chief Justice and the McLachlin Court to the Resolution of Key Common Law Controversies

Chief Justice McLachlin was instrumental in resolving controversy in a number of areas of private law. In their chapters, Bruce Feldthusen and Erika Chamberlain address McLachlin CJ's contribution to tort law. Feldthusen acknowledges her role in ensuring that tort law protects and advances the interests of women in ground-breaking areas such as sexual violence,[16] the law of consent,[17] and reproductive rights,[18] as well as protecting the interests of children through innovations in the law of vicarious liability for child sexual abuse.[19] He also discusses her contribution to revolutionary changes in the law of negligence – in particular, her interpretation of the role of proximity in the recognition of novel duties of care. Chamberlain also addresses aspects of negligence law, specifically the role of policy in determining the duties of care that individuals and corporations owe to others. This is an area of law that has been revolutionized in Canada by the adoption of the House of Lords' decision of *Anns v Merton LBC*,[20] rendered in 1977, by the Supreme Court of Canada in the 2001 case of *Cooper v Hobart*.[21]

The other principal area of private law that Supreme Court of Canada revolutionized was that of unjust enrichment, an important doctrine of equity that is employed in the law of restitution and trusts (constructive trust), and that has applications in areas such as family law and business. The wheels were set in motion by the decision of Laskin J in

14 *Ibid* at 116, citing *Van der Peet, supra* note 10 at para 247.

15 Larry Chartrand, "Eagle Soaring on the Emergent Winds of Indigenous Legal Authority" (2013) 18:1 Rev of Const Stud 49 at 76.

16 See e.g. *Norberg v Wynrib*, [1992] 2 SCR 226.

17 *Non-Marine Underwriters, Lloyd's of London v Scalera*, 2000 SCC 24.

18 *Winnipeg, supra* note 5; *Dobson (Litigation Guardian of) v Dobson*, [1999] 2 SCR 753.

19 *Bazley v Curry*, [1999] 2 SCR 534.

20 *Anns v Merton LBC*, [1977] UKHL 4, [1978] AC 728 [*Anns*].

21 *Cooper v Hobart*, 2001 SCC 79 [*Cooper*].

Murdoch v Murdoch and of Dickson J in *Pettkus v Becker*, which for the first time suggested that a constructive trust was the appropriate remedy for a woman who had contributed to the wealth of her long-time male partner before the relationship ended.[22] Until that point, a more limited remedy, the resulting trust, was available when one partner exploited the other economically and then left the partnership.[23] The Supreme Court of Canada has been instrumental in developing the law that underlies such a revolution, whose effects have spread to many common law jurisdictions, thereby providing a new tool in the courts' arsenal for remedying unfairness in domestic partnerships. Mitchell McInnes's chapter ably identifies the controversies in this area and the contributions made by the Supreme Court of Canada and Chief Justice McLachlin.

Lady Hale, in her chapter on the contributions of McLachlin CJ, discusses the influence that the Canadian approach to illegality[24] in tort, contract, and restitution claims has had on the law in the United Kingdom.[25] The principle of illegality states broadly that a person does not have a cause of action based on their illegal act. In *Hall v Hebert*, the Supreme Court of Canada dealt with a case in which the plaintiff had suffered serious head injuries when, while drunk, she tried to help her friend "roll start" a stalled car, which went out of control with her in the driver's seat, careened down a steep slope, and turned upside down. Determining whether a person who had engaged in illegal activity such as driving a car when drunk can be compensated for injuries suffered as a result of that activity raises controversial issues of responsibility.[26] Other cases in which the principle has been applied involve key public policy issues such as the protection of vulnerable populations. Thus in the UK case of *Hounga v Allen*, the Supreme Court of the United Kingdom had to decide whether a Nigerian victim of human trafficking, who was working illegally as a domestic in the United Kingdom, could sue in tort for being exploited by her employer, given that the domestic was in the country illegally.[27] It is clear that the Supreme Court of Canada's contribution to this area of law provided tools to deal with a

22 *Murdoch v Murdoch*, [1975] 1 SCR 423 [*Murdoch*]; *Pettkus v Becker*, [1980] 2 SCR 834 [*Pettkus*]. The principle of unjust enrichment provides the juristic basis for finding a constructive trust.

23 *Murdoch*, *supra* note 22, Martland J.

24 Often referred to by the Latin maxim "*ex turpi causa non oritur actio.*"

25 *Hounga v Allen*, [2014] UKSC 47, [2014] 1 WLR 2889 [*Hounga*].

26 *Hall v Hebert*, [1993] 2 SCR 159 [*Hall*].

27 *Hounga*, *supra* note 25.

thorny controversy. Lady Hale also mentions the Chief Justice's articulation of an approach to equitable compensation that,[28] while rejected in Canadian law, has found favour in the United Kingdom.[29]

Lawyers tend to think of the terms "common law" and "private law" as synonymous;[30] but many areas of public law have their roots in the common law, including the two areas addressed in this book: administrative law and criminal law. The roots of administrative law are to be found in the prerogative writs: tools used by common law courts to ensure that government decision makers do not overstep the boundaries of their decision-making authority.[31] What was a rather stagnant area of law based on a sclerotic concept of "jurisdiction" was revolutionized in 1979 by Justice Dickson's decision in *CUPE v NB Liquor Corporation*.[32] Since then, the area has exploded, and developments continue, not least of which is the Court's recent decision in *Canada (Minister of Citizenship and Immigration) v Vavilov*.[33] Adam Goldbenberg's chapter identifies the crux of controversy in this area during Chief Justice McLachlin's tenure: the test, called the "standard of review analysis," for determining how much scrutiny courts ought to give to a government decision. His chapter highlights the controversy at the heart of administrative law generally, which

---

28 *Canson Enterprises Ltd v Boughton & Co*, [1991] 3 SCR 534.

29 *Various claimants v Giambrone & Law (a firm)*, [2017] EWCA Civ 1193, [2018] PNLR 2.

30 This synonymy is likely derived from the fact that private law deals with the private rights of individuals while public law is the domain of laws enacted to pursue the public good, which of course is sometimes at odds with individual rights. See Alan Brudner, *The Unity of the Common Law: Studies in Hegelian Jurisprudence* (Berkeley and Los Angeles: University of California Press, 1995) at 2–3.

31 On this point, see the following comments of Justice Beetz in *Attorney General of Quebec v Labrecque and al*, [1980] 2 SCR 1057 at 1081–2:

> It must be remembered that in Anglo-Canadian law, administrative law does not constitute a complete and independent system, separate from the ordinary law and administered by specialized courts. On the contrary, it is the ordinary law, administered by the courts of law, which is made a part of public law and the provisions of which cover the public administrative authority, unless they are replaced by incompatible legislative provisions, or supplanted by rules peculiar to the royal prerogative, that group of powers and privileges belonging only to the Crown.
>
> It follows that faced with the necessity of qualifying and regulating a given legal relationship in public law, the jurist of the Anglo-Canadian tradition must necessarily carry out this function with the concepts and rules of the ordinary law, unless statute or prerogative require otherwise.

By "ordinary law," Beetz J is referring to common law, using a term from AVV Dicey.

32 *CUPE v NB Liquor Corporation*, [1979] 2 SCR 227 [*CUPE*].

33 *Canada (Minister of Citizenship and Immigration) v Vavilov*, 2019 SCC 65.

arises from the legitimacy of unelected judges reviewing the decisions of elected legislators and the government administrators they appoint, and which has important implications for the rule of law.

David Sandomierski's chapter considers the structural features of Chief Justice McLachlin's approach to the development of the common law and the resolution of difficult cases. In particular, Sandomierski posits that one of the animating features of Chief Justice McLachlin's judicial philosophy is the pursuit of the appropriate source of law, legal institution, or legal process, in the given circumstances – what he calls "selective deference." He then examines the application of this approach through a series of public and private law decisions: he outlines the question of "balance" raised by *Charter* adjudication,[34] explores how the Court mediates between competing branches of government,[35] and examines Chief Justice McLachlin's approach in applying the constructive trust in family property disputes.[36]

Criminal law also has its origins in English common law; indeed, in the United Kingdom, some areas of criminal law are still governed by the common law, though statutes have taken over in large part.[37] In Canada, the first *Criminal Code* was promulgated in 1892, and after the Second World War, courts were barred from creating new criminal offences.[38] However, this has not diminished the role of judges in interpreting and developing criminal law. Judges have created new defences, such as the defence of entrapment,[39] and they have broadened important aspects of certain defences, such as self-defence[40] and duress,[41] while narrowing others, such as the defence of provocation.[42]

34 These cases include *Hutterian Brethren of Wilson Colony v Alberta*, 2009 SCC 37; *Canada v Taylor*, [1990] 3 SCR 892; *Sauvé*, *supra* note 1; *RJR-MacDonald Inc v Canada*, [1995] 3 SCR 199.

35 *New Brunswick Broadcasting Co v Nova Scotia (Speaker of the House of Assembly)*, [1993] 1 SCR 319; *Harvey v New Brunswick (AG)*, [1996] 2 SCR 876; *Canada (Prime Minister) v Khadr*, [2010] 1 SCR 44.

36 *Rawluk v Rawluk*, [1990] 1 SCR 70 [*Rawluk*]; *Peter v Beblow*, [1993] 1 SCR 980 [*Peter*]; *Tataryn v Tataryn* [1994] 2 SCR 807.

37 Andrew Ashworth, *Principles of Criminal Law*, 4th ed (Oxford: Oxford University Press, 2003) at 6.

38 *Criminal Code of Canada*, RSC 1985, c C-46, s 9.

39 *R v Mack*, [1988] 2 SCR 903.

40 *R v Lavallee*, [1990] 1 SCR 852.

41 *R v Ruzic*, 2001 SCC 24. The case makes the defence available to a person even if the person threatening them is not immediately able to carry out the threat.

42 *R v Thibert*, [1996] 1 SCR 37 (clarifying that the defence is not available to a man who has been rejected by his romantic partner); *R v Tran*, 2010 SCC 58 (clarifying that the defence is not available where a man seeks out his estranged wife and her lover).

They have also played an important role in the law of criminal evidence, developing key common law rules such as those around the admissibility of hearsay. Indeed, the revolution arising from what is today called the "principled approach" to the admissibility of hearsay was brought about solely by the Supreme Court of Canada under the tenure of Chief Justice McLachlin.[43]

Three contibutors to this book address important areas of criminal law that have their roots in the common law. David Tanovich pulls together some lesser-known strands of the law of evidence to make a case for an approach to the admissibility of evidence that can fight against the implicit bias that has a disproportionate impact on marginalized groups such as racialized and Indigenous people. His chapter addresses controversial aspects of the law of evidence in two ways. First, he claims that the law of evidence is a potential source of systemic bias. Second, he argues that Chief Justice McLachlin has provided a viable basis for remedying this bias in some key decisions such as *Mitchell v MNR*,[44] which deals with the admissibility of traditional oral knowledge in a case involving Aboriginal rights, and *Seaboyer*,[45] which deals with the prevention of sexual assault stereotypes in sexual assault cases.

Matthew Gourlay addresses the perennial question of the proper role of criminal law in correcting "social ills": can the criminal law be used to penalize all anti-social conduct? Or must it be concerned with the harm that criminalization can impose on vulnerable groups? Gourlay argues that, in her early decisions, McLachlin J initially took a civil-libertarian approach that restricts the role of the state, and therefore of criminal law, to avoiding the worst harms. He points to her dissent in *R v Keegstra*, in which she argued that the hate speech provisions in the *Criminal Code* violated both the right to freedom of expression and the presumption of innocence in ways that could not be justified in a free and democratic society.[46] She thus argued that use of the criminal law may have to be restricted where countervailing constitutional rights are in issue. However, once she became Chief Justice in 2000, she led a court that took a different view: it required not only that the state's interest in preventing crime had to be balanced against other *rights*, but also that the government had the onus to demonstrate that criminalization did not harm marginalized groups. To support this view, Gourlay points to the controversial cases

43 *R v Khan*, [1990] 2 SCR 531 [*Khan*]; *R v Starr*, 2000 SCC 40; *R v Mapara*, 2005 SCC 23; *R v Khelawon*, 2006 SCC 57; *R v Baldree*, 2013 SCC 35; *R v Bradshaw*, 2017 SCC 35.

44 *Mitchell v MNR*, 2001 SCC 33 [*Mitchell*].

45 *R v Seaboyer; R v Gayme*, [1991] 2 SCR 577 [*Seaboyer*].

46 *R v Keegstra*, [1990] 3 SCR 697.

of *Bedford*,[47] *PHS*,[48] and *Carter*,[49] which deal, respectively, with prostitution/sex work, a supervised injection site, and assisted death. In his view, the Supreme Court's approach to these issues goes beyond a simple libertarian view that the state must refrain from limiting individual freedom, and instead adopts a more nuanced view requiring the courts to weigh the harms that criminalization can pose on those who engage in sex work, who are managing a drug addiction, or who are capable of making informed choices about when to die. Thus, if a prohibition on sex work harms those engaged in this work, it can violate their rights. Or if the laws that limit medically assisted death cause more suffering than they prevent, they too may be problematic.

Graham Mayeda addresses an aspect of criminal law that goes to the heart of its common law origins. He asks whether the common law still has any effect in criminal law following the codification of the latter and the introduction of the *Canadian Charter of Rights and Freedoms*. Both of these phenomena have led lawyers to consider criminal law "public law," and therefore to separate it from common law – which is today often restricted to private law. Mayeda argues that Canadian criminal law, especially as developed by Chief Justice McLachlin, is interpreted and developed by courts using a traditional common law method that favours incremental change rather than the wholesale change that might be considered "judicial legislation." His review of controversial decisions relating to the definition of murder and manslaughter,[50] the criminalization of HIV status,[51] the scope of fraud,[52] and the availability of the defence of self-defence,[53] demonstrates that the common law is as much a way of thinking about the law and resolving legal problems as it is a distinct area of law.

Eszter Bodnár's chapter on the concept of open justice raises the important issue of the publicity of the law, a key element of the rule of law identified by Lon Fuller in his important work *The Morality of Law*.[54] As Bodnár points out, the concept of open justice has deep roots in the common law and is related to the long-standing principle that "justice

47 *Bedford*, *supra* note 4.

48 *Canada (Attorney General) v PHS Community Services Society*, 2011 SCC 44.

49 *Carter*, *supra* note 3.

50 *R v Vaillancourt*, [1987] 2 SCR 636; *R v Martineau*, [1990] 2 SCR 633; *R v Creighton*, [1993] 3 SCR 3.

51 *R v Cuerrier*, [1998] 2 SCR 371; *R v Mabior*, 2012 SCC 47.

52 *R v Théroux*, [1993] 2 SCR 5.

53 *R v McIntosh*, [1995] 1 SCR 686.

54 Lon Fuller, *The Mortality of Law* (New Haven, CT: Yale University Press, 1969).

should not only be done, but should manifestly and undoubtedly be seen to be done."[55] Her chapter explores the common law concept of open justice and the justifications for this principle, which include judicial accountability, therapeutic justice, and the search for the truth. Bodnár then examines Chief Justice McLachlin's approach to the open justice principle in her judicial decisions and her speeches and published writings. Bodnár also considers how Chief Justice McLachlin's ideas about open justice were put into practice through her leadership roles as Chief Justice of the Supreme Court of Canada, as head of the judiciary in Canada.

In both private and public law, the jurisprudence of the Supreme Court of Canada during Chief Justice McLachlin's time on the Court, from 1989 to 2017, was highly innovative. Of course, some of these innovations created controversy, while others resolved them.

II. Unfinished Business: The Common Law as an Iterative Process of Adapting the Law to Changing Social Needs

While individual contributors focus on specific common law controversies, this book as a whole illustrates that the common law represents a process of constant adaptation of the law to changing social needs.[56] More controversially, the chapters demonstrate that the common law model of the law is an iterative process of change that can be used to understand every area of law, even those dominated by statutes. The generally accepted model presupposes that statutes, especially written constitutions, contain principles about which there is broad social agreement because they were adopted by elected legislators.[57] Others have suggested that this view is a

55 JJ Spigelman, "Seen to Be Done: The Principle of Open Justice – Part I" (2000) 74 Austl LJ 290.

56 Cardozo writes, "Every new case is an experiment; and if the accepted rule which seems applicable yields a result which is felt to be unjust, the rule is reconsidered" (*supra* note 6 at 23). Here, I take "unjust" to mean "unjust based on contemporary social standards of justice." Douglas E Edlin writes, "For the common law, judgments are individual statements of normative evaluation placed within an existing *and evolving system*, which are claimed as a contribution to ongoing public debate and to the articulation of public standards of governance" [emphasis added] ("Introduction," in Douglas E Edlin, ed, *Common Law Theory* (Cambridge: Cambridge University Press, 2007) 1 at 1–2).

57 Waluchow describes this view, which he calls "the Standard Case" for creating an entrenched charter or bill of rights, as "a means by which a society ties itself to the mast of its fundamental beliefs, values, commitments, and settled preferences" (*supra* note 1 at 118).

fiction, and that the process of interpreting all statutes is more akin to the common law method, which Waluchow describes as reflecting "the community's moral judgments in reflective equilibrium"[58] – i.e., a consensus about key moral questions arrived at through a process of public deliberation.[59] The common law is a body of law, but it is also a method for thinking about and resolving important legal questions; it is one way in which our society engages in ongoing deliberation.

The idea that all law is, or should be, based on the common law model may not seem controversial on its face; indeed, it is part of the "living tree" approach that the Supreme Court of Canada has taken to the Canadian Constitution.[60] But the view has been widely opposed by those who argue that unelected judges usurp the role of elected legislators if they consider every legal question before them to be part of an iterative process of adapting the law to current social situations.[61] After all, they argue, it is legislators, and not judges, who have the expertise and the legitimacy to make policy decisions about what our society needs or wants. On this view, the judge's principal function is simply to apply the law enacted in statutes, not bend and twist it by determining how statutes relate to the common law, supplementing it with the common law, or interpreting it to be consistent or inconsistent with the common law.[62] The problem is most acute where the statute in question is a constitutionalized bill of rights, because, as theorists such as Jeremy Waldron point out, permitting

58 *Ibid* at 270.

59 John Rawls, *A Theory of Justice* (Cambridge, MA: Harvard University Press, 1971) at 19–20.

60 First articulated by Lord Sankey LC in *Edwards v Attorney-General for Canada*, [1930] AC 124 (PC) at 136.

61 FL Morton & R Knopff, *The Charter Revolution and the Court Party* (Peterborough, ON: Broadview Press, 2000); R Bork, *Coercing Virtue: The Worldwide Rule of Judges* (Toronto: Vintage, 2002); C Manfredi, *Judicial Power and the Charter: Canada and the Paradox of Liberal Constitutionalism* (Oxford: Oxford University Press, 2001).

62 In *R v Jobidon*, [1991] 2 SCR 714, the majority reasons, penned by Gonthier J, argued that, while the *Criminal Code*, *supra* note 38, made no mention of limits on the defence of consent to assault, the common law restrictions on this defence had to be read into the statute. Sopinka and Stevenson JJ dissented, arguing that the *Code* was clear that consent was a good defence to all forms of assault and that "the absence of consent [as a defence] cannot be swept away by a robust application of judge-made policy" (at 774). Sopinka J went on to accuse the majority of what we would today call "judicial activism," writing that "[t]he effect of my colleague's approach is to create an offence where one does not exist under the terms of the *Code* by application of the common law" (at 774).

judges to interpret and apply constitutional norms risks transforming them into dictators.[63]

A far different view of the law considers statute laws to be part of the fabric of the law woven together with the thread of the common law. In his description of A.V. Dicey's view, T.R.S. Allan explains this model:

> Although Dicey's doctrine is often treated as a merely formal one, having no implications for the content of law, it is clear that it was intended to reflect and inform judicial practice. Parliamentary sovereignty was consistent with the rule of law because Acts of Parliament were subject to judicial interpretation; and the *judges could be trusted to interpret statutes in accordance with the general principles of the common law*.[64]

As Allan explains, it follows from this view that, while law may contain general principles articulated in a relatively abstract way, judges are performing a substantive function when they apply these abstract rules to specific situations. The rule of law requires an independent and impartial judiciary to ensure that ambiguous statutes are applied to specific situations in ways that benefit rather than harm citizens. Allan gives as an example the common law presumption that a criminal offence requires proof of subjective *mens rea*: "The common law presumptions in favour of requiring *mens rea* for criminal offences, and against retrospective laws, are necessary features of interpretation attuned to the requirements of the rule of law."[65]

If we use the common law conception of law as a model of law in general, law must be considered an evolving discourse, involving both statutes and common law rules, that aims at interpreting and adapting the rules found in both sources to our society's conception of justice. As Mark D. Walters writes, "[i]t is a discourse of reason that seeks a 'unity' of reason through an inductive ascent from particular manifestations of general principles to the general principles themselves, and then a descent back again to the level of specifics to articulate new rules or rights that cohere, in principle, with established rules and rights." It follows from this model that there are "points of convergence between written and unwritten law."[66]

---

63 Jeremy Waldron, "The Core of the Case against Judicial Review" (2006) 115 Yale LJ 1346; see David Dyzenhaus's critique of this view in "The Incoherence of Constitutional Positivism" in Grant Huscroft, ed, *Expounding the Constitution: Essays in Constitutional Theory* (Cambridge: Cambridge University Press, 2008) 138.

64 TRS Allan, "Constitutional Justice and the Concept of Law" in Huscroft, ed, *supra* note 63, 219 at 224 [emphasis added].

65 *Ibid.*

66 Mark D Walters, "Written Constitutions and Unwritten Constitutionalism" in Huscroft, ed, *supra* note 63, 245 at 254.

Many of the chapters in this book demonstrate that Chief Justice McLachlin considered the common law model to be the basic model for understanding the role of law in general, which in turn affected how she approached and, in many cases, resolved key legal controversies during her tenure on the Court.[67]

This view is not an orthodox one. Most lawyers operate on the basis that the law is divided into "private" and "public" law and that only private law is the domain of the common law.[68] It is also common to divide the law into judge-made law and statute law and to consider only the first to be common law.[69] However, while a number of the chapters do address controversies in private law, such as tort law and the law of unjust enrichment, others address areas of public law that have their origins in the common law, such as administrative law and criminal law, in which statutes play an increasingly important role. Thus, what the chapters in this book illustrate is that areas of public law in which statutes play a big part can still be considered areas of common law – but how so?

---

67 In explaining the coherence rationale for the illegality principle, McLachlin has written: "[T]he law must aspire to be a unified institution, the parts of which – contract, tort, the criminal law – must be in essential harmony" (*Hall*, *supra* note 26 at 176).

68 Alan Brudner explains that, "[f]or most of its history, the common law was an ordering of human interactions independent of the political order directed to common ends. It was a system of rules ordered not to a common good but to individual rights over one's person and property conceived as existing prior to any association for a common purpose" (*supra* note 30 at 2). Insofar as it was considered to pre-date the formation of the state as a public body, the common law was thus synonymous with private right and private law.

69 In *Egerton v Brownlow*, (1853) 4 HLC 1, Parke B wrote:

> It is the province of the judge to expound the law only; the written from the statutes, the unwritten or common law from the decisions of our predecessors and of our existing courts, from text writers of acknowledged authority, and upon the principles to be clearly deduced from them by sound reason and just inference; not to speculate upon what is best, in his opinion, for the advantage of the community. (123)

And TRS Allan explains:

> At first impression, the distinction between statute and common law may appear to entrench the division between competing ideals, leading in turn to the need for sharply differentiated styles of adjudication, according to the source of law involved. Enacted rules can enable us to ascertain most clearly what is lawfully required or permitted or prohibited: The canonical text reduces, even if it cannot eliminate, the scope for argument. Common law adjudication, by contrast, is more characteristic of equity; It permits a decision closely attuned to the particular circumstances, leaving wide discretion to the judge in making his appraisal.

("Text, Context, and Constitution: The Common Law as Public Reason" in Edlin, ed, *supra* note 56, 185 at 187.)

Some of the chapters demonstrate that the principles for understanding the relationship between statutes and judge-made law are themselves derived from common law. For instance, statutes such as the *Canadian Charter of Rights and Freedoms*,[70] the *Federal Courts Act*,[71] and provincial laws such as Ontario's *Judicial Review Procedure Act*[72] and *Statutory Procedures Act*[73] play a key role in administrative law and constitutional law, while Canadian criminal law is largely codified in statutes such as the *Criminal Code* and the *Controlled Drugs and Substances Act*.[74] Nonetheless, the rules of statutory interpretation give judges the ability to "fill gaps" in statutes with their own creations, or to interpret statutory provisions in light of the common law that the statutes codify or replace. Tanovich's chapter on the law of evidence is a good illustration of this. While there are statutory rules on the admissibility of evidence contained in statutes such as the *Canada Evidence Act*,[75] the common law has played an important role in adapting the law to modern social conditions. He points to a number of Supreme Court of Canada cases that have interpreted various rules on the admissibility of evidence in order to take into account the marginalization of witnesses such as children (*R v Khan*,[76] *R v W(R)*[77]), oral history in cases involving Indigenous communities (*Mitchell v MNR*),[78] and the evidence of women complainants in sexual assault cases (*R v Seaboyer*).[79] He suggests ways in which statutory rules such as that in section 12(1) of the *Canada Evidence Act* allowing an accused to be cross-examined on their prior criminal record should be interpreted by courts to take into account the marginalization of Indigenous and racialized defendants in criminal cases. The premise behind this argument is the continuity between statute and judge-made common law.

In their respective chapters on tort law, Feldthusen and Chamberlain also explore the question of the interplay of statute and common law, which the Court was forced to deal with in cases involving the liability of government organizations regulated by statute, such as the police in

70 *Canadian Charter of Rights and Freedoms*, Part I of the *Constitution Act 1982*, being Schedule B to the *Canada Act 1982* (UK), 1982, c 11.

71 *Federal Courts Act*, RSC 1985, c F-7.

72 *Judicial Review Procedure Act*, RSO 1990, c J.1.

73 *Statutory Procedures Act*, RSO 1990, c S.22.

74 *Criminal Code*, *supra* note 38; *Controlled Drugs and Substances Act*, SC 1996, c 19.

75 *Canada Evidence Act*, RSC 1985, c C-5.

76 *Khan*, *supra* note 43.

77 *R v W(R)*, [1992] 2 SCR 122.

78 *Mitchell*, *supra* note 44.

79 *Seaboyer*, *supra* note 45.

Hill v Hamilton-Wentworth Police Services Board,[80] the Registrar of Mortgage Brokers in *Cooper v Hobart,*[81] and Health Canada in *R v Imperial Tobacco.*[82] For instance, Chamberlain's analysis of tort cases involving government defendants demonstrates that the Court has moved toward a position where statutes are the only source of duties of government decision makers. And yet, the Court has also maintained the common law *Anns* framework for determining negligence liability, adapting it to claims against governments by allowing policy considerations under the second branch of the *Anns* test to trump private law considerations of proximity and foreseeability.

McInnes's chapter on unjust enrichment also demonstrates how the lines are blurred between common law concepts and statute law. In *Peel (Regional Municipality) v Canada,*[83] the Court dealt with a section of the *Juvenile Delinquents Act*[84] that gave family court judges the jurisdiction to place juveniles in group homes, bypassing the Children's Aid Society. The legislation also allowed the courts to require a municipality to reimburse the province and the federal government for some of the cost of these placements. When the legislation allowing direct placement by courts was found to be *ultra vires,* the municipality demanded repayment of the money. The Court considered whether the municipality had a claim in unjust enrichment. The case blurs the line between statute and common law in that the Court was required to consider whether a government was enriched if, through payments received from the municipality, it was able to achieve its legislative goals, or if it was "morally enriched" because its obligation to support juveniles was fulfilled. It concluded that only financial enrichments will be compensated. Moreover, the public law aspect of the case was accentuated by the fact that the municipality was seeking restitution as a form of remedy under section 24(1) of the *Charter,* having won its argument that the legislation was *ultra vires*. Here, the interplay of private and public law remedies required the Court to consider how common law remedies fill gaps in the statutory framework of the *Charter*.

Some chapters also illustrate the subtle way in which Canadian judges are influenced by "common law" thinking: while the common law advances by identifying and revising general principles as they are

---

80 *Hill v Hamilton-Wentworth Police Services Board,* 2007 SCC 41.

81 *Cooper, supra* note 21.

82 *R v Imperial Tobacco,* 2011 SCC 42 [*Imperial Tobacco*].

83 *Peel (Regional Municipality) v Canada,* [1992] 3 SCR 762.

84 *Juvenile Delinquents Act,* RSC 1970, c J-3.

applied in cases to particular fact scenarios, this does not mean that the principles are abstract regulative ideals, as they were traditionally regarded in civil law jurisdictions.[85] The principles of the common law are determined through induction from specific instances;[86] they are not first articulated abstractly and then applied to specific cases. The organic relationship between principle and specific instance in common law seems to colour the ways that Canadian judges think when addressing novel areas.

In his chapter exploring Chief Justice McLachlin's contributions to criminal law, Mayeda contrasts the common law method that she used in some well-known cases with the abstract Cartesian approach of her colleagues former Chief Justice Antonio Lamer and Justice Claire L'Heureux-Dubé, who were trained in the civil law tradition, and the policy-oriented approach of judges such as Justice Peter Cory. In the referenced cases, Justice McLachlin first derived the principle underlying past cases through inductive reasoning and then used analogical and deductive reasoning to apply it to novel fact scenarios.[87] As Mayeda explains, this method inherently limits innovation to incremental change and ensures the stability of the principles and values that underlie criminal law.

Tanovich's description of the emergence of the principled approach to the admission of hearsay evidence is interesting because it relies on cases that are "purely" common law, in the sense that they deal with rules that emerged only in case law, and cases that involve both the common law and statute, such as *Seaboyer*, in which section 276 of the *Criminal Code* was used as a statement of Canadian values that favoured the promotion of women's equality through the prevention

---

85 Catherine Valcke explains the difference between the positivism of the common law and civil law systems as follows: "While civil legal systems are rooted in positivism, this positivism is not of a bare Hobbesian kind whereby the legislator proceeds, entirely unconstrained, from a clean juridical slate; the positivism that roots civil legal systems is itself solidly rooted in ethical premises of Cartesian naturalism ... [T]hese premises ... permeate all aspects of civil legal materials and method" (Catherine Valcke, "Quebec Civil Law and Canadian Federalism" (1996) 21 Yale J Intl L 67 at 77); see also RA Macdonald, "Comments" (1980) 58 Can Bar Rev 185 at 188.

86 See Mayeda's discussion in Chapter 8 of Lord Diplock's description of the common law reasoning process in *Home Office v Dorset Yacht Co Ltd*, [1970] AC 1004 (HL (Eng)).

87 On the importance of analogical reasoning in the common law, see Gerald J Postema, "*A Similibus ad Similia:* Analogical Thinking in Law" in Edlin, ed, *supra* note 56, 102.

of impermissible sexual assault myths and stereotypes. In the Court's most recent decision on the application of section 276, Justice Moldaver, in concurring reasons, describes the decision in *Seaboyer* as articulating "common law principles,"[88] in regard, for instance, to how the prejudicial effects and probative value of evidence must be weighed before evidence is admitted.[89]

Chief Justice McLachlin acknowledged that both common law and statute must be sewn together by judges to create a complete legal regime that responds to changing social needs. Her judgments also demonstrated the iterative process at work: common law doctrines must take into account statutory developments and fill gaps where necessary. The example Sandomierski provides is that of unjust enrichment in the context of family law. Despite the radical introduction of the constructive trust and the doctrine of unjust enrichment to remedy the exploitation of women in the family law context in *Pettkus v Becker*,[90] McLachlin J recognized the need to respect legislators who also addressed the same issue in legislation such as the *Family Law Act, 1986*.[91] Thus in the *Rawluk* case,[92] McLachlin J disagreed with the majority that the new common law remedy of the constructive trust was the proper way to address potential unjust enrichment of the husband at the expense of the wife because a remedy was provided under the *Family Law Act, 1986*. However, in the subsequent case of *Peter v Beblow*, she recognized a woman's equitable interest in the family home because no remedy was provided by statute.[93] While the two decisions may seem somewhat controversial, Sandomierski demonstrates that they actually demonstrate a sensitivity to institutional competence in advancing social justice for women. Indeed, McLachlin J's recognition of changing social views was clearly demonstrated in *Peter v Beblow*, in which she incorporated into the law contemporary social concerns about the feminization of poverty by explicitly acknowledging that housekeeping and childrearing are activities that can give rise to a claim of unjust enrichment. She did this by integrating a public policy component into the third stage of the test for unjust enrichment, which

---

88 *R v Goldfinch*, 2019 SCC 38 at paras 142 and 148 and note 13. (In the note, Brown J (dissenting) explains that *Seaboyer* sets out "common law rules of evidence in sexual prosecutions.")

89 *R v Grant*, 2015 SCC 9 at para 19.

90 *Pettkus*, *supra* note 22.

91 *Family Law Act, 1986*, SO 1986, c 4.

92 *Rawluk*, *supra* note 36.

93 *Peter*, *supra* note 36.

considers whether there is a juristic reason for one party to have been enriched at the expense of the other. Sandomierski explains that the distinction between McLachlin J's reasons in *Rawluk* and *Peter* arises from two concerns: an appreciation for the proper categorization of distinct legal doctrines and attention to institutional competence. He goes on to conclude that her search for which source of law is most appropriate is driven by the idea that substantive fairness will be best achieved by respecting the proper and fair balance between diverse legal institutions.

Contributors suggest that there were some shifts in the Chief Justice's approach to judgment after she was appointed to head the Court in 2000. One way of describing this development is that it is a shift away from a common law approach toward a pragmatic approach in which political values weigh more highly. The chapters in this book that note this shift provide a fruitful basis for future research.

For instance, in his chapter on criminal law minimalism, Gourlay notes the shift in the Chief Justice's judgments from a preference for a civil libertarian position in which the criminal law must be limited where important countervailing interests such as free speech are in play (as in *Keegstra*) toward an approach in *Carter* and *Bedford* in which she takes what he describes as "a realist and pragmatist" approach that favours what he calls "criminal law minimalism" – the idea that the criminal law "must not do more harm than good." He finds it significant that the latter two decisions are part of "a general consensus," thus suggesting that her new leadership role required building consensus, which in turn affected the ways in which she argued cases and reasoned about the law. When one contrasts the Court's reasons in these later cases with her dissenting reasons in *Keegstra*, one is indeed struck by the common law method that she used in this earlier case. For while she does run through the historical and philosophical justifications for protecting free speech, she then turns to a discussion of how the right was developed in key Canadian cases, which demonstrate an incremental shift from limited protection of only political speech to a broader protection of freedom of expression as first articulated by Justice Rand in *Boucher*.[94] She thus anchored her dissent in how social change was reflected in incremental adjustments in Canadian case law to a new social consensus.

94 *Boucher v The King*, [1951] SCR 265.

III. Chief Justice McLachlin: A Common Law Judge

We have seen that Chief Justice McLachlin not only contributed to the development of important areas of the common law, she also used common law modes of reasoning in both private and common law cases, including cases that involved primarily judge-made rules and those that involved statutes or a mix of the two. The final theme that emerges in this book is about whether judges consciously adopt a particular "style" and, if so, what role their background plays in choosing it.

Do judges adopt a style – a particular way of reasoning about the law and justifying their decisions? The chapters in this book seem to support a positive answer to this question: before she became Chief Justice, Justice McLachlin adopted a way of thinking and reasoning that is characteristic of a common law judge and that differs from other "styles," such as a civilian style, a positivist style, a philosophical style, or a policy-oriented style. It was only later in her career, once she took on a new leadership role that required building consensus within a court that was fractured during the 1990s under the tenure of her predecessor, that her style changed toward a more pragmatic one that often relied on the articulation of general abstract principles rather than the use of the typical common law method of inductive reasoning to derive principles from previous cases and then apply these principles to new cases based on analogical and deductive reasoning.

While this book is by no means a biography of Beverley McLachlin or a comprehensive overview of all of her judgments, it indicates some important pathways for future research in this regard by providing indications of what her judgment style was and why she adopted it. Thus, this book is a small contribution to similar characterizations of the judgments of other retired Supreme Court judges contained in the increasing number of biographies and scholarly anthologies about them that have been published in the past thirty years, and that demonstrate the academic penchant to identify the "style of judgment" of a particular judge.

For instance, in a book celebrating the career of Justice Charles Gonthier, DeLloyd Guth described the retired judge's unique style, which was arguably the result of his bilingual, bicultural, and bijuridical background. For instance, Guth describes Justice Gonthier's style of reasoning and writing as fitting into "the unified Anglo-French common law tradition,"[95] developed

95 DeLloyd Guth, "Method and Matter in the Gonthier Legacy: Legal History and Judgment Writing, 1989–2003" in Michel Morin et al, eds, *Responsibility, Fraternity and Sustainability in Law: In Memory of the Honourable Charles Doherty Gonthier* (Markham, ON: LexisNexis, 2012) 39 at 44.

through the influence of two Quebec jurists with opposite styles: the comparative internationalist approach of his grandfather Charles Joseph Doherty, and the "monojuralist" civil law style of Pierre-Basile Mignault.[96] Gonthier J was not a consequentialist but a "proceduralist": he went where reasoning, the law, and the facts took him without undue consideration for policy issues.[97]

While Gonthier J was most influenced by the process of reasoning about the law, other judges were ideological: for them, the abstract principle or idea came first, and the law then had to be adapted to fit. Justice L'Heureux-Dubé, who adopted a feminist social justice approach (and "law and order" approach to criminal law cases), often found herself writing dissenting judgments as a result of her style of judgment. She explained the role of dissents as being "innovative yet, paradoxically, potentially stabilizing forces in the law, particularly when these opinions are oriented toward the future and invite dialogue with those who are unsatisfied with, or feel excluded by, the majority decision."[98] She in turn characterized the judgments of Chief Justice Lamer as being similarly ideological, writing that "[h]e was only for the criminal. He was a defence lawyer all his life, so he was a defence lawyer on the bench. He acted as if he were the Law Commission, not a judge. He didn't care what the law was. He just changed it to what he wanted it to be."[99]

While other judges valued many of the principles underlying the common law, such as stability,[100] they did not accept the common law as the sole model for all adjudication. Thus, Chief Justice Dickson set out his (and the Court's) judicial philosophy in regard to the interpretation of the *Canadian Charter of Rights and Freedoms* as a break from the past. Robert Sharpe and Kent Roach characterize his approach to the new constitutional document as "distinctively Canadian," from which it followed that the Court intended to "nudge Canadian judges away from their traditional adherence to English jurisprudence."[101] And yet, while this meant embracing some aspects of American law, this approach was

96 *Ibid* at 43.

97 *Ibid* at 46–7.

98 Claire L'Heureux-Dubé, *Claire L'Heureux-Dubé: A Life* (Vancouver: UBC Press, 2017) [*Claire L'Heureux-Dubé*] at 374–5, citing Claire L'Heureux-Dubé, "The Dissenting Opinion: Voice of the Future?" (2000) 28:3 Osgoode Hall LJ 495 at 498, 504.

99 *Claire L'Heureux-Dubé, supra* note 98 at 371, citing an interview with Justice L'Heureux-Dubé, Quebec City, 27–28 April 2009.

100 Robert J Sharpe & Kent Roach, *Brian Dickson: A Judge's Journey* (Toronto: University of Toronto Press, 2003) at 311.

101 *Ibid* at 317.

not intended to "lead to the 'Americanization' of Canadian law."[102] In some sense, this was an ideological approach to the law: "Dickson," Sharpe and Roach write, "strongly believed in the development of international human rights norms from which Canada could benefit and to which Canada could contribute."[103]

In their book collecting papers presented to honour Justice Louise Charron, Peter Oliver and Graham Mayeda characterize her style as didactic: her clear, well-reasoned judgments educated lawyers, the public, students, and other judges about the law that they contained.[104] They characterize the educative function of the law as follows:

> It seems natural that the role of education should appeal to judges. Perhaps this is due to the similar social role both teacher and judge are expected to play in society. Like the teacher, the judge is expected to speak with authority. She is generally respected in Canadian society, and she is a public servant producing a social good. She has a captive audience, although the judge's immediate audience – the legal community – is perhaps more attentive. There are crucial differences between a teacher and a judge, however. The judge is a mediator between two parties; a teacher is not. The consequence of this is that a judge is accountable, not just to society, but also to a very specific subset of society – the litigants. Also, the judge is, at least conceptually, a peer – a member of a community whose judgments should represent its values and reflect them in her reasons. In contrast, a teacher does not necessarily represent a community, but rather the doctrine being taught.[105]

A survey of Justice Charron's judgments during her tenure on the Supreme Court of Canada from 2004 to 2011 clearly indicates that her style – both her method of reasoning and her writing – reflected her role as legal educator and responsive community member.

Through the chapters in this book, it is possible to sketch Justice McLachlin's judicial style. Mayeda tackles this question head on in his chapter on the Chief Justice's contributions to criminal law during the turbulent 1990s, an era in which ideological disagreements were manifest. Mayeda contrasts Chief Justice McLachlin's common law

---

102 *Ibid*.

103 *Ibid* at 319.

104 Graham Mayeda & Peter Oliver, "Principles and Pragmatism: An Introduction" in Graham Mayeda & Peter Oliver, eds, *Principles and Pragmatism: Essays in Honour of Louise Charron* (Markham, ON: LexisNexis, 2014) 3.

105 *Ibid* at 5.

approach, which was incremental and principled, with that of other judges, such as Chief Justice Lamer, Justice L'Heureux-Dubé, and Justice Cory, who tended to take abstract principles as their point of departure rather than deriving the principle through induction from past cases.

Adam Goldenberg begins his chapter on administrative law by describing Chief Justice McLachlin's leadership style between 2000 and 2017, which shifted the culture of the Court from conflict to consensus. During that time, the Court moved away from multiple opinions to issuing a single majority opinion in as many cases as possible. He examines some of the reasons that lie behind the emergence of consensus, such as greater stability and certainty about the law. However, this search for stability and certainty did not come at the expense of principle, which he describes as a tool for ensuring that there is enough flexibility in administrative law (the subject of his chapter) to adapt it to changing times. Unfortunately, in the case of administrative law, the principles announced in the key case of *Dunsmuir v New Brunswick*[106] did not provide the stability and certainty the Court sought, thus suggesting that, while building consensus may have had certain advantages in terms of collegiality on the Court and clarity about the law, it may not have created a practical and enduring legal framework, perhaps because an abstract approach is too far removed from the way the judges required to apply it had learned administrative law in times prior to the revolution brought about by Justice Dickson in *CUPE v NB Liquor Corporation.*[107]

Tanovich's chapter elaborates on what he has called the "McLachlin Principle," which aimed at ensuring that the ever-evolving law of evidence would be responsive to concerns about systemic discrimination. He specifically documents the Chief Justice's commitment to a law that could adapt to the times in *R v Khan*, the case in which the Supreme Court of Canada first began to revise the traditional common law approach to hearsay toward a principled approach. In subsequent decisions such as *Seaboyer* (admissibility of evidence of sexual reputation in sexual assault cases) and *Mitchell v MNR* (admissibility of oral history in a case of Aboriginal rights), the Chief Justice continued to reform the law of evidence to "facilitate justice" rather than letting formalistic rules "stand in its way."[108]

106 *Dunsmuir v New Brunswick*, 2008 SCC 9.

107 *CUPE, supra* note 32.

108 *Mitchell, supra* note 44 at para 30.

Feldthusen's chapter characterizes Justice McLachlin as a pioneer in the protection of women through reforms in the law of battery and vicarious liability for child sexual abuse while at the same time conservatively restricting the tort liability of government and public authorities in key cases such as *Cooper v Hobart*[109] and *Edwards v Law Society of Upper Canada*.[110] He attributes this apparent contradiction to her profound respect for the constitutional separation of powers, which is consistent with the general characterization of Justice McLachlin as a "common law" judge by other contributors: while some might see the common law as inimical to the separation of powers by allowing judges to take over the legislative role, scholars have pointed out that the separation of powers – for instance, as contained in the United States Constitution – was no more than a step in the evolution of the traditional common law view on the subject.[111]

Chamberlain further develops Feldthusen's characterization of Justice McLachlin's style of judgment. She notes the tension between her willingness to challenge the policy arguments presented by government agencies arguing against liability in cases such as *Hill*, while at the same time being more deferential to the government in cases such as *Cooper*[112] and *Imperial Tobacco*.[113] Chamberlain's analysis of the cases dealing with policy-based arguments in tort law reinforces Feldthusen's view that public law values such as the separation of powers coloured the Chief Justice's thinking in this area. For example, in *Imperial Tobacco*, McLachlin CJ accepted that Health Canada could not be liable for its decision to promote low-tar cigarettes, because of the possibility of unlimited government liability and the immense cost this would entail.[114] She also accepted that the government was immune because its decision was one of policy that could not give rise to private law liability.[115] These are private law analogues of the types of arguments that one often sees in public law decisions under the application of the *Oakes* test: in the application of *Oakes*, courts are hesitant to probe too seriously the policy decisions of governments as long as these governmental decisions are rationally connected to the achievement of a legitimate policy goal and

109 *Cooper, supra* note 21.

110 *Edwards v Law Society of Upper Canada*, 2001 SCC 80.

111 James R Stoner Jr, "Natural Law, Common Law, and the Constitution" in Edlin, ed, *supra* note 56, 171 at 177.

112 *Cooper, supra* note 21.

113 *Imperial Tobacco, supra* note 82.

114 *Ibid* at paras 97–101.

115 *Ibid* at para 95.

the rights infringements are not disproportionate to that goal's achievement.[116] Chamberlain sees in these decisions instances of deference to government derived from the necessity of restricting the role of judges in accordance with the separation of powers.

Sandomierski focuses on one particular animating feature of Chief Justice McLachlin's judicial approach — the selection of which legal process, institution, or source is most appropriate in the given circumstances. In doing so, he decentres the "outcome" and "motivation" as elements of her philosophy. Through several public and private law examples, he illustrates that a salient feature of Chief Justice McLachlin's judicial philosophy is a due regard for the distinctive claim to legitimacy that a given legal institution or branch of government may have in a given circumstance. Sandomierski explains that the first question in the pursuit of justice is whether judicial intervention is appropriate.

McInnes's chapter on unjust enrichment also demonstrates the common law approach that the Chief Justice adopted, especially in the early part of her career. In his description of how the Court innovated in the law of restitution, he points out how McLachlin J, in her reasons in *Peel*, acknowledged both the need to look forward – to develop the law in a way that met changing social circumstances – while not forgetting the past, or the common law framework for compensation for unjust enrichment. She was not faced with a *tabula rasa* but, rather, was required to fit the new principled approach to restitution based on unjust enrichment within the principles animating the old categories of recovery.

Gourlay, in his characterization of the Chief Justice as an advocate of "criminal law minimalism" – the idea that the criminal law, being a blunt tool for controlling anti-social behaviour, should be used only when the harms of doing so do not outweigh the benefits – demonstrates that the civil libertarian streak so evident in her early judgments in cases such as *Keegstra*, *Zundel*, and *Rodriguez* is consistent with her style as a common law judge. Indeed, Douglas Husak, whose work advocates against overcriminalization (overuse of the criminal sanction to deal with social ills), derives the central test for weighing the competing interests at issue in many criminal cases from the common law. "Over time," Husak writes, "and through the trial and error distinctive

116 For an explanation of why the Supreme Court of Canada's approach to analysis under section 1 of the *Charter* may be overly deferential and hence unprincipled, see Graham Mayeda, "Between Principle and Pragmatism: The Decline of Principled Reasoning in the Jurisprudence of the McLachlin Court" in Sanda Rodgers & Sheila McIntyre, eds, *The Supreme Court of Canada and Social Justice: Commitment, Retrenchment or Retreat* (Markham, ON: LexisNexis, 2010) 41 at 81–7.

of the common law, courts have refined a test to determine the constitutionality of state actions that implicate those rights that are granted an intermediate level of protection."[117] Gourlay argues that it is this very test that the Chief Justice and the Supreme Court implemented in recent decisions dealing with the legality of the criminalization of suicide, sex-work/prostitution, and illegal drug use. In the cases that address these topics, the Court has essentially required the government to explain how certain criminal prohibitions promote an important policy that warrants the harms that criminalization imposes.

In her chapter on the Chief Justice's deep commitment to the principle of open justice, Bodnár takes a wider view of the Chief Justice's judicial style by looking beyond her judgments to her extrajudicial writings, speeches, and actions. Bodnár concludes that Chief Justice McLachlin took an activist approach to open justice, and that she underlined the importance of this concept not only in words but also through her actions. Bodnár considers Chief Justice McLachlin's era to be one of significant growth for the open justice principle. During this period, McLachlin substantially improved communications with the media, made written arguments available to the public online, increased the profile of the Court through speeches and interviews on a range of topics, and strengthened ties with judges from countries around the world.

IV. Conclusion

This book contributes to scholarship in three different ways: it documents key controversies in areas of the common law and explains how the Supreme Court of Canada and Chief Justice McLachlin, in particular, have addressed them; it illustrates the complexity of the phenomenon of the common law as a method of legal judgment that transgresses the traditional boundaries within which it has traditionally been confined by legal theorists and lawyers; and it provides an initial sketch of the Chief Justice's common law judicial style.

During her career on the Supreme Court of Canada, Chief Justice McLachlin contributed to fundamental changes in numerous areas of the law, many controversial. Chapters 2 (Hale), 3 (Feldthusen), 4 (Chamberlain), 5 (McInnes), and 6 (Sandomierski) analyse her contributions to

117 Douglas Husak, *Overcriminalization: The Limits of the Criminal Law* (Oxford: Oxford University Press, 2008) at 128.

private law, with a focus on tort law and the law of unjust enrichment. Chapters 7 (Tanovich), 8 (Mayeda), 9 (Gourlay), 10 (Goldenberg), and 11 (Bodnár) illustrate her common law approach to what is frequently considered "public law," including the law of evidence, criminal law, and administrative law. What emerges from these authors' analysis is the picture of a judge who took inspiration from the incremental and iterative nature of the common law and applied this approach, especially in the first half of her career on the Supreme Court, in both private and public law. Her approach highlights the porosity of what lawyers traditionally regard as rigid categories, such as private law and public law, common law and statute. Above all, Chief Justice McLachlin was sensitive to the need for the law to adapt to social change. She made this clear in a speech presented to the Council of the Canadian Bar Association on 11 August 2016, in which she wrote,

> I believe meeting the challenge of providing access to justice to ordinary Canadians must be a top priority, if we are to maintain public confidence in the justice system. If people are excluded from the system, if they conclude it exists only to serve the interests of the elites, they will turn away. Respect for the rule of law will diminish, and our society will be the poorer.[118]

However, adapting the law to social conditions must be done in a principled way that accords with the separation of powers and the limited role given to courts within the Canadian constitutional framework. Her common law approach to the law, which requires all decisions to be based on principles that emerge from the past while looking at the future, was well suited to integrating emerging social needs into the law in a way that respected the institutional role of courts.

---

118 Beverley McLachlin, "Remarks to the Council of the Canadian Bar Association at the Canadian Legal Conference" (Canadian Legal Conference, Ottawa, 11 August 2016), online: <https://scc-csc.ca/judges-juges/spe-dis/bm-2016-08-11-eng.aspx>.

2 Reflecting on the Legacy of Chief Justice McLachlin

LADY HALE, PRESIDENT OF THE SUPREME COURT OF THE UNITED KINGDOM

I. Introduction

We are all here to celebrate the legacy of your remarkable Chief Justice – a legacy that is inherited, not only by Canada, but also by other parts of the common law world – not least in the United Kingdom. In my country, her legacy is not just her jurisprudence, but also her shining embodiment of the virtues of diversity, and in particular gender diversity, in the judiciary.

II. Gender Diversity in the Judiciary

On 1 April 2003, less than 10 percent of the senior judiciary in England and Wales were women, but the judicial leaders – the Lord Chief Justice and Lord Chancellor – still believed in the "trickle up" theory, that eventually all the able young women joining the legal profession would trickle up to the top without anyone having to do anything very much to change the system. This was a system in which all appointments were recommended by the Lord Chancellor, mainly on the basis of his "secret soundings" among members of the existing judiciary – a recipe for cloning, even though it occasionally let a non-traditional candidate like me through the net.

Then, on 2 July 2003, Chief Justice McLachlin came to address a meeting organized by the Association of Women Barristers (of which I was then president), with the Association of Women Solicitors, in Committee Room 10 at the Houses of Parliament in London. The Lord Chief Justice of England and Wales was present. Chief Justice McLachlin explained why having more women on the bench was a good thing. She explained how this had been achieved in Canada only because of the concerted efforts of the legal profession, the judiciary, and the politicians to make a difference. She made a powerful case, and I think it hit home. Fifteen years later, we have an entirely different system of judicial appointments, independent of government and wholly merit based. We also have a much more diverse judiciary. We don't yet have the figures for 1 April 2018, but last year 22 percent of High Court judges and 24 percent of Court of Appeal judges were women – still far too low, but much more than double the 2003 figures. We even doubled the number of Supreme Court Justices – from one to two. Thank you, Chief Justice McLachlin – we owe a lot to you.

I remember that meeting for another reason, which I quoted in a recent judgment about the treatment of transgender women by Job Centre staff: "We lead women's lives: we have no choice."[1] Thus has the Chief Justice of Canada, the Rt Hon Beverley McLachlin, summed up the basic truth that women and men do indeed lead different lives. Our lives are different, not just because of the choices we make but because of the way that other people perceive and treat us. By using her words, I was able to acknowledge the centrality of gender in most people's lives and how desperately important it is for trans people to be recognized and related to wholly in their reassigned gender, the gender that they have always felt themselves to be.

Occasionally our gender may make a difference to our judging – and even to other people's judging, because casual, almost unconscious, sexism is difficult to voice when there is even one woman around to challenge it. But much of the time it makes no difference. The legacy that Chief Justice McLachlin has left to the law of the United Kingdom is not in areas where her gender might be thought to have played a part, but in the mainstream principles of public law, common law, and equity. There are four main areas where her judgments have regularly been cited in recent UK cases: proportionality, illegality, unjust enrichment and equitable compensation, and vicarious liability.[2]

III. Proportionality

Bank Mellat v Her Majesty's Treasury concerned the implementation of sanctions against those whose activities were thought to support the nuclear program in Iran.[3] The issue was whether excluding one particular

---

1 *R (C) v Secretary of State for Work and Pensions*, [2017] UKSC 72 at para 1.

2 I am most grateful to my judicial assistant, Penelope Gorman, for the help she has given me in finding these references.

3 *Bank Mellat v Her Majesty's Treasury*, [2013] UKSC 39 [*Bank Mellat*].

Iranian bank from the London financial markets was a proportionate means of protecting UK national interests from the threat posed by that nuclear program. Lord Sumption (for the majority) and Lord Reed (for the minority) both adopted a four-part analysis of proportionality along Canadian lines. Lord Reed described the analysis of Chief Justice Dickson in *R v Oakes*[4] as "the clearest and most influential judicial analysis of proportionality within the common law tradition of legal reasoning."[5] The benefit lay in breaking the concept down into distinct elements: (1) whether the objective of the measure is sufficiently important to justify the limitation of a protected right – or, as you would put it, is "pressing and substantial"; (2) whether the measure is rationally connected to that objective; and (3) whether a less intrusive measure could have been used without unacceptably compromising the attainment of the objective – or, as you would put it, whether it is "minimally impairing." But those three alone are not enough. The key concept is (4), as explained by Chief Justice McLachlin in *Alberta v Hutterian Brethren of Wilson Colony*,[6] a case about whether requiring everyone to have a photograph on their drivers' licence was a proportionate restriction of religious freedom. She wrote that, even if the objective is sufficiently important and the measure is rationally connected to that objective, and the objective cannot be achieved by a less intrusive measure, it still has to be asked whether the harm done by the limitation of a protected right is proportionate to the public benefit conferred by that limitation. In other words – do the ends justify the means? There will be some means that are so destructive of the right that they cannot be justified.

In the *Hutterian Brethren* case, Chief Justice McLachlin was concerned that this last and most important element had not featured strongly in Canadian jurisprudence until then. The same may be said of our own jurisprudence, which adopted the first three elements in the case of *de Freitas* in 1999,[7] but did not clearly acknowledge the fourth until much later.[8] It is now firmly established. Chief Justice McLachlin's explanation of the "meaningful distinction" between the first and fourth

4 *R v Oakes*, [1986] 1 SCR 103.

5 *Bank Mellat*, *supra* note 3 at para 74.

6 *Alberta v Hutterian Brethren of Wilson Colony*, 2009 SCC 37 [*Hutterian Brethren*].

7 *de Freitas v Permanent Secretary of the Ministry of Agriculture, Fisheries, Lands and Housing*, [1998] UKPC 30.

8 In *Huang v Secretary of State for the Home Department*, [2007] UKHL 11 at para 19, Lord Bingham stated that, "If insufficient attention has been paid to this requirement [striking a fair balance between the rights of the individual and the interests of the community] the failure should be made good."

elements of the inquiry was quoted again by Lord Kerr in *R (Lord Carlile of Berriew) v Secretary of State for the Home Department*,[9] a case about whether banning an Iranian dissident politician from coming to the United Kingdom to talk with politicians in the Houses of Parliament was a proportionate means of protecting the United Kingdom's "fragile but imperative" relations with Iran. Some might find it strange that our government was prepared to imperil those relations by severely restricting the activities of a major Iranian bank but not by allowing a Paris-based dissident to make a brief trip to the United Kingdom. We found the first disproportionate but the second not.

However useful it may be to break down the inquiry into its component parts, the reality is that answering the "ends versus means" or "individual versus community" question is always difficult: your court was divided in the *Hutterian Brethren* case, and ours was divided in both the *Bank Mellat* and *Lord Carlile* cases.

IV. Illegality

While our approach to proportionality is now well settled along Canadian lines, it has taken us longer to adopt a Canadian-style approach to the defence of illegality in tort, contract, and restitution claims. In *Hounga v Allen*,[10] one panel of the UK Supreme Court wrestled with a claim brought by a Nigerian victim of trafficking, brought to the United Kingdom to work illegally in domestic service and grossly ill-treated and exploited in breach of our labour laws until she managed to escape. It was accepted that she could not sue on the illegal contract of employment, but she sued for the statutory tort of race discrimination. But was her claim barred by the illegality? Lord Wilson asked, first, what is the aspect of public policy that founds the defence? And second, is there another aspect of public policy to which applying the defence would run counter? In answering the first question, he expressly adopted the analysis of Justice McLachlin in *Hall v Hebert*,[11] the case of the drunken driver injured by a mixture of his own and his passenger's carelessness. The basis of the power to bar recovery in tort, she said,

> lies in the duty of the courts to preserve the integrity of the legal system, and is exercisable only where this concern is in issue. This concern is in

9 *R (Lord Carlile of Berriew) v Secretary of State for the Home Department*, [2014] UKSC 60 at para 149.

10 *Hounga v Allen*, [2014] UKSC 47.

11 *Hall v Hebert*, [1993] 2 SCR 159.

> issue where a damage award in a civil suit would, in effect, allow a person to profit from illegal or wrongful conduct, or would permit evasion or rebate of a penalty prescribed by the criminal law. The idea common to these instances is that the law refuses to give by its right hand what it takes away by its left hand.[12]

Awarding compensation for injury to the claimant's feelings did not allow her to profit from her wrongful conduct; nor did it enable her to evade a penalty prescribed by the criminal law; nor did it compromise the integrity of the legal system by encouraging people like her to enter into illegal contracts of employment; on the contrary, denying her a remedy would compromise the integrity of the legal system by encouraging employers to exploit people in this way. (It also occurred to me that, even if she could not enforce her contract of employment, she ought to be able to claim a *quantum meruit* for the work that she had done.)

Meanwhile, another panel of the Supreme Court was deciding *Les Laboratoires Servier v Apotex Inc*,[13] a case with a Canadian connection. In brief, holders of a European patent for a particular drug and their licensed distributors obtained an interim injunction prohibiting the defendants from distributing the same drug. In return, they gave the usual undertaking to compensate the defendants for their loss if it later turned out that the injunction should not have been granted. The European patent was then held invalid, so damages were assessed at over £17 million. Meanwhile, a federal court in Canada had held that the defendants were in breach of a Canadian patent. Should this illegality bar their claim under the English undertaking? The Supreme Court was unanimous in holding that committing the tort of infringing a foreign patent was not "turpitude" for the purpose of the doctrine of illegality, and Lord Sumption referred to the "much- admired" judgment of Justice McLachlin in *Hall v Hebert*. But the judgments revealed a disagreement between Lord Sumption (with whom Lord Neuberger, Lord Mance, and Lord Clarke agreed), who espoused the "reliance test" adopted by the House of Lords in *Tinsley v Milligan* – does the claimant have to rely upon the illegality to found the claim? – and Lord Toulson, who favoured a more flexible test, based upon the "integrity of the legal system."[14]

---

12 *Ibid* at 169.

13 *Les Laboratoires Servier v Apotex Inc*, [2014] UKSC 55.

14 *Tinsley v Milligan*, [1993] UKHL 3.

That disagreement also featured in *Jetivia SA v Bilta (UK) Ltd*,[15] in which Lord Sumption continued to favour the *Tinsley v Milligan* approach and thought that *Hounga v Allen* turned on its special facts, while Lord Toulson and Lord Hodge favoured the more flexible approach, citing *Hounga v Allen* as an example. The disagreement did not have to be resolved in that case, but Lord Neuberger expressed the hope that an opportunity would soon come along for a panel of seven or nine to do so.

He did not have to wait long. We assembled a nine-justice panel for *Patel v Mirza*.[16] Mr Patel had transferred a large sum of money to Mr Mirza for the purpose of betting on the price of Royal Bank of Scotland shares, relying on information that Mr Mirza expected to obtain from contacts in the bank. This would have been illegal insider trading. But it never happened, because the inside information was not forthcoming. Mr Mirza refused to pay the money back, and Mr Patel sued. We held that he was entitled to his money back, on the basis that returning the money would simply return the parties to the position in which they were before the transaction and avoid the unjust enrichment that Mr Mirza would otherwise enjoy. The majority espoused the more flexible approach and rejected the "reliance test" espoused by the minority. *Hall v Hebert* featured extensively in Lord Toulson's review of the comparative law, and the "integrity of the legal system" approach was described as a "valuable insight." The majority approach involved considering (a) the underlying purpose of the prohibition transgressed; (b) any other public policies rendered ineffective or less effective by denying the claim; and (c) the possibility of overkill unless the law was applied with a sense of proportionality.

Lord Kerr agreed with this approach, although he did point out that Justice McLachlin had rejected the suggestion that the law of *ex turpi causa* should be replaced by a power to reject claims on grounds of public policy; but, he commented, what was the integrity of the legal system approach, if not a public policy consideration?[17] Yet, as I read *Hall v Hebert*, the real debate was not so much about the relevance of policy, but about whether it should be applied at the duty of care stage or as a bar at a later stage. *Hall v Hebert* was, of course, a tort case, whereas we have applied a version of that approach across the board, to claims in

15 *Jetivia SA v Bilta (UK) Ltd*, [2015] UKSC 23.

16 *Patel v Mirza*, [2016] UKSC 42.

17 The fullest account of the "valuable insight" in *Hall v Hebert* is, in fact, given by Lord Mance, who was in the minority.

tort, contract, and unjust enrichment. I wonder what the Chief Justice really thinks of our decision.

V. Unjust Enrichment and Equitable Compensation

We have recently been reminded of Chief Justice McLachlin's preference for principle over policy in the field of unjust enrichment. In *Peter v Beblow*, while upholding a claim for unjust enrichment brought by an unmarried cohabitant who had rendered domestic services for no reward, she warned: "There is a tendency on the part of some to view the action for unjust enrichment as a device doing what may seem fair between the parties. In the rush to substantive justice the principles are sometimes forgotten."[18] She proceeded to ask whether the defendant had been enriched to the detriment of the claimant and then whether there was a juristic basis for that enrichment – and it was under the third head that she considered that policy questions might arise.

Her dictum was cited by Lord Reed in *Investment Trust Companies v Revenue and Customs Commissioners*,[19] where the issue was whether the Revenue had been enriched at the expense of the company. Lord Reed cited Justice McLachlin when emphasizing that claims for unjust enrichment are matters of right, depending on rules of law, to be denied only on the basis of legal principle and not as a matter of discretion.

Her principled approach to unjust enrichment was also apparent in *Peel (Regional Municipality) v Canada; Peel (Regional Municipality) v Ontario*,[20] two citations from which appeared in *Benedetti v Sawiris*.[21] One was by Lord Clarke, quoting Goff and Jones's reference to her observation that the common law "places a premium on the right to choose how to spend one's money."[22] The other was by Lord Reed (dissenting), who referred to her statement that "[t]he concept of 'injustice' in the context of the law of restitution harkens back to the Aristotelean notion of correcting a balance or equilibrium that has been disrupted."[23] The case was about how the enrichment was to be valued – and Justice McLachlin was prayed in aid in support of both sides – the one arguing for a "subjective" approach of how much the defendant would be

18 *Peter v Beblow*, [1993] 1 SCR 980 at 988.

19 *Investment Trust Companies v Revenue and Customs Commissioners*, [2017] UKSC 29.

20 *Peel (Regional Municipality) v Canada; Peel (Regional Municipality) v Ontario*, [1992] 3 SCR 762.

21 *Benedetti v Sawiris*, [2013] UKSC 50.

22 *Ibid* at para 18.

23 *Ibid* at para 97.

willing to pay for the claimant's services and the other arguing for an "objective" approach of how much they were worth to him. The subjectivists won, but I am not sure which side Justice McLachlin would have favoured.

More significantly, in *Various claimants v Giambrone & Law (a firm)*,[24] the Court of Appeal has recently observed that Justice McLachlin's judgment in *Canson Enterprises Ltd v Boughton & Co*[25] has on a number of occasions been cited by English courts as reflecting the English law on equitable compensation. Lord Justice Jackson quoted her rejection of an analogy with damages in tort:[26]

> The basis of the fiduciary obligation and the rationale for equitable compensation are distinct from the tort of negligence and contract. In negligence and contract the parties are taken to be independent and equal actors, concerned primarily with their own self-interest ... The essence of a fiduciary relationship, by contrast, is that one party pledges herself to act in the best interests of the other. The fiduciary relationship has trust, not self-interest, at its core and when breach occurs, the balance favours the person wronged.

Another valuable insight, you may think. An Italian law firm, practising in London and Italy, received deposits paid by British and Irish purchasers of Italian properties "off plan" and released them to the Italian vendor and agent, despite having promised not to do so unless the guarantees required by Italian law had been supplied – which they were not. The Court held it irrelevant that the guarantees would have made no difference. The firm was ordered to repay the purchasers in full. We refused permission to appeal in December 2017.

VI. Vicarious Liability

Perhaps most influential of all has been Justice McLachlin's contribution to the development of the law of vicarious liability, in *Bazley v Curry*,[27] *Jacobi v Griffiths*,[28] and *John Doe v Bennett*.[29] We have all had to

---

24 *Various claimants v Giambrone & Law (a firm)*, [2017] EWCA Civ 1193 [*Giambrone & Law*].

25 *Canson Enterprises Ltd v Boughton & Co*, [1991] 3 SCR 534.

26 *Giambrone & Law*, *supra* note 24 at para 50.

27 *Bazley v Curry*, [1999] 2 SCR 534.

28 *Jacobi v Griffiths*, [1999] 2 SCR 570.

29 *John Doe v Bennett*, [2004] 1 SCR 436 [*Bennett*].

wrestle with the responsibility of institutions for sexual abuse perpetrated by people working within them. This affects both parts of the vicarious liability inquiry – the relationship between the institution and the perpetrator – which used to be a contract of employment – and the connection between that relationship and the acts complained of – which used to be summed up in the phrase "the course or scope of his employment." The answer to the latter question came first.

How could acts of sexual abuse possibly be within the scope of a person's employment? It was the last thing that the employer wanted him to do. *Bazley v Curry* and *Jacobi v Griffiths* supplied both the answer and the rationale – the answer was the "strong connection" test, and the rationale was the increased risk of harm arising out of the employer's enterprise. In *Lister v Hesley Hall*, the House of Lords adopted a "close connection" test modelled on the Canadian approach, Lord Steyn describing the judgments of Justice McLachlin as "luminous and illuminating" and a genuine advance on previous thinking.[30] The UK Supreme Court has recently applied that same approach in relation to an egregious act of violence carried out by a petrol station employee against a hapless customer.[31]

The answer to the first question was more troubling. Sadly, much sexual abuse has been perpetrated by priests, monks, and other clergy who work within organized religion but are not its employees in the technical sense. In *John Doe v Bennett*,[32] Chief Justice McLachlin held that the relationship of priest and diocese was sufficiently "akin to employment" to make the diocesan episcopal corporation vicariously liable for the priest's misdeeds. Once again, the rationale was the enterprise risk – "a person who puts a risky enterprise into the community may fairly be held responsible when those risks emerge and cause loss or injury to members of the public."[33] In *Various Claimants v Catholic Child Welfare Society*,[34] the UK Supreme Court held that the Institute of the Brothers of the Christian Schools (usually known as the Christian Brothers) was vicariously liable (jointly with the brothers' actual employers) for sexual abuse carried out by members of the Institute at a boarding school for delinquent boys, relying very heavily on the Canadian jurisprudence in doing so. More recently, we have applied

30 *Lister v Hesley Hall*, [2001] UKHL 22.

31 *Mohamud v WM Morrison Supermarkets plc*, [2016] UKSC 11.

32 *Bennett*, supra note 29.

33 *Ibid* at para 20.

34 *Various Claimants v Catholic Child Welfare Society*, [2012] UKSC 56.

the "akin to employment" test in the very different context of the work done by prisoners in a prison.[35]

But we have now gone even further than you have done. In *Armes v Nottinghamshire County Council*,[36] we found a local authority that had a child in their care vicariously liable for acts of physical and sexual abuse carried out by foster parents with whom the authority had placed the child. We distinguished the Canadian case of *KLB v British Columbia* on the basis that the English courts had not adopted deterrence as a reason for extending vicarious liability.[37] However, Lord Reed also observed that "[t]he most influential idea in modern times has been that it is just that an enterprise which takes the benefit of activities carried on by a person integrated into its organization should also bear the cost of harm wrongfully caused by that person in the course of those activities."[38] That influential idea can, of course, be traced back to *Bazley v Curry*, as can the idea of enterprise risk, which also played its part in our decision. The foster parents provided care as an integral part of the local authority's organization of its child care services. It was an activity carried on for the benefit of the local authority. And it created a relationship of authority and trust between the child and the foster parent in circumstances where close control could not be exercised, thus making the child particularly vulnerable to abuse. Ironically, therefore, while control used to be the watchword of vicarious liability, in that case it was the lack of control over a situation of the local authority's own making that led to it.

VII. Conclusion

There are many more cases than these in which first Justice and then Chief Justice McLachlin has been cited in our courts. Canada is probably the "go to" jurisdiction when we are looking at comparative law, followed by Australia, New Zealand, and Hong Kong, and, in some areas but not others, the United States and South Africa: so much so that, if we find that we are departing from recent Canadian authority, we are troubled about it.[39] Some of us were sorry that judgment had not

35 *Cox v Ministry of Justice*, [2016] UKSC 10.

36 *Armes v Nottinghamshire County Council*, [2017] UKSC 60 [*Armes*].

37 *KLB v British Columbia*, 2003 SCC 51.

38 *Armes*, *supra* note 36 at para 67.

39 For example, *Whitlock v Moree*, [2017] UKPC 44, where the Board was divided about the effect of banking documents on the beneficial interests in a joint bank account, especially in the light of *Niles v Lake*, [1947] SCR 291 and *Pecore v Pecore*, 2007 SCC 17.

been given in *Carter v Canada (Attorney General)* before we had to give judgment in our own assisted suicide case.[40]

One of the reasons why the approach of Canadian courts is of such interest to us, and to other courts outside Canada, may be your openness to cross-cultural influences. Your Supreme Court has been active in and encouraged the frequent use of foreign law. This may be, as Markesinis, Ackermann, and Fedtke suggest,[41] because your mixed cultural background has prepared you for a multi-cultural approach to law. Unlike the United States, you are more prone to a "dialogic" model. This includes reference not only to UK, Commonwealth, and American case law, but also to civilian systems. As they say:

> The Canadian universalism may thus demonstrate the confident state of an eclectic mind which does not see in transnational judicial dialogue a threat to national individuality or an impoverishment of the local legal culture but, on the contrary, a source of constant inspiration and reinforced judicial legitimacy.[42]

My few examples have shown that this is very much a two-way dialogue – from our point of view, we have probably learned more from you than the other way about, and Chief Justice McLachlin's valuable insights are a large part of the reason for that.

---

40 *Carter v Canada (Attorney General)*, 2015 SCC 5; *cf R (Nicklinson) v Ministry of Justice*, [2014] UKSC 38.

41 BS Markesinis, Laurie Ackermann & Jorg Fedtke, *Judicial Recourse to Foreign Law: A New Source of Inspiration* (London: UCL Press, 2006) at 84.

42 *Ibid*.

PART ONE

Controversies in Private Law

3 Justice Beverley McLachlin and Tort Law: The Good, the Bad, and the Puzzling

BRUCE FELDTHUSEN

I. Introduction

During her twenty-eight years on the Supreme Court, Justice McLachlin sat on all but 13 of the 145 torts cases that came before the Court.[1] Nine of the 13 she missed came between her initial appointment in 1989 and 1992. She was present for every tort hearing from jurisdictions other than Quebec between 1992 and 2002, and for every tort hearing from 2002 until she retired in 2017.

Her participation rate was about average for the judges who sat during that twenty-eight-year period, but her total number of cases was almost double that of any other common law judge because of her long tenure.

Justice McLachlin was in the majority in 82 percent of the torts cases on which she sat, 85 percent after she became Chief Justice. She gave the majority judgement in 26 percent of them. She wrote the majority decision for 34 cases of the 132 she heard and gave the judgment of the Court 20 times out of 132 cases heard.[2]

---

1 I have referred to Justice McLachlin when speaking generally of her as Justice McLachlin. I have referred to her as either J or CJ, as the case was, when discussing her decisions in particular cases.

2 I would like to thank my research assistant, Gavin Inkster, for compiling these statistics. He explains his methodology as follows:

> For every search, I defined the range as 1989 to the present. I included every case where the Court's analysis addressed whether or not a tort had occurred, or discussed the elements of a specific tort. To populate my list, I started by searching the QuickLaw database for every Supreme Court of Canada decision that contained the word "tort" and included every case that met the criteria. I cross-referenced my list with cases categorized as "torts" cases in the Judgements of the Supreme Court of Canada database by Lexum. The Lexum

It is possible to review in any detail only a small sample of Justice McLachlin's 132 tort decisions. I will begin with her most courageous and socially significant contribution, her unequivocal support for women, and for all victims of sexual battery. She stands, openly and forcefully, at the forefront of the outcomes in so many ground-breaking cases dealing with challenging subjects such as sexual violence, consent, motherhood, and vicarious liability for child sexual abuse. This contribution has not received the recognition it deserves.[3]

Next, I have chosen to concentrate on negligence law, where Justice McLachlin sat on every single one of the thirty-nine pure negligence cases that came to the Court during her tenure.[4] In particular, I will consider her more technical contributions to the law of negligence on the matter of proximity. Her views on proximity in the recognition of novel duties of care dominate thirty years of rapid growth in Canadian negligence law. They are of tremendous significance to tort lawyers. Unfortunately, I conclude that little or no meaningful progress was made on these questions during her time on the Court. In some respects, Canadian negligence law has regressed. Justice McLachlin's concept of proximity is a shape-shifter, and the two-step *Anns/Cooper* template for recognizing novel duties is a sham.[5]

Third, I will discuss three puzzlers – decisions that make no sense to me. They deal with the low standard of care required of investigating police officers when dealing with suspects;[6] the continuing unnecessary hurdles faced by victims of psychiatric harm to recover damages for provable injury;[7] and the reductions to damage awards for residential school survivors who have suffered sequential sexual batteries.[8]

---

categorized list did not appear to be exhaustive, so I ran the same "tort" keyword search through the entire Lexum database and found the same list of cases that appeared on QuickLaw. I re-assessed cases I had left off my list at this stage. Finally, I went through hard copies of the Supreme Court Reports at the Brian Dickson Law Library, searching for cases categorized as "Tort," "Negligence," "Damages," "Civil Liability" and "Banking."

3 Ironically, Justice McLachlin has been criticized for several of her important judgments involving the rights of women in criminal law. See e.g. for example Martha Schafer, "*Seaboyer v R*: A Case Comment," (1992) 5:1 CJWL 202 at 209–11.

4 Mr Inkster defined pure negligence cases as any case dealing only with duty, standard, causation, remoteness, damages (but *not* quantum), or defences to a negligence action.

5 See *infra*, Part III.c: "*Cooper v Hobart*: McLachlin CJ Wins the Day."

6 *Hill v Hamilton-Wentworth Police Services Board*, 2007 SCC 41 [*Hill*].

7 *Mustapha v Culligan of Canada Ltd*, 2008 SCC 27 [*Mustapha*].

8 *Blackwater v Plint*, 2005 SCC 58 [*Blackwater*].

It is difficult to identify general trends in Justice McLachlin's decisions beyond her crystal clear and precisely ordered writing style. Nevertheless, before beginning the discussion of the three topics noted above, it may be helpful to identify a few background tendencies that emerge generally.

First, some might argue that Justice McLachlin tended to defer to the government. In highway maintenance cases, she did invariably side with the government and other public authority defendants, beginning with her decision as the trial judge in *Just v British Columbia*.[9] She introduced the American doctrine of government policy immunity to Canada,[10] and kept it alive despite strong criticism from the House of Lords.[11] She sided with the public regulators in *Cooper v Hobart* and *Edwards v Law Society of Upper Canada*.[12] One could argue that she sided with the police and against wrongfully convicted suspects in *Hill*.[13] On the other hand, if we look at the *Charter* damage cases, McLachlin CJ decided against the government in *Ward, Henry,* and *Ernst*.[14] In *Henry*, an action against a public prosecutor for withholding important evidence from an accused, her dissenting judgment offered a strong endorsement of individual *Charter* rights, in contrast to the majority, which was content to water them down to promote an efficient public prosecution system.

I leave it to the reader to decide whether this body of work evidences a tendency to defer to the government. Except for *Hill*, for reasons I explain below, I have no quarrel with the results in any of these cases. I would put the general observation differently. Justice McLachlin has always respected the separate role of the courts and the legislatures, deferring not to government but to the constitutional separation of powers. When she felt the matter properly fell within the judicial sphere, she had no reluctance to rule against the government. One may disagree with how she chose to achieve this balance, but one should surely commend her for trying to strike it.

---

9 *Just v British Columbia*, (1985), 64 BCLR 349 (BCSC), [1985] 5 WWR 570 [*Just*].

10 *Ibid.*

11 *R v Imperial Tobacco Canada Ltd*, 2011 SCC 42 [*Imperial Tobacco*]. The House of Lords declared the "policy/operational distinction unworkable in difficult cases," a point said to be evidenced by the Canadian jurisprudence: *Stovin v Wise*, [1996] AC 923 (HL), [1996] 3 WLR 389 per Lord Hoffmann.

12 *Cooper v Hobart*, 2001 SCC 79 [*Cooper*]; *Edwards v Law Society of Upper Canada*, 2001 SCC 80.

13 *Hill, supra* note 6.

14 *Vancouver (City) v Ward*, 2010 SCC 27 [*Ward*]; *Henry v British Columbia (Attorney General)*, 2015 SCC 24 [*Henry*]; *Ernst v Alberta Energy Regulator*, 2017 SCC 1 [*Ernst*].

Was Justice McLachlin a rights-based judge or a policy maker?[15] Most of the evidence puts Justice McLachlin in the policy camp. She was always a strong supporter of the *Anns* case, the most influential policy decision ever in Canadian tort law.[16] Many of her judgments explicitly refer to and approve an activist policy-making role for judges. As will be noted, her unfailing tendency to strike down *prima facie* duties on policy grounds such as government immunity[17] or potential indeterminate liability[18] put her firmly in the policy camp. Yet, she did also rely on rights-based principles as opposed to consequentialist policies. Her decision on proximity in *Childs*, in which she applied the principle of autonomy to find no duty was owed by a social host who provided alcohol, is the best example.[19] *Henry*, the *Charter* damage decision, and *Norberg v Wynrib*, a consent to sexual relations decision, were others.[20] Perhaps it would be more accurate to describe her as a pragmatist, turning to rights or policy as she felt the occasion demanded. Justice McLachlin never took the distinction between principle and policy very seriously. And she proved as likely to raise policy arguments as rights-based principles at Step 1 of the *Anns/Cooper* template.[21]

---

15 At the risk of over-simplification, by policymaking I mean adopting a rule to achieve a particular purpose, such as deterrence of a perceived social problem, like shoddy residential housing construction in *Anns v Merton London Borough Council*, [1977] UKHL 4, [1978] AC 728 (HL) [*Anns*] or *Winnipeg Condominium Corp No 36 v Bird Construction*, [1995] 1 SCR 85, 121 DLR (4th) 193 [*Winnipeg Condominium*], for example. For an exceptional US example of judicial social engineering, see *Escola v Coca Cola Bottling Co of Fresno*, USA 150 P 2d 436 (1944). In contrast, Professor Fridman has suggested that policy in relation to proximity is simply "judicial policy," a matter of determining whether, based on the relationship between the parties, it is just and fair to impose a legal duty of care on the defendant. See GHL Fridman, *Canadian Law of Torts*, 3rd ed (Toronto: Lexis Nexis, 2012). See also GHL Fridman, *The Law of Torts in Canada*, 2nd ed (Toronto: Carswell, 2002) at 9. A rights-based approach would limit the considerations to interferences with recognized rights such as personal security and property damage, and exclude the judicial pursuit of external distributional policy goals. See also chapter 4 by Erika Chamberlain in the present volume for an excellent discussion of the contrasting policy and rights-based approaches. I am delighted to discover the many similarities between the conclusions I reach here and those that appear in Dean Chamberlain's chapter.

16 *Anns, supra* note 15.

17 *Imperial Tobacco, supra* note 11.

18 *Deloitte & Touche v Livent Inc (Receiver of)*, 2017 SCC 63 [*Livent*].

19 *Childs v Desormeaux*, 2006 SCC 18 [*Childs*].

20 *Henry, supra* note 14; *Norberg v Wynrib*, [1992] 2 SCR 226 [*Norberg*].

21 *Cooper, supra* note 12 at para 27; *Livent, supra* note 18 at para 167.

In tort, was Justice McLachlin a champion for the vulnerable members of society? The evidence is mixed. On the one hand, the fates of Mr Mustapha, the vulnerable immigrant victim of serious psychiatric harm, and of the wrongly incarcerated Mr Hill, an Indigenous man, discussed in two of the puzzler decisions below, strike me as inexplicably insensitive to the issues faced by members of minority groups.[22] I say inexplicably because Justice McLachlin rightly enjoyed a reputation as champion for the vulnerable in other areas of law. The case of Ms. Childs is more complicated. Nevertheless, the *Childs* decision focuses almost exclusively on the rights of the host and the rights of the drunk driver. The plight of Ms. Childs, who was seriously injured when the drunk driver had a car accident, figures little in the reasons for judgment. In contrast, Justice McLachlin was unequivocally supportive of women, and of all victims of sexual battery, the topic to which I now turn.

II. The Good: Rights of Women and Victims of Sexual Battery

What distinguishes Justice McLachlin's judgments affecting women is her transparent articulation of what it means to be a woman in Canadian law. If she saw sexism from other members of the Court, she called it out. Nor was she content to simply get the decision she wanted; she wrote several separate and more radical concurring reasons for judgment.

Her first exercise in leadership on issues affecting women arose in the 1992 case of *Norberg*.[23] This was a case in which a physician, in return for sexual favours, traded prescription drugs with a female patient whom he was treating for drug addiction. It was a 5–1 decision in the patient's favour – Sopinka J, in dissent, found that the patient had consented to the sexual encounters. The majority imposed liability in battery, giving an excellent interpretation of the power dynamics at work between a physician and a drug addict, which vitiated consent. McLachlin and L'Heureux-Dubé JJ gave a separate decision imposing liability for breach of fiduciary duty to which one cannot consent. Of significance for present purposes is not so much the doctrinal difference but the clarity with which the McLachlin and L'Heureux-Dubé JJ's judgment exposed and rejected the sexism inherent in many of the arguments made on behalf of the physician. The headnote provides a concise summary:

---

22 See *Mustapha, supra* note 7 and *Hill, supra* note 6.

23 *Norberg, supra* note 20.

> The short answer to the arguments based on wrongful conduct of the plaintiff is that she did nothing wrong in the context of this relationship. She was not a sinner, but a sick person, suffering from an addiction which proved to be uncontrollable in the absence of a professional drug rehabilitation program. The law might accuse the plaintiff of "double doctoring" and moralists might accuse her of licentiousness; but she did no wrong because not she but the doctor was responsible for this conduct. He had the power to cure her of her addiction, as her successful treatment after leaving his "care" demonstrated, but instead chose to use his power to keep her in her addicted state and to use her for his own sexual purposes. An application of the clean hands maxim here amounts to nothing more than "blaming the victim."

McLachlin J dealt with a number of cases in which the always controversial matter of abortion rights lurked in the background. First, she gave the judgment for a divided court in *Winnipeg Child and Family Services (Northwest Area) v G(DF)*.[24] A pregnant woman was addicted to glue sniffing, and the child welfare agency sought an order to take custody of the woman until her child was born. McLachlin J came right to her point:

> The law of Canada does not recognize the unborn child as a legal or juridical person. Once a child is born, alive and viable, the law may recognize that its existence began before birth for certain limited purposes. But the only right recognized is that of the born person. This is a general proposition, applicable to all aspects of the law, including the law of torts[25] . . . It follows that under the law as it presently stands, the fetus on whose behalf the agency purported to act in seeking the order for the respondent's detention was not a legal person and possessed no legal rights. If it was not a legal person and possessed no legal rights at the time of the application, then there was no legal person in whose interests the agency could act or in whose interests a court order could be made.[26]

She then offered a full and frank review of policy reasons why the common law should not be changed. On the topic of whether an unborn child could sue their mother, McLachlin J said:

24 *Winnipeg Child and Family Services (Northwest Area) v G(DF)*, [1997] 3 SCR 925.

25 *Ibid* at para 11.

26 *Ibid* at para 16.

> To permit an unborn child to sue its pregnant mother-to-be would introduce a radically new conception into the law; the unborn child and its mother as separate juristic persons in a mutually separable and antagonistic relation. Such a legal conception, moreover, is belied by the reality of the physical situation; for practical purposes, the unborn child and its mother-to-be are bonded in a union separable only by birth. Such a dramatic departure from the traditional legal characterization of the relationship between the unborn child and its future mother is better left to the legislature than effected by the courts.[27]

The question of whether a child born alive could sue its mother for injuries suffered in utero during a motor vehicle accident, when the mother was driving the car, came to the Supreme Court in *Dobson (Litigation Guardian of) v Dobson*.[28] Two judges held the child could sue. Four of the nine judges invoked similar policy arguments to hold that the child could not sue. McLachlin J, with whom L'Heureux-Dubé J agreed, gave a separate concurring judgment. Significantly, while approving of the policy-based approach of the majority, McLachlin J added a rights-based argument: liability for fetal injury by pregnant women would run contrary to two of the most fundamental *Charter* values – liberty and equality.[29]

Justice McLachlin's decision in *Non-Marine Underwriters, Lloyd's of London v Scalera* is a classic exposition of the right to personal security and, in particular, of a woman's right to control her own sexual autonomy.[30] In the United States and the United Kingdom, "battery" is defined as the intentional infliction of harmful or offensive contact upon the person of another without consent. This is not the definition in Canada. *Scalera* made clear that the plaintiff establishes the *prima facie* case of battery by proving direct contact. Period. No injury beyond contact is required. The direct contact is harmful or offensive in and of itself. The defendant may escape liability by proving the contact was neither intentional nor negligent. The defendant may also attempt to establish the affirmative defence that the plaintiff consented to the contact. In a 4–3 split majority decision, McLachlin J, speaking for the four, makes it clear that the law does not recognize a different rule for sexual battery.

Iacobucci J, speaking for the three, said that "putting the onus of proving lack of consent on the plaintiff simply recognizes that in the sexual

---

27 *Ibid* at para 29.

28 *Dobson (Litigation Guardian of) v Dobson*, [1999] 2 SCR 753.

29 *Ibid* at para 84.

30 *Non-Marine Underwriters, Lloyd's of London v Scalera*, 2000 SCC 24.

assault context, 'non-consensual' is equivalent to 'harmful or offensive'; and the latter has always been an element of the plaintiff's case."[31] He added, "Without denying the seriousness and frequency of sexual assault, the simple fact is that sexual activity – unlike being punched, stabbed, or shot – is usually consensual. It generally becomes harmful only if it is non-consensual, in the wider meaning of that word."[32] McLachlin J would have none of this. She opposed importing into tort law the difficulties with consent in sexual assault cases, including victim blaming, that have plagued the criminal law. The significance of her decision for victims of sexual assault is evident if one compares the approach in criminal law to the approach she outlines for tort law. Criminal law defines a crime from the perspective of the defendant's knowledge and intentions. Tort law defines the tort from the perspective of the victim's right to personal security. The point of departure is the inviolability of a person's body. This is in striking contrast to Iacobucci J's starting proposition that sexual contact is presumptively consensual.

One of McLachlin J's finest judgments was given on behalf of the Court in *Bazley v Curry*.[33] The plaintiff was a young boy who was sexually abused by an employee of a non-profit organization that operated a residential care facility for emotionally troubled children. The issue was whether the abuse had occurred in the course of employment, so as to justify the employer being held vicariously liable. The then-current law, known as the *Salmond* test, held that employers are vicariously liable for both employee acts authorized by the employer and unauthorized acts so connected with authorized acts that they may be regarded as modes (albeit improper modes) of doing authorized acts. This test was incomprehensible and tended to obscure the real issues in practice. The Court departed from the *Salmond* test and took a transparent enterprise-liability policy approach to the issue.[34] The idea was that enterprises that contributed to increasing the risk that their employees would commit torts would generally be better placed to bear and distribute the costs associated with the employees' acts than the typical victims. Assigning the costs of associated risk to the employer would then be reflected in a higher price for the employers' activity, which in turn would lower the enterprises' output and hence

---

31 *Ibid* at para 110.

32 *Ibid* at para 105.

33 *Bazley v Curry*, [1999] 2 SCR 534 [*Bazley*].

34 See Alan O Sykes, "The Boundaries of Vicarious Liability: An Economic Analysis of the Scope of Employment Rule and Related Legal Doctrines" (1988) 101:3 Harv L Rev 563. Binnie J would later say in *Jacobi v Griffiths*, [1999] 2 SCR 570 [*Jacobi*] that the Court had not intended to change the law in *Bazley*.

reduce the incidence of the risk. This was not a fault-based argument, but rather strict liability based on the goals of deterrence, loss spreading, and compensation. This policy perspective was surely appropriate, given that vicarious liability itself is inherently a legal policy designed to further the goals of compensation and deterrence in cases where the typical impecuniosity of the perpetrator thwarts them.[35] McLachlin J said:

> In summary, the test for vicarious liability for an employee's sexual abuse of a client should focus on whether the employer's enterprise and empowerment of the employee materially increased the risk of the sexual assault and hence the harm . . . Because of the peculiar exercises of power and trust that pervade cases such as child abuse, special attention should be paid to the existence of a power or dependency relationship, which on its own often creates a considerable risk of wrongdoing.[36]

The potentially sweeping scope of the *Bazley* decision was soon reined in by three other important Supreme Court decisions. The first was *Jacobi*, in a judgment released simultaneously with *Bazley*.[37] A brother, age eleven, and sister, age fourteen, were sexually abused by the director of an after-school non-residential drop-in centre for children. The Supreme Court, split 4–3, refused to impose vicarious liability. Both the majority and the dissent applied the *Bazley* test, but they differed forcefully on the outcome of that application.

McLachlin CJ gave the dissenting judgment on behalf of L'Heureux-Dubé and Bastarache JJ and herself. It suffices to say, for present purposes, that the dissenting justices believed the facts in *Jacobi* were ideally suited to support vicarious liability on the policy grounds discussed in *Bazley*. McLachlin CJ stuck to her guns. Binnie J gave the majority judgment on behalf of Cory, Iacobucci, and Major JJ, and himself. In Binnie J's view, the key distinctions between *Bazley* and *Jacobi* were between a parental relationship and friendship;[38] a private custodial setting and public visible setting; and a job-created authority to control children and the encouragement to create friendships. There was an underlying search for fault in the Binnie J judgment.

McLachlin CJ seemed to retreat from the groundbreaking decision in *Bazely* after that. She gave the judgment for the Court in *KLB v British*

35 John G Fleming, *The Law of Torts*, 2nd ed (Sydney: Law Book Co, 1957) at 323.

36 *Bazley, supra* note 33 at para 46.

37 *Jacobi, supra* note 34.

38 *Ibid* at para 58: "It was the job-created parent-like relationship that attracted vicarious liability in Children's Foundation."

Columbia,[39] declining to hold that the government was vicariously liable for child abuse committed by foster parents because it lacked sufficient control. She declined to join a brilliant dissent by Arbour J, perhaps realizing that the other members of the Court no longer favoured the broad strict-liability approach to vicarious liability she had articulated in *Bazley*. Later, the plaintiffs would suffer a similar setback in *EB v Order of the Oblates of Mary Immaculate in the Province of British Columbia*.[40] The plaintiff was sexually abused in a religious residential facility by a lay employee who was the school baker. The majority declined to hold the church employer vicariously liable. This time, Binnie J gave the majority judgment, and he was supported by McLachlin CJ and six others. Abella J dissented. In brief, the Order was not held vicariously liable because the baker "did not have authority to insinuate himself into the intimate life of the appellant or any of the other students."[41] The baker's "duties required no significant contact with the students, and his quarters where the sexual abuse took place was [*sic*] located in an area off limits to students."[42]

Today it is virtually impossible to hold an employer vicariously liable for an employee's criminal misconduct, particularly sexual misconduct. For example, in *Ivic v Lakovic*, the Ontario Court of Appeal declined to hold a taxi company vicariously liable for a sexual assault perpetrated by one of its employee drivers on a passenger in the taxi cab.[43] The decision provoked considerable interest and outrage in the community.[44] Nevertheless, application for leave to appeal to the Supreme Court of Canada was dismissed.[45]

III. The Bad: Proximity and the Two-Step Test for Recognition of Novel Duties of Care in Negligence

Negligence is a tort of relation. Prior to the decision in *Donoghue v Stevenson*,[46] the test for a sufficient relationship to ground a duty of care was privity, essentially a direct *ex ante* relationship between the parties.

---

39 *KLB v British Columbia*, 2003 SCC 51 [*KLB*].

40 *EB v Order of the Oblates of Mary Immaculate in the Province of British Columbia*, 2005 SCC 60.

41 *Ibid* at para 37.

42 *Ibid* at para 48.

43 *Ivic v Lakovic*, 2017 ONCA 446.

44 See e.g. Shannon Kari, "SCC May Look at Vicarious Liability Again" *Law Times* (2 October 2017), online: <www.lawtimesnews.com/author/shannon-kari/scc-may-look-at-vicarious-liability-again-14736/>.

45 Leave to appeal to SCC refused, 37718 (1 February 2018).

46 *Donoghue v Stevenson*, [1932] AC 562 (HL) [*Donoghue*].

Subsequently, the duty test became "double foreseeability": (1) was some harm reasonably foreseeable and (2) to a person who was a reasonably foreseeable plaintiff? The necessary relationship could be established by the accident itself.

The double foreseeability test remains today as a necessary and sufficient test for proximity in the "paradigmatic" negligence case – that is, one involving a direct act that causes physical harm.[47] Double foreseeability also remains a necessary, although not sufficient, test for cases outside the paradigm, such as those involving omissions rather than acts, or economic loss rather than physical damage. However, near the end of the twentieth century, the emerging question for Justice McLachlin and others became whether double foreseeability was a sufficient test for duty of care outside the paradigm.[48]

The point of departure for the modern notion of proximity in negligence law is Lord Wilberforce's two-step test for recognition of novel duties of care established in *Anns*:[49]

> (1) was the harm that occurred the reasonably foreseeable consequence of the defendant's act? and
> (2) are there reasons, notwithstanding the proximity between the parties established in the first part of this test, that tort liability should not be recognized here?

Equating proximity with foreseeability remained common until 2001.[50] In the transformative duty case of *Cooper v Hobart*, McLachlin CJ joined Major J to state unequivocally that foreseeability alone was insufficient to find a novel duty of care outside the paradigm.[51] The *Cooper* modification to *Anns* is as follows:

- Step One: The plaintiff may establish a prima facie duty of care based on a sufficiently proximate relationship between the parties. There are two aspects to proximity:

47 See *Cooper, supra* note 12 at para 36; *Childs, supra* note 19 at para 31.

48 See especially *Canadian National Railway Co v Norsk Pacific Steamship Co*, [1992] 1 SCR 1021 [*Norsk*] per McLachin J, discussed *infra*, and *Hercules Managements v Ernst & Young*, [1997] 2 SCR 165 [*Hercules*] per LaForest J, with whom McLachlin J concurred, discussed *infra*. In both these economic loss cases, the judges were clear that foreseeability alone was an insufficient test for proximity. In both cases, they simply chose the wrong substitute. See *infra*.

49 *Anns, supra* note 15, as stated in *Cooper, supra* note 12 at para 30.

50 See *Livent, supra* note 18.

51 *Cooper, supra* note 12 at paras 22, 30.

a) Double foreseeability; and
b) *Other considerations relevant to proximity* [emphasis added]

- Step Two: If the plaintiff establishes a prima facie duty of care at Step One, the defendant may rebut it by raising policy arguments to limit or negative the prima facie duty.

So far, the twenty-first century has been characterized by attempts to craft subject-matter-specific proximity tests in novel cases, especially those involving omissions, economic loss, and public defendants. Justice McLachlin took a leadership role on this issue.

a. Just v British Columbia: *The Road Not Taken*

McLachlin J was the trial judge in what would eventually become the influential Supreme Court decision in *Just v British Columbia*.[52] Just was injured and his daughter killed when a boulder rolled down a hill and onto a highway, striking his car. He sued the province for negligence in maintaining the highway.

Just arose well after the decision in *Anns*,[53] and well after *Anns* had been fawningly adopted by the Supreme Court in *Kamloops v Neilson*.[54] Nevertheless, McLachlin J did not mention proximity. McLachlin J cannot be criticized for this. At the time, proximity was assumed to mean foreseeability, a standard easily met by *Just*. Instead, she went directly to Step 2 *Anns* policy considerations and took the more radical step of introducing into Canadian law the American concept of government immunity for policy decisions to defeat the plaintiff's claim.[55] The history and substance of government immunity in the United States is substantially different from the relationship between the legislative and judicial branches in Canada.

The general rule that has emerged since *Cooper* is that proximity requires the plaintiff to have had an interaction with the public defendant in the context of a specific event or transaction, often an antecedent relationship, and always one that meaningfully differentiates that potential

52 *Just*, *supra* note 9.

53 *Anns*, *supra* note 15.

54 *Kamloops v Neilson*, [1984] 2 SCR 2 [*Kamloops*].

55 See generally, Bruce Feldthusen, "Public Authority Immunity from Negligence Liability: Uncertain, Unnecessary, and Unjustified" (2014) 92:2 Can Bar Rev 211. Although policy immunity is frequently invoked as an alternate reason to deny liability in the absence of a finding of proximity, there are very few times that immunity has been invoked to defeat a finding of proximity. McLachlin CJ's decision in *Imperial Tobacco*, *supra* note 11 is one of these rare instances.

plaintiff from other members of the class of foreseeable potential plaintiffs.[56] Being a member of the specific class that is the subject of the statutory regime will not suffice. There must be a closer relationship before the law will consider a negligence duty to the individual as opposed to a general public duty. Today, *Just* would probably have failed for want of proximity. Being one of thousands of highway users, and having had no specific interaction with the government department to distinguish him from the other users, *Just* would not meet the proximity threshold.

Just eventually went to the Supreme Court, where the issues were as McLachlin J had framed them.[57] Proximity was mentioned only briefly and treated as a synonym for foreseeability. The bulk of the reasons for judgment turned on immunity. The Supreme Court held that the government did not enjoy immunity in respect of the exercise of its discretionary powers to maintain the highway. In two suspiciously similar subsequent decisions, *Brown* and *Swinamer*, the Court employed the immunity concept to dismiss actions against public authorities.[58] McLachlin J sat on both and agreed with the outcomes in both.

The concept of government immunity has been criticized as uncertain, unnecessary, and unjustified.[59] Nevertheless, in my opinion, McLachlin J's instincts to deny the claim in *Just* were entirely correct. What would have made a tremendous difference is if she had dismissed the claim for want of proximity. Instead, in addition to introducing the problematic concept of immunity, *Just* became a leading authority for what has been called the "Good Public Samaritan" rule, which holds that, once a public authority begins to exercise a statutory power, it owes a duty of care in negligence to those affected. This unique public duty derived from the *Anns* decision has now been discredited in the United Kingdom.[60] It

56 *Hill, supra* note 6 per McLachlin CJ at para 31. See *Taylor v Canada (AG)*, 2012 ONCA 479 for a good summary of the case law.

57 *Just v British Columbia*, [1989] 2 SCR 1228.

58 *Brown v British Columbia*, [1994] 1 SCR 420 [*Brown*]; *Swinamer v Nova Scotia*, [1994] 1 SCR 445 [*Swinamer*].

59 Feldthusen, *supra* note 55. The House of Lords declared immunity based on the "policy/operational distinction unworkable in difficult cases, a point said to be evidenced by the Canadian jurisprudence: *Stovin v Wise*, [1996] AC 923 (HL), per Lord Hoffmann."

60 *Michael v The Chief Constable of South Wales Police*, [2015] UKSC 2 [*Michael*]; *Robinson v Chief Constable of West Yorkshire Police*, [2018] UKSC 4. By "unique," I mean a duty imposed on a public actor that would not be imposed on a private defendant in an analogous situation. Generally speaking, private parties do not owe a duty to confer a benefit on another. McLachlin CJ would later summarize the law to this effect in *Childs*, *supra* note 19.

is both constitutionally objectionable and irrational. If the "Good Public Samaritan" rule were adopted across the board as a test of sufficient proximity in government defendant cases, the separation of powers between the courts and the legislatures would no longer exist as we know it.[61] Instead, we are left with a different objection. Judges are careful not to overwhelm the traditional realm of the legislators across the board. Today the Good Public Samaritan principle is applied selectively, but unpredictably, on an *ad hoc* basis. It is doubtful that McLachlin J foresaw, let alone intended, these developments when she decided the *Just* case, but her judgment certainly made a significant contribution to their birth and evolution. If, instead, Canada abandoned the Good Public Samaritan rule altogether, there would be no need for immunity, and public authority negligence law would be considerably easier to apply.

b. Canadian National Railway Co v Norsk Pacific Steamship Co*: Proximity's Coming-Out Party*

Seven years after *Just*, McLachlin J was no longer ignoring the need for a robust concept of proximity. On the contrary, in *Norsk* she revealed herself as proximity's champion in the Supreme Court.[62] She and La-Forest J went head to head. LaForest J articulated numerous specific policy goals that supported an exclusionary rule for relational economic loss that had existed for over a century. McLachlin J argued for a case-by-case approach based on proximity. In *Norsk,* she held for Canadian National Railways (CNR), finding proximity based on the relationship between CNR, Norsk, and the accident in question.[63]

In *Norsk,* a ship damaged a rail bridge owned by Canada. The bridge was used primarily by CNR under a contractual arrangement with the government, but also by two other railways. CNR sued to recover the cost of re-routing its trains during the bridge repairs made necessary by the defendant's actions. This is a category of pure economic loss called contractual relational economic loss. CNR succeeded. McLachlin

61 See Bruce Feldthusen, "10 Reasons to Reject Unique Public Duties of Care in Negligence" in Margaret Hall, ed, *The Canadian Law of Obligations: Private Law for the 21st Century and Beyond* (Toronto: LexisNexis, 2018) 25.

62 *Norsk, supra* note 48.

63 In brief, "proximity" is the notion of a sufficiently close relationship between the parties to justify holding one to owe a duty of care to another. "Distributional" or "instrumentalist policy" refers to specific social goals such as deterrence that might justify or preclude a particular rule, as opposed to a particular relationship. The distinction is developed further in the discussion of *Cooper, infra.*

J gave the majority judgment in favour of CNR on behalf of herself and two others. LaForest J gave the dissenting judgment on behalf of himself and two others. Stevenson J gave a separate judgment in favour of CNR. Insofar as proximity was concerned, *Norsk* was a pyrrhic victory for McLachlin J. Stevenson J held for CNR, but he also sided with LaForest J in rejecting unequivocally McLachlin J's attempt to ground the duty in proximity. Thus, four of the seven judges described proximity as a purely conclusory label.[64]

McLachlin J quoted from the judgment of Deane J in *Sutherland Shire Council v Heyman* to attempt to supply a general definition of proximity.[65] Such attempts are bound to fail. Proximity is a concept that identifies a *specific* relationship as being sufficiently close as to justify a duty of care in the circumstances of the case. Any general description of proximity is destined to result in the term being used as a conclusory label, not as a legal test. A test for proximity must be developed in the particular case, or at least particular type of case. Proximity is going to be different in *Norsk* than in *Hercules* or *Childs,* and so on. Ironically, elsewhere in *Norsk,* McLachlin J acknowledges this.[66]

In my opinion, her problem in *Norsk* was not in trying to develop a specific test of proximity for relational economic loss, but in failing to develop a meaningful proximity test on the facts of *Norsk.* McLachlin J considered a number of factors: damaging the bridge created the danger of physical injury to CNR's property; CNR had a close connection with the damaged property, including the fact that CNR's property was in close proximity to the bridge; CNR's property could not be enjoyed without the link of the bridge; and CNR supplied materials, inspection, and consulting services for the bridge, was its preponderant user, and was recognized in the periodic negotiations surrounding the closing of the bridge. She concluded that CNR was in a "joint venture" with the owner of the bridge and that to deny recovery in such circumstances would be to deny it to a person who, for practical purposes, is in the same position as if they owned the property physically damaged.

None of these facts justify a finding of proximity. It is insufficient that a proximate relationship can merely be distinguished from other relationships. It must be "special" in a way that *justifies* holding the defendant liable.[67] Most of the facts relied upon by McLachlin J to find proximity justify nothing. Many do not distinguish CNR from other

64 *Norsk, supra* note 48 at para 162.

65 *Sutherland Shire Council v Heyman,* [1985] 50 ALR 1, 157 CLR 424 at 55–6.

66 *Norsk, supra* note 48 at para 257.

67 *Childs, supra* note 19, quoted *infra,* Part III (d).

users of the bridge. And while a true "joint venture" might justify finding proximity, surely such a joint venture must be one in which the parties share the risks and rewards.[68]

Nevertheless, one has to admire McLachlin J's groundbreaking efforts to introduce a meaningful proximity concept into Canadian negligence law. One also has to admire her continuing determination to infuse Canadian negligence law with an important element of proximity thereafter. Nowhere is this determination more evident than in the case of *Bow Valley Husky (Bermuda) Ltd v Saint John Shipbuilding Ltd.*[69] This case involved *inter alia* another claim for relational economic loss. The Court unanimously rejected the claim and, in so doing, elected to follow LaForest J's judgment in *Norsk*, not McLachlin J's.[70]

The various sets of reasons in *Bow Valley* hint at considerable tension among the members of the Court, as well as another clear rejection of the proximity approach. This makes the discussion of *Cooper* immediately below all the more interesting. In effect, in the *Cooper* decision McLachlin CJ succeeded in resurrecting her discredited proximity approach from *Norsk*. Her proximity approach would dominate Canadian negligence law from 2001 until at least 2017.[71]

c. Cooper v Hobart: *McLachlin CJ Wins the Day*

McLachlin CJ and Major J gave the judgment for the Court in *Cooper v Hobart*, probably the most influential negligence judgment in Canadian history.[72] *Cooper* effectively revived McLachlin CJ's ideas about proximity first raised but rejected in *Norsk* and rejected again in *Bow Valley*.[73] Her personal influence on the question of proximity in *Cooper* is obvious.

The best thing about the *Cooper* decision is that it broke from *Anns* by making it abundantly clear that the proximity inquiry at Step 1 must

68 See *R171 Enterprises Ltd v Sunrise Construction Ltd (cob Sunrise Homes Ltd)*, 2005 BCSC 1081 [*Sunrise Construction*]; *Fraser v Westminer Canada Ltd*, 2003 NSCA 76 [*Fraser*]; and *Pembina County Water Resource District v Manitoba*, 2008 FC 1390 [*Pembina*].

69 *Bow Valley Husky (Bermuda) Ltd v Saint John Shipbuilding Ltd*, [1997] 3 SCR 1210 [*Bow Valley*].

70 *Ibid* at paras 112, 113. Iacobucci J described the LaForest J approach as one that adopted a general exclusionary rule with limited categorical exceptions. "Joint venture," strictly defined, was one of those categorical exceptions.

71 A break with this trend is evident in *Livent*, *supra* note 18.

72 *Cooper*, *supra* note 12.

73 *Norsk*, *supra* note 48 and *Bow Valley*, *supra* note 69.

include additional indicators of proximity beyond foreseeability alone. Although *Cooper* appeared to emphasize the concept of proximity, it did little to elucidate it. The Court correctly identified proximity as a question of relationship: is the relationship between the parties sufficiently close to make it just to impose a duty of care on the defendant toward the plaintiff?[74] McLachlin CJ's reasons offered a list of factors that might be relevant to a finding of proximity, much as she had done in *Norsk.*[75] She did not explain how any of them might justify a finding of relational proximity. As in *Norsk,* she failed to connect the dots. She then admitted that such generalities are useless.[76] The Court conceded that proximity must be defined in the particular case.[77] Given that there was absolutely no *ex ante* or transaction-specific relationship between the regulator and persons in the plaintiffs' position, in fact or contemplated by the legislation, the facts of *Cooper* were not helpful for this purpose. It would have been more useful to simply dismiss the claim because there was no evidence of any meaningful relationship, and reserve discussion of what would constitute proximity for a case where proximity was found.

Cooper also completely undermined the concept of *relational* proximity that it had purported to adopt by treating and describing relational proximity as "relational policy."[78] Professor Fridman has suggested that policy in relation to proximity is simply "judicial policy," a matter of determining whether, given the relationship between the parties, it is just and fair to impose a legal duty of care on the defendant.[79] The majority in *Deloitte & Touche v Livent* took a similar approach.[80] A search for proximity along these lines would be helpful. However, using the word "policy" to describe such a search is unnecessary and ambiguous. In fact, the Supreme Court jurisprudence indicates that relational policy at Step 1 often goes well beyond Fridman's idea of judicial policy to include instrumentalist distributive policy.[81]

---

74 *Cooper, supra* note 12 at paras 31, 34, 42.

75 *Norsk, supra* note 48 at para 34.

76 *Cooper, supra* note 12 at para 35.

77 *Ibid.*

78 *Ibid* at para 30.

79 Fridman, *supra* note 15.

80 *Livent, supra* note 18 at para 38.

81 Consider deterrence, a widely accepted instrumentalist "aim" of tort law. Courts can impose the cost of product-defect accidents on manufacturers in the hope that prospective liability will encourage safer manufacturing, and that increased product prices would reduce demand for the product and hence reduce the number of product-defect accidents. These are instrumentalist distributive policies.

Rights-based theorists will probably have a deeper concern.[82] They would argue that proximity should not be used as a policy tool. Either one is in a proximate relationship and hence it is "right" to recognize a *prima facie* duty, or one is not. Novel duties should not be constructed by policy arguments, however "good" the policy might seem. This is the role of the legislative branch. Such an approach leaves considerably less scope for Step 2 in the duty analysis.[83] In contrast, many, including certainly McLachlin CJ, support a distributive policy-making role for the courts. McLachlin CJ is refreshingly candid about this.[84] So be it, but why refer to it as proximity?

One might praise the retention of the two-step template for recognizing novel duties on the ground that it brings consistency to the analysis. However, the *Cooper* Court held that it really did not matter whether policy arguments were raised at Step 1 or Step 2.[85] This is an inevitable consequence of jumbling relational proximity and distributional policy together. Of course, it does matter, conceptually and practically.[86] What is the point of a two-step test otherwise?

We can assess them as good or bad policies. This is a common approach in the United States. See, for example, *Greenman v Yuba Power Products*, USA 59 Cal 2d 57 (SC 1963). In Canada, see *Winnipeg Condominium*, *supra* note 15. In contrast, a corrective justice rights-based approach justifies liability based on the defendant's unreasonable interference with the plaintiff's rights, personal and proprietary. This is a matter of right and wrong, not good and bad. There may be a deterrent impact of a rights-based approach, but that is not the "aim" of the liability rule. In fact, there is no instrumentalist aim to negligence law under a rights-based approach. Corrective justice achieved through unmediated interaction between the defendant and plaintiff is the end in itself. *Donoghue*, *supra* note 46 is better explained as a rights-based decision than as a policy decision. So too is the concept of "proximity." Compensation is also often referred to as an "aim" of tort law, but the term is ambiguous. Tort is not an insurance scheme. Compensatory damages awarded on the restitutionary principle are central to a corrective justice approach.

82 Among the rights-based torts scholars who have been influential in Canada, see Ernest J Weinrib, "The Disintegration of Duty" (2006) 31:2 Adv Q 212 [Weinrib, "Disintegration"]; Ernest J Weinrib, *The Idea of Private Law* (Cambridge, MA: Harvard University Press, 1995); Allan Beever, "A Rights-Based Approach to the Recovery of Economic Loss in Negligence" (2004) 4:1 OUCLJ 25 at 37–8; Allan Beever, *Rediscovering the Law of Negligence* (Oxford: Hart Publishing, 2007) at 211; and Russell Brown, *Pure Economic Loss in Canadian Negligence Law* (Toronto: LexisNexis, 2011).

83 See the discussion of *Livent*, *infra* Part III.f.

84 *Cooper*, *supra* note 12 at paras 25–6.

85 *Ibid* at para 27. A subtle retreat from this position may have been intended in *Bow Valley*, *supra* note 69 at para 53.

86 See *Livent*, *supra* note 18. The onus of proof supposedly rests with the plaintiff at Step 1 and with the defendant at Step 2.

Finally, the *Cooper* decision introduces unnecessary confusion about the relationship between regulatory legislation and common law negligence. The Court said:

> In this case, the factors giving rise to proximity, if they exist, must arise from the statute under which the Registrar is appointed. That statute is the only source of his duties, private or public. Apart from that statute, he is in no different position than the ordinary man or woman on the street. If a duty to investors with regulated mortgage brokers is to be found, it must be in the statute.[87]

The legislature may create expressly a right to claim damages from a regulator. This would be a statutory cause of action, not a common law tort. There was no such provision in *Cooper*. The legislation may mandate certain types of interactions between members of the protected class and the regulator that a common law court *might* take into account in deciding whether to recognize the relationship as a proximate relationship.[88] There was nothing like this in *Cooper*. There may also be cases in which a court might have found meaningful proximity but for the fact that to do so would undermine the public purpose of the statute.[89] *Cooper* is not such a case. There is simply no potentially meaningful relationship of proximity in *Cooper* that had to be rejected in deference to the legislature. Given all this, the relatively lengthy discussion of the specific provisions of the legislation to prove that the purpose of the legislation was to protect the public interest, not the private interests of investors, muddles the analysis.[90] All regulatory statutes have a public protection dimension, so simply identifying this is unhelpful. Instead, this part of the decision reads as if the Court is searching for an *implied* statutory cause of action, something the Court itself has held is impermissible in Canada.[91]

---

87 *Cooper, supra* note 12 at para 43. This is an interesting passage in the context of the Good Public Samaritan rule discussed above. McLachlin CJ is obviously prepared to recognize this principle based on the relevant legislation, but her methodology is at best obscure and at worst faulty.

88 See e.g. *Hill, supra* note 6; and *Williams v Toronto (City)*, 2016 ONCA 666 [*Williams*].

89 See e.g. *Syl Apps Secure Treatment Centre v BD*, 2007 SCC 38 [*Syl Apps*].

90 *Cooper, supra* note 12 at paras 42–50.

91 *R v Saskatchewan Wheat Pool*, [1983] 1 SCR 205 [*Saskatchewan*]; *Odhavji Estate v Woodhouse*, 2003 SCC 69 [*Odhavji*]. Such liability was also emphasized in *Michael, supra* note 60. See also Lewis Klar, "The Tort Liability of the Crown: Back to Canada v Saskatchewan Wheat Pool" (2007) 32:3 Adv Q 293 and Lewis Klar, "The Proximity Hurdle in Negligence Actions against Public Authorities" (2018) 84 SCLR 3.

d. Childs v Desormeaux: *Pure Proximity*

The possibility of social host liability was the issue in *Childs v Desormeaux*.[92] This was a pure proximity-based decision, not a policy decision, and, in my opinion, one of McLachlin CJ's finest decisions on duty of care.

The defendants served a small amount of alcohol to their guests at a house party. In addition, guests brought their own alcohol. One guest, Desormeaux, was well- known to the hosts, as was his tendency to consume alcohol to excess and then drive on the highway. On the night in question he did both. He left the host's home and caused a serious accident, killing one of the passengers in the other vehicle and seriously injuring the rest.

The trial judge held that Child's injuries were foreseeable to the hosts and that there was sufficient proximity between them to ground a duty of care. He dismissed the action on Step 2 *Cooper* grounds – policy reasons to deny a duty of care despite a finding of proximity at Step 1. The Court of Appeal disagreed that there was sufficient foreseeability to found a *prima facie* duty based on proximity and did not, therefore, consider Step 2 policy concerns. At the time, the liability of alcohol providers was in its developing stages, and the idea that a social host might be liable to third parties was controversial within and outside of the legal community. People anxiously awaited the decision of the Supreme Court.

I. FORESEEABILITY

McLachlin CJ dismissed Childs' claim because the plaintiff did not prove the hosts actually knew Desormeaux was intoxicated, and therefore they could not foresee he would injure Childs. There are few more elastic terms posing as concrete tests in tort law than foreseeability. One can easily and reasonably go either way on the foreseeability question in *Childs*. The beauty of the foreseeability finding – and, to be clear, it was a judgment of the entire Court – is that it completely depoliticized the issues raised by potential social host liability. The foreseeability approach allowed the Court to dispense entirely with a Step 2 overt policy analysis. As a result, neither rights-based theorists nor conservative politicians could complain about policy activism on the *Childs* court. Nor could policy activists quarrel with the particular policy implications of an apparently factual determination. I have no idea if this was McLachlin CJ's intention, but it is not necessarily an inappropriate goal for a Chief Justice to pursue on an issue like social host liability. Drunk

92 *Childs, supra* note 19.

driving was, and remains, on the federal and provincial political agendas. The courts continue to address it incrementally.[93]

II. PROXIMITY BEYOND FORESEEABILITY

Moving beyond foreseeability, McLachlin CJ took a less cluttered approach to proximity in *Childs* than she had in previous decisions. First, she provided a succinct general guideline for proximity that is more focused than the "list of factors" approach used in *Norsk* or *Cooper.* She stated: "The law of negligence not only considers the plaintiff's loss, but explains why it is just and fair to impose the cost of that loss on the particular defendant before the court. The proximity requirement captures this two-sided face of negligence."[94]

Second, she moved directly to the specific issue of proximity raised in *Childs*. The plaintiff was seeking to impose an affirmative duty on the part of the social hosts to protect her from the misconduct of a guest, an allegation of non-feasance, not misfeasance. McLachlin CJ provided a succinct review of the exceptional situations in which the common law has imposed affirmative duties to benefit another, a welcome contribution to this important question from the Supreme Court. She identified this as a Step 1 question of proximity. She based her finding of insufficient proximity on the principle of autonomy, the autonomy of the host who had not created the risk, and the autonomy of the guest to consume alcohol unsupervised.[95]

Finally, and significantly given what would later transpire in *Deloitte & Touche v Livent*,[96] she concluded as follows: "Having concluded that a prima facie duty of care has not been established, I find it unnecessary to consider whether any duty would be negated by policy considerations at the second stage of the Anns test."[97]

e. Hill v Hamilton-Wentworth Police Services Board*: Back to the Past*

In *Hill v Hamilton-Wentworth Police Services Board*, McLachlin CJ gave the majority judgment for the Court in a 6–3 decision to recognize a

93 Interestingly, a want of foreseeability was again relied on by the Court in a similar case involving a commercial alcohol provider, *Stewart v Pettie*, [1995] 1 SCR 131 at para 55 [*Stewart*]. Major J gave the judgment for the Court, of which McLachlin J was a member. See also *Rankin (Rankin's Garage & Sales) v JJ*, 2018 SCC 19 [*Rankin*].

94 *Childs, supra* note 19 at para 25.

95 *Ibid* at paras 39, 45.

96 *Livant, supra* note 18.

97 *Childs, supra* note 19 at para 48.

groundbreaking duty of care owed by police to suspects of crime to investigate the case against them with due care.[98] Her proximity analysis looks more like that in *Norsk* and *Cooper* than in *Childs*. We see the stand-alone list of relevant factors and the jump from these to the proximity conclusion.[99] We see the indifference to the distinction between Step 1 proximity considerations and Step 2 policy considerations.[100] The key proximity question was whether a private law duty to the suspect would conflict with the duties owed to the public by the police. This was treated as a Step 2 policy question.[101] She noted that negligent police investigations have contributed to failures of the justice system, such as wrongful convictions or institutional racism.[102] These are certainly important policy matters, but not matters of proximity. The illusion of a structured two-part approach to novel duties of care became again a basket of undifferentiated observations, and a conclusion.

f. Deloitte & Touche v Livent: *The End of* Anns*?*

In *Deloitte & Touche v Livent*,[103] the majority of the Supreme Court, with McLachlin CJ dissenting on a different point, held that the Court had stated the wrong proximity test for negligent misrepresentation in an earlier decision, *Hercules v Ernst & Young*.[104] According to *Hercules*, proximity arose when (a) the defendant ought reasonably to foresee that the plaintiff will rely on the defendant's representation, and (b) reliance by the plaintiff would, in the particular circumstances of the case, be reasonable. With a professional auditor as a defendant, this amounts to a simple foreseeability test. This cast the net so widely in *Hercules* that it was necessary to adopt a further "end and aim" test to limit potentially indeterminate liability at Step 2.[105] *Livent* redefined the proximity test as

98 *Hill*, *supra* note 6.
99 *Ibid* at paras 24, 25, 27.
100 *Ibid* at para 31.
101 *Ibid* at para 43. The minority saw it as a proximity question. So too did the full Court in *Syl Apps*, *supra* note 89, decided only months earlier, with which McLachlin CJ had agreed.
102 *Hill*, *supra* note 6 at para 36.
103 *Livent*, *supra* note 18.
104 *Hercules*, *supra* note 48. In fact, the Court in *Livent* was gentler, suggesting that *Hercules* was decided at a time when foreseeability was the proximity test and that this had subsequently been modified by *Cooper*. As I read *Hercules*, LaForest J was well aware that he needed a richer proximity test than foreseeability, but he simply chose the wrong one.
105 This phrase was used by Cardozo J in *Glanzer v Shepard*, 135 NE 275 (NYCA 1922) and cited with approval in *Hercules*, *supra* note 48 at para 38. It limits the ambit

follows: Where the defendant undertakes to provide a representation or service in circumstances that invite the plaintiff's reasonable reliance, the defendant becomes obligated to take reasonable care.[106]

Justice McLachlin had relied frequently on the *Hercules* decision over her career. *Hercules* employed the *Anns* approach. It was an early example of the recognition that proximity meant more than foreseeability, at least for economic loss. It was also an example of how courts would frequently need to limit potentially indeterminate liability at Step 2. This may explain why McLachlin J gave the new duty formulation in *Livent* only her indifferent approval in passing.[107] Her dissenting judgment was more concerned with the practical question of the scope of the defendant's liability than about the theoretically proper proximity test. On this point, a strong and significant disagreement grounded in competing notions of proximity arose between the majority and dissent.

In brief, the majority pointed out that the scope of liability was determined at the proximity stage. In misrepresentation, the scope of liability would be determined by what the defendant undertook and on what it was reasonable for the plaintiff to rely. The Court stated that only rarely would a residual issue of indeterminate liability survive a proper proximity analysis.[108] It is, after all, bizarre to speak of a relationship that causes an indeterminacy problem as a proximate relationship. It followed that there remained no residual concern about indeterminate liability to be raised at Step 2. In contrast, McLachlin CJ said little about

---

of liability in misrepresentation to the purpose for which the representation was made and in the context of the transaction in which it was made. The test is common in the United States and elsewhere but, as part of the proximity analysis, not as a reason to restrict a pre-existing *prima facie* duty as in *Hercules*.

106 *Livent, supra* note 18 at para 30.

107 *Ibid* at para 167.

108 *Ibid* at paras 42–4. The most famous expression of the indeterminacy problem, a concern about "a liability in an indeterminate amount for an indeterminate time to an indeterminate class," may be found in *Ultramares Corporation v Touche*, 174 NE 441 (NYCA 1932) (Cardozo CJ). It has been argued that these concerns were expressed to suggest that there was an error in the duty analysis if such exposure existed, not expressed for the purpose of limiting the exposure generated by the (improper) duty formulation. Cardozo CJ presumably would have found *Hercules* a good example of his point. See Jason W Neyers, "*Donoghue v Stevenson* and the Rescue Doctrine: A Public Justification of Recovery in Situations Involving the Negligent Supply of Dangerous Structures" (1999) 49:4 UTLJ 475, citing Peter Benson, "The Basis for Excluding Liability for Economic Loss in Tort Law," in D Owen, ed, *Philosophical Foundations of Tort Law* (Oxford: Clarendon Press, 1995) 427; R Bernstein, *Economic Loss* (London: Longman, 1993) 14; Weinrib, "Disintegration," *supra* note 82 at 231.

proximity and a lot about indeterminacy, reminiscent of the *Hercules* approach. I predict that the majority approach, a rights-based approach with a limited role for judicial policy-making, will carry the day going forward in misrepresentation and beyond.

IV. Three Puzzling Decisions

a. Back to Hill v Hamilton Wentworth Police

Earlier I discussed the groundbreaking decision in *Hill*, in which a duty of care was held to be owed by an investigating police officer to a criminal suspect.[109] This was only part of the story. The majority went on to hold that the police did not breach the standard of care. Hill's action failed. The majority held that publication of Hill's photo, incomplete records of witness interviews, interviewing two witnesses together, and failing to blind-test photos were not good practices by today's standards, but the evidence did not establish that a reasonable officer at the time would not have followed similar practices. Really? The Court dismissed the significance of the fact that Hill was in custody while many similar offences were committed. The Court also excused the failure of the police to include any Indigenous men in the line-up except Mr Hill himself. Just what would be an unreasonable investigation if this was not? Not surprisingly, the only reported application of *Hill* to impose liability for negligent investigation by a police officer was reversed on appeal.[110] To me, the finding on standard of care in *Hill* rendered the entire duty analysis an important symbolic, but otherwise pointless, exercise.

b. Blackwater v Plint

In *Blackwater v Plint*, damages awarded in a sexual abuse claim brought by a residential school survivor were reduced to reflect that the plaintiff had been previously abused by a different independent tortfeasor.[111] This decision seems to conflict with other Supreme Court decisions that do not make a deduction for indivisible harm suffered in sequential standard personal injury cases.

---

109 *Hill, supra* note 6.

110 *495793 Ontario Ltd. (Central Auto Parts) v Barclay*, 2014 ONSC 3517; rev'd *495793 Ontario Ltd (Central Auto Parts) v Barclay*, 2016 ONCA 656.

111 *Blackwater, supra* note 8.

The plaintiff was entitled to be compensated for abuse suffered at residential school. However, the question of quantification was a difficult one because the plaintiff had been abused by independent tortfeasors prior to the abuse that was the subject of this suit. The tortfeasor is required to compensate for only the difference between the plaintiff's original position – that is, immediately before the defendant's tort – and the position after the tort. So, to determine the original position, it was necessary to determine how much of the plaintiff's emotional damage was present before the tort in question.

The problem is that often, including in *Blackwater*, the original position cannot be determined because the loss is, as a practical matter, indivisible. One simply cannot determine who caused what divisible components of the total harm. In *Athey v Leonati*, for example, there were several contributing successive tortious causes of the plaintiff's back injury.[112] However, the back injury was indivisible. As a practical matter, the Court could not attribute different parts or degrees of the injury to any particular tortfeasor. In *Athey*, the Supreme Court ruled that each tortfeasor would be jointly and severally liable for the full extent of the indivisible harm.[113] Admittedly, *Athey* dealt with causation, and *Blackwater* with quantification, but either way the damage is indivisible, and the result in *Blackwater* is therefore arbitrary.

In *Blackwater*, like in *Athey*, the trial judge could not attribute the plaintiff's emotional damage to the different tortfeasors. The damage was indivisible. The judge assumed that the prior abuse must have contributed somehow to the injury, but there was no evidence to support that. He made an arbitrary deduction to reflect his hunch. McLachlin CJ for the Court approved this. She noted the judge had tried his best. Personally, I prefer the *Athey* approach. I certainly regret having one rule for standard back injuries and another for survivors of sexual abuse, including abuse suffered at residential schools.[114] I wish McLachlin CJ had had another opportunity to resolve this.

c. *Mustapha v Culligan of Canada*

In *Mustapha v Culligan of Canada*, the plaintiff was a regular bottled water customer of Culligan.[115] One day he discovered a dead fly and part

112 *Athey v Leonati*, [1996] 3 SCR 458 [*Athey*].

113 McLachlin CJ approved this aspect of the *Athey* decision in another sexual battery case, *EDG v Hammer*, 2003 SCC 52 at para 31.

114 See also *KLB*, *supra* note 39 at paras 60–1.

115 *Mustapha*, *supra* note 7.

of another in an unopened water bottle. He subsequently developed a major depressive disorder. There was no question that his injuries were real, serious, and caused by discovering the contaminated water. He sued Culligan for psychiatric injury and succeeded at trial. The Court of Appeal overturned the judgment on the basis that the injury was not reasonably foreseeable. At the Supreme Court, McLachlin CJ writing for the full Court, agreed.

Prior to this decision, recovery for psychiatric harm had been constrained by a special duty of care. It must have been reasonably foreseeable that a mental injury would *occur to a person of ordinary fortitude*. McLachlin CJ held that the duty test for psychiatric damage would henceforth be double foreseeability, the same as for where a consumable food product causes other physical harm. So far so good. At the duty stage, this is *Donoghue* all over again.[116] However, McLachlin CJ did not abandon the former special duty requirement of ordinary fortitude. She simply transformed this into a remoteness rule. Any suggestion that psychiatric damage is now to be regarded as simply one form of physical harm was effectively reversed at the remoteness stage. The Supreme Court held that Mr Mustapha's injuries were too remote because it was not foreseeable that what happened to him would have happened to a person of ordinary fortitude.

The test for remoteness in ordinary physical damage cases is whether one can foresee the precise kind of harm. There is considerable leeway in defining the precise kind of harm. Under the ordinary physical damage rules, one need not foresee the *manner* in which the precise kind of harm was suffered. Nor need one foresee the *degree* of the precise kind of harm (psychiatric injury?), which was admittedly extreme in this case, merely some (psychiatric?) injury. McLachlin CJ held that the degree of foreseeability was too low to support recovery in this case, a conclusion of fact with which I disagree. It is not clear to me why insects are less repulsive than snails.

One of the strengths of McLachlin CJ's proximity analyses in other cases is her insistence that the imposition of liability must depend both on the harm to the plaintiff and on whether it is fair to transfer the loss to the defendant.[117] *Wagon Mound (No 2)*, which she cited, requires the courts to balance the justification for a defendant's conduct and the cost of avoidance against the low probability of harm before making a finding of remoteness.[118] There is no justification for the defendant's

116 *Donoghue, supra* note 46.

117 *Childs, supra* note 19 at para 25; *Cooper, supra* note 12 at paras 34–5.

118 *Overseas Tankship (UK) Ltd v The Miller SS Co Pty Ltd*, [1967] 1 AC 617 (*sub nom Wagon Mound (No 2)*).

conduct. Including Mustapha in the scope of the risk adds nothing to the avoidance cost. What is so unfair about requiring a commercial seller to compensate consumers for a provable serious injury when, in breach of its duty of care, it supplies the consumer with insect-infected drinking water in a closed container? What happened to the law's traditional concern for food safety? If the injury suffered by Mustapha is as rare as the Court suggested, where is the floodgates problem?

The most disappointing aspect of McLachlin CJ's *Mustapha* decision is the retention of the requirement that particularly vulnerable plaintiffs may be defined out of the range of legal protection by the "person of ordinary fortitude" requirement. People are differently abled. This is no such thing as ordinary fortitude across the board. Persons have different "cultural" experiences.[119] Disability and sensitivity are often foreseeable. The House of Lords recognized this with respect to blind persons more than fifty years ago.[120] I suggest that the *Mustapha* decision is nothing more than a continuation of the law's longstanding failure to accord psychiatric injury and persons with mental disabilities the full protection of tort law.[121]

V. Conclusions

There is no evidence that Justice McLachlin is an ideologue of any sort.

Her greatest achievement in tort law was her strong and principled approach to the rights of women and victims of sexual abuse. Her track

---

119 The trial judge relied in part on "the background of Mr. Mustapha in the Middle East, where the devotion to and concern for the family is at a higher level than is found in North America, and the higher level of cleanliness and avoidance of insects practiced by this family than is usual, including taking food to and from an outdoor barbecue in covered containers, and covering the depressed top of the Culligan water dispenser with a plate, to preserve cleanliness when the bottle was removed. These things, in my view predisposed Mr. Mustapha for the reaction that occurred." *Mustapha v Culligan of Canada Ltd*, [2005] OJ No. 1469 at para 211 (Quicklaw). In the Supreme Court, McLachlin CJ said: "Instead of asking whether it was foreseeable that the defendant's conduct would have injured a person of ordinary fortitude, the trial judge applied a subjective standard, taking into account Mr. Mustapha's 'previous history' and 'particular circumstances' (at para 227), including a number of 'cultural factors' such as his unusual concern over cleanliness, and the health and well-being of his family. This was an error." *Mustapha, supra* note 7 at para 18.

120 *Haley v London Electricity Board*, [1965] AC 778, [1964] 3 WLR 479.

121 Subsequently, in *Saadati v Moorhead*, 2017 SCC 28 the Court made great progress in normalizing the recovery for psychiatric harm. Unfortunately, *Mustapha* was left untouched.

record on so many controversial social issues in these areas is remarkable. One senses her personal commitment to advancing these rights. She was ahead of her time.

In contrast is the failure to develop a meaningful, clear, and consistent definition of proximity in negligence law. Given the centrality of the proximity concept to negligence law, this is a major failing. This, however, is a failing of the entire Court, not particularly of Justice McLachlin's. It is also a forgivable failing, albeit a serious one.

When one is contemplating surgery, experts advise selecting a well-trained specialist in the particular area, and a specialist who performs the procedure regularly and often. As far as I know, with the exception of the relatively recently appointed Justice Brown, no members of the McLachlin-era Court had special expertise in tort law. And as the chronological summary of proximity decisions reveals, the court deals with the issue of proximity so rarely that it is unfair to expect a mature and sophisticated negligence jurisprudence to develop. McLachlin CJ had to deal with many more important social issues than those raised in a typical tort suit. She had to manage the court.

I am not suggesting that torts expertise be an important condition for a Supreme Court judicial appointment, nor that the Court grant leave in more tort cases and fewer public law cases, for example. I would simply suggest that some type of institutional reform – perhaps specialized courts for specific areas of law and all the extra funding that would require – would probably be necessary to obtain judicial excellence in every branch of Canadian law. Given the realities of the present demands on the justices, I commend them all for making the best of it.

4 Evaluating Chief Justice McLachlin's Decisions on "Residual Policy Considerations" in Negligence

ERIKA CHAMBERLAIN

I. Introduction

During her time as Chief Justice, Beverley McLachlin led the Supreme Court of Canada through a formative period in the law of negligence. Among other key developments,[1] the court developed a uniquely Canadian version of the *Anns* test for novel duties of care in its 2001 decision in *Cooper v Hobart*.[2] That test consists of three main elements: foreseeability, proximity, and residual policy considerations. This chapter focuses on the last element; in particular, it examines the former Chief Justice's opinions on residual policy considerations as they were applied in leading claims against public authorities.[3]

The decisions in *Cooper*, *Hill v Hamilton-Wentworth Regional Police Services Board*, and *R v Imperial Tobacco* demonstrate a spectrum of approaches to assessing residual policy considerations as they pertain to the regulatory, investigative, and policy-making functions of public

---

1 Including reformulated tests for causation (*Resurfice Corp v Hanke*, 2007 SCC 7; *Clements v Clements*, 2012 SCC 32) and recovery for mental injury (*Mustapha v Culligan of Canada Ltd*, 2008 SCC 27; *Saadati v Moorhead*, 2017 SCC 28).

2 *Cooper v Hobart*, 2001 SCC 79 [*Cooper*].

3 This is admittedly a small sample of McLachlin CJ's decisions. As noted in Professor Bruce Feldthusen's contribution to this volume (see Chapter 3), McLachlin CJ wrote over fifty torts decisions during her time at the Supreme Court of Canada. They are nevertheless worth a close reading, as they have shaped the Court's interpretation of core policy immunity.

As a matter of interest, a recent empirical study of duty decisions in the highest courts of Canada, Australia, and the United Kingdom found that the Supreme Court of Canada dismissed negligence claims at the residual policy stage 32 percent of the time between 1985 and 2015. See James Plunkett, *The Duty of Care in Negligence* (Oxford: Hart Publishing, 2018) at 187.

bodies.[4] In *Hill*, McLachlin CJ was refreshingly sceptical about police arguments that a duty of care toward suspects under investigation would interfere with their exercise of discretion, create a chilling effect, or divert resources from other critical police functions. She expressed concern about denying potential redress to plaintiffs based on speculative policy arguments. Yet, in both *Cooper* and *Imperial Tobacco*, McLachlin CJ showed deference to regulators and policy-makers who were reputed to engage in a balancing of competing interests and did not give their residual policy considerations similar scrutiny.

While the distinctions among these defendants are largely consistent with precedent and are reasonably justifiable, they reveal an underlying tension about the types of public actors that the court finds worthy of deference. In *Imperial Tobacco*, the Court was willing to extend so-called policy immunity even where foreseeable harm and a relationship of proximity were established. Moreover, the Court accepted the defendant's arguments about the risk of indeterminate liability at face value, with none of the scepticism that was evident in *Hill*.

The treatment of these defendants also highlights some inconsistency in the Supreme Court's evaluation of the respective statutory frameworks in which they operate and suggests that the Court's reasoning may be strongly result-driven. As Professor Feldthusen points out in his contribution to this volume, it is not clear what leads the Court to conclude that one defendant's statutory duties are owed to the public at large, while another defendant's duties can support a proximate relationship with individual plaintiffs.[5] Similarly, as I argue in this chapter, the Court has not consistently applied its definition of "core policy" decisions to the conduct of public authority defendants. In turn, these tendencies call into question the considerable weight that has been placed on the relevant statutory framework since the decision in *Cooper* (a weight that has been criticized by several scholars, most notably Professor Lewis Klar).[6] In my view, therefore, McLachlin CJ's decisions

---

4 *Cooper, supra* note 2; *Hill v Hamilton-Wentworth Regional Police Services Board*, 2007 SCC 41 [*Hill*]; *R v Imperial Tobacco*, 2011 SCC 42 [*Imperial Tobacco*]. I take comfort that Professor Feldthusen is similarly puzzled by these decisions, and particularly their shifting references to policy in claims arising from alleged regulatory negligence. This underlies much of his general critique of the two-step test for duty. See Chapter 3 in this volume.

5 He also notes that the Court has been inconsistent as to whether this is a proximity issue or a residual policy consideration.

6 See Lewis Klar, "The Tort Liability of the Crown: Back to *Saskatchewan Wheat Pool*" (2007) 32:3 Adv Q 293; and Lewis Klar, "*Syl Apps Secure Treatment Centre v B.D.*: Looking for Proximity within Statutory Provisions" (2007) 86:3 Can Bar Rev 337.

on residual policy considerations represent some of her most and least compelling duty analyses.

Apart from their relevance to the assessment of McLachlin CJ's significant contributions to Canadian tort law, these cases inform broader debates about the appropriateness of using policy-based reasoning in the law of negligence.[7] As Professor Ernest Weinrib has noted, the analysis of residual policy considerations is almost completely one-sided (focusing on factors that could negative liability), and can amount to "judicial confiscation of what was rightly due to the plaintiff in order to subsidize policy objectives unilaterally favourable to the defendant and those similarly situated."[8] The influence of policy considerations in public authority negligence cases also reflects the encroachment of public law values into private law, and thus has the potential to contradict the traditional Diceyan notion of equal treatment for public and private defendants.[9] The clear, though not universal, trend following *Cooper* is that public authority defendants will be found not to owe a duty of care to those who suffer loss as a result of their negligence.

II. Defining Residual Policy Considerations

In *Cooper*, the Court described two different sets of policy considerations that are relevant to identifying novel duties of care. At the proximity stage of the duty analysis, a court should examine the closeness of the relationship between the plaintiff and defendant, which involves questions of "policy, in the broad sense of that word."[10] In contrast, policy considerations at the "residual" stage deal with the broader effects on society:

> These are not concerned with the relationship between the parties, but with the effect of recognizing a duty of care on other legal obligations, the

---

7 See e.g. Robert Stevens, *Torts and Rights* (Oxford: Oxford University Press, 2007) at 14 (arguing that the courts do not have the political legitimacy or technical competence to assess policy or social considerations), and Allan Beever, *Rediscovering the Law of Negligence* (Oxford: Hart Publishing, 2007) at 142.

8 Ernest J Weinrib, "The Disintegration of Duty" (2006) 31:2 Adv Q 212 at 235.

9 See AV Dicey, *The Law of the Constitution*, 10th ed (London: Macmillan, 1959) at 193. Diceyan principles can also come into play as part of the proximity analysis, with the court finding insufficient proximity because a private law defendant would owe no similar duty to the plaintiff; for example, regulating an industry is a function performed uniquely by public defendants.

10 *Cooper, supra* note 2 at para 30. This is probably one of the most perplexing phrases in the judgment.

> legal system and society more generally. Does the law already provide a remedy? Would recognition of the duty of care create the spectre of unlimited liability to an unlimited class? Are there other reasons of broad policy that suggest that the duty of care should not be recognized?[11]

Presumably, these policy considerations are limited only by lawyers' creativity and their ability to persuade the court that the broader implications of recognizing a new duty of care would be more detrimental than beneficial.

For the most part, it is the defendant's task to raise residual policy considerations that negate any *prima facie* duty of care established at Stage 1 of the *Cooper* analysis. Indeed, in *Childs v Desormeaux*,[12] McLachlin CJ clarified that, "once the plaintiff establishes a *prima facie* duty of care, the evidentiary burden of showing countervailing policy considerations shifts to the defendant, following the general rule that the party asserting a point should be required to establish it."[13] While the plaintiff may also raise policy considerations to support a *prima facie* duty, these are typically of lesser importance.[14]

Because they are meant to address concerns beyond the relationship between the parties to the dispute, they are sometimes referred to as "community welfare" considerations.[15] This is especially relevant in public authority negligence cases. As described below, the residual policy considerations that most often arise in public authority cases are the "chilling effect" of recognizing a duty, the risk of indeterminate liability, and the immunity of public authorities for their core policy decisions. Typically, then, they focus on the ways that imposing a duty of care would interfere with the public authority's ability to perform its functions and the inappropriateness of the courts' second-guessing

---

11 *Ibid* at para 37. See also Andrew Robertson, "Policy-based Reasoning in Duty of Care Cases" (2013) 33:1 LS 119, where he makes a similar distinction between policy arguments based on interpersonal justice and those based on community welfare considerations.

12 *Childs v Desormeaux*, 2006 SCC 18 [*Childs*].

13 *Ibid* at para 13.

14 See Robertson, *supra* note 11 at 131–2. Robertson, who completed an empirical study of ninety-two duty cases decided in England and Canada in the years 2008 and 2009, found that only one of the cases mentioned policy considerations weighing in favour of a duty. That case was *Donaldson v John Doe*, 2009 BCCA 38, which involved the liability of commercial alcohol providers.

15 Andrew Robertson, "Constraints on Policy-based Reasoning in Private Law" in Andrew Robertson & Tang Hang Wu, eds, *The Goals of Private* Law (Oxford: Hart Publishing, 2009) 261 at 263.

their actions. While this reasoning is often rationalized based on the separation of powers, it is clearly a line of defence that is not available for private defendants. Similarly, it is sometimes suggested that the courts are not competent to assess the complexity of government decision-making, an argument that may well be over-stated, given the sophistication of other negligence claims regularly decided by the courts (e.g., medical malpractice or complex commercial matters).

III. Application in Key Public Authority Cases

a. *Hill v Hamilton-Wentworth Regional Police Services Board*

In *Hill*, the Supreme Court of Canada became the highest court in the Commonwealth to recognize that police owe a duty of care to suspects under investigation.[16] The plaintiff had been tried and convicted of robbery in the mid-1990s. The evidence against him consisted primarily of eyewitness identification. Although he was eventually acquitted on appeal, he had spent twenty months in jail. He sued, *inter alia*, the police for their alleged negligence in carrying out the investigation. The allegations of negligence included: that police had published a photo identifying him as a suspect early in the investigation, thereby tainting subsequent eyewitness identifications, and that police had failed to thoroughly investigate information suggesting that other persons might have committed the robberies. Perhaps most egregiously, police had conducted a photo line-up using Hill (an Indigenous man) and eleven Caucasian foils.

Since the alleged duty of care between police and criminal suspects was a novel one, the Court engaged in the analysis outlined in *Cooper*. While the majority's analysis of proximity in the case was less than illuminating,[17] its analysis of residual policy considerations was highly commendable. McLachlin CJ proceeded through the various arguments raised by the police and found that each was either unsubstantiated and/or unpersuasive.

I. THE DISCRETIONARY NATURE OF POLICE INVESTIGATIONS

While McLachlin CJ acknowledged that criminal investigations require the exercise of discretion, she found that this did not distinguish

16 For additional discussion, see Erika Chamberlain, "Negligent Investigation: Tort Law as Police Ombudsman" in Andrew Robertson & Tang Hang Wu, eds, *The Goals of Private Law* (Oxford: Hart Publishing, 2009) 283.

17 See Erika Chamberlain, "Negligent Investigation: The End of Malicious Prosecution in Canada?" (2008) 124:2 Law Q Rev 205.

the police from other professionals.[18] For example, medicine also involves the exercise of "discretion, intuition and occasionally hunch," but this does not render doctors immune to negligence.[19] Also, given the demise of barristers' immunity throughout much of the Commonwealth,[20] it would be difficult to justify the continued immunity of police, alone, among the professions. McLachlin CJ further reasoned that the discretion exercised by police was hardly unrestrained: there are various statutory, constitutional, and common law obligations that direct how police can exercise their discretion in a democratic society. To hold them to a standard of reasonableness is merely to affirm their professional standards. Indeed, if it had been found that police exercised their discretion in a discriminatory manner on account of Hill's ethnicity, few would argue that this had been a valid exercise of their discretion. McLachlin CJ rightly concluded that the discretionary nature of police functions should not serve to exclude them entirely from scrutiny in negligence.

Any concerns police had about the exercise of discretion, the majority found, could be addressed by reference to the standard of care. The standard adopted in *Hill* – that of a reasonable police officer in the circumstances – was highly deferential and took into account the discretion inherent in many police functions.[21] At the same time, the standard of care must account for the potentially serious harms that might flow from the negligent conduct of investigations: the arrest and imprisonment of innocent persons.[22] While police should be given some leeway to pursue investigations as they see fit, the potential consequences for the suspect demand that the police act reasonably in the circumstances.

In *Hill*, the police were ultimately absolved of liability based on this relatively generous standard of care. The majority prefaced its analysis by noting that police practices have improved since 1995 and that the defendants' conduct should be judged by the standards prevailing at that time.[23] With respect to the photo line-up, the majority accepted the trial

18 *Hill, supra* note 4 at paras 51–4.
19 *Ibid* at para 53.
20 *JS Hall and Co v Simons*, [2000] 3 WLR 543 (HL); *Chamberlains v Lai*, [2006] NZSC 70. Canadian barristers have been subject to negligence claims for considerably longer: *Leslie v Ball* (1863), 22 UCQB 522 (Upper Canada Queen's Bench); *Wade v Ball* (1870), 20 UCCP 302 (Upper Canada Court of Common Pleas); and *Demarco v Ungaro* (1979), 95 DLR (3d) 385 (Ont HCJ).
21 *Hill, supra* note 4 at para 73.
22 *Ibid* at para 72.
23 *Ibid* at para 77.

judge's finding that there were no rules regarding line-ups in 1995. While a modern-day police officer would likely use foils of the same race as the suspect, the defendants' conduct was not unreasonable in its day.[24] This conclusion sits uneasily with many: it seems a matter of common sense that the foils in a line-up should be the same race as the suspect. Nevertheless, some of the foils had similar skin tones and facial features to Hill, so his race did not make him obviously stand out. On the facts, the trial judge and the majorities of the Court of Appeal and Supreme Court all concluded that the racial composition of the line-up did not result in unfairness.[25]

The other main allegation of negligence was that police downplayed evidence that another perpetrator might have been responsible for the crimes. They arrested and charged Hill even though they had tips implicating others, and then proceeded with the case against him even though the robberies continued while he was in custody. Although another suspect was identified and charged with some of the robberies, the lead detective did not seek to delay Hill's trial to permit a further investigation. McLachlin CJ conceded that, "[h]ad Detective Loft conducted further investigation, it is likely the case against Hill would have collapsed. Had he re-interviewed the eyewitnesses, for example, and shown them [the other suspect's] photo, it is probable that matters would have turned out otherwise; when the witnesses were eventually shown the photo of [the other suspect], they recanted their identification of Hill as the robber."[26] In spite of this observation, McLachlin CJ found that the detective's conduct fell within the acceptable range of police discretion.[27] She stressed that, in 1995, "awareness of the danger of wrongful convictions was less acute than it is today."[28] Thus, the majority concluded that the detective met the standard of a reasonable officer in the circumstances. This fairly deferential standard suggests that police need not be seriously concerned about the courts second guessing their investigatory discretion.

II. THE THREAT OF DEFENSIVE POLICING

The defendants in *Hill* also raised the argument, often successful in other Commonwealth courts,[29] that imposing a duty of care on police

24 *Ibid* at para 80.

25 One wonders whether the courts would come to a similar conclusion now in light of the Truth and Reconciliation Commission and recent scrutiny involving the interaction of Indigenous persons with the criminal justice system.

26 *Hill, supra* note 4 at para 83.

27 *Ibid* at para 88.

28 *Ibid*.

29 See the leading English case of *Hill v Chief Constable of West Yorkshire*, [1989] 1 AC 53 (HL), whose principles have repeatedly been upheld: *Elguzouli-Daf v*

would force them to carry out their investigations in a defensive manner. Also known as the "chilling effect," this argument insinuates that police will be fearful of vigorously pursuing all lines of investigation, lest the suspects bring civil claims after the fact. Charron J's dissenting opinion suggested that a duty toward suspects would discourage police from laying charges "except in cases where the evidence is overwhelming."[30] However, the majority found that this argument was speculative and that the record did not support the assertion that potential tort liability would alter police behaviour. Instead, the majority cited literature indicating the tort liability had no chilling effect.[31] Further, the majority reiterated that the standard was only that of reasonableness. While McLachlin CJ acknowledged that "police might become more careful in conducting investigations if a duty of care in tort is recognized," she concluded that "this is not necessarily a bad thing."[32]

Arguments about a potential chilling effect on police are sometimes framed in terms of a conflict of duties: if police are found to owe a private law duty to suspects, they may prefer individual suspects' interests to their broader public duty to thoroughly pursue criminal investigations. The dissenters in *Hill* cited this conflict as a reason not to recognize a duty of care.[33] Charron J explained that "the overly cautious approach that may result from the imposition of conflicting duties would seriously undermine *society's interest* in having the police investigate crime and apprehend offenders."[34]

The dissenters' reasoning is consistent with the reasoning of the English courts, except that the English cases have primarily been brought by victims of crime whose pleas to police for protection went unheeded. For example, in *Smith v Chief Constable of Sussex Police*,[35] the plaintiff had been assaulted by his estranged partner, who was taken into custody but not prosecuted. The plaintiff subsequently received numerous threats, which he reported to police, but they took virtually no action in response. Ultimately, the plaintiff was attacked by his partner with

---

Commissioner of Police of the Metropolis, [1995] QB 335 at 349 (Eng CA); *Cran v New South Wales* (2004), 62 NSWLR 95 (CA) at para 48; *Brooks v Commissioner of Police for the Metropolis*, [2005] UKHL 24 at para 30; and *Michael v Chief Constable of South Wales Police*, [2015] UKSC 2 at para 121.

30 *Hill, supra* note 4 at para 152.

31 *Ibid* at para 57.

32 *Ibid* at para 56.

33 *Ibid* at para 140.

34 *Ibid* at para 142 (emphasis in original).

35 *Smith v Chief Constable of Sussex Police*, [2008] UKHL 50 [*Smith*].

a claw hammer, leaving him with a fractured skull and brain damage. Although the House of Lords acknowledged that there had been a "highly regrettable failure [by police] to react to a prolonged campaign … threatening the use of extreme criminal violence,"[36] they declined to impose a duty of care due to fear that it would impede the ability of police to carry out their public functions.[37]

As is discussed in Part IV below, the Supreme Court of Canada has been somewhat inconsistent in its application of this policy factor. In *Hill*, the majority was not persuaded that the alleged conflict of duties had "a real potential for negative policy consequences," and warned that a duty of care "should not be denied on speculative grounds."[38] Yet, in *Cooper*, they found the potential for conflicting duties to be fatal to the plaintiff's claim, with no clear evidence to support that conclusion.

III. FLOODGATES

Finally, the police in *Hill* resorted to the argument that recognizing a duty of care toward suspects would result in a flood of litigation. Even worse, they argued, lawsuits could be brought by factually guilty parties who managed to avoid conviction on a technicality.[39] Unlike many Commonwealth courts, which have accepted this argument without supporting evidence,[40] the majority of the Supreme Court concluded that the threat of floodgates was not credibly substantiated. McLachlin CJ noted that both Ontario and Quebec had already recognized claims for negligent investigation, and neither province had experienced a glut of litigation. She also seemed critical of the defendants for raising this argument in the abstract without providing supporting data. Pointing to "a relatively small number of lawsuits, the cost of which are unknown, with effects on the police that have not been measured," was not sufficient to negate the *prima facie* duty of care.[41]

Regarding the possibility of recovery by factually guilty parties, McLachlin CJ concluded that the chance of such "injustice" was not any greater than in other tort actions. The tort system is not perfect. For

36 *Ibid* at para 72.

37 *Ibid* at para 73. Lord Hope wrote, "the interests of the wider community must prevail over those of the individual." *Ibid* at para 75.

38 *Hill, supra* note 4 at para 43.

39 The dissenting judges found this argument persuasive, noting that it would be difficult to determine which plaintiffs should rightfully recover without introducing a verdict of "factually innocent" into Canada's criminal justice system.

40 See the cases listed in *supra* note 29.

41 *Hill, supra* note 4 at para 61.

example, a "person who recovers against her doctor for medical malpractice may, despite having proved illness in court, have in fact been malingering."[42] No one would suggest, however, that such a possibility should lead to blanket immunity for medical practitioners. Further, McLachlin CJ stressed that the possibility of erroneous awards would be minimized by the other safeguards in the tort process, noting especially the difficulties of proving causation in negligent investigation cases (i.e., that the suspect would not have been charged at all but for the police negligence). Indeed, these factors have made negligent investigation claims nearly unwinnable for plaintiffs in the fifteen years since *Hill*.[43]

It is noteworthy that the Supreme Court challenged the police's rather bald argument regarding the floodgates of litigation. The courts have too easily accepted this argument in the past, on the assumption that any suspect who is exonerated will subsequently bring a civil claim against the police. This assumption ignores that most suspected criminals lack the financial resources to pursue lengthy litigation against the state and that most are probably relieved to be rid of the justice system once acquitted. Given the deferential standard adopted in *Hill*, it seems that only the most obvious cases of negligence will succeed in any event.

In summary, McLachlin CJ's majority opinion in *Hill* was refreshingly critical of the standard police arguments in favour of immunity during investigations. The majority rightly scrutinized these arguments and dismissed them in so far as they were speculative. *Hill* took seriously the argument that residual policy considerations should be evaluated carefully, because they drive an otherwise meritorious case from the courts, and usually set a precedent that will prevent similar claims in the future.

b. Cooper v Hobart

The Court's decision in *Cooper* demonstrates a very different approach to the analysis of residual policy considerations. The plaintiff in that case was an investor who suffered economic loss due to the misconduct

---

42 *Ibid* at para 63.

43 For more recent cases, see *Jarrett v Halifax (Regional Municipality)*, 2014 NSSC 116; *JH v Windsor Police Services Board et al*, 2017 ONSC 6507; and *Roda v Toronto Police Services Board*, 2016 ONSC 743, aff'd 2017 ONCA 768. See generally Erika Chamberlain, "Negligent Investigation: Faint Hope for the Wrongly Accused?" (2011) 39:2 Adv Q 153.

of a registered mortgage broker; she sued the Registrar of Mortgage Brokers, alleging that, had the Registrar taken more timely action against the relevant broker's registration, the plaintiff (and other investors) would not have suffered as much of a loss. The court concluded that there was insufficient proximity to recognize the alleged duty of care. In particular, the statutory framework suggested that the Registrar owed duties to the public at large, rather than to individual investors.[44] The Registrar had to balance factors like public access to capital through mortgage financing, and maintaining public confidence in the system by taking action against unsuitable brokers. The Court suggested that these factors required "delicate balancing," such that a private law duty toward individual investors was precluded.[45]

This conclusion itself was a matter of policy. As indicated, McLachlin CJ and Major J described the proximity analysis as involving, somewhat cryptically, "questions of policy, in the broad sense of that word."[46] Professor Weinrib has criticized the Court's analysis of proximity in *Cooper* as being one-sided: "[t]he judgment did not compare the interests of the investors with the interests of the Registrar of Mortgage Brokers ... The exercise in question was not one of balancing policies or interests but of specifying the nature of the Registrar's duty through analysis of the institutional framework created by the statute."[47] At no point did the Court explicitly consider how the interests of investors were factored into the analysis, or explain why they should be left remediless against the Registrar's negligence. It was merely asserted that this result was preferable for the Registrar's functioning and the public as a whole.

Having dismissed the plaintiff's claim at the proximity stage, it is understandable that the Court's analysis of residual policy considerations was brief (only four paragraphs). Nevertheless, unlike its sceptical attitude in *Hill*, the Court in *Cooper* accepted without question that the recognition of a duty between the Registrar of Mortgage Brokers and individual investors would give rise to indeterminate liability. Specifically, there was no way for the Registrar to control either the number of investors or the value of their investments.[48]

Further, the Court suggested that it would be inappropriate to create an "insurance scheme" for investors' losses by shifting them to the taxpaying

44 *Cooper*, *supra* note 2 at para 44.
45 *Ibid* at para 49.
46 *Ibid* at para 30.
47 Weinrib, *supra* note 8 at 247–8.
48 *Cooper*, *supra* note 2 at para 54.

public through the Registrar's liability.[49] This policy argument is not uncommon in public authority cases, particularly those involving pure economic loss.[50] It is not especially compelling. While one can appreciate that a finding of liability would put pressure on public resources, that is not, in itself, a justification for putting the entire burden of the Registrar's negligence on investors. This is particularly true given that one of the main purposes of the statutory framework is to protect investors from the risks posed by unsuitable mortgage brokers. It could be argued, for instance, that the losses suffered by the investors were not the result of risky or aggressive investing choices, but of their reliance on the broker's registration as a marker that it was suitable to act as such. Liability, thus, does not "insure" investors against poor investment decisions but, rather, compensates them for their reasonable reliance on the impression of investment security negligently created (or maintained) by the defendant Registrar.

Moreover, while the taxpaying public would presumably prefer that their taxes not be used to pay damages, this does not mean that the losses should be borne by the plaintiffs alone. The taxpaying public may well prefer that the Registrar not act negligently. Finally, this policy consideration boils down to an argument that tort damages divert financial resources from other uses; accepting it in public authority cases suggests that those harmed by public authority negligence should sacrifice their needs for the greater public good. In contrast, private defendants do not have access to the argument that tort liability will cut into their profits or harm their shareholders or creditors. This distinction could well be justifiable; however, it should not be accepted without question.

As additional residual policy considerations, the court in *Cooper* noted that the Registrar's functions were quasi-judicial (in that they involved the power to investigate complaints against brokers, and to suspend and revoke their registration) and involved questions of the public interest. McLachlin CJ and Major J wrote: "the Registrar must make difficult discretionary decisions in the area of public policy, decisions which command deference."[51] While immunity for quasi-judicial decisions is well established and is not questioned here,[52] one may legitimately

49 *Ibid* at para 55.

50 See e.g. *Martel Building Ltd v Canada*, 2000 SCC 60; *Ross v British Columbia Lottery Corporation*, 2014 BCSC 320.

51 *Cooper, supra* note 2 at para 53.

52 See *Everett v Griffiths*, [1921] 1 AC 631 (HL), and *Calvert v Law Society of Upper Canada* (1981), 121 DLR (3d) 169 (Ont HC). But see Robert J Sadler, "Judicial and Quasi-Judicial Immunities: A Remedy Denied" (1982) 4:4 Melbourne UL Rev 508, and John Murphy, "Rethinking Tortious Immunity for Judicial Acts" (2013) 33:3 LS 455.

ask whether the Registrar's decisions truly involve questions of public policy that should command deference or render them immune from negligence liability. The primary functions of the Registrar are to ensure that registered mortgage brokers are suitable to engage in that business. The Registrar does not make high-level decisions about financial policy in the province, engage in resource allocation, or balance social or political considerations. If the Court's interpretation of "public interest" in *Cooper* were broadly adopted, immunity for policy decisions would extend to a vast number of public officers. That concern is revisited in the discussion of *Imperial Tobacco*, below.

c. R v Imperial Tobacco

The *Imperial Tobacco* case involved a series of claims and cross-claims; for present purposes, it is sufficient to focus on the tobacco companies' third-party claim against Health Canada in negligent misrepresentation.[53] This claim was based on the allegation that Health Canada misrepresented the health benefits of low-tar and light cigarettes, encouraging both the companies to sell them and consumers to smoke them. This ultimately made the companies susceptible to liability toward affected smokers in tort and, under a provincial costs recovery statute, for their related health-care costs.[54] The Supreme Court found that there was no established duty of care in the situation where the government made representations to an industry and that a *Cooper* analysis was therefore required.

The Court was prepared to find a proximate relationship between Health Canada and the tobacco companies based on the history of their interactions. Specifically, Health Canada went beyond its duties as regulator and acted as "designer, developer, promoter and licensor of tobacco strains."[55] It regularly gave advice and recommendations to tobacco companies, and so it was reasonable for the companies to rely on its representation that low-tar cigarettes were less harmful than regular cigarettes. McLachlin CJ summarized: "what is alleged is not simply that broad powers of regulation were brought to bear on the tobacco industry, but that Canada assumed the role of adviser to a finite number of manufacturers and that there were commercial relationships entered into between Canada and the companies based in part on the advice

53 The claims for failure to warn and negligent design were also dismissed for public policy reasons.

54 *Tobacco Damages and Health Care Costs Recovery Act*, SBC 2000, c 30.

55 *Imperial Tobacco*, *supra* note 4 at para 54.

given to the companies by government officials."[56] This was sufficient to bring Health Canada into a proximate relationship with the tobacco companies, giving rise to a *prima facie* duty of care. Nevertheless, this duty was negated by residual policy considerations under Stage 2 of the *Cooper* analysis, namely, that Health Canada's actions were expressions of public policy, and that imposing a duty could give rise to indeterminate liability.

I. IMMUNITY FOR GOVERNMENT POLICY DECISIONS

Imperial Tobacco is well-known for its restatement of immunity for the "core policy" decisions of public authorities.[57] After reviewing the somewhat notorious jurisprudence on the distinction between policy and operational decisions,[58] the Court concluded that "'core policy' government decisions protected from suit are decisions as to a course or principle of action that are based on public policy considerations, such as economic, social and political factors, provided they are neither irrational nor taken in bad faith."[59] Applied to the facts, the Court found that Health Canada's decision to promote low-tar cigarettes as being a less harmful alternative to regular cigarettes was part of its broader policy to protect the health of Canadians, and was based on social and economic considerations (including the "individual and institutional costs associated with tobacco-related disease").[60]

There are several bases on which this conclusion can be challenged,[61] and they illustrate the continuing disutility of policy immunity for making determinations of duty. In particular, the Court's conclusion seems

---

56 *Ibid* at para 53.

57 See Lewis Klar, "*R v Imperial Tobacco Ltd*: More Restrictions on Public Authority Tort Liability" (2012) 50:1 Alb L Rev 157 at 168, where he argues that the judgment did nothing to clarify the policy/operational dichotomy. In contrast, Feldthusen believes that McLachlin CJ provided an "excellent" restatement, and that "it is doubtful one could improve upon it." Bruce Feldthusen, "Public Authority Immunity from Negligence Liability: Uncertain, Unnecessary, and Unjustified" (2013) 92:2 Can Bar Rev 211 at 217.

58 *Imperial Tobacco, supra* note 4 at para 72*ff*. McLachlin CJ wrote, "The question of what constitutes a policy decision that is generally protected from negligence liability is a vexed one, upon which much judicial ink has been spilled." See also SH Bailey & MJ Bowman, "The Policy/Operational Dichotomy: A Cuckoo in the Nest" (1986) 45:3 Cambridge LJ 430; Peter W Hogg, Patrick J Monahan & Wade K Wright, *Liability of the Crown*, 4th ed (Toronto: Carswell, 2011) at 228–30; and *Paradis Honey Ltd v Canada*, 2015 FCA 89.

59 *Imperial Tobacco*, supra note 4 at para 90.

60 *Ibid* at para 95.

61 See generally Feldthusen, *supra* note 57.

predetermined by the way that it chose to frame the government's activity: "Health Canada was acting out of concern for the health of Canadians, pursuant to its *policy* of encouraging smokers to switch to low-tar cigarettes ... Health Canada had a *policy* to warn the public about the hazardous effects of smoking, and to encourage healthier smoking habits among Canadians."[62] Respectfully, the government's conduct in *Imperial Tobacco* was not self-evidently a matter of policy. As Professor Feldthusen has argued, the policy could instead have been defined as one of harm reduction or health promotion; the decision to promote low-tar cigarettes was an *implementation* of that over-arching policy.[63] Further, it is not entirely clear what financial or political considerations had to be balanced in deciding to promote a dangerous product as a more healthful alternative to regular cigarettes.

The broader criticism of the decision in *Imperial Tobacco* is that it extended immunity to Health Canada even though it had found a proximate relationship between the parties. Since the decision in *Cooper*, most duty analyses have focused on the question of proximity, and have avoided the difficulties posed by the policy/operational distinction. This is especially true for the cases based on allegations that the government failed to properly regulate an industry or to confer certain benefits on members of the public.[64] Typically, there are insufficient interactions between the government and the plaintiff to establish proximity: the plaintiff is but one member of the public whom the defendant needs to keep in mind, and the defendant needs to balance the competing needs of various constituencies.[65]

However, in *Imperial Tobacco*, the Court *had* found sufficiently direct interactions between the parties to ground proximity, so its conclusions on policy immunity are perplexing. The government was not obviously allocating scarce resources or otherwise balancing competing interests. It deliberately encouraged tobacco companies to manufacture and promote, and smokers to consume, low-tar cigarettes. Further, a private party who engaged in a similar act of promoting unhealthy products would presumably be found to owe a duty of care (in fact, this was the underlying claim against the tobacco companies in *Imperial Tobacco*).

62 *Imperial Tobacco, supra* note 4 at para 94 (emphasis added).

63 Feldthusen, *supra* note 57 at 218.

64 See generally Bruce Feldthusen, "Failure to Confer Discretionary Public Benefits: The Case for Complete Negligence Immunity" (1997) 5 Tort L Rev 17.

65 See e.g. *Eliopoulos v Ontario (Minister of Health & Long Term Care)* (2006), 82 OR (3d) 321 (CA), 276 DLR (4th) 411; *Attis v Canada (Minister of Health)*, 2008 ONCA 660; *Los Angeles Salad Company v Canadian Food Inspection Agency*, 2013 BCCA 34.

A private party defendant would not be able to hide behind policy immunity. Therefore, under a Diceyan approach to negligence liability (i.e., that governments should be liable to the same extent as a private party – no more and no less),[66] there is no reason for the government to be immune altogether.[67] One could possibly argue that the defendant's actions were reasonable, given the state of knowledge at the time, but this should not preclude a finding of duty altogether.

II. INDETERMINATE LIABILITY

In addition to dismissing the tobacco companies' claim on account of policy immunity, McLachlin CJ suggested that the risk of indeterminate liability was "fatal" to their case.[68] Referring to the indeterminate liability analysis in *Cooper*, she noted that Health Canada had no control over smokers and, thus, no way to limit its liability. This argument seems misguided. By analogy to this reasoning, manufacturers would also be able to avoid liability for their products: they have no effective means of controlling who buys them or how they are used. But manufacturers are liable both for defective products and for products that pose risks when they are used improperly by consumers.[69] Health Canada's liability was no more indeterminate than this. The Court seems to have fallen into the somewhat amateur trap of confusing extensive liability with indeterminate liability.[70] This was most likely coloured by the fact that the dollar amounts were substantial, and would have strained the public purse (and perhaps relieved the costs of tobacco companies, who are not exactly sympathetic players in this litigation).

In addition, McLachlin CJ stressed that indeterminate liability arguments are especially persuasive in claims involving pure economic

---

66 See Dicey, *supra* note 9 at 193. This is the basis of most Crown liability legislation, which allows the Crown to be sued as though it were a private citizen. See Hogg *et al*, *supra* note 58 at 2–4.

67 See Feldthusen, *supra* note 57 at 230–1, where he notes that policy immunity is intended to recognize the unique functions of government and also the non-justiciability of policy decisions. These factors do not apply in situations where a private party in the same position would be found liable.

68 *Imperial Tobacco*, *supra* note 4 at para 99.

69 With respect to defective products, see *Hollis v Dow Corning*, [1995] 4 SCR 634. Regarding risks and improperly used products, see e.g. *Walford v Jacuzzi Canada Ltd*, 2007 ONCA 729 (involving the common practice of backyard pool users to ignore warnings not to enter the water head-first).

70 It appears that this point was argued, unsuccessfully, by the plaintiffs. See *Imperial Tobacco*, *supra* note 4 at para 98, and *R v Imperial Tobacco*, 2011 SCC 42 (Factum of the Respondent on Appeal and Factum of the Appellant on Cross-Appeal), Supreme Court File No 33559 (10 January 2011) at para 139.

loss.[71] Typically, this argument arises in economic loss claims involving negligent misstatement (where it is difficult for the defendant to control how the statement is repeated and used by a range of different parties),[72] or those involving consequential or "relational" economic loss (where it is difficult to control how many third parties will suffer loss following harm to a primary party).[73] In each of those situations, indeterminate liability can be overcome by proximity considerations, such as the requirements in negligent misstatement that the defendant knew the plaintiff would rely on its statement and assumed responsibility for the consequences of that reliance.[74] Again, it is odd that the Court concluded that there was indeterminate liability in the face of a proximate relationship. Health Canada knew exactly who would rely on its statements and had created a relationship where such reliance was reasonable.

IV. Residual Policy Considerations and Current Tort Theories

The decisions reviewed above reveal an inconsistent approach to the assessment of residual policy considerations in public authority negligence cases. Accordingly, they can provide fodder for current scholarly debates about the appropriate role of policy considerations in private law. The discussion below provides an overview of the predominant schools of thought on this issue and then discusses their applicability to McLachlin CJ's spectrum of deference and her variable willingness to allow public policy considerations to trump private law rights.

On the one hand, most rights theorists claim that policy considerations have no place in private law, and that they involve the courts in questions that they are neither qualified nor legitimated to answer.[75] Policy-based reasoning is more properly the purview of the legislature, they argue, and only serves to introduce incoherence and uncertainty into the common law. According to these critics, the courts should confine themselves to asking whether the plaintiff had a legally recognized right that was wrongfully infringed by the defendant. They raise alarm against what Allan Beever has described as a "policy-based free-for-all."[76]

---

71 *Imperial Tobacco, supra* note 4 at para 100.

72 *Hercules Management v Ernst & Young,* [1997] 2 SCR 165 [*Hercules Management*].

73 *Bow Valley Husky (Bermuda) Ltd v Saint John Shipbuilding Ltd,* [1997] 3 SCR 1210. See also McLachlin CJ's dissent in *Deloitte & Touche v Livent Inc (Receiver of),* 2017 SCC 63.

74 *Hercules Management, supra* note 72.

75 See e.g. Stevens, *supra* note 7 at 308–9.

76 Beever, *supra* note 7 at 142.

Moreover, rights theorists argue that, if a private law right exists, it should not be extinguished on the basis that its remedy would have broader social implications or would be detrimental to the way that the defendant carries out its activities.[77] They question how courts can weigh the justice of recovery for the plaintiff (established by foreseeable harm and a proximate relationship) against the residual policy factors raised by the defendant, which are extrinsic to the relationship between the parties. Professor Weinrib asks, "How is this balancing of incommensurables to be done?"[78] For these scholars, the two-stage approach in *Cooper* improperly invites courts to restrict the rights of private litigants based on community welfare considerations.

When it comes to public authority negligence, three aspects of rights theory are especially important. First, rights theorists tend toward conservatism in their description of legally recognized rights, typically limiting them to long-standing common law rights like bodily security, property, and reputation.[79] Second, they generally subscribe to the Diceyan principle that public actors should have the same private law obligations as other citizens.[80] This means that they recognize "special" duties for public actors only to the extent that they are clearly established by statute, which is exceedingly rare.

Third, rights theorists tend to be hostile to affirmative duties; apart from situations involving assumptions of responsibility, we do not have a right to demand that others make us better off.[81] They further apply Dicey's theory to conclude that, if we do not have such rights "against the world," we cannot have them against public actors, either.[82] Thus, rights theorists lean against the liability of public authorities, especially if the claim is said to involve a "gratuitous benefit."[83] For example, they might argue that

77 Weinrib, *supra* note 8 at 235.

78 *Ibid* at 236.

79 Stevens, *supra* note 7 at 5, quoting Cave J in *Allen v Flood*, [1898] 1 AC 1 (HL). For critique, see Roderick Bagshaw, "Tort Law, Concepts and What Really Matters," in Andrew Robertson & Tang Hang Wu, eds, *The Goals of Private Law* (Oxford: Hart Publishing, 2009) 254.

80 See Feldthusen, *supra* note 64.

81 Stevens, *supra* note 7 at 9.

82 *Ibid* at 221. But see Jane Stapleton, "Duty of Care Factors: A Selection from the Judicial Menus" in Jane Stapleton & Peter Cane, eds, *The Law of Obligations: Essays in Celebration of John Fleming* (Oxford: Clarendon Press, 1998) 59; Harold Luntz, "The Use of Policy in Negligence Cases in the High Court of Australia" in Michael Bryan, ed, *Private Law in Theory and Practice* (London: Routledge-Cavendish, 2006) 55; and John Murphy, "Rights, Reductionism and Tort Law" (2008) 28:2 Oxford J Leg Stud 393.

83 Stevens, *supra* note 7 at 9.

a mortgage regulator provides a gratuitous service to investors, which cannot give rise to a private law claim if it is performed negligently; the government could just as well decide not to regulate the industry at all, and the plaintiff could not complain about the lack of regulation.[84]

These types of arguments tend to be considered at the proximity stage of the duty analysis, as they relate more directly to the relationship between the parties – that is, what obligations the defendant owes to the plaintiff, and what the plaintiff can legally expect the defendant to do. (Rights theorists would argue that, if the plaintiff's rights are defined with sufficient restraint, there should be no need to resort to residual policy factors to cut them back.)[85] All of this leads rights theorists to conclude that courts should very rarely establish new duties of care owed by public authorities, and that policy considerations should have no role in their analyses.

In contrast, instrumentalist scholars view the social effects of law as an important component of common law decision-making. Law and economics scholars, for example, view tort law as promoting economically efficient behaviour, which is better for society as a whole. Others suggest that tort has important deterrent or care-inducing functions.[86] A manufacturer's duty to warn of risks associated with its products is a prime example, as it provides a financial incentive for manufacturers to protect consumers from injury and keep abreast of new risks that come to light. Instrumentalists are not averse to the use of public policy considerations to either support or negate the recognition of new duties of care.[87]

Finally, some scholars take an intermediate approach, labelled by Professor Andrew Robertson as "pluralist."[88] Under this approach, which maps well onto the two-stage test outlined in *Cooper*, the duty analysis

> is primarily concerned with identifying the circumstances in which one person has a right against another that the second person be mindful

84 At least not in the courts. They could complain through political processes.

85 See Stevens, *supra* note 7 at 224–5.

86 Allen Linden, "Torts Tomorrow: Empowering the Injured" in Nicholas Mullany & Allen Linden, eds, *Torts Tomorrow: A Tribute to John Fleming* (Sydney: LBC Information Services, 1998) 321.

87 See e.g. Stelios Tofaris and Sandy Steel, "Negligence Liability for Omissions and the Police" (2016) 75:1 Cambridge LJ 128.

88 Andrew Robertson, "Rights, Pluralism, and the Duty of Care" in Donal Nolan & Andrew Robertson, eds, *Rights and Private Law* (Oxford: Hart Publishing, 2012) 435 at 440.

> of the first person's legitimate interests. This approach recognises that relational considerations, or questions of interpersonal justice, are the principal determinants of the duty of care question. It is pluralist, however, in the sense that community welfare considerations can come into play in a secondary way to negate the duty of care in certain limited circumstances.[89]

Thus, this approach prioritizes the plaintiff's rights but leaves room for policy considerations to over-ride them in appropriate circumstances. Robertson is also sceptical of the concern that policy considerations introduce chaos into private law, noting that their use is heavily constrained by common law method and convention.[90] Therefore, policy is not the unruly horse or incoherent influence that rights theorists make it out to be.

The three decisions examined in this chapter apply, at various times, aspects of the rights-based, instrumentalist, and pluralist approaches; in so doing, they suggest that McLachlin CJ did not have a coherent theoretical approach to public authority negligence liability and that her reasoning was at least partially result-driven. One could conclude that rights theorists are therefore correct in condemning the use of policy reasoning in these cases, as it introduces uncertainty and confusion in the law. At the same time, the results in these cases suggest that the Supreme Court is generally deferential toward public decision-makers and is not employing policy considerations to insert itself into political decisions.

Indeed, somewhat ironically, policy is most often used in these decisions as a means of *showing* deference to public decision-makers. In *Cooper*, this was evident in both the proximity and residual policy stages; in *Imperial Tobacco*, it was manifested in the conclusion that the government's action was a core policy decision that was non-justiciable in negligence. In other words, the Court accepted that it was not appropriately situated to assess the public actor's conduct. The outlier is *Hill*, where McLachlin CJ showed scant deference to the police (at least at the duty stage). She was emphatic that residual policy considerations could not negate a duty if they were merely speculative and put the police to a relatively onerous burden of persuasion. What justifies this spectrum of deference? Why single out police as needing to prove that

89 *Ibid* at 440–1.

90 Andrew Robertson, "Constraints on Policy-Based Reasoning in Private Law" in Andrew Robertson & Tang Hang Wu, eds, *The Goals of Private Law* (Oxford: Hart Publishing, 2009) 261.

their arguments were based on more than speculation, and then accept the other defendants' policy arguments at face value?

From the perspective of institutional competence, it seems natural for courts to assess whether a criminal investigation falls below the standard of reasonable care; they regularly engage in similar analyses in criminal and *Charter* cases. Nevertheless, their competence in the three cases seems a matter of degree, rather than substance. It would not be far-fetched for a court to conclude that the promotion of low-tar cigarettes as a healthier alternative to regular cigarettes was a negligent misstatement, or that the Registrar of Mortgage Brokers did not adequately supervise or investigate the misconduct of a registered broker. Such conclusions do not stretch the Courts' competence and would not obviously involve the courts' usurping the role of the government.

In terms of interpersonal factors (i.e., proximity), there are two obvious factual distinctions between *Hill* and the other cases. First, the defendants in *Hill* had a closer personal interaction with the plaintiff; and second, the harm was a loss of liberty, rather than economic loss. (More pragmatically, though not explicit in the judgments, the wrongly convicted elicit greater sympathy than either disappointed investors or tobacco companies.) From a rights-based perspective, it might also be critical that the defendants' actions actively caused harm (imprisonment) to the plaintiff; the police were not simply withholding a gratuitous benefit. Further, as Dicey might put it, police and private citizens are equally liable when they wrongly imprison others.

A final distinguishing factor was the statutory framework, which, since *Cooper*, has been the primary focus in public authority negligence cases. Like rights theorists, the Supreme Court of Canada has relied on the statutory framework to determine whether a public authority should owe a duty above and beyond what is owed by the ordinary person; in *Cooper*, McLachlin CJ and Major J wrote, "Th[e] statute is the only source of [the Registrar's] duties, private or public. Apart from that statute, he is in no different position than the ordinary man or woman on the street."[91]

However, a close analysis of the statutory frameworks in these cases reveals that the Court's assessment of the relevant statutory frameworks is inconsistent and appears result-driven. Consider the statutory frameworks in *Hill* and *Cooper*. The statutory duties owed by police include the fairly open-ended "preserving the peace," "maintaining law and order," "preventing crimes and other offences," and "assisting victims

91 *Cooper, supra* note 2 at para 43.

of crime."[92] These duties clearly have a public element to them, and there is no doubt that police must balance competing interests when allocating human and financial resources to crime prevention, investigations, and the apprehension of criminal suspects. The statute does not obviously single out any individual as having an enforceable right against police. Yet, the majority in *Hill* did not really discuss whether these over-arching statutory duties would preclude a private law duty of care toward suspects, and confidently concluded that the interests of the suspect and the general public were aligned.

Turning to *Cooper*, the Registrar of Mortgage Brokers' statutory duties seem to be framed more narrowly. The Registrar "must keep a register" of brokers, "must grant registration" to a broker who is suitable, and may investigate a broker's affairs, suspend or revoke registrations, and so on.[93] These duties seem more confined to particular tasks than to over-arching public duties, and they appear to be susceptible to an objective standard of care. Moreover, there are clearly some individuals who stand to suffer loss if the Registrar performs its tasks negligently. Yet in *Cooper*, the Court concluded that the Registrar's duties are owed "to the public as a whole" and involve a "delicate balancing" of "a myriad of competing interests."[94] The Registrar's actions must "[instil] public confidence in the system."[95]

It is hard to see how the Court could interpret these statutes so differently, and to conclude that the Registrar is engaged in policy-making that is immune from negligence liability. Indeed, the scope of the Registrar's investigative powers seems much narrower than that of police. The range of individuals who can be "targeted" by an investigation is smaller, and such an investigation is limited to a defined set of issues. Further, the conduct of an investigation by the Registrar does not significantly detract resources from activities equivalent to police patrols or other public safety or crime prevention initiatives. The Registrar's mandate is much more circumscribed.

The related issue of "conflicting duties" also arises in these cases.[96] As noted, this argument suggests that, if the defendant is found to owe a private law duty of care, this will conflict with its broader duties to

---

92 See e.g. *Police Services Act*, RSO 1990, c P.15, s 42(1); *Police Act*, SNB 1977, c P-9.2, s 12(1).

93 See *Mortgage Brokers Act*, RSBC 1996, c 313, as reviewed in *Cooper*, *supra* note 2 at paras 44–9.

94 *Cooper*, *supra* note 2 at para 49.

95 *Ibid*.

96 See Feldthusen, *supra* note 63.

the public as a whole. Fearing liability, the defendant will tend to prefer the interests of private parties and neglect its public law duties. One author has described this policy concern as a "myth."[97] It certainly appears to be a risk that is over-stated. When a defendant is tasked with regulating a particular industry, the broader public interest will presumably often align with those who are directly tied to that industry and who risk suffering harm if the defendant is negligent in exercising its regulatory functions. In *Cooper*, for example, it is difficult to see how the public interest would conflict with the Registrar's obligation to investigate and suspend the registrations of unsuitable mortgage brokers in a timely manner, unless easy access to mortgage financing is more important than the trustworthiness of the financiers.[98]

Moreover, this is exactly the type of potential conflict that the majority dismissed in *Hill*. Unlike its Commonwealth counterparts, which frequently state that a police duty toward suspects would conflict with their general duties to protect the public and investigate crime, the court in *Hill* concluded that a duty toward suspects was generally consistent with the public duties of police. McLachlin CJ reasoned that an officer's public duty to investigate crime was not "unconstrained" and must be exercised in accordance with lawful standards.[99] Further, both the public and the suspect have an interest that investigations be conducted diligently.[100] Finally, for a conflict of duties to negate a *prima facie* duty of care, it must have a "real potential for negative policy consequences."[101] McLachlin CJ found that this potential did not exist in *Hill*.

Nevertheless, in *Cooper*, McLachlin CJ and Major J concluded that the potential for conflicting duties mandated that a private law duty not be recognized. They reasoned, summarily: a private law duty of care toward investors "would no doubt come at the expense of other important interests, of efficiency and finally at the expense of public confidence in the system as a whole."[102] It seems fair to question whether

97 Jasmine van Schouwen, "The King Can Still Do No Wrong: A Critical Perspective on the Crown's Private Law Duty of Care in Canada" (2016) 24:3 Tort L Rev 159 at 171.

98 *Ibid* at 159, referring to the liability of health and environmental regulators: "what is the 'public health' or 'public safety' that regulators are so often mandated to protect, if not the health and safety of those members of the public directly affected by the activities which regulators exist to oversee?"

99 *Hill, supra* note 4 at para 41.

100 *Ibid.*

101 *Ibid* at para 43.

102 *Cooper, supra* note 2 at para 50.

the court based this conclusion on any evidence of "a real potential for negative policy consequences."[103] For example, how often will the investigation and possible deregistration of unsuitable mortgage brokers not align with the public interest? How different is this from the situation in *Hill*? As van Schouwen recently noted, "Just as the public shares the interest of suspects in diligent investigation in accordance with the law [as in *Hill*], the public also shares the interest of those members of society who are vulnerable to harm from regulated activities in diligent regulation according to the law."[104]

Ultimately, the spectrum of deference shown in these cases is not as defensible as it might first appear. McLachlin CJ's interpretation of the relevant statutory frameworks and her application of policy immunity gave a privilege to regulatory and administrative decision-makers over police, on the unsubstantiated grounds that their decisions involved a more delicate balancing of interests. This meant that the plaintiffs' rights were sacrificed for a poorly defined public good.

This leads to rights theorists' second main criticism of policy-based reasoning, which is that it allows community interests to potentially usurp the established rights of plaintiffs. In this respect, McLachlin CJ's decisions demonstrate a range of alignment with rights theory and pluralist approaches. Of course, the two-stage test in *Cooper* mandates that residual policy considerations be assessed, which will always be offensive to rights theorists. Nevertheless, McLachlin CJ's rigorous assessment of such considerations in *Hill* showed a refusal to negate a *prima facie* duty on the basis of speculative policy concerns. The plaintiff's right not to be wrongfully arrested had sufficient importance that community concerns like the risk of defensive policing were insufficient to displace it.

On the other hand, in both *Cooper* and *Imperial Tobacco*, McLachlin CJ showed her willingness to negate a *prima facie* duty based on the infamous "spectre" of indeterminate liability. In public authority cases, arguments about indeterminate liability often go hand in hand with the suggestion that imposing a duty of care would put a significant strain on the public purse, and, thus, it is better for society if the duty

103 *Hill*, *supra* note 4 at para 48.

104 van Schouwen, *supra* note 97 at 173. See also Lorian Hardcastle, "Government Liability for Negligence in the Health Sector: A Critique of the Canadian Jurisprudence" (2012) 37:2 Queen's LJ 525, where the author makes similar arguments about the Ontario courts' refusal to recognize a duty of care because of potential conflicts with the broader public interest.

is negated.[105] There is a hint of this in *Cooper*, at least.[106] But it is hard to justify why plaintiffs who were in a proximate relationship with government, as in *Imperial Tobacco*, and who suffered harm as a result of the government's negligence, should be denied compensation just because the government harmed many other people in the same way. Returning to Dicey's theory, we would not accept the same argument from a private sector defendant; indeed, tobacco companies cannot escape liability simply because many people were misled into smoking low-tar cigarettes. If we are going to absolve public authorities of liability in these situations, the Court should directly confront this inconsistency and explain why the injured parties should be required to bear the losses alone.

In this vein, Professor Klar has suggested that indeterminate liability arguments should no longer be persuasive in Canadian law, given the requirements of foreseeability and especially proximity.[107] If the relationship between the parties was sufficiently "close and direct" that it seems "fair, just and reasonable" to impose a *prima facie* duty of care, it is hard to imagine how liability could, at the same time, be indeterminate.[108] Professor Feldthusen has argued equally persuasively that the requirement of proximity has rendered policy immunity incoherent and unjustified in duty analysis.[109] As discussed above, the defendants in *Cooper* and *Imperial Tobacco* were not making decisions that were impossible to assess on an objective standard.

In sum, McLachlin CJ's decisions in these three cases demonstrate that *Cooper*'s two-stage test can lead to unpredictable results in public authority cases, depending on the rigour with which the Court assesses residual policy considerations and on the underlying deference shown to decision-makers. This may leave both rights theorists and instrumentalists unsatisfied. For rights theorists, the decisions are incoherent, and could more reliably be decided based on whether the plaintiffs had a right to demand that the defendants look out for their private interests. Nevertheless, the main thrust of the decisions is still one of

105 The obvious question is why the government did not choose to limit its own liability through statute.

106 *Cooper*, *supra* note 2 at para 55, particularly because the loss is economic.

107 Klar, *supra* note 57 at 168–70.

108 Klar's logic was accepted by the majority in the more recent case of *Deloitte & Touche v Livent (Receiver of)*, 2017 SCC 63 at paras 43–4, where the dissenting opinion of McLachlin CJ was roundly criticized by the majority for its perceived miscategorization of extensive liability as indeterminate.

109 See Feldthusen, *supra* note 57.

deference toward public decision-makers, which should placate rights theorists to some degree. For instrumentalists, the decisions are frustrating because, while they consider community welfare factors, they do so in an inconsistent way. In *Cooper* and *Imperial Tobacco,* the Court was quick to relieve the defendants from internalizing the costs of their negligence and to place those costs on the plaintiffs, alone. Given the implications for the plaintiffs' *prima facie* rights, this deference – itself a policy decision of sorts – ought to have been more thoroughly and transparently explained, and balanced against the benefits of holding regulators accountable for their negligence.

5 Controversy Resolved: Chief Justice McLachlin, Personal Autonomy, and Unjust Enrichment

MITCHELL MCINNES

I. Introduction

Chief Justice McLachlin's tenure on the bench – spanning nearly four decades – was a period of profound change in Canadian law. The most notable developments occurred in the public sphere. In the pre-*Charter* era, same-sex marriage was almost unthinkable,[1] abortion was subject to legal prohibitions,[2] assisting suicide was unlawful,[3] incarcerated murderers were not entitled to vote,[4] activities associated with prostitution were broadly criminalized,[5] and if anyone had actually proposed constitutionally protected "safe-injection sites,"[6] the idea would have been regarded as risible. That list is easily extended.

Though less familiar to most Canadians, private law experienced similar shifts. The *Charter*'s direct impact was limited,[7] but social movements and legal theories encouraged reform. In tort, the duty of care in negligence first expanded and then contracted,[8] the concept of causation was repeatedly revisited,[9] traditionally draconian defences were substantially softened,[10] and restrictions on liability for psychological

1 *Reference re Same-Sex Marriage*, 2004 SCC 79.
2 *R v Morgentaler*, [1988] 1 SCR 30.
3 *Rodriguez v British Columbia (Attorney General)*, [1993] 3 SCR 519 (McLachlin J dissenting); *cf Carter v Canada (Attorney General)*, 2015 SCC 5.
4 *Sauvé v Canada (Attorney General)*, [1993] 2 SCR 438.
5 *Canada (Attorney General) v Bedford*, 2013 SCC 72.
6 *Canada (Attorney General) v PHS Community Services Society*, 2011 SCC 44.
7 *RWDSU v Dolphin Delivery Ltd*, [1986] 2 SCR 573; *Dobson (Litigation Guardian of) v Dobson*, [1999] 2 SCR 753.
8 *Kamloops v Nielsen*, [1984] 2 SCR 2; *Cooper v Hobart*, 2001 SCC 79.
9 *Myers v Peel County Board of Education*, [1981] 2 SCR 21; *Snell v Farrell*, [1990] 2 SCR 311; *Resurfice Corp v Hanke*, 2007 SCC 7; *Clements v Clements*, 2012 SCC 32.
10 *Hall v Hebert*, [1993] 2 SCR 159; *Dube v Labar*, [1986] 1 SCR 649; *Crocker v Sundance Northwest Resorts Ltd*, [1988] 1 SCR 1186.

losses were eliminated.[11] In contract law, an important exception was carved out of the privity doctrine,[12] an organizing principle of good faith and a duty of honest performance were recognized,[13] attempts were made to rationalize the rules governing exclusion clauses,[14] and evolving attitudes about mental health expanded the scope of damages for intangible injuries.[15] And in property law, there was a dramatic increase in the incidence of remedial trusts,[16] new perspectives on Aboriginal title emerged,[17] *de facto* expropriations became actionable,[18] and the availability of specific performance for contractual rights to purchase land was curtailed.[19]

However profound and far-reaching, none of these private law developments compare – quantitatively or qualitatively – to the changes experienced within the law of unjust enrichment.[20] Despite roots that

---

11 *Mustapha v Culligan of Canada Ltd*, 2008 SCC 27; *Saadati v Moorhead*, 2017 SCC 28.

12 *London Drugs Ltd v Kuehne & Nagel International Ltd*, [1992] 3 SCR 299; *Fraser River Pile & Dredge Ltd v Can-Dive Services Ltd*, [1999] 3 SCR 108.

13 *Bhasin v Hrynew*, 2014 SCC 71.

14 *Hunter Engineering Co v Syncrude Canada Ltd*, [1989] 1 SCR 426; *Tercon Contractors Ltd v British Columbia (Transportation and Highways)*, 2010 SCC 4.

15 *Fidler v Sun Life Assurance Co of Canada*, 2006 SCC 30; *Honda Canada Inc v Keays*, 2008 SCC 39.

16 *Pettkus v Becker*, [1980] 2 SCR 834 [*Pettkus*]; *Soulos v Korkontzilas*, [1997] 2 SCR 217.

17 *Delgamuukw v British Columbia*, [1997] 3 SCR 1010; *Tsilhqot'in Nation v British Columbia*, 2014 SCC 44.

18 *Canadian Pacific Railway Co v Vancouver (City)*, 2006 SCC 5; *R v Tener*, [1985] 1 SCR 533.

19 *Semelhago v Paramadevan*, [1996] 2 SCR 415; *cf Southcott Estates Inc v Toronto Catholic District School Board*, 2012 SCC 51.

20 One complication must be eliminated at the outset. The terms "unjust enrichment" and "restitution" are frustratingly ambiguous. This chapter defines them narrowly. "Unjust enrichment" is the three-part cause of action that invariably requires proof of an *enrichment* to the defendant, a *corresponding deprivation* to the plaintiff, and an *absence of juristic reason* for the transfer between the parties. That claim is animated by the goal of reversing transfers that, regardless of any wrongdoing, lack legally recognizable justifications. If liability occurs, it invariably entails true "restitution." While the remedy may be personal or proprietary, it must be measured by the benefit that moved from the plaintiff to the defendant. The plaintiff recovers no more than was actually lost; the defendant gives back no more than was actually gained.

Unfortunately, the same terms are also used in connection with an entirely distinct phenomenon: see *Cinar Corp v Robinson*, 2013 SCC 73 at para 86; *Lac Minerals Ltd v International Corona Resources Ltd*, [1989] 2 SCR 574 at 618. That phenomenon is animated by the desire to strip wrongful profits rather than reverse unwarranted gains. The cause of action is not the three-part claim in unjust enrichment, but rather some form of civil wrongdoing – e.g. an equitable wrong, a proprietary tort, or an exceptional breach of contract. (The courts have yet to explain why the phenomenon is supported by some civil wrongs but not others.) The "unjust enrichment" becomes

reach back centuries, and notwithstanding something of a rebirth in 1954,[21] the cause of action's constituent elements were not formalized until 1980, and another quarter century passed before the nature of injustice was settled.[22] And even those events merely highlight a much greater phenomenon. Beginning in 1985, unjust enrichment enjoyed a run of unprecedented growth throughout the Commonwealth. The rapid rise of administrative law in the post-war period may provide a legitimate comparison on the public law side,[23] but within private law, no subject has ever grown so far, so fast. The explanation for that phenomenon is examined elsewhere.[24] The important point for present purposes is that the Chief Justice's judicial tenure overlapped almost perfectly with the emergence of the modern law of unjust enrichment.

The remarkable development of unjust enrichment was possible only because a number of potentially divisive controversies were settled relatively early. Though she seldom receives credit, McLachlin J played a critical role in resolving one of those debates.

---

manifest at the remedial stage, when the plaintiff elects to have relief measured not by its own loss (i.e., compensation), but rather by the benefit that the defendant obtained through the wrong. That is true, for instance, if the defendant committed a breach of confidence by improperly selling a beverage made from the plaintiff's secret recipe: *Cadbury Schweppes Inc v FBI Foods Ltd*, [1999] 1 SCR 142. That response is often called "restitution," but that term is misleading. The court does not compel the defendant to "give back" a benefit received from the plaintiff. It demands that the defendant "give up" the benefits that it obtained from its customers by violating the claimant's rights. As courts have begun to acknowledge, the proper term is "disgorgement": *Atlantic Lottery Corp Inc v Babstock*, 2020 SCC 19 at para 27; *Indutech Canada Ltd v Gibbs Pipe Distributors Ltd*, 2011 ABQB 38 at para 507, aff'd 2013 ABCA 111; *Nunavut Tunngavik Inc v Canada (Attorney General)*, 2012 NUCJ 11 at para 308; *Chatfield v Bell Mobility Inc*, 2016 SKQB 364 at para 43; *Jin v Ren*, 2015 ABQB 115 at para 86.

21 *Moses v Macferlan*, (1760) 2 Burr 1005, 97 ER 676 (KB); *Deglman v Guaranty Trust Co of Canada and Constantineau*, [1954] SCR 725.

22 *Pettkus, supra* note 16; *Garland v Consumers' Gas Co*, 2004 SCC 25 [*Garland*].

23 J Jowell, "Administrative Law" in Vernon Bogdanor, ed, *The British Constitution in the Twentieth Century* (Oxford: Oxford University Press, 2003).

24 Unjust enrichment's remarkable evolution was possible only because Robert Goff and Gareth Jones had undertaken the monumental task of collecting the diverse strands of restitutionary liability into a single text: Robert Goff & Gareth H. Jones, *The Law of Restitution* (London: Sweet & Maxwell, 1966); see also American Law Institute, *Restatement of the Law of Restitution: Quasi Contracts and Constructive Trusts* (St. Paul: American Law Institute, 1937). The subject truly caught fire, however, only after Peter Birks' masterwork sparked a generation of outstanding scholars: Peter Birks, *An Introduction to the Law of Restitution* (Oxford: Clarendon, 1985). Many of the great developments in the area began life as Oxbridge doctoral dissertations. For a comparative history, see Mitchell McInnes, *The Canadian Law of Unjust Enrichment and Restitution* (Markham, ON: LexisNexis, 2014) at 71–9.

The primary risk associated with restitutionary liability lies in the imposition of unfair burdens upon innocent recipients. That risk might be addressed directly through the element of injustice. On that approach, liability could be restricted to wrongdoers. As McLachlin J implicitly recognized, however, the risk is far better managed upfront. A nuanced conception of enrichment simultaneously provides protection where it is needed and facilitates a generous conception of recoverability. Part II of this chapter examines that risk and outlines two ways in which it may be managed. Part III explains the Chief Justice's role in formulating an autonomy-focused conception of enrichment that facilitates a broad right to reverse unintentional or ineffective transfers.

II. The Risk of Restitution

While it has been said that "any civilised system of law is bound to provide remedies for ... unjust enrichment,"[25] the operative phrase requires definition. The basis upon which transfers are deemed "unjust," and hence reversible, must be determined. At the broadest level, there are two possibilities, representing different strategies for managing the risk of unfair burdens.

The first model protects innocent recipients by limiting liability to wrongdoers. It begins with the observation that, aside from consent-based obligations (e.g. contracts) and anomalies (e.g. maritime salvage), wrongdoing constitutes the only justification for overriding the defendant's autonomy and extracting relief. The court must be satisfied with the recipient's culpability.[26] Within the context of unjust enrichment, that means that the plaintiff must prove that the defendant received the impugned enrichment with at least constructive knowledge that payment was expected.[27] If that

25 *Fibrosa Spolka Akcyjna v Fairbairn Lawson Combe Barbour Ltd*, [1942] UKHL 4 at 61.

26 Stephen Smith, "Justifying the Law of Unjust Enrichment" (2001) 79:7 Tex L Rev 2177 at 2194; Nicholas J. McBride & Paul McGrath, "The Nature of Restitution" (1995) 15:1 Oxford J Leg Stud 33 at 38 ("Being unjustly enriched is not sufficient to give rise to the restitutionary duty ... [T]he restitutionary duty should not arise before the defendant has acquired knowledge of his being unjustly enriched"). Professor Weinrib's position is ambiguous: Ernest Weinrib, *The Idea of Private Law* (Cambridge, MA: Harvard University Press, 1995) at 133–42; Ernest Weinrib, "The Gains and Losses of Corrective Justice" (1994) 44:2 Duke LJ 277. He appears to hold that liability is possible if the defendant innocently *received* a benefit, as long as he subsequently *retained* it despite knowledge of the plaintiff's claim.

27 *Citadel General Assurance Co v Lloyds Bank Canada*, [1997] 3 SCR 805 at para 51 [*Citadel*]; *cf Kingstreet Investments Ltd v New Brunswick (Department of Finance)*, 2007 SCC 1 at para 58 [*Kingstreet*].

standard is met, the risk of intolerable hardship disappears. Any claim that restitution would create injustice is defeated by the fact that the defendant culpably participated in the underlying event. If the defendant wanted to avoid responsibility, something should have been said prior to the transfer.

The competing model is built on a theory of true strict liability.[28] There is no need for proof that the defendant was culpably complicit in the receipt or retention of the enrichment. Depending upon the precise test of injustice that the jurisdiction employs, it is enough that either the plaintiff's intention was vitiated or the transfer failed to fulfill a legally recognized purpose.[29] As a result, a restitutionary

---

28 "Strict liability" is an ambiguous phrase. In the context of civil wrongs, it means that liability may be imposed for the breach of an obligation that was neither deliberate nor negligent (e.g. breach of contract, trespass, breach of fiduciary duty). In the context of unjust enrichment, it means that liability may be imposed even though the defendant did not breach any obligation.

29 Until 2004, Canadian courts followed the common law tradition by requiring proof of *unjust factors* – i.e., positive reasons for restitution. Typically, as in cases of mistake or compulsion, that reason consisted of the claimant's impaired intention. Because of their commitment to personal autonomy and private property, the courts were prepared to reverse transfers that were not a function of free will. In *Garland*, however, the Supreme Court of Canada adopted a civilian-inspired test of injustice that is triggered by the absence of *juristic reasons*: *supra* note 22; *cf Pettkus, supra* note 16 at 848. Personal autonomy and private property remain paramount, but they are protected by a regime that reverses any transfer that did not serve a juridical purpose, such as a contract or a gift or an enforceable obligation. That development is immensely important, but it does not affect the analysis in this chapter. Both tests of injustice entail strict liability; each is viable only because the recipient's autonomy is protected at the enrichment stage of analysis.

Although she did not participate in the appeal, the Chief Justice was well connected to *Garland*. To begin, she had experience with the new approach. While the substantive test was not adopted until 2004, the language of "juristic reason" first appeared in Canadian common law a quarter century earlier. In 1977, Beetz J explained that the civilian action for unjustified enrichment requires proof of, *inter alia*, an "absence of justification": *Cie Immobilière Viger v L Guiguère Inc*, [1977] 2 SCR 67 at 77. Having concurred in that judgment, Dickson J similarly spoke of an "absence of juristic reason" in *Rathwell v Rathwell*, [1978] 2 SCR 436 at 455 and again in *Pettkus, supra* note 16 at 848. Although most Canadian judges, including Dickson J, actually continued to address the issue of injustice through the lens of unjust factors, some judges occasionally reasoned in terms of juristic reasons. That was true of McLachlin J in *Peter v Beblow*, [1993] 1 SCR 980 at 991 [*Peter*]. The defendant was enriched by the receipt of the plaintiff's domestic and childcare services, and that enrichment was unjust because the plaintiff had not acted with a donative intent and because "a common law spouse generally owes no duty at common law, in equity or by statute to perform work or services for her partner."

The Chief Justice's influence on *Garland* is also evident from Iacobucci J's endorsement of her statement that Canadian law strikes a compromise between employing the generalized principle of unjust enrichment and relying upon "categories" of recovery: *Garland, supra* note 22 at para 44; *Peel (Regional Municipality)*

obligation may crystallize even before the defendant is aware of the transfer.[30]

The great danger with true strict liability, of course, is that it may adversely affect an entirely innocent recipient. It threatens to burden the defendant with the price of something that was neither requested nor desired. That model consequently is viable only if the defendant's interests can be protected outside the element of injustice. That need is filled by a nuanced notion of enrichment.[31] Following the Chief Justice's lead, an enrichment requires proof of more than an objective benefit. As explained in Part III, the plaintiff must demonstrate that liability – if ultimately imposed – would be consistent with the defendant's freedom of choice. There is no risk of hardship because restitution is confined to (1) benefits for which the defendant chose to accept financial responsibility, and (2) benefits that, by their very nature, respect personal autonomy.

III. Fault-based Liability versus Strict Liability

Accepting that the risk of unfair burdens can be managed by either model of unjust enrichment, it becomes necessary to elect between the two. Both precedent and principle favour strict liability.

---

v Canada, [1992] 3 SCR 762 at 804 [*Peel*]. (Iacobucci J did not observe, however, that her "traditional categories" involved unjust factors, whereas his "established categories" consisted of juristic reasons.)

Finally, the contents of *Garland*'s second stage can be traced to the Chief Justice. Iacobucci J held that, even if none of the "established categories" of juristic reason explain an impugned transfer, the defendant may demonstrate some other reason — guided by the parties' reasonable expectations and public policy — for denying restitution: *Garland*, *supra* note 22 at para 44. A decade earlier, McLachlin J had said that the issue of injustice is informed by public policy and, more controversially, that "the fundamental concern" in "every case" of unjust enrichment "is the legitimate expectation of the parties": *Peter*, *supra* at 990.

30 Interest and limitations periods presumptively run from the time of receipt: *Air Canada v Ontario (Liquor Control Board)*, [1997] 2 SCR 581 at 611–12 [*Air Canada*], cited in *Kleinwort Benson Ltd v Lincoln City Council*, [1999] 2 AC 349 (HL (Eng) at 386, 409 [*Kleinwort*].

31 Just as the legal concept of enrichment protects the defendant's freedom of choice at the time of receipt, the change of position defence serves the same function at the time of trial. Canadian courts have an unfortunate tendency to view the defence as a discretionary tool for "balancing the equities," but restitution ought to be reduced only to the extent that the defendant suffered a disenrichment that was not the product of free choice: McInnes, *supra* note 24 at 1495–1502. The overriding concern, as always, is personal autonomy.

While there are calls for culpability,[32] especially among older authorities,[33] it has been authoritatively held that restitutionary liability is strict.[34] *Air Canada v Ontario (Liquor Control Board)* affirmed that proposition is Canada.[35] The defendant province imposed a "fee" on airlines operating within its borders. Pleased with the results, it continued to demand payment even after it discovered that the imposition constituted an indirect, and hence *ultra vires*, tax. The Ontario Court of Appeal recognized a general right to restitution, but held that the defendant was not liable with respect to the early payments that it honestly received in good faith. In the Supreme Court of Canada, Iacobucci J rejected that "compromise" approach and ordered restitution of all the payments.[36]

Principle overwhelmingly points in the same direction.[37] Because the fault-based model is confined to cases of culpability, it often provides protection when none is needed. Strict liability, in contrast, sensitively

---

32 Canadian courts occasionally fail to appreciate the logic of strict liability: *Citadel, supra* note 27 (defendant's constructive knowledge required for the equitable form of unjust enrichment known as "knowing receipt"); *cf* "That would make no sense": Lord Nicholls' assessment of the anomalous fault requirement, *Royal Brunei Airlines Sdn Bhd v Tan*, [1995] UKPC 4 at 385.

33 *Royal Bank v The King*, [1931] 2 DLR 685 (MBQB) at 688–9; rejected by *Central Guaranty Trust Co v Dixdale Mortgage Investment Corp*, [1994] 24 OR (3d) 506 (CA) at para 41, 121 DLR (4th) 53 [*Dixdale*].

34 *Kleinwort, supra* note 30 at 386, 409; *Lipkin Gorman (a firm) v Karpnale Ltd*, [1988] UKHL 12 at 578; *El Ajou v Dollar Land Holdings plc*, [1993] EWCA Civ 4; *AFLS v Hills Industries Limited & Anor*, [2014] HCA 14 at para 83; *David Securities Pty Ltd v Commonwealth Bank of Australia*, (1992) 175 CLR 353 (HCA) at 389.

35 *Air Canada, supra* note 30. See also *Horch v Horch*, 2017 MBCA 97 at para 53.

36 *Air Canada, supra* note 30 at para 80. Under the controversial decision in *Kingstreet, supra* note 27, the dispute would be resolved by a unique public law action. The reasoning in *Air Canada* nevertheless continues to explain the private law claim of unjust enrichment.

37 In addition to the more substantive arguments presented in the text, a fault-based conception of unjust enrichment also suffers from a curious redundancy. Civil wrongs typically entail primary and secondary obligations that differ in content. The tort of defamation provides an example. The primary obligation tells the defendant, "You must not publish false statements that diminish the plaintiff's reputation." If that obligation is breached, the defendant normally becomes subject to a secondary obligation that takes the forms of a judgment debt. The plaintiff becomes entitled to receive damages that reflect the resulting loss. Though related, the two obligations are distinct. Their satisfaction requires very different acts. Examples could be easily multiplied.

A fault-based model of unjust enrichment would not follow the same pattern. Instead, the two obligations – primary and secondary – would be essentially identical: "You must restore the unjust enrichment. If you fail to do so, you will be required to restore the unjust enrichment."

denies relief only when restitution would actually cause hardship. That difference is easily illustrated in the context of unrequested services.

Unlike other forms of enrichment, such as money and property, services can never be restored. Once they have been performed, the time for choice has passed. As Baron Pollock famously observed, "One cleans another's shoes; what can that other do but put them on?"[38] Questions of culpability, in other words, cannot arise when unrequested services are conferred on unwitting recipients. There can be no finding of fault if knowledge of the relevant facts arrives too late for the defendant to exercise a moral choice between rejecting a benefit and receiving it for a price.

As the strict liability model recognizes, however, unrequested services do occasionally warrant relief. Granted, it is hard to imagine a valid claim arising from a simple shoeshine, but the picture looks very different if a service clearly exceeds the *de minimis* threshold. Consider a common-enough example. While the defendant was away on vacation and unaware of the tragedy, a loved one died, and the defendant became legally obligated to dispose of the body.[39] Prepared to lend a hand but unwilling to give a gift, the plaintiff intervened and did the decent thing, and then demanded payment upon the defendant's return. Despite having done nothing wrong, the defendant should be compelled to pay restitution. Since the burial obligation necessarily entailed an expense, personal autonomy is sufficiently respected if recovery is capped at the amount that the defendant would have spent if informed of the facts in a timely way.

Even if the impugned transfer involves money rather than services, a fault requirement may create injustice if the funds are dissipated before the recipient acquires the relevant knowledge. Assume that the plaintiff mistakenly transfers $5,000 to the defendant. Honestly oblivious to the error, the defendant uses those funds, rather than another $5,000 that had been put aside for the purpose, to pay rent. At that point, it is too late for the plaintiff to fix the defendant with knowledge of the mistake. Because nothing remains from the impugned transfer, the defendant cannot be blamed for failing to return the money, and liability is precluded under a fault-based scheme.[40] That protection, however, is unnecessary and

38 *Taylor v Laird*, (1856) 25 LJ Ex 329 at 332.

39 *Schara Tzedeck v Royal Trust Co*, [1953] 1 SCR 31; *Pearce v Diensthuber* (1977), 17 OR (2d) 401, 81 DLR (3d) 286; *Chernichan v Chernichan Estate*, 2001 ABQB 913; *Holowaychuk v Lopushinsky*, 2015 ABQB 63; *Sargent & Son Ltd v Buday*, [2000] OJ No. 5476 (Ont. SCJ); *cf D'Agostino v D'Agostino* (10 June 2014), Oshawa 80518/12 (Ont Sup Ct (Sm Cl Div)).

40 A less ambitious form of fault-based liability would hold the defendant fully liable for the enrichment received, but defer the restitutionary obligation until the

unjust. While the original funds no longer exist,[41] the plaintiff continues to be deprived of $5,000, and the defendant continues to be abstractly enriched to the same extent. Under a regime of strict lability, both parties will hold the positions they would have occupied but for the mistaken payment. The defendant can satisfy judgment with the funds that were intended to pay the rent, and the claimant will be made whole.[42] Restitution would effectively re-create the world of the *status quo ante.*

IV. The Test of Enrichment

However desirable, the strict liability model of unjust enrichment is possible only if the risk of unfair hardship can be managed without a fault requirement. The key lies in a surprisingly subtle notion of enrichment.

The first element in the restitutionary claim serves at least three functions. Most obviously, the defendant's enrichment, coupled with the plaintiff's corresponding deprivation, establishes a transfer between the parties.[43] If the transfer is determined to be unjust, then, as the Chief Justice once explained,[44] the defendant is uniquely identified as the source of the plaintiff's remedial rights under the Aristotelian notion of corrective justice.

Second, the enrichment, together with the deprivation, determines the quantum of recovery if liability is imposed. Exceptions aside, restitution is effected personally rather than proprietarily. Even if an

---

defendant was fixed with the requisite knowledge. That model, however, would be fault-based in name only. Assuming that the quantum of recovery was assessed at the time of receipt, liability would be strict, albeit delayed. In a restitutionary context, knowledge-based fault makes sense only if the defendant exercised a meaningful choice to receive or retain the impugned benefit: *Agip (Africa) Ltd v Jackson,* [1990] 1 EWCA Civ 2 at 291, cited in *Citadel, supra* note 27 at paras 25, 42.

41 More precisely, the money that was mistakenly transferred between the parties may now be found in the hands of the defendant's landlord. It is likely, however, that the landlord qualified as a *bona fide* purchaser for value and thereby became immune to both personal and proprietary relief: McInnes, *supra* note 24 c 38.

42 That analysis would not hold true if, instead of using the enrichment to pay a necessary expense, the defendant had spent the money on something exceptional, such as a once-in-a-lifetime vacation. Strict liability presumptively would require restitution, but the defendant ultimately would be protected by the change of position defence. Interestingly, as previously observed, that defence is animated by the same principles that inform the nuanced notion of enrichment: *supra* at note 31.

43 *PriceWaterhouseCoopers v Bank of Montreal*, 2017 NLTD(G) 43.

44 *Peel, supra* note 29 at 804.

enrichment consists of property that the defendant received and at least traceably retains, the plaintiff is seldom entitled to recover the thing itself. The court simply declares a debt. And while judges do the best they can with frequently incomplete evidence,[45] relief will be denied if the exercise is intolerably speculative. It is not uncommon for a judge to recognize an unjust enrichment but refuse restitution because the plaintiff failed to adduce sufficient proof of its value.[46]

The final function served by the enrichment element is easily overlooked, but it is indispensable to a regime of strict liability. The test of enrichment is formulated to protect the recipient's freedom of choice. The plaintiff must establish either that the defendant chose to incur the risk of liability or that, given the circumstances, there was no choice to make. Once that requirement has been met, the court can proceed, confident in the knowledge that the defendant will not be adversely affected, relative to the *status quo ante*, even if liability ultimately is imposed.

Collecting together the principles that the Chief Justice identified, and employing restitutionary terms of art,[47] that goal is achieved through a three-stage analysis:

- The plaintiff must prove that the defendant received an *objective benefit*.
- The defendant *prima facie* is entitled to *subjectively devalue* that benefit.
- The plaintiff must overcome subjective devaluation by demonstrating – through the concept of *request*, *free acceptance*, or *incontrovertible benefit* – that restitution, if awarded, would respect the defendant's autonomy.

a. Objective Benefit

While it is tempting to say that *any* type of benefit can lead to restitution, the range of possibilities is necessarily narrower. As McLachlin J observed, the "word 'enrichment' ... connotes a tangible benefit."[48]

45 *Porteous v Nuekomm*, 2015 BCSC 1171 at para 107; *Gari Holdings Ltd v Langham Credit Union Ltd*, 2005 SKCA 97 at para 50.

46 *Henderson (Trustee of) v Pitters*, 2014 ONSC 6227 at para 49; *Forestier SL Inc v Gestion Unibec Inc*, 2017 QCCA 998 at para 41; *Gill Tech Framing Ltd v Gill*, 2012 BCSC 1913 at para 261; *Ghanati v Chemist Holdings Ltd*, 2017 BCSC 1921 at para 27; *Hamelin v Mousseau*, 2018 ONSC 276 at para 64; *Benedetti v Sawiris*, [2013] UKSC 50 at para 115 [*Benedetti*].

47 See especially *Peel*, *supra* note 29; *Peter*, *supra* note 29.

48 *Peel*, *supra* note 29 at 790. Similarly, in *Peter*, McLachlin J lamented the tendency for "the simple questions of 'benefit' and 'detriment' to become infused with moral

"Tangible" here refers not to the capacity for physical touch,[49] but rather to the capacity for monetary valuation. Accordingly, while it may be positive or negative (i.e., an accretion of wealth or a discharged debt),[50] an enrichment must possess market value.[51] In that sense, the courts have "consistently taken a straightforward economic approach to the first two elements of the action in unjust enrichment."[52]

The explanation for limiting relief to *objective* enrichments pertains to the recipient's autonomy. As previously said, restitutionary liability normally consists of a personal debt. Market value is required for the calculation of that debt, but, significantly, it also shields the innocent recipient from hardship. The court will impose a monetary obligation only insofar as the defendant received something of monetary value. Consequently, while resources may be redistributed, an episode of unjust enrichment never reduces the totality of the defendant's wealth.

Take a simple example. The defendant has $5,000 in cash but owes $2,000 in rent to a landlord. As a result of an error, the plaintiff transfers $2,000 to the landlord, who accepts the payment in discharge of the defendant's debt. The landlord drops out of the picture. The court will calculate the market value of the enrichment at $2,000 and impose liability for that amount. Crucially, the defendant will be none the worse for wear even after satisfying judgment. Although it will consist of a simple sum of money ($3,000), rather than a larger sum offset by a debt ($5,000 – $2,000), the defendant's net value remains the same ($3,000). Significantly, however, that equation would not hold true if the concept of enrichment were extended to encompass benefits, such as love and affection, that the law refuses to value monetarily.[53] Restitution would

---

and policy questions" that are better addressed under the label of "injustice": *supra* note 29 at 988.

49 Were it otherwise, restitutionary relief would not be available with respect to services. That obviously is not the case: *Carleton (County) v Ottawa (City)*, [1965] SCR 663 [*Carleton*].

50 *Peel, supra* note 29 at 790.

51 The same is true of the deprivation when the transfer is read from the plaintiff's perspective.

52 *Peter, supra* note 29 at 990. McLachlin J also referred to "enrichment and deprivation" as being "morally neutral in themselves."

53 While courts are prepared to recognize other types of ephemeral benefits (e.g. concerts, lectures) as enrichments, they consistently refuse to treat love and affection as marketable commodities. That is why, whatever their psychological and cultural value, love and affection cannot function as contractual consideration: *Thomas v Thomas*, (1842) 2 QB 851; *Loranger v Haines* (1921), 50 OLR 268 (CA). Of course, as McLachlin J observed in *Peter*, while love and affection are not enrichments in themselves, such feelings may motivate a person to perform services (e.g.

hurt. Despite receiving neither money nor money's worth, the defendant would be liable to pay money.[54] That analysis emerges from *Peel (Regional Municipality) v Canada.*[55]

Proceeding under section 20 of the *Juvenile Delinquents Act,*[56] judges in Ontario routinely committed errant children to group homes and ordered the relevant municipalities to pay the associated costs. After successfully having those orders declared *ultra vires*, the municipalities sought to recover the value of their payments from the provincial and federal governments. In a remarkable judgment, McLachlin J examined the first element of the restitutionary action and denied liability. There was no enrichment. The municipalities had offered two arguments. They began by claiming that, if the invalid orders had not been issued, the courts would have dealt with the delinquents in ways that would have cost the federal and provincial governments money. McLachlin J found that proposition to be intolerably speculative. The *Act* allowed Family Court judges to pick from a long list of dispositions, but only some of those options would have cast a financial burden on the defendants. The municipalities consequently were reduced to arguing that, regardless of financial implications, their payments left Canada *politically* enriched insofar as its legislative goals were advanced, and Ontario *morally* enriched insofar as the province was obliged, in conscience, to help the children. McLachlin J rejected that argument because it could not be translated into economic terms. The defendants may have been enriched, but not in a legally relevant sense.[57]

b. Subjective Devaluation

The enrichment analysis must require more than an objective benefit. As McLachlin J explained in *Peel,*[58] the common law "was founded on a philosophy of robust individualism which expected every person to look

---

child-rearing, housekeeping) that do have market value, and consequently may support restitutionary relief: *Peter, supra* note 29 at 989–90.

54 Canadian courts occasionally improperly proceed on the basis of intangible (i.e., non-marketable) benefits: *Clarkson v McCrossen Estate* (1995), 122 DLR (4th) 239 at 249, [1995] 6 WWR 28 (BCCA); *Everard v Devereaux*, 2004 NLSCTD 158 at para 79.

55 *Peel, supra* note 29.

56 *Juvenile Delinquents Act*, RSC 1970, c J-3.

57 See also *628356 Saskatchewan Ltd v Water Security Agency*, 2018 SKQB 4 at paras 37–8; *Halvorson v British Columbia (Medical Services Commission)*, 2001 BCSC 632 at para 85.

58 *Peel, supra* note 29 at 785–6. See also *Falcke v Scottish Imperial Insurance Co* (1886), 34 Ch 234 (CA) at 248 (that "Liabilities are not to be forced upon people behind their backs any more than you can confer a benefit upon a man against his will").

out after his or her own interests and which place[d] a premium on the right to choose how to spend one's money." Granted, "robust individualism" is no longer a phrase that leaps to mind in connection with Anglo-Canadian culture. In some corners of private law, however, courts do continue to vigilantly protect freedom of choice. Within the law of unjust enrichment, that policy operates through *subjective devaluation*.[59]

The doctrine allows the recipient of an objective benefit to resist liability by subjectively devaluing the purported enrichment. That phrase, unfortunately, is somewhat misleading. It suggests that the defendant's personal perception of the benefit is determinative. On that understanding, liability is possible if, but only if, the defendant feels enriched by the transfer.[60] In truth, however, an enrichment may be refused recognition even if the recipient admits to being delighted with the transfer.[61] The relevant question is whether that party freely chose to accept financial responsibility for the impugned benefit. In effect, subjective devaluation allows the defendant to turn to the claimant and say, "[I]t is not your job to make my choices."[62] There is a crucial difference between being happy with a benefit and being willing to pay for it.[63]

---

59 The phrase has yet to be uttered by the Supreme Court of Canada, but it is well supported at lower levels: *Stevested Machinery & Engineering Ltd v Metso Paper Ltd*, 2014 BCCA 91 at paras 57, 60 [*Stevested*]; *Salna v Awad*, 2011 ABCA 20 at para 33 [*Salna*]; *Middlesex Condominium Corp 229 v WMJO Ltd*, 2015 ONSC 3879 at para 137; *Sherbeth v Sherbeth*, 2007 MBQB 50 at paras 22–3, 27 [*Sherbeth*].

60 *Olchowy v McKay*, [1996] 1 WWR 36 (Sask QB) at 46.

61 *Lakin v Nuttal* (1879), 3 SCR 685 at 696; *Benedetti, supra* note 46 at paras 26, 113. Posner J expressed the idea with characteristic flair in *Indiana Lumbermans Mutual Insurance Co v Reinsurance Results Inc*, 513 F (3d) 652 at 656 (7th Cir 2008): "If while you are sitting on your porch sipping Margaritas a trio of itinerant musicians serenades you with mandolin, lute, and hautboy, you have no obligation, in the absence of a contract, to pay them for their performance no matter how much you enjoyed it."

62 *Magical Waters Fountain Ltd v Sarnia (City)* (1990), 74 OR (2d) 682 at 691, 73 DLR (4th) 734 (Ont Gen Div), rev'd on other grounds (1992), 8 OR (3d) 689 (CA). Canadian law demands a correspondence between the defendant's enrichment and the plaintiff's deprivation. That requirement is usually reckoned objectively. The benefit that passes between the parties has market value. The enrichment concept, however, encompasses a subjective element as well. Is there anything similar on the plaintiff's side of the equation? That question may receive one of two answers. First, it may be enough that the enrichment and the deprivation correspond objectively. Despite operating within the enrichment inquiry, subjective devaluation may serve a distinct function in protecting vulnerable recipients. Alternatively, it may be that a similar element of subjectivity is active on the claimant's side but is addressed elsewhere in the test for liability. Just as the risk of liability must be consistent with the defendant's autonomy interest, so, too, restitution is available only if it fairly reflects the choices that the claimant made. That most obviously

c. Personal Autonomy

Given the recipient's right to subjectively devalue an objective benefit, the recognition of an enrichment ultimately turns on the plaintiff's ability to demonstrate that a restitutionary obligation can be reconciled with the defendant's autonomy. Broadly speaking, successful claims fall into two categories. The evidence may prove either that (1) the defendant actually chose to assume the risk of financial responsibility, or (2) as McLachlin J said, the "principle of freedom of choice [was] a spent force" because, in the circumstances, the defendant had no choice to make.[64]

I. CHOICE EXERCISED

The first category is relatively uncontroversial. A person who actually chose to accept the risk of financial responsibility for a benefit cannot plausibly resist liability by saying, "[I]t is not your job to make my choices." The court can recognize an enrichment secure in the knowledge that, even if the plaintiff satisfies the other elements of liability, restitution will merely reflect a spending priority that the defendant chose to incur.

A. Request. A choice may be exercised actively or passively. An active choice constitutes a request. Of course, if the request led to an enforceable contract, then there is no role for restitution. Contract trumps unjust enrichment. The circumstances, however, may preclude the operation of a contract. The parties may lack the requisite intention, one or both may be incapacitated, the terms may be insufficiently uncertain, performance may be frustrated, the agreement may be discharged for breach, and so on. In those situations, unjust enrichment likely represents the only alternative source of relief.

For the most part, the restitutionary concept of request is straightforward. At least in commercial contexts, a request normally conveys both a desire to receive and a willingness to pay. Complications nevertheless may arise. The key, in each instance, is to ask whether the recipient genuinely accepted the risk of liability. That is not the case if,

---

means that the court will deny recovery if an enrichment was conferred with a donative intention, but a similar principle also informs the incidental benefit doctrine: McInnes, *supra* note 24 at c 41.

63 Injustice occurs when that point is ignored: *Estok v Heguy* (1963), 40 DLR (2d) 88, 43 WWR (ns) 167 (BCSC); *Sanderson v Campsall*, 2000 BCSC 583 at para 10 [*Sanderson*].

64 *Peel*, *supra* note 29 at 799.

for instance, a benefit was requested in the belief that the plaintiff was prepared to act gratuitously[65] or that the cost would fall on some third party.[66] Moreover, although the proposition may surprise those who rarely encounter the law of unjust enrichment, all of that is true even if the defendant carelessly failed to appreciate the plaintiff's expectation of payment. Just as a mistaken payment may be reversed despite the payor's negligence,[67] so too the concept of enrichment respects the recipient's honest, albeit incorrect, perception. Personal autonomy is paramount. As to hidden consequences, an apparent choice is really no choice at all.

Other difficulties are generally resolved on the same basis.[68] A request supports recognition of an enrichment only to the *extent* that the defendant believed payment was required. Accordingly, if the defendant requested a benefit in the belief that it cost $X, relief will be capped at that amount even if the plaintiff expected to charge $X + Y.[69] Of course, the defendant's expectation must be formed in good faith. Recognition of an enrichment will not be defeated merely because the defendant intended to deliberately disappoint the claimant. Restitution will be available if, for instance, a criminal on the lam points a pistol at a mechanic and demands free car repairs.[70]

---

65 That may be true if the defendant believed that the claimant, having previously rendered defective services under a contract, was prepared to bear the non-contractual expense of making things right: *Moncton (City) v Stephen* (1956), 5 DLR (2d) 722 (NBSC (AD)).

66 That may be true if an injured worker requests medical services in the belief that the cost is covered by insurance: *Tang v Jarrett* (2009), 251 OAC 123 (Ont Sup Ct (Div Ct)); *Toronto Healthcare Clinic Inc v Stein* (2017), Toronto SC-14-35749-00 (Ont Sup Ct (Sm Cl Div)).

67 *Kelly v Solari* (1841), 9 M & W 54, 152 ER 24 (Exch); *Dixdale, supra* note 33.

68 Some issues remain unresolved. Accepting that the value of a requested benefit can be subjectively devalued down to the price that the defendant expected to pay, can the process ever work in the opposite direction? If the plaintiff normally charges $X for a service, but the defendant requests performance in the expectation of paying $X + Y, will the claimant ultimately receive the higher amount? That question has yet to be heard in a Canadian court, but the United Kingdom's Supreme Court considered the idea of *subjective overvaluation* to be misguided: *Benedetti, supra* note 46. Subjective devaluation, the court explained, serves the crucial policy goal of protecting personal autonomy. Without it, innocent recipients would often be unfairly prejudiced by a regime of strict liability. Subjective overvaluation simply is not needed for that purpose.

69 *Hills v Snell*, 104 Mass 173 (Mass Sup Jud Ct 1870); *McKeown v Cavalier Yachts Pty Ltd* (1988), 13 NSWLR 303 (SC).

70 *Webster v Robbins Parking Service Ltd*, 2016 BCSC 1863; *720654 Alberta Ltd v El Hajj*, 2011 ABPC 64.

B. Free Acceptance. A choice can be expressed actively through a request or passively through *free acceptance*. The latter concept was authoritatively formulated in *Pettkus v Becker*: "[W]here one person ... prejudices herself in the reasonable expectation of receiving an interest in property and the other person ... freely accepts benefits conferred by the first person in circumstances where he knows or ought to have known of that reasonable expectation, it would be unjust to allow the recipient of the benefit to retain it."[71]

Many of the same rules and principles govern both concepts. For instance, just as a benefit may be requested in the belief that it is available free of charge, so too the defendant's decision to acquiesce in receipt may be premised on the assumption that the plaintiff is offering a gift. If so, then the court will not recognize an enrichment, even if the claimant actually expected payment.[72] The result will be the same if the defendant did not enjoy a reasonable opportunity to reject the proffered benefit. Assume, for instance, that a football team is unable to host games unless it arranges adequate policing. The police department, however, drives a hard bargain: twice the required number of officers – at twice the price – or nothing at all. If the club yields to the pressure and the police subsequently sue for restitution, the enrichment may be limited to the number and the cost of the officers that were actually required. While the team acquiesced (in a colloquial sense) to the surplus officers, it never genuinely accepted the associated cost.[73]

Despite those similarities, there are significant differences between request and free acceptance as tests of enrichment.[74] To begin, a request can usually be interpreted as both a desire to receive and a willingness to pay. People don't ask for things that they don't want. Free acceptance

71 *Pettkus, supra* note 16 at 849. Though most often encountered in cohabitational property disputes, the free acceptance doctrine is equally available in other circumstances: *Sharwood & Co v Municipal Financial Corp* (2001), 53 OR (3d) 470, 197 DLR (4th) 477 (CA) [*Sharwood*].

72 *A fortiori* if the plaintiff conferred a benefit despite the defendant's prior refusal to pay: *1318847 Ontario Ltd v Laval Tool & Mould Ltd*, 2015 ONSC 2664; *Bookmakers' Afternoon Greyhound Services Ltd v Gilbert*, [1994] FSR 723 (Ch).

73 *Chief Constable of Greater Manchester Police v Wigan Athletic AFC Ltd*, [2008] EWCA 1449.

74 Free acceptance previously served a dual function in Canadian law. In addition to establishing an *enrichment*, it could also demonstrate the *injustice* of a transfer. The issue of injustice traditionally required proof of an *unjust factor* — i.e., a positive reason for reversing a transfer. That reason usually consisted of the plaintiff's impaired intention, as in cases of mistake or compulsion. The enrichment was recoverable because the plaintiff did not truly intend to part with it. Occasionally,

cannot support the same conclusion. Assume that the defendant, despite knowing that payment is expected, sits back and says nothing as the plaintiff confers a benefit. That acquiescence *may* reflect the defendant's desire to receive, but it equally may indicate utter indifference. Consequently, for the purposes of enrichment, free acceptance cannot be read, like request, as a positive decision to bear the risk of financial responsibility.

That difficulty is not necessarily fatal. Free acceptance was never intended to identify positively desired benefits.[75] It serves instead to overcome subjective devaluation. Presented with an opportunity to reasonably reject a benefit for which the plaintiff will expect payment,[76] the defendant is put to a choice: speak up or run the risk of liability.

A related difficulty is not so easily overcome. A passively exercised choice is a genuine choice. It accordingly makes sense to deny the plea of subjective devaluation if the defendant chose to receive a benefit despite actually knowing that the plaintiff expected payment. As employed by Canadian courts, however, the doctrine of free acceptance goes one step further. It operates as long as the defendant "knows or ought to have known" of the plaintiff's expectation.[77] The inclusion of constructive knowledge sits uneasily within a test of enrichment that emphasizes personal autonomy. A person who passively received a benefit and should have known, but did not know, that payment was expected, cannot sensibly be said to have exercised a choice to accept

---

however, the focus fell on the other side of the transfer. The positive reason for restitution was the defendant's unconscientious behaviour in freely accepting a benefit, despite knowing of the plaintiff's non-gratuitous intention, but refusing payment: *Pettkus, supra* note 16. The test of injustice, however, fundamentally changed in *Garland, supra* note 22. Instead of imposing liability only if there is an unjust factor that positively calls for recovery, Canadian law is now prepared to reverse any transfer that lacks a *juristic reason*: see discussion *supra*, at note 29. Consequently, while free acceptance continues to serve as a test of enrichment, it has nothing to say on the issue of injustice: *Kerr v Baranow*, 2011 SCC 10 at paras 120–1.

75 Peter Birks, "In Defence of Free Acceptance" in A.S. Burrows, ed, *Essays on the Law of Restitution* (Oxford: Clarendon, 1991) 105 at 128–32.

76 The plaintiff's state of mind is important. If a benefit is genuinely conferred with a gratuitous intention, then the defendant's acquiescence will not allow the claimant to retroactively turn a gift into a liability: *Malik (Estate of) v State Petroleum Corp*, 2009 BCCA 505. And if the plaintiff, intending to be paid, confers a benefit despite knowing that the defendant is unwilling to bear the cost, relief will be barred by the doctrine of officiousness: McInnes, *supra* note 24 at c 42.

77 *Pettkus, supra* note 16 at 849; *Sorochan v Sorochan*, [1986] 2 SCR 38 at 46; *Peter, supra* note 29 at 1017.

the risk of financial responsibility. The doctrine of free acceptance consequently should be confined to instances of actual knowledge (including recklessness and wilful blindness).[78]

II. INCONTROVERTIBLE BENEFIT

Subjective devaluation can be overcome on the basis of either the defendant's conduct or the nature of the benefit itself. The former is true in cases of request and free acceptance. The latter involves the doctrine of *incontrovertible benefit*.

McLachlin J provided the leading statement – domestic or international – on point in *Peel*.[79] "Where the benefit is not clear and manifest," she began, "it would be wrong to make the defendant pay, since he or she might well have preferred to decline the benefit if given a choice." An incontrovertible benefit, however, "is a benefit which is demonstrably apparent and not subject to debate or conjecture."[80] It is "not the antithesis of freedom of choice," because it "exists when freedom of choice as a problem is absent."[81]

The principle was clear, but when McLachlin J wrote in 1992, the details were unsettled. The challenge was two-fold. Since the modern law of unjust enrichment was still in its formative period, it was necessary to ensure that the governing rules produced appropriate results. In the context of enrichment, that meant striking a sensitive balance between facilitating recovery and protecting personal autonomy. That task was further complicated by the need to look both forwards and backwards.

---

78 The doctrine's scope could be extended slightly without becoming unprincipled. Since they cannot be restored *in specie*, beneficial services require that the defendant's knowledge be assessed upon receipt. Goods, in contrast, generally persist for some time after conferral. It should be sufficient that the defendant learned of the plaintiff's non-gratuitous intention before the goods deteriorated or were consumed. The nature of goods has encouraged English judges to carve out a third conduct-based test of enrichment: *readily returnable benefit*. Regardless of the defendant's knowledge at the time of receipt, a plea of subjective devaluation will not prevail as long as the goods obtained from the claimant can reasonably be restored: *McDonald v Coys of Kensington Ltd*, [2004] EWCA Civ 47 at paras 35–6; *Harrison v Madejski*, [2014] EWCA Civ 361. Canadian courts generally come to the same conclusions by rolling such cases into the free acceptance doctrine.

79 *Peel*, *supra* note 29. See also *Benedetti*, *supra* note 46 at para 25; *Sempra Metals Ltd v IRC*, [2007] UKHL 34 at para 232 [*Sempra*]; *Lumbers v W Cook Builders Pty Ltd (in liquidation)*, [2008] HCA 27 at paras 53, 75.

80 *Peel*, *supra* note 29 at 795.

81 *Ibid* at 795-6, quoting JR Maurice Gautreau, "When Are Enrichments Unjust?" (1989) 10:3 Adv Q 258 at 270–1.

The Supreme Court of Canada was charged with the responsibility of articulating rules to take restitutionary liability into the twenty-first century, but it was constrained, to some extent, by the need to fit its decisions within the historical framework. Unjust enrichment was experiencing a renaissance – it was not being written from a *tabula rasa.*

McLachlin J's judgment in *Peel* reflects those circumstances.[82] Rather than attempt a comprehensive statement of the incontrovertible benefit doctrine, she sketched an outline and identified areas of uncertainty. Following Goff and Jones, she recognized that an incontrovertible benefit may exist if the defendant has either "gained a demonstrable financial benefit or [was] saved an inevitable expense."[83] The claimant in *Peel* relied on the second branch of that test. It argued that the concept of "inevitable expense" should extend beyond the traditional category of legally enforceable debts and "require only that the plaintiff's payments have discharged a political, social or moral responsibility ... for which the defendant was primarily liable."[84] McLachlin J took the proposal seriously and canvassed several possibilities: the law might insist on an expense that was "inevitable" or "necessary" or perhaps merely "likely."[85] In the end, however, she believed that adoption of a lenient test would intolerably undermine personal autonomy and would effectively deprive the defendant of the right to allocate its resources.[86]

Whatever McLachlin J's judgment in *Peel* lacked in details, it embedded the incontrovertible benefit doctrine into Canadian law and

---

82 McLachlin J began by identifying three sets of tensions that are inherent in the modern law of unjust enrichment: theoretical, jurisprudential, and philosophical. In each instance, opposing forces pull in opposite directions. On the one side, "the traditional 'category' approach" prioritizes the need for "certainty" and is informed by historical notions of "robust individualism"; on the other side, "the 'principled' approach'" looks beyond established heads of liability to "allow recovery where ... retention ... would ... be unjust" and, where necessary, "shrinks from the harsh consequences of individualism and seeks to effect justice where fairness requires": *Peel, supra* note 29 at 784–6. That perception was understandable given the state of the literature in 1992, but one important misstep is now clear. The "principled" approach described in *Peel* comes dangerously close to the type of "palm tree justice" that rightly concerned McLachlin J: *supra* note 29 at 802. Today, *ad hoc* discretion remains a trap for the unwary and the overzealous, but courts and commentators have succeeded in formulating a principled approach to unjust enrichment that is capable of consistently securing just results without sacrificing certainty and predictability.

83 *Peel, supra* note 29 at 797, quoting Goff and Jones, *supra* note 24 at 21–2.

84 *Peel, supra* note 29 at 792.

85 *Ibid* at 799.

86 *Ibid* at 796.

established the guiding principles.[87] From that basis, the concept has evolved. Although the proposition has yet to receive judicial imprimatur, courts eventually will find that the three categories of incontrovertible benefit all turn on the unique characteristics of money.

A. Money. As the very means by which the law recognizes and expresses value, money is immune to subjective devaluation.[88] It is always valuable, and it is equally valuable regardless of who holds it. A $20 bill is worth precisely the same whether it sits in the plaintiff's purse or the defendant's pocket. Moreover, because of its fungibility, money can be restored even if the defendant no longer holds the same notes and coins that were received from the plaintiff: one $20 bill is as good as the next. Accordingly, while issues arise at the margins,[89] the receipt of money is the paradigm of an incontrovertible benefit.

---

87 The judgment's influence has not been limited to Canada: *Benedetti, supra* note 46 at paras 18, 97; *Roy v Lagona*, [2010] VSC 250 at para 316.

88 *BP Exploration Co (Libya) Ltd v Hunt (No 2)*, [1979] 1 WLR 783 (QB) Goff J ("Money has the peculiar character of a universal medium of exchange. By its receipt, the recipient inevitably is benefitted" at 799).

89 An especially difficult issue concerns interest. A judicially recognized right to restitution normally carries a statutory right to simple interest: e.g. *Courts of Justice Act*, RSO 1990, c C.43, ss 128, 129. The far more difficult question is whether the successful claimant should be entitled to compound interest. For a period, at least, the prospects were promising.

Although Canadian law has yet to authoritatively move beyond simple interest (*cf Bank of America Canada v Mutual Trust Co*, 2002 SCC 43; *Ermineskin Indian Band and Nation v Canada (Attorney General)*, 2009 SCC 9), the House of Lords endorsed a broad right to compound interest in 2007: *Sempra, supra* 79. A transfer of money was said to carry a dual benefit. In addition to the principal sum, the plaintiff was said to provide the defendant with the opportunity to put those funds to work. The court calculated that "use value" as the amount that it would have commercially cost the defendant to obtain the same opportunity in the market place – i.e., compound interest. Lord Nicholls went so far as to say that, "[i]n principle, this claim is unanswerable ... Nobody has suggested a good reason why ... an award of compound interest should be denied": *Sempra*, at paras 102, 112.

Ten years later, the United Kingdom's Supreme Court resiled from that view: *Littlewoods Ltd v HMRC*, [2017] UKSC 70; *Prudential Assurance Co Ltd v HMRC*, [2018] UKSC 39 [*Prudential*]. It is difficult to predict the implications of those cases. The decisions were coloured by the fact that European Union law prevented Parliament from amending a limitation period that allowed claims dating back to the United Kingdom's entry into the Union in 1973. That quirk, coupled with the exponential growth possible under compound interest, threatened to cost the public purse £5 billion in *Prudential* and a whopping £17 billion in *Littlewoods*. Moreover, much of the Supreme Court's reasoning turned on its interpretation of domestic statutes

B. Inevitable Expense. As McLachlin J recognized in *Peel*,[90] an incontrovertible benefit may also arise if the plaintiff discharged an inevitable expense on the defendant's behalf. The underlying necessity may be legal or factual in origin. The first possibility is simpler because legally enforceable debts generally leave no scope for discretion. Taxes, for instance, normally must be paid in specific amounts by specific dates. Factually necessary expenses are more troublesome because, strictly speaking, very few things in life are necessary.[91] Judges consequently have to balance the plaintiff's interest in recovery against the defendant's interest in autonomy in order to decide what level of probability constitutes practical necessity.[92]

The important point, for present purposes, is that *if* the court determines that a necessary expense has been saved, then it can recognize an incontrovertible benefit. It is *as if* the plaintiff conferred a monetary enrichment upon the defendant. Being relieved of a $5,000 burden is essentially the same as receiving $5,000.[93] The resources that the defendant could have used to discharge the inevitable expense can be used instead to satisfy the plaintiff's judgment. And while it is true that liability leaves the defendant with no choice but to make restitution, it also is true that the defendant had no choice but to honour the original obligation. Liability accordingly leaves the defendant none the worse for wear.[94]

---

and judgments of the European Court of Justice. Compound interest was rejected as a matter of unjust enrichment only because of the belief that the use value received under a mistaken payment is not a benefit that the defendant obtains "at the expense of" the plaintiff, "in the relevant sense" of that phrase: *Prudential* at para 74. That analysis may not appeal to Canadian judges, who view the element of "expense" or "deprivation" quite differently than do their English counterparts.

90 *Peel, supra* note 29.

91 *Malette v Shulman* (1987), 47 DLR (4th) 18, 63 OR (2d) 243 (Ont HCJ) (life-saving blood transfusion need not be accepted).

92 *Carrington Petroleum & Fertilizers Ltd v Imperial Oil Ltd*, 2003 ABQB 545; *Matheson v Smiley*, [1932] 2 DLR 787, [1932] 1 WWR 758 (MB CA); *Craven-Ellis v Canons Ltd*, [1936] 2 KB 403 (CA).

93 *Carleton, supra* note 49; *Davey v Rur Mun Cornwallis*, [1931] 2 DLR 80 (MB CA).

94 There is some need for caution. To ensure proper respect for personal autonomy, the value of the incontrovertible benefit must accurately reflect the defendant's circumstances. If the defendant was peculiarly capable of discharging a debt below market value, then the enrichment must be discounted as well: *Gould v Gould Estate*, 2009 BCSC 1528. Likewise, recovery must be capped if, in satisfying a need, the plaintiff plumped for luxury even though the defendant would have settled for economy: *Hutzal v Hutzal (Administratrix)*, [1942] 2 WWR 492 (SK KB).

C. Realizable Financial Gain. Finally, just as the receipt of money trumps subjective devaluation, so, too, an incontrovertible benefit exists if the plaintiff provided goods or services that the defendant has turned into money.[95] Suppose, for instance, that the plaintiff mistakenly repairs the defendant's widget and thereby raises its value from $5,000 to $7,000. The defendant immediately sells the widget in its improved state for the greater amount. There is no room for subjective devaluation because it is *as if* the defendant received $2,000 cash from the plaintiff. Liability allows for the restoration of the *status quo ante.* Even after the claimant recovers the value of the mistaken services, the defendant can use the remaining $5,000 to buy a replacement for the widget in its original condition.

The situation becomes far more difficult if the facts merely disclose a *realizable* financial gain – i.e., if, because of the plaintiff's services, the defendant *could* sell an enhanced asset for profit, but has not yet done so. To what extent should the courts protect freedom of choice? Is it enough that the services *could* be turned into cash? Should the recognition of an enrichment require proof that the defendant *probably* will realize a financial gain in the future? At least in theory, if the improved asset is sold, the defendant can pay restitution to the plaintiff and buy a replacement for the original item. But what if that item is unique or holds great sentimental value for the defendant? Should liability ever be imposed if, practically speaking, selling a cherished asset is the only way for the defendant to obtain enough money to satisfy judgment?

There are no easy answers, precisely because opinions about personal autonomy vary.[96] Nevertheless, although the issue has never received the attention that is deserves, Canadian judges have taken a surprisingly relaxed approach. Even when the plaintiff has substantially improved the defendant's land – i.e., even when the threat to freedom of choice is apt to be greatest – courts have recognized enrichments on the basis of realizable financial gains.[97] Those decisions are

95 *Peel, supra* note 29 at 797–800; *Sanderson, supra* note 63; *Sharwood, supra* note 71; *Salna, supra* note 59; *Gidney v Shank* (1995), 101 Man R (2d) 197 (QB), rev'd on other grounds (1995), 107 Man R (2d) 208 (CA); *Greenwood v Bennett,* [1962] 1 QB 195 (CA).

96 Academic opinion is divided across a broad continuum. The various positions are discussed in McInnes, *supra* note 24 118–23.

97 *Sherbeth, supra* note 59; *MacLellan v Morash,* 2006 NSSC 101; *Love v Schumacher Estate,* 2014 ONSC 4080; *Servello v Servello,* 2014 ONSC 5035; *Idle-O Apartments Inc v Charlyn Investments Ltd,* 2013 BCSC 2158, var'd on other grounds 2014 BCCA 451; *Clarke v Johnson,* 2014 ONCA 237; *Dutertre Manufacturing Inc v Palliser Regional Park Authority,* 2012 SKQB 335; *Murphy v MacDonald,* 2009 PESC 30; *Simonin v Simonin Estate,* 2010 ONCA 900.

not philosophically indefensible, but they certainly go well beyond the traditional cases, and they arguably leave too little room for personal autonomy.[98] If enrichments are to be recognized, courts should perhaps make greater use of proprietary remedies that facilitate a more sensitive balance between the parties' competing interests.[99]

V. Conclusion

While the Chief Justice's retirement had a significant impact on Canadian law, her legacy will soften the blow. The judgments that she delivered during nearly forty years on the bench will shape the law for generations to come, as will the philosophy of personal autonomy that informed them. That focus on the individual features prominently in public law contexts, but it shaped the Chief Justice's analysis of private law issues as well.

The central challenge for the modern law of unjust enrichment lies in the need to balance the plaintiff's interest in reversing unjustified transfers and the defendant's interest in freedom of choice. As McLachlin J explained in *Peel*,[100] the solution to that problem is found in the element of enrichment. By requiring proof of a tangible benefit that accords with the recipient's right of autonomy, she protected the defendant from the risk of hardship and thereby facilitated the adoption of a generous regime of strict liability. In that respect, while a great deal of work remains to be done, Chief Justice McLachlin leaves the law of unjust enrichment in excellent condition.

98 Claims for unrequested improvements to land were historically subject to the stringent requirements of the proprietary estoppel doctrine. Without any discussion on point, Canadian courts now routinely analyse such claims in terms of unjust enrichment and readily treat increased market value as an enrichment: Mitchell McInnes, "Improvements to Land, Equity, Proprietary Estoppel, and Unjust Enrichment" (2016) 2:2 Can J Comparative & Contemporary L 421.

99 *Re Gareau Estate* (1995), 9 ETR (2d) 25 (Ont Ct J (Gen Div)) (improved asset subject to equitable lien exercisable if and when financial gain realized through sale); *Stevested, supra* note 59; *cf Sullivan v Lee* (1994), 95 BCLR (2d) 195 (SC).

100 *Peel, supra* note 29.

6 Selective Deference and the Judicial Role: Chief Justice McLachlin's Legacy for Law and Legal Education

DAVID SANDOMIERSKI

I. Introduction

The legal consciousness of common law Canada can, in some sense, be described as straddling the sceptical position of the United States and the fidelity to doctrine of the United Kingdom.[1] That characterization would, at least, be a sensible and logical extrapolation of our bifurcated legal genealogy: we have inherited and received the law of England, yet our commercial and cultural allegiances flow strongly to our southern neighbour. One might expect, therefore, the sceptical position of American legal realism, and its intellectual heirs, to figure prominently in how we conceive judicial language. The American scholarly traditions, in varying degrees of hyperbole, describe judicial language as mere rhetoric, or politics by other means.[2] Careful judicial tests can be seen as empty verbiage, vessels for the propagation of ideology, the

I am grateful to Wade Wright for helpful comments on an earlier draft, and to the organizers of this conference for the opportunity to continue my reflections on Chief Justice McLachlin's legacy. Discussions at the symposium with David Wiseman and Marie-Claire Belleau also helped me develop the ideas for this chapter. I would like to acknowledge the superb research assistance of Emily Denomme and Madeleine Douglas, JD students at Western Law, as well as the financial support of the Faculty of Law. The comments by the anonymous reviewer were also very helpful.

1 See Philip Girard, "The Making of the Canadian Legal Profession: A Hybrid Heritage" (2014) 21:2 IJLP 145; David Sandomierski, *Aspiration and Reality in Legal Education* (Toronto: University of Toronto Press, 2020).

2 Richard A Posner, *Economic Analysis of Law*, 4th ed (Boston: Little, Brown, 1992) at 23; Elizabeth Mensch, "The History of Mainstream Legal Thought" in David Kairys, ed, *The Politics of Law: A Progressive Critique*, rev ed (New York: Pantheon Books, 1990) 33; Duncan Kennedy, "Politicizing the Classroom" (1995) 4 Rev L Women's Stud 84.

pursuit of personal preference, or the advancement of preferred policy outcomes.

The counterpoint to this posture toward judicial reasoning is an approach that "takes doctrine seriously," that considers judges' words and carefully constructed tests as genuine attempts to produce rules and principles meant to actually guide decision making.[3] There is a long tradition, even within the common law, of searching for "principle" and its distinction from "policy" – even if those two terms can run into one another.[4] Nevertheless, the Herculean ideal of the judge who represents society's values and deploys rationality to uphold the rule of law – to ensure that differential outcomes are decided on a rational and systematic basis – is one of the hallmarks of the common law.

In this chapter, I want to tap into this somewhat reverent view of adjudication and judicial language. Like a good number of today's law teachers, I had the opportunity to clerk with a judge at an impressionable moment in my intellectual development. The spirit of this chapter blossomed over the course of my year clerking for Chief Justice McLachlin in 2008–9 at the Supreme Court of Canada. I observed a person exercising her judicial responsibility with a great deal of concern for her appropriate role. Ideology, a hidden agenda, and a desire for particular political or policy outcomes all seemed remote from how she appeared to work. Admittedly, I was not privy to her inner thoughts or most of her deliberations. Yet, when you speak to someone in chambers at the end of a winter day and witness her genuine struggle to choose, among conflicting sources of law, which authority is most appropriate to emphasize, whatever sceptical voices might have been whispering in your ear tend to fade into the background.

What follows is my attempt to elucidate one feature of Chief Justice McLachlin's legal thought, from a vantage point that de-emphasizes ideology and focuses not so much on the outcomes of cases (or any imputed motive to achieve such outcomes), but rather on the structural features of her reasoning. To even posit the "structural features" of reasoning already appears to abandon certain realist preoccupations with what judges do as opposed to what they say.[5] I do not intend here to

3 See e.g. Daniel Markovits, *Contract Law and Legal Methods* (New York: Foundation Press, 2012) at x–xii for a discussion on what taking doctrine seriously means and how it can be conceived of as an outlier position in the United States.

4 SM Waddams, *Principle and Policy in Contract Law: Competing or Complementary Concepts?* (Cambridge: Cambridge University Press, 2011) at 216–17, 223.

5 See e.g. Oliver Wendell Holmes, "The Path of the Law" (1997) 110: 5 Harv L Rev 1006; Karl N Llewellyn, *The Bramble Bush: On Our Law and Its Study* (New York:

stake the ground for such a permanent abandonment; rather, I engage in such an abandonment as a means of understanding one particular aspect of the legacy of Canada's longest-serving Chief Justice.

One animating feature of Chief Justice McLachlin's judicial philosophy is the pursuit of the appropriate source of law, legal institution, or legal process, in the given circumstances. In this view, the judge's role is not to impose their own sense of what is just or right, but rather to determine, when different sources of legal authority yield different results, which one is most appropriate in the given situation. The act of selecting from among different sources of law – judicial equitable intervention, contract, legislation – is, in this view, the pre-eminent role of the judge.

This is not to say that Chief Justice McLachlin is indifferent to outcomes or never deploys consequentialist reasoning in arriving at decisions. Nor am I suggesting that, in certain circumstances, she may not be motivated by deep moral intuitions.[6] All of these influences are undoubtedly present in the activity of any human judge. However, I am emphasizing that the question of "selective deference" – the selection of which legal process, institution, or source is most appropriate in the given circumstances – is a central, maybe even prior, consideration in many of her judicial and extrajudicial writings. In decentring the *outcome* and *motivation* elements of her philosophy, I hope to highlight how this procedural aspect of judging is one that can be taken "seriously," not sceptically, and is one that serves the underlying aims of justice and fairness. This perception of the judicial role, moreover, is ultimately informed by the twin authorities of democracy and the rule of law.

a. The Sceptical Predisposition

What is involved in "taking seriously" a judge's words? In part, it means to suspend one's suspicions and predispositions. Philosophies of adjudication can be experienced as a matter of faith: I either *believe* that a judge's words represent a genuine attempt to deal with an issue from a rational and (to the extent possible) objective fashion, or I

Oceana, 1960) 3; LL Fuller and William R Perdue, Jr, "The Reliance Interest in Contract Damages: 1" (1936) 46:1 Yale LJ 52; SM Waddams, "Unconscionability in Contracts" (1976) 39:4 Mod L Rev 369. See generally Joseph William Singer, "Legal Realism Now" (1988) 76: 2 Cal L Rev 465.

6 See e.g. *Reference Re Assisted Human Reproduction Act*, 2010 SCC 61; *R v Keegstra*, [1990] 3 SCR 697.

believe that such claims to objectivity are false, that rationality is a contestable standard, and that judicial justifications pale in relevance to consequences or outcomes. It seems daunting to reconcile these opposing faiths – although, as I argue elsewhere, reconciling ourselves to the somewhat ambivalent nature of our commitments about law would be a worthwhile endeavour.[7] But in the absence of reconciliation, suspension can be useful.

The sceptic might argue that assertions about the "delicate work" of the courts are merely attempts to justify judicial encroachment on the domain of the legislature.[8] However, if one suspends this prior disposition, and reads such pronouncements earnestly, one can identify the seeds of a deeper, principled concern for selective deference in Chief Justice McLachlin's writings. Consider, for example, her speech to the Empire Club of Canada in 2016, on democracy and the judiciary. In it, she recounts the "delicate work" that "required judges to balance interests and calibrate outcomes in a way that was both respectful of the role of elected legislators and administrators on the one hand, and true to the country's constitutional guarantees on the other."[9] This respect runs deep in her philosophy: she articulated it as Chief Justice and demonstrated it in her judicial writings throughout her career.

The remainder of this chapter explores the respect that Chief Justice McLachlin demonstrates toward the legislative branch, as a means of teasing out a substructural element of her judicial philosophy. My claim is that the archetypal question of the relationship between the courts and Parliament is not merely a result of the enactment of the *Charter*. Rather, Chief Justice McLachlin's concern for balance in the context of *Charter* adjudication reflects a deep and pervasive preoccupation with the

7 See Sandomierski, *supra* note 1, c 6.

8 Critics of judicial activism following the introduction of the *Charter* would fall into this category. See e.g. Peter H Russell, "The Political Purposes of the Canadian Charter of Rights and Freedoms" (1983) 16:1 Can Bar Rev 30; M Mandel, *The Charter of Rights and the Legalization of Politics in Canada* (Toronto: Wall and Thompson, 1989). Events in Ontario in the fall of 2018 – in particular, comments from the Premier over the proposed (but ultimately withdrawn) legislation that would have invoked the notwithstanding clause because "I was elected. The judge was appointed." – appear to revive this debate. See e.g. Jennifer Pagliaro & Robert Benzie, "Ford Plans to Invoke Notwithstanding Clause for First Time in Province's History and Will Call Back Legislature on Bill 5," *Toronto Star* (10 September 2018), online: <www.thestar.com/news/toronto-election/2018/09/10/superior-court-judge-strikes-down-legislation-cutting-the-size-of-toronto-city-council.html>.

9 Beverley McLachlin, "Canada's Legal System at 150: Democracy and the Judiciary" (speech delivered at the Empire Club of Canada, 3 June 2016), online: <www.scc-csc.ca/judges-juges/spe-dis/bm-2016-06-03-eng.aspx>.

diverse roles that different institutions play in the legal order. A salient feature of her judicial philosophy is due regard for the distinctive claim to legitimacy that a given legal institution – or branch of government – may have in a given circumstance. In this conception, the judge's responsibility is more to be the arbiter among competing claims for legitimacy than it is to consider intervention as the presumptive method of achieving justice. The pursuit of justice is first filtered through the question of *whether* judicial intervention is appropriate. This technique upholds the proper role of the judiciary within the separation of powers. It is an expression of the judge's unique role as arbiter, and it is never indifferent to the question of substantive justice. It operationalizes deeper commitments about the sources of legitimacy – democracy and coherent legal rationality – for the exercise of power.

To illustrate this idea, I begin by outlining the archetypal question of "balance" raised by *Charter* adjudication. I then explore the macro question of the separation of powers and how Chief Justice McLachlin articulated this preference for selective deference as a matter of extra-*Charter* constitutional philosophy. Finally, I focus on a particular corner of her private law adjudication – her early decisions on the role of the constructive trust in family property disputes – to show how notions of balance and institutional appropriateness guide her in determining when to intervene to achieve substantive justice for private parties. In selecting these examples, I have sought out instances in which her philosophy of "selective deference" appears to be most explicit. There are, no doubt, other cases that lend support to this interpretation, and yet others that might challenge it. This chapter, therefore, can neither claim to be an exhaustive survey nor to refute other plausible characterizations of her judicial philosophy. Nonetheless, it attempts to highlight one strand of her thinking, relying on a series of decisions drawn from across her jurisprudence. The selected decisions demonstrate an appreciation of the judicial role as being to implement (by having to select among) the constitutional values of democracy and the rule of law.

II. *Charter* Adjudication as the Archetypal Occasion for Selective Deference

As the excerpt from Chief Justice McLachlin's speech to the Empire Club quoted above demonstrates, an essential feature of *Charter* adjudication is the determination of the appropriate balance to be struck between the courts and the legislatures. As she candidly announced in an earlier speech, adjudicating *Charter* claims necessarily involves "invading the domain of social policy, once perceived as the exclusive right of

Parliament and the legislature."[10] This candidness exposes an underlying humility, an awareness of the inherent limits of courts' "lack [of] resources for gathering and collating information and opinion available to the legislatures."[11]

Thus, *Charter* issues invite her at times to comment on the importance of deferring to Parliament, as she did in *Alberta v Hutterian Brethren of Wilson Colony*.[12] In that case McLachlin CJ, for the majority, found Alberta's legislative requirement of a photo drivers' licence to be a justifiable limit on freedom of religion. She writes that deference should be accorded to legislatures when the matter "concerned complex social issues where the legislature may be better positioned than the courts to choose among a range of alternatives."[13]

Conversely, other *Charter* cases see her taking on the judicial responsibility, in a constitutional democracy, to resist the will of the legislature. She is sometimes reluctant to defer to the legislature in circumstances where constitutional interests are at play. In the free speech cases, for example, she consistently held that laws limiting the scope of section 2(b) protection were unduly broad. In *Canada v Taylor*,[14] in partial dissent, she found section 13(1) of the *Canadian Human Rights Act*,[15] which prevented the dissemination of materials that were "likely to expose a person or persons to hatred or contempt," to be overly broad. She wrote:

> There may be good reasons to defer to legislative judgment on the appropriate balance between furthering equality and safeguarding free expression, particularly in the context of a human rights statute. The problem here, however, is that no serious attempt to strike such a balance appears to have been made … The effort made to accommodate the right of free expression is insufficient.[16]

She is even more definitive about the inappropriateness of deference at times when legislatures purport to "limit fundamental rights." In

---

10 Beverley McLachlin, "The Role of Judges in Modern Society" (speech delivered at the Fourth Worldwide Common Law Judiciary Conference, Vancouver, 5 May 2001), online: <www.scc-csc.ca/judges-juges/spe-dis/bm-2001-05-05-eng.aspx>.

11 *Ibid.*

12 *Alberta v Hutterian Brethren of Wilson Colony*, 2009 SCC 37 [*Hutterian*].

13 *Ibid* at para 53.

14 *Canada v Taylor*, [1990] 3 SCR 892 [*Taylor*].

15 *Canadian Human Rights Act*, RSC 1985, c H-6.

16 *Taylor*, *supra* note 14 at 966, 968.

Sauvé v Canada,[17] Chief Justice McLachlin, for a 5–4 majority, found a law that disenfranchised inmates serving more than two years to be unconstitutional:

> The right to vote is fundamental to our democracy and the rule of law and cannot be lightly set aside. Limits on it require not deference, but careful examination. This is not a matter of substituting the Court's philosophical preference for that of the legislature, but of ensuring that the legislature's proffered justification is supported by logic and common sense …
>
> Deference may be appropriate on a decision involving competing social and political policies. It is not appropriate, however, on a decision to limit fundamental rights. This case is not merely a competition between competing social philosophies. It represents a conflict between the right of citizens to vote … and Parliament's denial of that right … It is for the courts, unaffected by the shifting winds of public opinion and electoral interests, to safeguard the right to vote guaranteed by section 3 of the Charter.[18]

Similarly, in *RJR-Macdonald Inc v Canada*,[19] in rejecting the government's scheme of banning tobacco advertising, Justice McLachlin (as she then was) insisted on the need for evidence to demonstrably justify limits on freedom of expression. In doing so, she outlined the role of the courts in giving "force and meaning" to constitutional rights, which may sometimes require them to "confront the tide of popular public opinion" – but she also specifically addressed how deference is to be selectively deployed depending on the circumstances: "[T]he situation which the law is attempting to redress may affect the degree of deference which the court should accord to Parliament's choice. The difficulty of devising legislative solutions to social problems which may be only incompletely understood may also affect the degree of deference that the courts accord to Parliament or the Legislature."[20]

Determining the appropriate amount of deference is directly connected to understanding the diverse roles and responsibilities of the courts and Parliament:

> Parliament has its role: to choose the appropriate response to social problems within the limiting framework of the Constitution. But the courts

17 *Sauvé v Canada*, 2002 SCC 68.
18 *Ibid* at paras 9, 13.
19 *RJR-Macdonald Inc v Canada*, [1995] 3 SCR 199 [*RJR-Macdonald*].
20 *Ibid* at para 135.

> also have a role: to determine, objectively and impartially, whether Parliament's choice falls within the limiting framework of the Constitution. The courts are no more permitted to abdicate their responsibility than is Parliament. To carry judicial deference to the point of accepting Parliament's view simply on the basis that the problem is serious and the solution difficult, would be to diminish the role of the courts in the constitutional process and to weaken the structure of rights upon which our constitution and our nation is founded.[21]

In *Charter* litigation, therefore, the decision of whether to defer or not has to do, in part, with the importance of the right: "how 'fundamental'" it is, the degree of intrusion, the extent to which competing policy issues are at play, and how complex an approach Parliament has taken. The more the question requires a complex response to policy matters, the more deference is apparently owed; the more the intrusion can be characterized as the denial of a fundamental right, the less deference is required.[22]

---

21 *Ibid* at para 136. Chief Justice McLachlin used very similar language in her concurring decision in *Chaoulli v Quebec (Attorney General)*, 2005 SCC 35 [*Chaoulli*], in which she ruled against the Government of Quebec, finding that the prohibition on private medical insurance contravenes section 7 and is not saved by section 1 ("The fact that the matter is complex, contentious or laden with social values does not mean that the courts can abdicate the responsibility vested in them by our Constitution to review legislation for *Charter* compliance when citizens challenge it"). Similarly, in *Canada (Attorney General) v PHS Community Services Society*, 2011 SCC 44 [*PHS*], McLachlin CJ (writing for a unanimous court) vigorously refuted the Minister of Health's refusal to grant a supervised drug injection site an exemption from the *Controlled Drugs and Substances Act.* In light of the overwhelming evidence of the effectiveness of injection sites, she held that the exercise of discretion to *not* to grant an exemption contravened section 7 and was not saved by section 1.

22 These trends might also go a way to accounting for multiple cases in which McLachlin CJ declined to defer to Parliament or executive action in the section 7 cases, including not only *PHS* and *Chaoulli*, *supra* note 21, but also *Canada (Attorney General) v Bedford*, 2013 SCC 72 [*Bedford*] and *Carter v Canada (Attorney General)*, 2015 SCC 5 [*Carter*]. In *Carter*, it was the "absolute prohibition" on assisted death – and the fact that it "could not be described as a 'complex regulatory response'" – that "reduced" "the degree of deference owed to Parliament" (at para 98). In *Chaoulli*, McLachlin CJ likewise rejected a blanket prohibition – in this case, on the purchasing of private healthcare insurance – stating that "the mere fact that [the] question may have policy recommendations does not permit us to avoid answering it" and making a point that "the conclusions of other bodies on other material cannot ... relieve the courts of their obligation to review government action for consistency with the *Charter* on the evidence before them" (at paras 108, 151).
In both *Bedford* and *PHS*, McLachlin CJ, writing for the Court, found that the deprivation of life, liberty, or security of the person is not in accordance with the

Another contributing factor, with respect to *Charter* remedies, is the fiscal impact of a judicial intervention. Such is the interpretation of Lawrence David in his article "Resource Allocation and Judicial Deference on Charter Review."[23] David argues that the McLachlin Court deferred more readily in cases where the financial impact of recognizing a *Charter* right would be substantial. For example, in *British Columbia (AG) v Christie*,[24] the Court refused to find that section 10(b) created a general right to state-funded counsel in all proceedings engaging legal rights or obligations. As David writes: "A judicially mandated state provision of legal services ... would represent an undue intrusion into matters reserved for the legislature ... [I]ts imposition by judicial fiat would arguably have been undemocratic. For this reason ... the McLachlin Court has exercised significant deference where recognizing a positive Charter right would interfere with the allocation of public funds."[25]

David expands the list of situations in which greater deference is owed to include those in which impugned provisions are "the result of polycentric decision-making by the legislature" and in which the government cites fiscal impact as one justification for limiting rights.[26] While the court may look "sceptic[ally]" at claims by a government relying solely on fiscal impact, when fiscal impact is part of a host of policy factors, deference is usually accorded at the minimal impairment

---

principles of fundamental justice. These cases can be considered as manifestations of her preoccupation with each branch's appropriate role. In finding that, in *PHS*, the Minister's decision was both arbitrary and grossly disproportionate, and, in *Bedford*, that the legislative provisions at issue were grossly disproportionate or overbroad, McLachlin CJ spent a good deal of effort in distinguishing the principles of fundamental justice (*Bedford* at paras 110–13; *PHS* at 129–35). This concern for the doctrinal integrity of these categories reflects her preoccupation with the work of deciding whether or not to defer to a government or legislature: "The question of deference arises under the principles of fundamental justice" (*Bedford* at para 90). In such cases, McLachlin CJ writes, accepting the argumentation of Peter Hogg and Hamish Stewart, the Court "accepts the legislative objective" but declares that the law is not a "rational means to achieve the objective" (*Bedford* at para 107). The imposition of standards of rationality, over which courts, as guardians of the rule of law, have expertise, may be thought to legitimately overturn legislative or executive action. On the importance of doctrinal integrity to the judicial role, see Part IV, below. On the relationship between the rule of law and legal rationality, see Sandomierski, *supra* note 1 at 220–3.

23 Lawrence David, "Resource Allocation and Judicial Deference on Charter Review: The Price of Rights Protection According to the McLachlin Court" (2015) 73:1 UT Fac L Rev 35.

24 *British Columbia (AG) v Christie*, 2007 SCC 21.

25 David, *supra* note 23 at 45.

26 *Ibid* at 39.

stage of the *Oakes* test.[27] Further, fiscal impact appears to influence the Court in determining which kind of remedy to grant.[28] In all, David argues that *Charter* remedies attract the greatest level of deference, an expression of the principle that "the remedy that will best vindicate the infringement of a given Charter protection is not always within the courts' constitutional or institutional competence."[29]

Themes of legitimacy, democratic accountability, the separation of powers, and institutional competence all, therefore, figure heavily in decisions as to whether to defer to legislatures when *Charter* rights are at play. These themes are, in a sense, the natural precipitate of the constitutional reforms of the *Charter*, and no judge, when faced with the challenge of adjudicating the state's purported limitation of rights, could have avoided them. However, the above examples disclose not merely a rote recitation of standard themes. They are seemingly written in earnest, with a genuine desire to identify the appropriate judicial role in a given situation.

Figuring out how and when a court should intervene holds a special place in Chief Justice McLachlin's judicial philosophy. It is not just engaged in the discrete instance of adjudicating constitutional rights; rather, the articulations of the problem in such instances signal a deeper, more thoroughgoing preoccupation about the judicial role. That preoccupation insists that judging is essentially, and *always*, a search for legitimacy and the appropriate institutional role. This search is most manifest in the cases on the separation of powers.

III. Separation of Powers

The search for legitimacy among different institutions is evident in cases where the Court is specifically asked to mediate between competing branches of government. These cases, while still on constitutional issues, differ from *Charter* cases in that the Court is not being asked to rule as to whether a right is limited and whether the limitation is justified. Instead, it is called on to referee, or potentially rewrite, the rules of the game between branches of government.

David Schneiderman outlines Chief Justice McLachlin's tendency to "be hesitant to encroach on the political branches." By investigating the decisions written by Chief Justice McLachlin, and those to which she ascribes her name, on the questions of parliamentary privileges and

27 *Ibid* at 47–8.
28 *Ibid* at 39.
29 *Ibid* at 54.

executive prerogatives, Schneiderman reveals a "marked reluctance on the part of the McLachlin Court to upset what is characterized as a constitutional balance."[30]

Most notably, in *New Brunswick Broadcasting Co v Nova Scotia (Speaker of the House of Assembly)*,[31] Justice McLachlin (as she then was) sided with the Nova Scotia legislature, which had denied permission to the New Brunswick company to televise proceedings of the legislature by invoking parliamentary privilege. The broadcasting corporation launched a section 2(b) *Charter* challenge in response. In upholding the legislature's ability to exercise its privilege in this fashion, Justice McLachlin outlined the legal basis for "curial deference to the action of the House of Assembly": in addition to the preamble of the Constitution and historical tradition, "legislatures must be presumed to possess such constitutional powers as are necessary for their proper functioning."[32] Since "one part of the Constitution cannot be abrogated or diminished by another part of the Constitution," the *Charter* could not be used to defeat the constitutional power the Legislature has to "exclude strangers from its chamber."[33] She characterized this power of exclusion as "necessary in modern Canadian democracy":

> The legislative chamber is at the core of the system of representative government. It is of the highest importance that the debate in that chamber not be disturbed or inhibited in any way … It follows that the Assembly must have the right, if it is to function effectively, to exclude strangers. The rule that the legislative assembly should have the exclusive right to control the conditions in which that debate takes place is thus of great importance, not only for the autonomy of the legislative body, but to ensure its effective functioning.[34]

Here, Justice McLachlin places the principle of democracy at the forefront of her decision to defer to the legislative assembly, much as she would a decade later in *Sauvé*. The democratic principle serves as a justification for establishing the constitutional status of the privilege. This concern for democracy also reveals a deep appreciation of the

30 David Schneiderman, "The Separation of Powers and Constitutional Balance at the McLachlin Court" (2018) 86:2 SCLR 137 at 165.

31 *New Brunswick Broadcasting Co v Nova Scotia (Speaker of the House of Assembly)*, [1993] 1 SCR 319.

32 *Ibid* at 374–5.

33 *Ibid* at 373.

34 *Ibid* at 387.

complementary and shared functions of different branches of government. After arguing for the constitutional status of the privilege, Justice McLachlin opines:

> I add this. Our democratic government consists of several branches: the Crown, as represented by the Governor General and the provincial counterparts of that office; the legislative body; the executive; and the courts. It is fundamental to the working of government as a whole that all these parts play their proper role. It is equally fundamental that no one of them overstep its bounds, that each show proper deference for the legitimate sphere of activity of the other.[35]

Three years later, McLachlin J cited this passage in another parliamentary privilege case: *Harvey v New Brunswick (Attorney General)*.[36] At issue in that case was whether the expulsion and disqualification of a member of the legislative assembly, pursuant to a provision of the *Elections Act*,[37] for having induced a minor to vote, contravened the appellant's section 3 right to be qualified for membership in the assembly. Justice McLachlin (as she then was), siding with a unanimous court but writing for just herself and Justice L'Heureux-Dubé, again reiterated that parliamentary privileges are not "subject" to the *Charter*. Both privilege and the *Charter* have constitutional status, so "[w]here apparent conflicts between different constitutional principles arise, the proper approach is not to resolve the conflict by subordinating one principle to the other, but rather to attempt to reconcile them."[38]

She then goes on to read the democratic guarantees of section 3 in a "purposive" way, finding that they support the "fundamental constitutional right of Parliament and the legislatures to regulate their own proceedings."[39] Section 3 could limit Parliament's ability to expel or disqualify members for reasons outside the scope of parliamentary privilege; courts must "inquire into the legitimacy of a claim of parliamentary privilege" and potentially determine that expulsion or disqualification is done on "invalid grounds."[40] But, as with the power to exclude the public from its chamber, once a court finds that "an act or ruling of the legislature … properly falls within the domain of

35 *Ibid* at 389 [emphasis added].
36 *Harvey v New Brunswick (Attorney General)*, [1996] 2 SCR 876 [*Harvey*].
37 *Elections Act*, RSNB 1973, c E3.
38 *Harvey*, *supra* note 36 at para 69.
39 *Ibid* at para 70.
40 *Ibid* at para 71.

parliamentary privilege ..., they must leave the matter to the legislature."[41] For Schneiderman, the *Harvey* case represents "an extreme instance of the sort of respect ... McLachlin CJC believed was due [to legislatures] based on an interpretation of old Parliamentary law."[42]

The question of whether, and when, to defer, therefore, is not only one regarding the legitimacy of courts in potentially overriding the policy choices of elected representatives. It is also a question that goes to the heart of the allocation of responsibility to separate branches of government. Getting the balance right is important not only because it will enhance the legitimacy of the courts, but also because it will realize the overriding principle of democratic government. In situations such as these, McLachlin CJ demonstrates a candid earnestness about the question of deference that is difficult to reconcile with a sceptical interpretation that judges opportunistically defer or intervene according to their own policy preferences. Moreover, the concern for a proper constitutional balance seems to run contrary to interpretations that "deference" is a strategy of disclaiming responsibility for "political" decisions. Decisions such as *New Brunswick Broadcasting* suggest that Justice McLachlin, years before being elevated to Chief Justice, was intensely and genuinely concerned with the proper judicial role, and that questions of whether to defer are best viewed through that macro-institutional, democratic-government, lens.

After reviewing these cases, Schneiderman turns to cases in which Chief Justice McLachlin demonstrates a similar willingness to defer to the executive in areas traditionally falling within the royal prerogative over foreign affairs.[43] Like privileges, prerogatives are historical mechanisms by which a branch of government claims a degree of autonomy over certain decisions. In cases in which the executive claims to be acting pursuant to such prerogative, McLachlin and "the Court" under her as Chief Justice have indicated a willingness to defer to these as well, again demonstrating a desire to respect the distinct contribution and sphere of authority of each branch of government.

Two cases are particularly instructive. In *Kindler v Canada*,[44] Justice McLachlin (as she then was) determined that, in deciding whether to extradite a person to a foreign country, the *Charter* did not require the Canadian government to seek assurances that the death penalty will not be

41 *Ibid* at para 74.
42 Schneiderman, *supra* note 30.
43 *Ibid* at 32–40.
44 *Kindler v Canada*, [1991] 2 SCR 779.

carried out. Justice McLachlin's articulation of the deference owed to the executive in such instances recalls the deference observed in the privilege cases:

> In recognition of the various and complex considerations which necessarily enter into the extradition process, this Court has developed a more cautious approach in the review of executive decisions in the extradition area, holding that judicial scrutiny should not be over-exacting ... The reviewing court must recognize that extradition involves interests and complexities with which judges may not be well equipped to deal. The superior placement of the executive to assess and consider the competing interests involved in particular extradition cases suggests that courts should be especially careful before striking down provisions conferring discretion on the executive. Thus the court must be "extremely circumspect" to avoid undue interference with an area where the executive is well placed to make these sorts of decisions.[45]

More recently, the Court confirmed the deference owed to the executive in its use of the prerogative over foreign affairs. In *Canada (Prime Minister) v Khadr*,[46] although the Court found that the Canadian government breached Omar Khadr's section 7 rights in collaborating with the US government in connection with his unlawful detention at Guantanamo Bay, it refused

---

45 *Ibid* at 849 (emphasis added). Ten years later, the Court came to the opposite conclusion in *United States v Burns*, 2001 SCC 7, finding that the failure to seek assurances constituted an unjustified infringement of section 7 in all but "exceptional" cases. While that case clearly demonstrates a departure – in result – from the deference showed in *Kindler*, the Court is careful to note that the "balancing process" from *Kindler* still applies (*ibid* at paras 64–7). The Court remains careful to map out the different spheres of authority for the executive and the judiciary: "The only issue under the Charter is whether, as a matter of constitutional law, the Minister had the power to decide as he did. The *Charter* does not give the Court a general mandate to set Canada's foreign policy on extradition. Yet the Court is the guardian of the Constitution and death penalty cases are uniquely bound up with basic constitutional values" (*ibid* at para 35). It is the evolving factual context around a myriad of factors relating to the criminal justice system since *Kindler* that caused the Court to resolve the balance in the opposite direction, not a different approach taken to the relative roles of the two institutions. The continued concern with institutional appropriateness in *United States v Burns* can also be seen in its emphasis on the distinction between "general public policy" and "the inherent domain of the judiciary as guardian of the justice system" that it employs, drawing on *Re BC Motor Vehicle Act*, [1985] 2 SCR 486, in describing the "basic tenets" of the legal system (*United States v Burns* at paras 70–1).

46 *Canada (Prime Minister) v Khadr*, 2010 SCC 3.

to order the government to request Khadr's repatriation to Canada. The Court found that this remedy was precluded by the prerogative over foreign affairs, and instead ordered declarative relief. The Court wrote that, while the exercise of this prerogative is not "exempt from constitutional scrutiny," the power of the courts to review it is "limited" and "narrow":

> [J]udicial review of the exercise of the prerogative power for constitutionality remains sensitive to the fact that the executive branch of government is responsible for decisions under this power, and that the executive is better placed to make such decisions within a range of constitutional options. The government must have flexibility in deciding how its duties under the power are to be charged.[47]

These decisions provide two additional examples of Chief Justice McLachlin (either individually or through the Court) emphasizing the distinct contributions of each branch. The inclination to defer (manifested in the limited power of review or in being "careful" about striking down provisions conferring discretion) apparently flows jointly from claims of capacity (different branches are better at different types of activity) and responsibility (a branch is worthier of deference when the question touches an area of core responsibilities). The executive in both cases deserves flexibility (and deference) because it is more equipped to make a decision and because it has, historically, had exclusive dominion over the matter at hand.

Privileges and prerogatives are particularly acute opportunities to highlight the distinct contributions of each branch and the resulting allocation of authority among them. Because they explicitly establish a *prima facie* legal basis of autonomy, privileges and prerogatives directly invite the question of the extent of that autonomy in extra-*Charter* constitutional contexts. Various postures could have been open to a court adjudicating these constitutional claims. A judge could have perfunctorily acknowledged the historical claims of autonomy but asserted a novel entitlement (by virtue of the *Charter*) to aggressively intervene. Alternatively, a judge could have disclaimed judicial responsibility in favour of greater deference (as, for example, Justice Nadon of the Federal Court of Appeal did in *Khadr*).[48] What we see in Chief Justice

47 *Ibid* at paras 37–8.

48 *Khadr v Canada (Prime Minister)*, 2009 FCA 246 at para 106 ("Why Canada has taken that position is, in my respectful view, not for us to criticize or inquire into. Whether Canada should seek Mr. Khadr's repatriation at the present is a matter best left to the Executive.").

McLachlin's particular posture is a balancing of these two approaches, drawn from an apparent sense that each branch is due respect in a meaningful way because it has a distinct claim on the subject matter, and because supra-constitutional virtues – democracy and the rule of law – necessitated an appropriate balance.

Such an inclination for balance and "selective deference" is, however, not unique to Chief Justice McLachlin's constitutional jurisprudence, where the questions are more obvious. A similar respect for the distinct contributions of different legal institutions can be seen in her private law jurisprudence. A unifying thread between her public and private law decisions may thus be a concern for institutional appropriateness.

The next section attempts to demonstrate how prevalent the question of selective deference is in a subset of Chief Justice McLachlin's private law jurisprudence: decisions over family property division. The direct subject matter of these cases is not, as it is in the constitutional cases, the appropriate allocation of authority among competing branches of government. Instead, the prevailing question is how best to achieve substantive fairness for the private parties in dispute. Yet the method of arriving at substantive fairness draws on the preoccupations with appropriate allocation of responsibility observable in the constitutional cases. In these cases, Chief Justice McLachlin demonstrates a prior preoccupation with choosing the appropriate institution for resolving the problem of substantive fairness. Equitable intervention is a real possibility, but it is meaningfully constrained by a concern for doctrinal integrity and by the preference for deferring to statute when the legislature has purported to deal with the underlying issue.

IV. Selective Deference in Chief Justice McLachlin's Private Law Jurisprudence: Family Property Disputes

A court faced with the task of allocating private parties' entitlements may use all manner of justificatory strategies to explain its approach. One common strategy is to argue on grounds of "institutional competence" that the court is either well placed to equitably intervene or, to the contrary, is ill-suited because the question is "better left to the legislatures." There are numerous examples of judicial statements in Canadian law of strong articulations from both sides of the debate.[49]

This tendency to make arguments about institutional competence has been attacked by some who suggest that the claim that a decision is

---

49 See e.g. *Harrison v Carswell*, [1976] 2 SCR 200; *Re Noble and Wolf*, [1948] OR 579, [1948] 4 DLR 123 (SC); *Re Drummond Wren*, [1945] OR 778, [1945] 4 DLR 674 (SC).

best left to the legislatures is a politically charged abdication of responsibility. As Duncan Kennedy writes:

> The premise of the institutional competence argument is that judges do not have the equipment they would need if they were to try to determine the likely consequences of their decisions for the total pattern of social activity ... Only the legislature is competent to carry out such investigations. Judges should therefore restrict themselves to general prescriptions.
>
> The premise of the political question gambit is that there is a radical distinction between the activity of following rules and that of applying standards. Standards refer directly to the substantive values or purposes of the community. They involve "value judgments." Since value judgments are inherently arbitrary and subjective, they should be made only according to majority vote ...
>
> Together, the institutional competence and political question arguments would produce a regime in which judges did nothing but formulate and apply formally realizable general rules. This procedure would minimize both the institutionally inappropriate investigation of the likely results of decision[s] and the inherently legislative activity of making value judgments ...
>
> [B]oth of these gambits are prototypically individualist. Each is an argument for nonintervention, for judicial passivity in the face of breach of altruistic duty.[50]

Although Chief Justice McLachlin does make recourse to both "institutional competence" and "political question" argumentative strategies, I do not believe that Kennedy's critique is apt in her case. Her resort to institutional appropriateness is not a technique to avoid making substantive determinations about fairness or distribution. Instead, the search for which source of law is most appropriate in the given circumstances is driven by the idea that substantive fairness will best be achieved by respecting the proper and fair balance between diverse legal institutions. Her judicial philosophy, in other words, encompasses a deep respect for the capacity of each legal institution to achieve substantively fair outcomes, and it acknowledges that the proper exercise of judicial authority is to decide, in the given circumstances, which process is most appropriate.

Exercising this selective deference is another manifestation of her more macro concern for the distinct roles of different branches of

50 Duncan Kennedy, "Form and Substance in Private Law Adjudication" (1976) 89:8 Harv L Rev 1685 at 1752–3.

government – each legal institution has its place, and, in different circumstances, one or the other will have a superior claim to authority. Chief Justice McLachlin's decisions in family property law celebrate judicial independence not by asserting the judge's licence to intervene, but by thoughtfully, rationally, and justifiably parsing when judicial intervention is the most appropriate technique, faced with the alternative of allowing other legal sources, such as statute or contract, to predominate. Her approach simultaneously manifests ideals associated with the adjudicative process and judicial branch of government – independence and respect for the rule of law – and illustrates a deep respect for the plurality of legal processes.

A starting point for understanding Chief Justice McLachlin's approach to adjudication in this branch of law is the seminal case of *Peter v Beblow*.[51] There, upon the breakdown of a common law relationship, the appellant, Catherine Peter, who had performed an extensive array of housekeeping and childrearing duties over fifteen years, was awarded title to the family home, pursuant to a constructive trust. It was a unanimous result for the Court, with two concurring decisions. Justice McLachlin (as she then was), while agreeing in the result with Justice Cory – who in emphatic terms described the policy reasons in favour of recognizing contributions that serve to "make a home" – outlined her preference for following appropriate channels of reasoning.[52] This decision demonstrates Justice McLachlin's willingness to invoke the Court's equitable jurisdiction when necessary to achieve substantive justice, but in a way that highlights the importance of established doctrinal categories. Moreover, it is an instance where the Court's equity jurisdiction "trumps" certain inferences that could be made of apparently contradictory legislative enactments.

Justice McLachlin signalled early on in the decision her belief that a judge, in pursuing equitable justice, must nevertheless remain bounded by categorical guidelines: "There is a tendency on the part of some to view the action for unjust enrichment as a device for doing whatever may seem fair between the parties. In the rush to substantive justice, the principles are sometimes forgotten."[53] She went on to clarify two important principles of which the other justices (below and in the Supreme Court) had, in her view, run afoul. The first of these is that the "moral and policy questions [that] require the Court to make value judgments" are best constrained to one step of the unjust enrichment analysis, the

51 *Peter v Beblow*, [1993] 1 SCR 980 [*Peter*].
52 *Ibid* at 1016.
53 *Ibid* at para 988.

determination that there be no "juristic reason" for the enrichment.[54] Justice McLachlin then went on to refute the claim that housekeeping and childrearing do not create equitable claims, calling the notion "a pernicious one that systematically devalues the contributions which women tend to make to the family economy. It has contributed to the phenomenon of the feminization of poverty."[55] Her substantive reasons resembled those of Justice Cory, but it was important to Justice McLachlin that they be considered at the right stage to justify a different set of reasons.

Second, Justice McLachlin took issue with the choice of remedy in unjust enrichment cases, as between monetary awards and the constructive trust. Unlike Justice Cory, who deemed it fit to apply different standards in family and commercial cases, Justice McLachlin insisted that the doctrinal requirements for applying a constructive trust – that there be a "proprietary link" – should be identical in all situations.[56] This consistency does not preclude courts exercising "flexibility and common sense," but it does require a standard rule in all situations: "In short, the concern for clarity and doctrinal integrity with which this Court has long been preoccupied in this area mandates that the basic principles governing the rights and remedies for unjust enrichment remain the same for all cases."[57]

Justice McLachlin's majority opinion – she wrote for four of seven judges in this case – invites a number of reflections about her judicial philosophy. She is willing to invoke the Court's power of equity to intervene. At the same time, this equitable jurisdiction is not a blank slate to pursue justice by whatever means. Doctrinal clarity and integrity are paramount – not only, one could argue, as brakes on the power to equitably intervene, but also as the expression of the underlying equitable power. With judicial power comes responsibility to maintain consistent categories. Or correlatively, power is justified by its responsible use. Finally, because the equitable power is exercised in a restrained and disciplined manner, it may be somewhat immune to arguments that ask the Court to defer because of some *imputed* legislative intent. Justice

---

54 *Ibid* at paras 989–90 (such considerations "properly find their place … at this stage [where] the court must consider whether the enrichment and detriment, morally neutral in themselves, are 'unjust'"). The Supreme Court of Canada has recently affirmed the idea that policy considerations are properly considered at the juristic reason stage of the analysis. See *Kerr v Baranow; Vanasse v Seguin*, 2011 SCC 10, per Cromwell J (for a unanimous court, including McLachlin CJ).

55 *Peter*, *supra* note 51 at 993.

56 *Ibid* at 996–7.

57 *Ibid*.

McLachlin specifically rejected, in *Peter*, the argument "that, because the legislature has chosen to exclude unmarried couples from the right to claim an interest in the matrimonial assets on the basis of contribution to the relationship, the court should not use the equitable doctrine of unjust enrichment to remedy the situation … It is precisely where an injustice arises without a legal remedy that equity finds a role."[58] Justice McLachlin clearly pursued substantive fairness in this case – recognizing the woman's equitable interest in the family home – while remaining alert to the issues of institutional competence. She did not seem vulnerable to overblown arguments in favour of legislative deference, yet at the same time considered the judicial power of intervention a limited one whose limitations serve to bolster the Court's claim to legitimately intervene through equity.

By contrast, other family property law decisions show the future Chief Justice declining to intervene equitably in deference to the legislature. In *Rawluk v Rawluk*,[59] for example, which was decided three years earlier than *Peter*, Justice McLachlin (as she then was) in dissent found that a constructive trust was *not* available to a divorced woman in a marriage. In that case, the issue was not whether the required elements of the constructive trust were met – both parties conceded that they were – but rather whether the remedies provided by the Ontario *Family Law Act, 1986* somehow prevented the operation of the constructive trust. This was a live issue in the case because the *Act* provided for equal division of family assets valued at the date of separation. The properties in question were held by the husband, and between the date of separation and the trial action, the properties increased substantially in value. Because the properties were valued at the date of separation, the wife was unable to participate in the increase in value. Justice Cory, writing for the majority of the seven-member Court, found that the provisions of the *Family Law Act, 1986*, did not "oust" the availability of the constructive trust remedy and, accordingly, upheld the lower court decisions that had awarded Mrs Rawluk a one-half interest in the contested property.[60]

Justice McLachlin, by contrast, considered whether the remedy of the constructive trust was "necessary and appropriate" in light of the other remedies provided for by the *Family Law Act, 1986*.[61] For her, the question was not whether the act "ousted" the availability of the remedy – she found that it did not and that, in disputes prior to separation, it might be

58 *Ibid* at 994.

59 *Rawluk v Rawluk*, [1990] 1 SCR 70 [*Rawluk*].

60 *Ibid* at 89–90.

61 *Rawluk*, supra note 59.

available – but that the legislature's approach to remedying the unjust enrichment obviated the availability of the remedy of constructive trust.[62]

Two related concerns contribute to this analysis. First, recalling *Peter*, it expresses an appreciation for the proper categorization of distinct legal doctrines. She begins by determining that the constructive trust is essentially a "general equitable remedy for unjust enrichment" and not a "substantive institution."[63] As a result, it is "discretionary and dependent on the inadequacy of other remedies for the unjust enrichment in question."[64] She cites with approval the statement that, if the constructive trust were to be "employed where personal remedies would suffice, it [would threaten] to upset the operation of other doctrines."[65] Thus, as with *Peter*, there is a concern for respecting the appropriate categories of existing doctrines, analogous to the concern that "the principles must not be forgotten" in the "rush to justice."

She then goes on to apply this question of inadequacy to the legislative scheme at hand, drawing on another underlying concern: that of institutional competence. Justice McLachlin starts her decision by framing it as a "balance between the constructive trust as a remedy for unjust enrichment and statutory schemes for the division of matrimonial property."[66] The second half of her judgment is dedicated to discerning the statutory scheme and ultimately finding that it "sets up a comprehensive statutory scheme ... [that] addresses the question of unjust enrichment between spouses by providing a monetary equalization payment."[67] This remedy "makes it unnecessary to resort to the doctrine of constructive trust," in part because "the statutory remedy and the remedy of the constructive trust are ... directed to the same end."[68] Moreover, the true interest pursued – allowing the wife to participate in the increase in value of the property since valuation – could, in principle, be addressed by the statutory provision for modifying the valuation.[69] Indeed, she would have disposed of the case by referring it to the trial judge to do precisely that.[70]

The concerns here are reminiscent of the cases discussed above. Although Justice McLachlin is attentive to the underlying interest, she

62 *Ibid*.
63 *Ibid* at 101–2.
64 *Ibid* at 103–4.
65 *Ibid* at 106 citing DWM Waters, *The Law of Trusts in Canada*, 2nd ed (Toronto: Carswell, 1984) at 393.
66 *Rawluk*, supra note 59 at 98.
67 *Ibid* at 108.
68 *Ibid* at 109.
69 *Ibid*.
70 *Ibid* at 113.

will not pursue the "most" just outcome by any means. Judicial equitable intervention is important and powerful, but is meaningfully constrained by the principles of doctrinal integrity and deference to legislatures. Where an equivalent outcome can potentially be achieved by recourse to legislation, that route is to be preferred even if it is not the "best" outcome.[71] In *Rawluk*, since the *Family Law Act, 1986* does not apply to common law spouses, it was argued that, were the legislation to preclude the constructive trust remedy, then married spouses would be worse off relative to common law spouses despite the legislature's intent to protect married spouses. Justice McLachlin responded that this was not a valid reason for disturbing doctrinal integrity: "The fact that that remedy may not be as advantageous in some cases as the remedy of constructive trust does not justify the court in altering the doctrine of constructive trust."[72]

In a case four years later regarding the variation of a will, Justice McLachlin (as she then was) had occasion again to explore the relationship between legislative intent and the judicial power to intervene. In *Tataryn v Tataryn*,[73] a male testator excluded his older, estranged son entirely from his estate. To ensure that his surviving wife (the excluded son's mother) did not counteract his wishes, the testator also restricted the wife's entitlements by providing her with a mere life interest in the

---

71 A similar issue had arisen a year earlier in *Watkins v Olafson*, [1989] 2 SCR 750, where McLachlin J (as she then was), for a unanimous court, overturned an order by the Manitoba Court of Appeal for a periodic payment scheme for tort damages, in departure from settled practices of awarding lump sum payments. There, McLachlin J rejected the departure on the grounds that reform in this area would have to await legislative intervention. Her deferential attitude is apparent:

> Generally speaking, the judiciary is bound to apply the rules of law found in the legislation and in the precedents. Over time, the law in any given area may change; but the process of change is a slow and incremental one, based largely on the mechanism of extending an existing principle to new circumstances …
>
> There are sound reasons supporting this judicial reluctance to dramatically recast established rules of law … [T]he court may not be in a position to appreciate fully the economic and policy issues underlying the choice it is asked to make … [T]here is the long-established principle that in a constitutional democracy it is the legislature, as the elected branch of government, which should assume the major responsibility for law reform.
>
> Considerations such as these suggest that major revisions of the law are best left to the legislature. ([1989] 2 SCR 750 at 760–1)

72 *Rawluk, supra* note 59 at 112. *Cf Quebec (Attorney General) v A*, 2013 SCC 5, per McLachlin CJ (upholding the Quebec National Assembly's differential treatment of common law and married spouses in the case of property division and spousal support, in part due to Quebec's "unique history and social situation," at para 413).

73 *Tataryn v Tataryn*, [1994] 2 SCR 807 [*Tataryn*].

family home, and by setting her up as a beneficiary of a discretionary trust to be administered by their younger (favoured) son. The wife sought a variation of the will under the 1920 statute, the *Wills Variation Act*,[74] which gave judges power to order a provision that "it thinks adequate, just and equitable" in cases where a testator did not make adequate provision for the testator's wife, husband, or children.

In this case, Justice McLachlin felt it appropriate to intervene. Writing for a unanimous court, she ordered that title to the matrimonial home and the bulk of the residue of the estate be given to the surviving wife. In exercising this discretion, she relied heavily on her understanding of legislative intent. Going back to Parliamentary debates, she cited the legislative intent as being to "ameliorate social conditions within the Province."[75] She found that the "generosity of the language suggests that the legislature was attempting to craft a formula which would permit the courts to make orders which are just in the specific circumstances and in light of contemporary standards."[76] This interpretation led her to find that the "adequate, just, and equitable" language empowered a court to reflect both legal and moral obligations owed by the testator in the award, which could address more than mere need or "maintenance" obligations.[77]

What is interesting for our purposes is how Justice McLachlin grounded the extensive equitable power – the expansive reading that "more than" need is permitted – in legislative scheme and intent. She cited bifurcating lines of jurisprudence that disagree on whether the *Wills Variation Act* enables variations based only on need or on more generous considerations, but her ultimate source of authority in resolving this divergence was the legislature itself, not some inherent jurisdiction of the court. Indeed, her assessment that "contemporary" justice be sought is drawn from the principle that "a statute is always speaking" and that "the Act must be read in light of modern values and expectations."[78] Moreover, the pursuit of contemporary justice, in this case, is drawn not only from a vague sense of contemporary values, but from specific recent doctrines: she included the law of constructive trust elaborated in the recent cases of *Peter v Beblow* and *Pettkus v Becker* as one source of the legal obligations leading to her generous award.[79]

74 Originally *An Act to Secure Adequate Provision for the Maintenance of the Wife and Children of a Testator*, SBC 1920, c 94.

75 *Tataryn*, *supra* note 73 at 815.

76 *Ibid* at 814.

77 *Ibid* at 820–1.

78 *Ibid* at 814–15.

79 *Ibid* at 821–2. See *Pettkus v Becker*, [1980] 2 SCR 834.

The pursuit of substantive justice in this vision is guided by the pre-existing channels of the law. She disciplined her own decision on whether to intervene by the norms and prescriptions of two pre-existing sources of authority: the common law (through a concern for doctrinal integrity) and the legislature (its enactment and an interpretive philosophy in favour of purposive reading). Underlying this self-imposed restriction on intervention is a two-pronged institutional consideration. First, the existing norms and standards of each branch bear on the individual justice's latitude to intervene. Proper channels must be observed; the principles must not be forgotten. Second, inasmuch as the content of these norms is important, a prior question is always which institution should trump the other. Justice McLachlin demonstrates a tendency to defer to a legislature's attempt to solve a problem over the common law, where the interests aimed at are the same.[80] However, this argument does not automatically win in every case: she rejects the *expressio unius exclusius alterius*–type arguments that a more stringent fidelity to legislative enactment might otherwise have yielded. Questions of institutional competence are prior questions, always disciplining the fundamental goal of achieving justice, but they are not facile predictors of outcomes. The judge inhabits her cloak of office by considering these questions carefully and ultimately exercising judgment as to which branch should prevail in the given circumstances.

V. Chief Justice McLachlin's Legacy for Law and Legal Education

The above analysis suggests that one of Chief Justice McLachlin's legacies is a distinctive vision of the judicial role, one composed of various constituent features. This pursuit of justice is both substantive and contextual in the sense that it inquires into *actual* effects of a given law, whether those effects be individual (such as depriving a citizen of the ability to vote) or systemic (such as the "feminization of poverty"). The proper judicial pursuit is not, in other words, one that can ignore distributive consequences, and thus is not entirely denuded of political import.

The pursuit of this justice is, however, structured by a series of constraints that flow from a deep appreciation of the diverse roles played by each branch of government. The prior judicial exercise is determining which legal institution ought to have the ultimate authority in a given instance. What may motivate this exercise of selective deference

---

80 *Rawluk, supra* note 59 at 110.

among different branches is an appreciation of each branch's ultimate ground of authority. In our constitutional structure, there are at least two sources of authority. One is democratic. Chief Justice McLachlin demonstrates a deep and overriding commitment to democracy. We see this in the cases that more narrowly uphold democratic rights, as in *Sauvé*. We see it when she defers to legislatures in cases of policy differences or fiscal impact in balancing rights infringements, or when they have purported to address a distributive problem in a particular way. We see it in deference to the executive and legislature over their prerogatives and privileges. And, we see it in her respect for the constitutional balance produced by the bargain of constitutional negotiation among democratically elected drafters. Democracy is the value that justifies precluding individual judicial intervention, even if a "more" just or fair situation (in the given circumstance) might flow from such intervention.

If democracy conditions judicial intervention, so does the rule of law: the requirement that law operates in a rational and coherent way. Equitable intervention, which might otherwise be thought of as the most malleable and discretionary form of intervention ("the size of the Chancellor's foot"), provides no free pass to achieve a desired result. As demonstrated in her disagreements with Justice Cory in the family property law cases, individual justice ought not to be obtained at the expense of doctrinal integrity. One gets the sense that for Chief Justice McLachlin, that would not be justice at all. On this view, the judge's power to equitably intervene may be considered legitimate only to the extent that it is exercised in a rational way that maintains the internal consistency of judge-made rules. Internal coherence, or rationality, is at once the source of the legitimacy of power and the criterion for its exercise. It is also probably, at root, the source of justification for the existence of the judicial branch of government and the judiciary's sacrosanct independence.

The judge, in exercising this tremendously privileged independence, does so as a steward of the two primordial values that underpin our system of government. Democracy and governance through a rational and coherent law are the ultimate ends to be pursued in any individual act of judging.[81] The process of selective deference operationalizes this rather abstract judicial responsibility.

81 There may be other primordial values at play. Although the examples chosen for this chapter do not allow us to explore it further, it is very possible that freedom of contract is one of these values.

Conceiving oneself as a steward of these primordial values is a fitting exercise for Canada's longest-serving Chief Justice. That role requires an astute understanding of the different branches of government, and an appreciation of the purposes (and limits) of judicial independence. The examples in this chapter illustrate how the spirit of the office of Chief Justice surfaces in her writings, both before and after her ascension to the role.

They also, however, inform an understanding of the lawyer and of legal education – there is only one Chief Justice, after all, but many lawyers and even more jurists. The practice of selective deference illustrates that the judicial activity is broad and concerns itself with diverse legal processes. In this regard, Chief Justice McLachlin's legacy may be felt beyond the many and varied doctrinal areas of the law she influenced during her decades on the bench. We might apply the spirit of selective deference to expanding the range of legal processes to which students in law school are exposed. Whenever they defer to a legislature, or the executive, a judge is acting on some theory of the contribution that each branch of government has to offer. A corollary of this theory is that the paradigmatic legal processes – legislative and adjudicative – have distinctive contributions to legal decision making and reflect distinctive activities that lawyers engage in.[82]

Paradoxically, perhaps, careful study and pedagogical engagement with Chief Justice McLachlin's jurisprudence can use the paradigmatic artifact of the adjudicative process – the appellate decision – to paint a more diverse picture of the processes, values, and activities that are central to law. The analogue to the judge asking, as a prior question, which branch of government ought to be accorded the presumptive authority in attaining justice in an individual case, is the lawyer (or law student) asking, at the outset, which legal process is best suited to achieve a given end. It is a long-standing criticism of legal education that, in focusing exclusively on adjudication and litigation, we tend to focus on pathological cases – instances where something went wrong. Study only the resolution of disputes, and every legal problem may look like a dispute. (Equipped only with a hammer, everything looks like a nail.) A consideration of the diverse forms of government can shed light on other principles that inform legal ordering.[83]

Chief Justice McLachlin's outsized influence, as both judicial author and in the role of Chief Justice, provides a promising opportunity to

82 See generally David Sandomierski, "Catalytic Agents? Lon Fuller, James Milner, and the Lawyer as Social Architect, 1950–1969" (2021) 71 UTLJ 91.

83 *Cf* Angela Swan, Nicholas C Bala & Jakub Adamski, *Contracts: Cases, Notes and Materials*, 10th ed (Markham, ON: LexisNexis Canada, 2020) at 14–19.

shift the balance within legal education from a focus almost exclusively on adjudication, to, in the words of Lon Fuller, the "rule-creative, structure-giving role" of the lawyer.[84] She demonstrates that the act of judging requires respect for diverse modes of law, and from that commitment legal educators can take creative inspiration. They can explore the mutually informative values of democracy and the rule of law, the countervailing but perennially coupled theories of realism and formalism, and the multitudinous contributions of adjudication and legislation. In light of these expansive possibilities, it is safe to say that Chief Justice McLachlin's legacy has only just begun.

84 Lon L Fuller, "What the Law Schools Can Contribute to the Making of Lawyers" (1948) 1 J Leg Ed 189 at 192–3.

PART TWO

Controversies in Public Law

7 Combatting Stereotyping and Facilitating Justice: Chief Justice McLachlin's Vision for the Law of Evidence

DAVID M. TANOVICH

I. Introduction

Beverley McLachlin is the architect of a flexible, socially conscious, and principled approach to evidence admissibility in Canada. Her jurisprudence has infused the law of evidence with tools that enable it to adapt to new situations and to be aware of and reflect concerns for systemic issues, all with an eye to ensuring it can fulfil its regulatory purpose of facilitating justice. I will call this the "McLachlin principle." This chapter explores the foundations of that approach in two early McLachlin decisions – *R v Khan*[1] and *R v Seaboyer*[2] – and then in *Mitchell v MNR*, where, as Chief Justice, she set out, for the first time in a Supreme Court decision, a theory of evidence admissibility.[3]

After examining this evidence trilogy, the chapter will consider the application of the McLachlin principle in the context of defence applications to limit cross-examination of an accused on their prior criminal record under *R v Corbett*.[4] Section 12(1) of the *Canada Evidence Act* permits

I wish to thank the peer reviewers for their helpful comments and Terra Duchene (Windsor Law 2019) for her careful editing.

1 *R v Khan*, [1990] 2 SCR 531 [*Khan*].

2 *R v Seaboyer*, [1991] 2 SCR 577 [*Seaboyer*].

3 *Mitchell v MNR*, 2001 SCC 33 [*Mitchell*].

4 *R v Corbett*, [1988] 1 SCR 670 [*Corbett*]. In *Corbett*, the trial judge permitted the Crown to cross-examine the accused, charged with murder, on his prior conviction for murder. The accused challenged section 12 of the *Canada Evidence Act*, RSC 1985, c C-5, arguing that its application to an accused violated the presumption of innocence and fair trial guarantees under section 11(d) of the *Charter*. The accused argued that section 12 jeopardized a fair trial because it allowed the Crown to introduce what would otherwise be presumptively inadmissible bad character evidence, thereby opening the door for a jury to misuse the evidence, even with an instruction from the trial judge. The misuse would be using the evidence to conclude that the accused is a bad person who has a propensity to commit criminal offences.

all witnesses, including an accused, to be cross-examined on their criminal record, and our common law has, for the most part uncritically, accepted that a criminal record is relevant to a witness's credibility and whether they are prepared to abide by their oath or affirmation to tell the truth.[5] As then Chief Justice Dickson held in *Corbett*, "what lies behind s. 12 is a legislative judgment that prior convictions do bear upon the credibility of a witness … There can surely be little argument that a prior criminal record is a fact which, to some extent at least, bears upon the credibility of a witness."[6]

In *Corbett*, the Supreme Court of Canada upheld the constitutionality of section 12(1) by reading into the provision a judicial discretion to prohibit or limit cross-examination on a prior record.[7] *Corbett* was decided in 1988, and, since then, we have become more aware of the existence and manifestations of systemic racism, particularly as it relates to Indigenous and Black communities and the criminal justice system.[8] Chief Justice McLachlin has recognized this social reality in both *Sauvé v Canada (Chief Electoral Officer)* and *R v Williams*.[9] Despite this consciousness, little, if any, attention has been given in our trial and

---

5 Section 12(1) of the *Canada Evidence Act*, *ibid*, reads:

> A witness may be questioned as to whether the witness has been convicted of any offence, excluding any offence designated as a contravention under the *Contraventions Act*, but including such an offence where the conviction was entered after a trial on an indictment.

6 *Corbett*, *supra* note 4 at 685.

7 *Ibid* at 692, 699, 745. Chief Justice Dickson characterized this discretion as applying "in those unusual circumstances where a mechanical application of s. 12 would undermine the right to a fair trial" (at 692). The majority also noted that other safeguards protected the fairness of the accused's trial. These safeguards include the obligation of the trial judge to provide a limiting instruction (i.e., that the record could be used only as impeachment evidence and not as evidence of a propensity to commit the offence) and the inability of the prosecution to get into details about the underlying facts giving rise to the conviction or to ask whether the accused testified in the earlier case(s) (at 691, 696–7).

8 The existence of systemic racism has been acknowledged in a number of Supreme Court of Canada and provincial appellate decisions, including *R v Le*, 2019 SCC 34 at paras 82–97 [*Le*]; *R v Barton*, 2019 SCC 33 at paras 195–204 [*Barton*]; *Ewert v Canada*, 2018 SCC 30 at para 57; *R v Ipeelee*, 2012 SCC 13 at paras 59–60 and 67; *R v Spence*, 2005 SCC 71 at paras 1, 5, 30–4 [*Spence*]; *R v Gladue*, [1999] 1 SCR 688 at paras 61–5 [*Gladue*]; *R v Williams*, [1998] 1 SCR 1128 at paras 58–9 [*Williams*]; and *R v Parks* (1993), 15 OR (3d) 324, 84 CCC (3d) 353 (ON CA) [*Parks*]. In *Spence*, for example, Justice Binnie, for the Court, began his judgment noting that "[t]he administration of justice has faced up to the fact that racial prejudice and discrimination are intractable features of our society and must be squarely addressed" (at para 1).

9 *Sauvé v Canada (Chief Electoral Officer)*, 2002 SCC 68 [*Sauvé*]; *Williams*, *supra* note 8.

appellate courts to how social conditions and bias are relevant in thinking about admissibility under *Corbett*. Enter the McLachlin principle.

The chapter now turns to a discussion of Justice McLachlin's jurisprudence and how it can be used to impact *Corbett* applications and stimulate future consideration of how evidence law can adapt to better facilitate justice in cases involving Indigenous and racialized participants.[10]

II. The McLachlin Evidence Trilogy

a. R v Khan *(1990)*

The McLachlin principle can be traced back to the 1990 decision in *R v Khan*, a sexual assault case involving hearsay evidence from a three-and-a-half-year-old child.[11] At trial, the complainant (then four and a half years old) was deemed to be incompetent to testify. The Crown conceded that she was not competent to give sworn testimony, and the trial judge concluded that she could not give unsworn testimony because of her very young age.[12] The prosecution was left with the complainant's out-of-court statement, made to her mother fifteen minutes after they had left the accused's medical office, and a mixed semen-saliva stain on the complainant's blouse that was consistent with what she told her mother had happened. However, the trial judge concluded that the cogent and reliable hearsay evidence was inadmissible because it did not fall under the narrow spontaneous utterance exception to the hearsay exclusionary rule.[13] Dr Khan was acquitted.

When the case reached the Supreme Court of Canada, Justice McLachlin, as she then was, recognized the need for a critical re-evaluation of the

10 See e.g. David M Tanovich, "Safeguarding Trials from Racial Bias," *Policy Options* (2 October 2018), online: <policyoptions.irpp.org/magazines/october-2018/safeguarding-trials-from-racial-bias/>.

11 *Khan, supra* note 1. Hearsay evidence is an out-of-court statement led at trial for the truth of its contents. It is presumptively inadmissible.

12 In 2005, Parliament abolished the presumption of incompetency for witnesses under the age of fourteen and the requirement that they demonstrate an understanding of the oath or duty to tell the truth. See Bill C-2, now *An act to amend the Criminal Code (protection of children and other vulnerable persons) and the Canada Evidence Act*, SC 2005, c 32. Today, witnesses under the age of fourteen can testify upon promising to tell the truth (*Canada Evidence Act, supra* note 4, s 16.1).

13 Before *Khan*, hearsay admissibility depended upon its falling under a common law or statutory exception.

common law's traditional approach to hearsay, because it "frequently proved unduly inflexible in dealing with new situations and new needs in the law."[14] She saw this as an appropriate context to reconsider the rule, because of "the increasing number of prosecutions for sexual offences against children and the hardships that often attend requiring children to retell and relive the frequently traumatic events surrounding the episode."[15]

Khan firmly established an approach to hearsay evidence in criminal cases that would be "rooted in the principle and the policy underlying the hearsay rule,"[16] an approach grounded in assessing necessity and reliability. On the facts of the case, Justice McLachlin held that the hearsay evidence was admissible. It was necessary, given the trial judge's refusal to allow the girl to testify, and it was reliable, given her lack of motive to lie, the corroborative forensic evidence, and the "fact that she could not be expected to have knowledge of such sexual acts[, which] imbues her statement with its own peculiar stamp of reliability."[17]

Khan represented the Court's adoption, for the first time in a criminal case, of a principled approach to hearsay admissibility.[18] While the case concerned hearsay evidence from child witnesses, it opened the door to the Supreme Court considering the viability of traditional hearsay exceptions and exclusions in a series of subsequent cases.[19]

---

14 *Khan, supra* note 1 at 540.

15 *Ibid.* The concern with how the law of evidence impacts access to the evidence of vulnerable witnesses such as children or witnesses with disabilities in sexual assault cases can be seen in a number of McLachlin decisions such as *R v W(R)*, [1992] 2 SCR 122 [*W(R)*] (assessing the credibility of children) and *R v DAI*, 2012 SCC 5 [*DAI*] (disability and testimonial competence). In *DAI*, for example, she observed: "Sexual assault is an evil. Too frequently, its victims are the vulnerable in our society – children and the mentally handicapped. Yet rules of evidence and criminal procedure, based on the norm of the average witness, may make it difficult for these victims to testify in courts of law" (para 1).

16 *Khan, supra* note 1 at 540.

17 *Ibid* at 542.

18 As then Chief Justice Lamer noted in *R v Smith*, [1992] 2 SCR 915 at 930, *Khan* "should be understood as the triumph of a principled analysis over a set of ossified judicially created categories." The Court would later apply a principled approach to the admissibility of expert evidence and similar fact evidence in *R v Mohan*, [1994] 2 SCR 9 and *R v Handy*, 2002 SCC 56.

19 For example, in *R v B(KG)*, [1993] 1 SCR 740, the Court held that prior inconsistent statements, which traditionally were admissible only to impeach credibility, could be used for the truth of their contents, such as where they were video-taped, under oath, and where the declarant was available for cross-examination. In *R v Starr*, [2000] 2 SCR 144, the Court added substantive content to the state of mind or present intentions hearsay exception. And finally, in *R v Khelawon*, 2006 SCC 57, the Court relied on *Khan* to overrule precedent that corroborative evidence could not be used in assessing threshold reliability.

b. R v Seaboyer *(1991)*

One year later, in *R v Seaboyer*, the Supreme Court was asked to address the constitutionality of the rape shield law in section 276 of the *Criminal Code*.[20] The accused argued that the provision was framed in such narrow terms as to violate his right to make full answer and defence under section 7 of the *Charter* by depriving him of relevant evidence. The case also provided the Court with an opportunity to address the scope of a trial judge's jurisdiction to exclude otherwise admissible evidence (i.e., exclusionary discretion). Justice McLachlin, as she then was, wrote the majority opinion.

On the issue of exclusionary discretion, she applied a principled approach, recognizing that such a discretion was critical to protect the integrity and fairness of the adjudicative process. She settled conflicting precedent and confirmed that the parameters of the discretion for Crown evidence was a balancing of probative value and prejudicial effect.[21] Crown evidence would be excluded where the accused could satisfy the trial judge that the prejudicial effect of the evidence outweighed its probative value.

Justice McLachlin further recognized that the exercise of exclusionary discretion had to be sensitive to the different contexts in which it would be applied. In cases involving a motion to exclude defence evidence, she highlighted the need to be cognizant of the dangers of wrongful convictions. After referencing the wrongful conviction of Donald Marshall,[22] she noted that courts must be "cautious in restricting the power of the

---

20 *Criminal Code*, RSC 1985, c C-46, formerly s 246.6, *as am* SC 1987, c 24, s 12. "Rape shield laws" are legal rules that limit the admissibility of a complainant's prior sexual history as evidence in sexual assault cases. They emerged because, at common law, defence counsel could introduce this evidence, and the trier of fact could use it to negatively assess the complainant's credibility and to conclude that the complainant was more likely to have consented because of engaging in that conduct in the past. Section 276 was enacted in 1983.

21 *Probative value* refers to the strength of the logical connection between the evidence and a material fact. *Prejudicial effect* refers to the danger that the evidence might be used for an improper purpose. For example, *moral prejudice* arises where the jury uses bad character evidence to conclude that the accused is a bad person and therefore more likely to have committed the offence. *Reasoning prejudice* arises where the evidence triggers stereotypical or other problematic assumptions that distort the reasoning process.

22 Donald Marshall, who was Indigenous, was wrongfully convicted of murder. He served eleven years before his conviction was overturned. See *R v Marshall* (1983), 57 NSR (2d) 286 (NS CA). A Royal Commission concluded in 1989 that racism had played a role in his wrongful conviction. See Nova Scotia, *Royal Commission on the Donald Marshall, Jr., Prosecution: Digest of Findings and Recommendations* (Halifax: Royal Commission on the Donald Marshall, Jr, Prosecution, 1989) (Chairman Chief Justice T. Alexander Hickman).

accused to call evidence in his or her defence, a reluctance founded in the fundamental tenet of our judicial system that an innocent person must not be convicted."[23] She thus narrowed the discretion to exclude relevant defence evidence to cases where the Crown could establish that the prejudicial effect *substantially* outweighs the probative value of the evidence.[24]

As noted earlier, *Seaboyer* was a sexual assault case about evidence of a complainant's prior sexual activity and the constitutionality of a legislative provision (section 276 of the *Criminal Code*) that limited its admissibility. Justice McLachlin recognized that this was a context that raised legitimate concerns about "outmoded, sexist-based" stereotypes, penalizing "those complainants who did not fit the stereotype of the 'good woman'" and permitting cross-examinations that caused "embarrassment or discomfort to the complainant."[25]

Justice McLachlin ultimately struck down section 276 on fair trial grounds, because it unduly restricted the ability of a judge to admit relevant defence evidence that did not trigger "illegitimate inferences from other sexual conduct that the complainant is more likely to have consented to the act or less likely to be telling the truth."[26] However, she replaced it with a common law regime that would largely be adopted by Parliament when it re-enacted section 276 a year later.[27] In so doing, she held that, given the concerns raised by prior sexual history evidence, trial judges had to assess the evidence with a "high degree of sensitivity"[28] and that "a sensitive and responsive exercise of discretion by the judiciary will reduce and even eliminate the concerns which provoked legislation such as s. 276."[29] She further noted that the "discretion must be exercised to ensure that neither the *in camera* procedure nor the trial become forums for demeaning and abusive conduct by defence counsel."[30] And, perhaps most significantly, she extended the scope of our rape shield protection to evidence of prior sexual history with the accused – something that section 276 had not

23 *Seaboyer, supra* note 2 at 611.
24 *Ibid.* For subsequent Supreme Court cases recognizing this narrower discretion, see *R v Shearing*, 2002 SCC 58 and *R v Grant*, 2015 SCC 9.
25 *Seaboyer, supra* note 2 at 598, 605.
26 *Ibid* at 621, 625.
27 Indeed, in *R v Darrach*, 2000 SCC 46, a decision that upheld the constitutionality of the new section 276, the Supreme Court observed that it "essentially codifies the decision in *Seaboyer*" (at para 1).
28 *Seaboyer, supra* note 2 at 634.
29 *Ibid.*
30 *Ibid.*

addressed.[31] Parliament followed her lead and included this evidence as part of the exclusionary coverage of the new section 276.[32]

c. Mitchell v MNR *(2001)*

Ten years later, in *Mitchell v MNR*, the Supreme Court had to decide whether the Mohawks of Akwesasne had a right to bring goods into Canada from the United States without paying customs duties because section 35(1) of the *Constitution Act* recognizes and affirms Aboriginal rights.[33] The case turned on the admissibility and sufficiency of the evidence of the Aboriginal right claimed. Grand Chief Mitchell sought to rely, in part, on oral history evidence of Elders. Now Chief Justice, Beverley McLachlin penned the opinion for the majority of the Court. She began by observing that "Aboriginal right claims give rise to unique and inherent evidentiary difficulties. Claimants are called upon to demonstrate features of their pre-contact society, across a gulf of centuries and without the aid of written records."[34]

In holding that the oral history evidence was admissible in this case, Chief Justice McLachlin set out a coherent theory of evidence admissibility using the building blocks she had relied on in *Khan* and *Seaboyer*. After highlighting that the rules of evidence are "animated by broad, flexible principles, applied purposively to promote truth-finding and fairness,"[35] and that they should "facilitate justice, not stand in its way,"[36] she identified the following drivers of admissibility: *usefulness*, *reasonable reliability*, and *exclusionary discretion*. As she put it:

---

31 *Ibid* at 633–5. There is research to suggest that this type of evidence is highly prejudicial. As Schuller and Klippenstine note, "participants were more likely to blame the victim and trivialize the sexual assault when the couple had a history of consensual intercourse" and that, "as the sexual intimacy of the couple increases, people are more likely to be focussed on the behaviour of the woman and question the validity of her claim." Regina A Schuller and Marc A Klippenstine, "The Impact of Complainant Sexual History Evidence on Jurors' Decisions: Considerations for a Psychological Perspective" (2004) 10:3 Psych Pub Pol & Law 321 at 329–30.

32 Not all jurisdictions include sexual history evidence with the accused as part of their rape shield provision. See e.g. *R v A*, [2001] UKHL 25, where this part of *Seaboyer* was rejected by the House of Lords. See also Rule 412(b)(1)(b) of the *Federal Rules of Evidence* [*Fed R Evid*] in the United States, which exempts prior sexual history evidence with the accused as part of Rule 412's rape shield provision.

33 *Constitution Act, 1982*, s 35(1), being Schedule B to the *Canada Act 1982* (UK), 1982, c 11.

34 *Mitchell*, *supra* note 3 at para 27.

35 *Ibid* at para 30.

36 *Ibid.*

> Underlying the diverse rules on the admissibility of evidence are three simple ideas. First, the evidence must be useful in the sense of tending to prove a fact relevant to the issues in the case. Second, the evidence must be reasonably reliable; unreliable evidence may hinder the search for the truth more than help it. Third, even useful and reasonably reliable evidence may be excluded in the discretion of the trial judge if its probative value is overshadowed by its potential for prejudice.[37]

The identification of "reasonable reliability" by Chief Justice McLachlin is significant. It reflects her concern with ensuring that the rules of evidence facilitate the search for truth and protect against wrongful convictions. Generally speaking, our courts have not been prepared to embrace this as a threshold requirement, treating reliability, outside of exclusionary rules like hearsay and expert opinion evidence, as a question of weight rather than admissibility.[38] One recent exception to this is *R v Hart*, where the Supreme Court was tasked with creating a regulatory regime for the admissibility of confessions obtained during Mr Big police sting operations.[39] Justice Moldaver, for the majority, held, "[i]n this context, the confession's probative value turns on an assessment of its reliability."[40] It is unfortunate that the Court in *Hart* did not look to Chief Justice McLachlin's decision in *Mitchell*, which provided jurisprudential support for the approach the Court ultimately adopted. In light of *Mitchell*, and now *Hart*, it "seems clear that where there is reason to be concerned about the reliability of a particular type of evidence, a trial judge must now ensure that there is sufficient threshold reliability in the particular case to give the evidence the necessary probative value to warrant its admission."[41]

---

37 *Ibid.* It is unfortunate that, despite its importance, *Mitchell* does not appear to have ever been cited in an appellate criminal law evidence decision (a Quicklaw search noting the decision was conducted on 27 January 2019).

38 See e.g. *R v Mezzo*, [1986] 1 SCR 802; *R v Buric*, [1997] 1 SCR 535.

39 *R v Hart*, 2014 SCC 52 [*Hart*]. Mr Big stings are an elaborate endeavour where the police pose as a fictitious crime organization in an effort to convince a target to join in and eventually confess to an undercover officer posing as a crime boss (Mr Big) in order to move up within the organization. See Adelina Iftene, "The 'Hart' of the (Mr.) Big Problem" (2016) 63:1&2 CLQ 178.

40 *Hart*, *supra* note 39 at para 85.

41 David M Tanovich, "*R v Hart*: A Welcome New Emphasis on Reliability and Admissibility" (2014) 12 CR (7th) 298 at 303. Other commentators have also recognized that *Hart* and *Mitchell* have given increased prominence to thinking about threshold reliability to protect against wrongful convictions. See Louis P Strezos, "Unreasonable Verdicts and Tainted Eyewitness Identification Evidence: Let's Start Thinking about Probative Value" (2018) 47 CR (7th) 376; Nikos Harris, "Justice for All: The Implications of *Hart* and *Hay* for *Vetrovec* Witnesses," (2015) 22 CR (7th) 105.

Returning to her admissibility framework, Chief Justice McLachlin urged courts in *Mitchell* to be cognizant of the inherent subjectivity of the inquiry and to ensure that the judicial lens is conscious of the broader social context. As she noted:

> In determining the usefulness and reliability of oral histories, judges must resist facile assumptions based on Eurocentric traditions of gathering and passing on historical facts and traditions. Oral histories reflect the distinctive perspectives and cultures of the communities from which they originate and should not be discounted simply because they do not conform to the expectations of the non-aboriginal perspective.[42]

Mitchell is thus a call to action for incorporating relevant social context into the admissibility mix to ensure that our rules of evidence are applied in a culturally competent manner. What do I mean by "cultural competence"? The late professor Rose Voyvodic defined "cultural competence" as one's ability to "(1) recognize an awareness of humans, and oneself, as cultural beings who are prone to stereotyping; (2) acknowledge the harmful effects of discriminatory thinking and behaviour upon human interaction; and (3) acquire and perform the skills necessary to lessen the effect of these influences in order to serve the pursuit of justice."[43]

This acknowledgment of and taking steps to prevent stereotyping are vital components of McLachlin's "socially conscious" approach to law. It is a much-needed approach, given the inherent subjectivity of admitting and weighing evidence. The law of evidence is predominantly driven by inductive reasoning – relying on what we identify as common sense, logic, and generalization about human experience to decide questions of admissibility and to evaluate evidence. Inductive reasoning is largely a subjective enterprise, as it relies on the perspective of judges, in the case of applying precedent, or of the decision maker or trier of fact's common sense and understanding of how the world operates in any particular case.[44] This is exactly the danger that the Chief Justice was

---

42 *Mitchell*, *supra* note 3 at para 34.

43 Rose Voyvodic, "Lawyers Meet the Social Context: Understanding Cultural Competence" (2005) 84:3 Can Bar Rev 564.

44 See David M Tanovich, "Regulating Inductive Reasoning in Sexual Assault Cases," in *To Ensure that Justice Is Done: Essays in Memory of Marc Rosenberg*, ed Benjamin L Berger, Emma Cunliffe & James Stribopoulos (Toronto: Carswell, 2017) 75–7. See also David M Tanovich, "*Angelis*: Inductive Reasoning, Post-Offence Conduct and Intimate Femicide" (2013) 99 CR (6th) 338.

referring to in *Mitchell* – the discounting of the usefulness or reliability of Aboriginal oral history simply because that methodology does not conform to the expectations of non-Aboriginal perspectives.

We see this in her earlier decision in *W(R)*, where then Justice McLachlin observed, in relation to how courts should evaluate the testimony of children, that we must "approach the evidence of children not from the perspective of rigid stereotypes, but ... taking into account the strengths and weaknesses which characterize the evidence offered in the particular case."[45] Cultural competence is an awareness of the reality that inductive reasoning is a breeding ground for implicit bias as well as discriminatory and unreliable fact-finding, and that we need to take steps to protect the trial process from it. So how, then, can the McLachlin approach to evidence impact admissibility under *Corbett*?

III. Race, Stereotyping, and Section 12(1)

As noted earlier, in *Corbett*, the Supreme Court of Canada read in a discretion to section 12(1) of the *Canada Evidence Act* to limit cross-examination on an accused's criminal record. Justice LaForest, for the majority on this point, recognized a number of relevant factors for a trial judge to take into account when deciding whether to exercise that discretion, including:

- the nature of the prior conviction: offences relating to dishonesty are more probative of the issue of credibility;
- the similarity of the prior conviction to the charge(s) facing the accused: the more similar, the greater the danger that the jury will use the evidence for an improper purpose;
- the recency or remoteness of the prior conviction; and
- other relevant considerations, including whether the cross-examination is necessary to respond to a defence attack on the criminal record of the Crown witnesses, as occurred in *Corbett*.[46]

Corbett has generated hundreds of reported cases dealing with the application of these factors.[47] As of the writing of this chapter, there

45 *W(R)*, *supra* note 15 at 134.

46 For a comprehensive discussion of *Corbett*, see S Casey Hill, David M Tanovich & Louis P Strezos, eds, *McWilliams' Canadian Criminal Evidence*, 5th ed (Toronto: Thomson Reuters, 2018), 9:30.20.20.20.

47 See the discussion in Peter Sankoff, "*Corbett* Revisited: A Fairer Approach to the Admission of an Accused's Prior Criminal Record in Cross-Examination" (2006) 51:4

appears to be no reported case, however, that has considered the impact of stereotyping and racism in thinking about how to apply *Corbett*.[48]

In "'The Mis-Characterization of the Negro': A Race Critique of the Prior Conviction Impeachment Rule," Montré D. Carodine discusses the nature and impact of racial bias in the United States in the context of cross-examining an accused on his criminal record pursuant to Rule 609 of the *Federal Rules of Evidence*[49] (the equivalent to section 12(1) of the *Canada Evidence Act*):

> [R]ace plays a role in the continued viability of the "ancient assumption" that once someone is convicted of a crime, he is forever untrustworthy … Because of the mass incarceration of minority defendants, particularly Black defendants, race should be of paramount concern to scholars critiquing the theory and practice of impeachment with prior convictions. It is simply not enough to critique the rule as if it were race neutral.

CLQ 400; Peter Sankoff, "*Corbett*, Crimes of Dishonesty and the Credibility Contest: Challenging the Accepted Wisdom of What Makes a Prior Conviction Probative" (2006) 10:3 CLQ 215; and Peter Sankoff, "*R v Laing*: Two Major Steps Backward on *Corbett* Applications" (2017) 33 CR (7th) 33 at 64.

48 A Quicklaw search (January 2019) with the key words "Corbett," "criminal record," and "racism," and "Corbett" and "stereotyping" revealed no relevant cases.

49 Fed R Evid, *supra* note 32, Rule 609 reads:

Rule 609 – Impeachment by Evidence of a Criminal Conviction

(a) In General. The following rules apply to attacking a witness's character for truthfulness by evidence of a criminal conviction:

(1) for a crime that, in the convicting jurisdiction, was punishable by death or by imprisonment for more than one year, the evidence:

(A) must be admitted, subject to *Rule 403*, in a civil case or in a criminal case in which the witness is not a defendant; and

(B) must be admitted in a criminal case in which the witness is a defendant, if the probative value of the evidence outweighs its prejudicial effect to that defendant; and

(2) for any crime regardless of the punishment, the evidence must be admitted if the court can readily determine that establishing the elements of the crime required proving – or the witness's admitting – a dishonest act or false statement.

(b) Limit on Using the Evidence After 10 Years. This subdivision (b) applies if more than 10 years have passed since the witness's conviction or release from confinement for it, whichever is later. Evidence of the conviction is admissible only if:

(1) its probative value, supported by specific facts and circumstances, substantially outweighs its prejudicial effect; and

(2) the proponent gives an adverse party reasonable written notice of the intent to use it so that the party has a fair opportunity to contest its use.

> A rule such as Rule 609, which almost ensures convictions based simply on a defendant's prior record, is particularly disturbing when one considers the plight of Blacks in the criminal justice system. Once a Black person is convicted of a crime (a likely scenario given the current statistics), that conviction will help to convict him again if he is ever charged with another crime (another very likely outcome given the "repeat offender" statistics for Blacks). Rules such as Rule 609 keep Blacks ensnared in the criminal system, perpetuating the criminalization of a staggering percentage of the Black population.[50]

Anna Roberts makes a similar point:

> Critics have noted the disparate effects of this rule on vulnerable groups. First, impeachment by prior conviction not only resembles a second punishment, but also, like other consequences of conviction, threatens to ensure that those who have one conviction face tremendous obstacles in avoiding a second one. Second, due to uneven distributions of criminal convictions, and because of race-based assumptions of guilt, the rule disproportionately affects people of color.[51]

Applying *Mitchell*'s cultural competence lens, social conditions and racial bias should be a relevant consideration in the application of *Corbett*. Interestingly, support comes from two non-evidence McLachlin decisions: *Sauvé* and *Williams*.

a. Sauvé v Canada (Chief Electoral Officer) *(2002)*

The issue in *Sauvé* was the constitutionality of the denial of the right to vote for federally incarcerated inmates. The government conceded that the prohibition contained in section 51(e) of the *Canada Elections Act* violated section 3 of the *Charter*.[52] The issue before the Supreme Court was whether it constituted a reasonable limit under section 1 of the *Charter*. In concluding that it did not, Chief Justice McLachlin

---

50 Montré D Carodine, "'The Mis-Characterization of the Negro': A Race Critique of the Prior Conviction Impeachment Rule" (2009) 84:2 Indiana LJ 521 at 525–6 [footnotes omitted].

51 Anna Roberts, "Impeachment by Unreliable Conviction" (2014) 55:2 Boston College LR 576 [footnotes omitted]. See also Anna Roberts, "Reclaiming the Importance of the Defendant's Testimony: Prior Conviction Impeachment and the Fight against Implicit Stereotyping" (2016) 83:2 Univ of Chicago LR 835.

52 *Canada Elections Act*, *supra* note 4, s 51(e).

recognized that the "negative effects of s. 51(e) upon prisoners have a disproportionate impact on Canada's already disadvantaged Aboriginal population, whose overrepresentation in prisons reflects a crisis in the Canadian criminal justice system,"[53] because, to the "extent that the disproportionate number of Aboriginal people in penitentiaries reflects factors such as higher rates of poverty and institutionalized alienation from mainstream society, penitentiary imprisonment may not be a fair or appropriate marker of the degree of individual culpability."[54]

One could argue, based on *Sauvé*, that we should be cautious about being too willing to infer that the criminal record of an Indigenous or racialized individual is a reliable indicator of their willingness to be truthful when testifying. The Canadian Civil Liberties Association makes this exact point in the context of prior criminal records and judicial interim release in its report *Set Up to Fail: Bail and the Revolving Door of Pre-Trial Detention*,[55] wherein the authors note that "courts should view prior convictions as systemically motivated rather than as intentional disregard for the law, particularly in relation to prior breaches of court orders."[56]

The need for courts to recognize this social reality in applying *Corbett* is evident, given the very troubling statement by the trial judge in the oft-cited *Corbett* case of *R v Saroya*.[57] In that case, a trial judge permitted the Crown to cross-examine an accused, who appears to be racialized, on his criminal record, observing that "[a] man wears the chains he forges in life."[58] In addition to the very problematic image of slavery and colonialism that this judicial comment invokes, Chief Justice McLachlin in *Sauvé* reminds us that, for Indigenous and racialized individuals, the "chains" are more often imposed by modern-day social conditions rather than the product of free will. While the Court of Appeal for Ontario held that the trial judge had misstated part of the *Corbett* test, it failed to comment on this statement by the judge.

In addition, Indigenous, Black, and Brown offenders are disproportionately impacted by the cross-examination rule, given that they are

---

53 *Sauvé, supra* note 9 at para 60 [footnotes omitted].

54 *Ibid.*

55 Abby Deshman and Nicole Myers, *Set Up to Fail: Bail and the Revolving Door of Pre-Trial Detention* (Toronto: Canadian Civil Liberties Association, 2014), online: <ccla.org/dev/v5/_doc/CCLA_set_up_to_fail.pdf>.

56 *Ibid* at 78.

57 *R v Saroya* (1994), 36 CR (4th) 253, 76 OAC 25 (Ont CA). As of 27 January 2019, the case has been cited in sixty decisions (Quicklaw database).

58 *R v Saroya* (1992), 18 CR (4th) 198 (Ont Ct J (Gen Div)) at para 14. I draw the conclusion that the accused is racialized based on his name, Iqbal Singh Saroya.

over-policed.[59] Because of this reality, they are more likely to have a record for street crimes or police interaction crimes than is a similarly situated white offender. Thus, a criminal record is arguably less an indication of the accused's commitment to veracity and more about another manifestation of structural racism.

b. R v Williams *(1998)*

In *Williams*, the issue was whether the accused, who was Indigenous, was denied a fair trial because of the refusal of the trial judge to allow a race-based challenge for cause.[60] Justice McLachlin, as she then was, agreed that it was an unfair trial. In holding that the accused was entitled to challenge prospective jurors for racial bias, she recognized the existence of systemic racism – and, in particular, anti-Indigenous bias – in the criminal justice system. She held that "racism against aboriginals includes stereotypes that relate to credibility, worthiness and criminal propensity,"[61] and that

> [r]acist stereotypes may affect how jurors assess the credibility of the accused. Bias can shape the information received during the course of the trial to conform with the bias … Jurors harbouring racial prejudices may consider those of the accused's race less worthy or perceive a link between those of the accused's race and crime in general. In this manner, subconscious racism may make it easier to conclude that a black

---

59 For judicial recognition of over-policing of Black, Indigenous, and other racialized communities, and other issues of race and criminal justice, see *Le, supra* note 8 at paras 74–97; *McKay v Toronto Police Services Board*, 2011 HRTO 499. See also the discussion in Lorne Foster et al, *Racial Profiling and Human Rights in Canada: The New Legal Landscape* (Toronto: Irwin Law, 2018).

60 An accused is entitled to challenge prospective jurors for cause under the *Criminal Code* when they can establish a realistic potential of partiality based on race. Williams wanted to ask each prospective juror the following questions:

> 1. Would your ability to judge the evidence in the case without bias, prejudice, or partiality be affected by the fact that the person charged is an Indian?
> 2. Would your ability to judge the evidence in the case without bias, prejudice, or partiality be affected by the fact that the person charged is an Indian and the complainant is white?

Williams was initially allowed to ask these questions, and twelve out of the forty-three potential jurors questioned were dismissed for racial bias. However, a mistrial was declared because of procedural issues surrounding the jury selection process. Williams was not allowed to challenge for cause based on racial bias at his new trial.

61 *Williams, supra* note 8 at para 58.

or aboriginal accused engaged in the crime regardless of the race of the complainant.[62]

All of this can be used to support an argument that the prejudicial effect of allowing cross-examination on an Indigenous or a Black or other racialized accused's criminal record will be significant, as the record is likely to trigger unconscious bias, especially where the crime corresponds to the stereotype.

In *Corbett*, the Supreme Court left open the possibility that other relevant considerations could inform the exercise of discretion read into section 12(1) of the *Canada Evidence Act*. Justice La Forest noted that it was "impossible to provide an exhaustive catalogue of the factors that are relevant in assessing the probative value or potential prejudice of such evidence."[63] So how could *Corbett* be applied in cases involving Indigenous or Black or Brown accused? I would argue that a strict application of *Corbett* should be applied and that cross-examination on a prior criminal record should rarely take place. Returning back to the *Corbett* factors and infusing them with the McLachlin principle and her decisions in *Sauvé* and *Williams* leaves one with the following considerations:

- **The nature of the prior conviction:** Does it relate to property offences, guns, gangs, drugs, breach of recognizance, or obstructing/assaulting police? If yes, there should be no cross-examination on it. Indigenous, Black, and Brown communities are over-policed in relation to these offences, and, therefore, these convictions are likely the result of differential policing and racial profiling. These are also offences that are likely to trigger stereotypes about young men in these communities.

62 *Ibid* at para 28. Similarly, in *Spence*, *supra* note 8, the Supreme Court quoted with approval the recognition, in *Parks*, *supra* note 8, of systemic anti-Black racism in our criminal justice system. Justice Binnie, for the Court, held (at paras 31–2):

Doherty J.A. concluded on the first step that "[r]acism, and in particular anti-black racism, is a part of our community's psyche" (p. 369). He continued:

> A significant segment of our community holds overtly racist views. A much larger segment subconsciously operates on the basis of negative racial stereotypes. Furthermore, our institutions, including the criminal justice system, reflect and perpetuate those negative stereotypes. These elements combine to infect our society as a whole with the evil of racism. Blacks are among the primary victims of that evil. (p. 369)

The studies cited by Doherty JA amply support his conclusion that the use of negative racist stereotypes is widespread in our society. (A more recent Angus Reid poll suggested that 45 percent of Canadians identify visible minorities, particularly Blacks and Vietnamese, with crime: see *Koh* at paras 9 and 22).

63 *Corbett*, *supra* note 4 at para 154.

- **The similarity of the prior conviction to the current charge:** If similar, there should be no cross-examination on it, as racial bias increases the likelihood of propensity reasoning.
- **Other relevant considerations, including whether there are racial dynamics to the case:** One consideration would be, for example, where the Crown's case rests largely on the evidence of a white complainant or on police testimony – in other words, cases where some jurors might view or construct the case as one of "us versus them." If that is the case, there should be no eliciting of the prior criminal record.

IV. Conclusion

In *Williams*, Chief Justice McLachlin recognized that the effects of racism are "as invasive and elusive as they are corrosive."[64] In her 2002 extra-judicial piece "Racism and the Law: The Canadian Experience," she urged that "courts can and should take proactive steps to recognize racism and prevent it from compromising trials and thereby marring the justice system."[65] This perspective was echoed recently in *Barton*, where the Supreme Court noted that "our criminal justice system and all participants within it should take reasonable steps to address systemic biases, prejudices, and stereotypes ... head on."[66] In her more than two decades on the Supreme Court of Canada, Beverley McLachlin crafted an approach to the law of evidence that can regulate implicit bias and ensure that it does not mar the justice system. A good start is for our courts to start applying the McLachlin principle to *Corbett* applications involving Indigenous and racialized accused. By doing so, we can begin to give effect to her vision of a law of evidence capable of combatting stereotyping and facilitating justice.

---

64 *Williams*, *supra* note 8 at para 22. She further held (at para 21 [footnotes omitted]) that:

> [R]acial prejudice interfering with jurors' impartiality is a form of discrimination. It involves making distinctions on the basis of class or category without regard to individual merit. It rests on preconceptions and unchallenged assumptions that unconsciously shape the daily behaviour of individuals. Buried deep in the human psyche, these preconceptions cannot be easily and effectively identified and set aside, even if one wishes to do so. For this reason, it cannot be assumed that judicial directions to act impartially will always effectively counter racial prejudice.

65 The Right Honourable Beverley McLachlin, "Racism and the Law: The Canadian Experience" (2002) 1 JL & Equality 22.

66 *Barton*, *supra* note 8 at para 200. The issue in *Barton* was stereotypes against Indigenous women and sex workers. The Court proposed judicial instructions to address this issue in future cases (at para 201).

8 The Continuity of Private and Public Law Reasoning in Chief Justice McLachlin's Criminal Law Judgments

GRAHAM MAYEDA

I. Introduction

Humans are fascinated and puzzled by the night sky, and we have imagined many ways to bring order to the apparent chaos that we see when we look up on a clear night. The law is somewhat like this: it is a chaotic universe in which the stars, galaxies, and black holes consist of judgments, professional and academic commentary, and the everyday understanding of the law in practice. Each of us finds our own way to create order within this chaos: some search out unifying principles; others discern an evolutionary structure in which past judgments give rise to present ones; still others see the law as periods of calm punctuated by revolutions. In the case of judges, having a general way of framing the chaotic universe of the law seems particularly important, given their role in creating the next star or galaxy and avoiding black holes. Examining the judgments of Chief Justice McLachlin, one can discern a style of reasoning that hints at the structure she has given to the law. This chapter attempts to describe that structure, which I argue is based on a common law model of principled incremental change.

Commentators and the public often begin from the premise that judges have particular political views to which they give effect in their judgments.[1] For instance, in his portrait of Chief Justice McLachlin in the *Globe and Mail*, Sean Fine describes her as a "classic liberal."[2] While

1 James Stribopoulos & Moin A Yahya, "Does a Judge's Party of Appointment or Gender Matter to Case Outcomes? An Empirical Study of the Court of Appeal for Ontario" (2007) 45:2 Osgoode Hall LJ 315; Benjamin Alarie & Andrew James Green, "Policy Preference Change and Appointments to the Supreme Court of Canada" (2009) 47:1 Osgoode Hall LJ 1.

2 Sean Fine, "How Beverley McLachlin Found Her Bliss: Where She Came From and What She Leaves Behind," *Globe and Mail* (12 January 2018), online: <https://

this might be an accurate characterization of her judgments, which have generally promoted liberal democracy, a study of them suggests that she did not set out to promote a particular set of values. Instead, she adopted a method of interpretation and reasoning to solve legal problems; the promotion of liberal values was simply the result of using this methodology, because the common law is itself based on these values.[3] Thus it is not that the Chief Justice is a "classic liberal," but rather that her judgments are a development of classic liberal ideas *as a result of* her deployment of a particular mode of legal reasoning and legal problem solving in them.

Theorists and public law jurists frequently separate public and private law and ascribe to each area a unique form of reasoning. Public lawyers tend to consider the law to be the deployment of public law values – broad principles that can be found in constitutions, both written and unwritten. Private lawyers tend to view principles as emerging organically as a result of the evolutionary development of the law.[4] But this division is artificial, as the Chief Justice's criminal law judgments in the 1990s demonstrate. In the cases from this period examined in this

---

www.theglobeandmail.com/news/national/beverley-mclachlin-profile/article 37588525/>. Fine writes, "[a]fter a few short years on the court, [the Chief Justice] had made it clear where she was headed: She was a classical liberal – embracing an essentially conservative view that protected individual freedoms, whether of speech or of control over one's death, against encroachments from the state. And conversely, on the small-l liberal side, she displayed a willingness to view legal claims from the vantage point of the vulnerable."

3 For a stimulating account of the relationship between the rule of law, a fundamental principle of the common law, and liberalism, see Brian Z Tamanaha, "The Dark Side of the Relationship between the Rule of Law and Liberalism" (2008) 3:3 NYUJ L & Liberty 516; see also David Dyzenhaus's discussion of Ronald Dworkin's account of the relationship between the rule of law and liberal principles in "The Rule of Law as the Rule of Liberal Principle" in Arthur Ripstein, ed, *Ronald Dworkin* (Cambridge: Cambridge University Press, 2007) 56. Dyzenhaus explains that, while there are many varieties of "liberals," libertarian liberals, whose interest is primarily the protection of negative freedom, and "egalitarian liberals," who consider the protection of equality to be the primary goal of the legal system, both share the view that core liberal principles should be protected from "majoritarian decision making" (at 70–1). I think this accords well with the liberal democratic values that Fine identifies with Justice McLachlin's jurisprudence.

4 For a classic statement of the private law view, see *Home Office v Dorset Yacht Co Ltd*, [1970] AC 1004 at 1140 (HL (Eng)) [*Dorset Yacht*]; Ernest J Weinrib describes this method in "The Disintegration of Duty" in M Stuart Madden, ed, *Exploring Tort Law* (Cambridge: Cambridge University Press) 143 at 181–2; see also Graham Mayeda, "Uncommonly Common: The Nature of Common Law Judgment" (2006) 19:1 Can JL & Jur 107.

chapter, we will see that a common law method for interpreting and reasoning about the law can be deployed in both private and public law cases, making it a legal method that unifies what are often erroneously considered separate fields.

The identification of a particular method of reasoning as characteristic of the Chief Justice's criminal law judgments is not intended to cast her approach as mechanistic or to suggest that she did not have an eye on the result. The common law method is itself based on liberal values, and so using it necessarily evokes them; but the method is also open to social change, and so it has the flexibility to adapt to new social and political circumstances. Common law reasoning demands cogent and logical argument; but it also requires the practitioner to identify the norms that provide unity to judgments about a particular issue through time. It is also essential that a judge using the method be willing to reflect on how these norms should adapt to the times. The method does not directly promote specific political or social values, but it does incorporate them into law in so far as they are necessary for interpreting and applying it in a way that is appropriate today.[5]

The common law approach to public law that emerges from the Chief Justice's public law jurisprudence does not fit any particular theoretical model. She is not Ronald Dworkin's Hercules, deciding hard cases by applying political norms in a novel way to conquer new situations:[6] the Chief Justice did not intentionally deploy political norms in the legal field. She is also not a natural law theorist who applies universal norms to particular cases. Some have characterized the "McLachlin Court" between 2002 and 2017 as "deferential," devoted to deferring to the political judgment of legislators.[7] In my assessment, this is also a mischaracterization: the Chief Justice is not a positivist in the sense that the label of "deference" implies.[8] The judicial method she deploys does not

5 Ronald Dworkin explains that there is "positive law" (the "law in the books" and the law "declared in the clear statements of statutes and past court decisions") and the "full law," which he describes as "the set of principles of political morality that taken together provide the best interpretation of the positive law" ("Law's Ambitions for Itself" (1985) 71:2 Virginia L Rev 176).

6 Ronald Dworkin uses this metaphor in *Taking Rights Seriously* (Cambridge, MA: Harvard University Press, 1977).

7 Sheila McIntyre, "The Equality Jurisprudence of the McLachlin Court: Back to the 70s" in Sanda Rodgers and Sheila McIntyre, eds, *The Supreme Court of Canada and Social Justice: Commitment, Retrenchment or Retreat* (Toronto: LexisNexis, 2010) 129.

8 For a discussion of the role of deference at the Supreme Court of Canada, see Kent Roach, *The Supreme Court on Trial: Judicial Activism or Democratic Dialogue* (Toronto: Irwin Law, 2001).

require judges to simply identify and then give effect to legislators' intentions;[9] rather, the method recognizes that interpreting law inevitably depends on weaving the words of legislators into the fabric of the law.[10] This is a traditional common law approach, which aims at integrating new cases with the old by means of expansion or contraction of a principle derived from the latter.

Following this introduction, this chapter has three parts. In the first part (II), I describe the principal theories about the nature of public law adjudication, which include theories that separate public and private (common) law and theories that consider the two to be integrated. At the end of that section, I propose as a hypothesis that the Chief Justice's approach to public law acknowledges a continuity between public and private law that manifests as a particular mode of interpreting and reasoning about law. In the next part, I survey a few of the Chief Justice's public law judgments from the 1990s with a particular focus on criminal law judgments. I have chosen this focus for two reasons: first, the Chief Justice's contribution to criminal law has had a significant influence on the Court's approach to criminal law in this century;[11] second, I focus on criminal law because it is a paradigmatic example of public law, and yet it has its origins in the common law, making it a perfect illustration of the continuity of public and common law. In the last part, I zoom out from an analysis of specific judgments and draw in broad strokes the features of the Chief Justice's approach to public law adjudication. As we will see, it is characterized by a particular form of legal reasoning rather than a commitment to specific substantive political and social values. However, a consequence of the Chief Justice's method has been

---

9 Jeremy Bentham, a classic positivist, used legislation as his model for legality. Thus the common law was only truly law, he argued, to the degree that it resembled statute and was created and enforced by an exercise of public power (JH Burns & HLA Hart, eds, *Comment on the Commentaries and a Fragment on Government* (London: Athlone Press, 1977) at 232); see also Mayeda, *supra* note 4 at 109; David Dyzenhaus, "Process and Substance as Aspects of the Public Law Form" (2015) 74:2 Cambridge LJ 284 at 292.

10 In my view, this is very different than what Dworkin proposed, which is to interpret legislation in light of constitutional norms (*supra* note 6 at 108; see also Dyzenhaus, *supra* note 3 at 64).

11 For an assessment of the McLachlin Court's contribution to criminal law, see Don Stuart, "Criminal Justice in the McLachlin Court: Many More Kudos than Brickbats" in David A Wright & Adam M Dodek, eds, *Public Law at the McLachlin Court: The First Decade* (Toronto: Irwin Law, 2011) 329. For a critical assessment of the Supreme Court's record from the perspective of the protection of equality, see Elizabeth Sheehy, "Equality and Supreme Court Criminal Jurisprudence: Never the Twain Shall Meet" in Rodgers & McIntyre, eds, *supra* note 7.

to support and further develop the liberal democratic norms that are the foundation of the common law and, in modern times, public law.

Why examine the use of common law reasoning in public law? First, Chief Justice McLachlin's criminal law judgments during the first ten years of her career on the Supreme Court of Canada adopted this approach, which differed markedly from that of other judges who also wrote in this area, such as Chief Justice Antonio Lamer and Justice Peter Cory. Second, the subject is of theoretical interest because the common law approach to public law is currently out of fashion. In this regard, the Chief Justice's judgments from this period demonstrate how to use this approach in actual judgments and permit us to evaluate its utility.

II. Theories about the Continuity and Discontinuity between Public and Private Law

Theories about the nature of public law fall into roughly two categories: theories that separate public law from private law,[12] and theories that recognize the continuity between the two. The thesis of this chapter is that Justice McLachlin's judgments in criminal law cases, a classic area of public law,[13] use common law reasoning, and are thus an example of the Chief Justice's tacit acceptance of the continuity of public and private law. In this regard, her judgments differ in approach from

---

12 A very forceful statement of the division between the two was made by Lord Woolf of Barnes, who wrote:

> We have now a developed set of distinct public law principles which are of general application, independent of private law and comparable to those of civil jurisdictions; that, while the principles are enforced by the High Court, with its extensive private law jurisdiction and not a separate supreme public or administrative law tribunal, the High Court when applying those principles is not exercising its normal jurisdiction. It is exercising a quite separate jurisdiction: its inherent power to review administrative action. ("Droit Public: English Style" (1995) Public L 57.)

13 By a "classic area of public law," I mean that modern Canadian criminal law is contained mainly in statute, and so its legitimacy is derived from the legitimacy of the state in creating and enforcing it. Malcolm Thorburn explains that a public law account of criminal law "conceives of the operations of the criminal justice system ... as concerned with the basic question of public law: when the use of state power is legitimate" ("Criminal Law as Public Law" in RA Duff & Stuart Green, eds, *Philosophical Foundations of Criminal* Law (Oxford: Oxford University Press, 2011) 21 at 24). Of course, as we will see, the origins of the criminal law are in the common law, and even its modern development is characterized by a fusion of common law and public law reasoning.

those of other judges who are less sensitive to the incrementalism that characterizes the common law. Before providing evidence to support this thesis, let us first examine various theories about the separation between private and public law and describe the peculiar features of common law reasoning.

The separation of public and private law has a long history in the United Kingdom and its former colonies, and the distinction subsists to this day. For instance, in *Vancouver (City) v Ward*,[14] a case in which Ward sued the City of Vancouver and the Province of British Columbia for breaching his *Charter* right to be secure from unreasonable search and seizure, the Supreme Court of Canada was careful to distinguish private law damages from constitutional (public law) damages. It quoted Thomas J, then a judge of the New Zealand Court of Appeal, who explained that an action for public law damages "is not a private law action in the nature of a tort claim for which the state is vicariously liable but [a distinct] public law action directly against the state for which the state is primarily liable."[15] The policy considerations relevant to an award of public law damages are different than those relevant in private law; for instance, the harm caused to society and the need to deter public officials from committing future breaches of the Constitution can be taken into account in the public law context, although they are not relevant in tort law.[16]

The division between public law and private law, common in civil law jurisdictions, has its origins in Roman law. In Justinian's *Digest*, we read, "There are two branches of legal study: public and private law. Public law is that which respects the establishment of the Roman commonwealth, private that which respects individuals' interests, some matters being of public and others of private interest."[17] In common law jurisdictions, the distinction emerged only once the statute came into regular use for creating law. Indeed, many areas of what we now consider classic public law, such as administrative law and criminal law, have their origins in the common law. However, as statute law became more prevalent, contemporary legal scholars distinguished between the source of authority of statute and of common law. For instance, Blackstone wrote that the authority of statute derived from

14 *Vancouver (City) v Ward*, 2010 SCC 27 [*Vancouver v Ward*].

15 *Dunlea v Attorney-General*, [2000] NZCA 84, [2000] 3 NZLR 136 at para 81; quoted in *Vancouver v Ward*, *supra* note 14 at para 22.

16 *Vancouver v Ward*, *supra* note 14 at paras 28–9.

17 Alan Watson, *The Digest of Justinian*, vol 1 (Philadelphia: University of Pennsylvania Press, 2009) at D, 1, 1, 1, 2.

the "intrinsic authority" of Parliament,[18] while the authority of common law rules derived from their "long and immemorial usage, and by their universal reception throughout the kingdom."[19] Further, disputes arising out of statutes were subject to a different form of adjudication than was common with disputes in the common law. As T.R.S. Allan explains,

> the distinction between statute and common law may appear to entrench the division between competing ideals, leading in turn to the need for sharply differentiated styles of adjudication, according to the source of law involved. Enacted rules can enable us to ascertain most clearly what is lawfully required or permitted or prohibited: the canonical text reduces, even if it cannot eliminate, the scope for argument. Common law adjudication, by contrast, is more characteristic of equity: it permits a decision closely attuned to the particular circumstances, leaving wide discretion to the judge in making his appraisal.[20]

Legal theorists soon seized on the difference between statute and common law to further drive a wedge between statute law, which was considered primarily public in nature, and common law, which was viewed as dealing predominantly with disputes between private parties. Famous proponents of the difference between statute and common law were Thomas Hobbes and Jeremy Bentham. Thus, Hobbes wrote in his *Dialogue*, "Statutes are not Philosophy as is the Common-Law, and other disputable Arts, but are Commands, or Prohibitions,"[21] by which he meant that statutes set out the law in a publicly accessible manner, whereas common law rules were merely "philosophy," i.e., the "private conjectures" of judges.[22] In a similar vein, Bentham explained that

---

18 William Blackstone, *Commentaries on the Laws of England*, vol 1 (New York, 1827) at 54; see the discussion of this in Jeffrey Goldsworthy, "The Myth of the Common Law Constitution" in Douglas E Edlin, ed, *Common Law Theory* (Cambridge: Cambridge University Press, 2007) 204 at 227–8.

19 Blackstone, *supra* note 18 at 42.

20 TRS Allan, "Text, Context, and Constitution: The Common Law as Public Reason" in Douglas E Edlin, ed, *Common Law Theory* (Cambridge: Cambridge University Press, 2007) 185 at 187. Allan goes on to point out that the difference is not always clear, because the interpretation of statutes often involves consideration of factors also relevant to deciding specific cases, as occurs in the common law.

21 Thomas Hobbes, *Dialogue between a Philosopher and a Student of the Common Laws of England*, ed Joseph Cropsey (Chicago: University of Chicago Press, 1971) at 69.

22 Gerald J Postema, *The Oxford Handbook of Jurisprudence and Philosophy of Law* (Oxford: Oxford University Press, 2004) at 616.

common law is not authoritative precisely because common law rules are inferences from a set of cases none of which may explicitly set out the rule.[23] In contrast, proper law, by which he meant primarily statute law, is an expression of the lawmaker's volition.[24]

Martin Loughlin is a modern advocate of the separation between public law and private law.[25] In *Foundations of Public Law*, he explains that public law is animated by the political principles that support a particular sovereign state.[26] On this view, "[p]olitical right might … be conceived to be the 'true' law of the state. Public law – the law of governmental ordering – becomes the expression of political right."[27] A judge who adopts this approach to public law would first identify the principles such as liberty, respect for diversity, democracy, and so on that underlie and support the state, and then, having identified them, would deploy them in public law judgments. Loughlin himself identifies two such principles: power and liberty. According to Loughlin, public law is a system that actualizes through legal practice the tension between these principles.[28] He contrasts this approach with that of Immanuel Kant and his proponents, for whom principles are derived from morality rather than being political principles.[29]

In contrast to theories that separate public law from private (common) law are theories that acknowledge the continuity between them. These largely fall into two categories: theories in which the continuity of public and private law is based on the fact that they share certain basic values, and theories in which the continuity is explained by a shared practice, such as a form of reasoning or shared institutions (for instance, generalist courts that decide both public and private law matters). The first category has many adherents, from natural law theorists to human rights theorists: natural law theorists recognize certain universal moral

23 Jeremy Bentham, *Of Laws in General*, ed HLA Hart (London: Athlone Press, 1970) at 152–3, 192.

24 *Ibid* at 43, 9–10; also HLA Hart, "Bentham's *Of Laws in* General" (1971) Cambrian L Rev 24 at 28.

25 Loughlin writes that the public law is "an autonomous subject operating in accordance with its own distinctive method" (Martin Loughlin, *The Idea of Public Law* (Oxford: Oxford University Press, 2010) at 153). By this he means that law is "an expression of sovereignty" rather than "a restriction on it" (at 133); it is "an expression of the immanent precepts of an autonomous discourse of politics" (at 145).

26 Martin Loughlin, *The Foundations of Public Law* (Oxford: Oxford University Press, 2010) at 86.

27 *Ibid* at 159.

28 *Ibid* at 178.

29 *Ibid* at 87.

principles as fundamental to both systems; human rights theorists derive these principles not from natural law but from generally accepted contemporary values such as those that underlie human rights or those that are contained in basic tenets of certain legal systems. Natural law theorists include John Finnis, who derives the basic rights of a legal system from the obligation to participate in a human community that is committed to achieving the common goods that he identifies.[30] In contrast, Ronald Dworkin rejects a natural law approach in favour of one in which valid judicial decisions are those that are consistent with the values underlying the liberal democratic system as a whole.[31] Lon Fuller's approach is similar to Dworkin's, but he locates the source of norms not in the principles of liberal democracy but rather in the very nature of law itself.[32]

Mark D. Walters points to the views of A.V. Dicey as an example of a theorist who posits that the continuity of public and private law is based on a shared form of reasoning rather than on shared values. According to Walters, Dicey was of the view that public law relies on a particular mode of legal interpretation and reasoning derived from the common law.[33] He writes, "embedded implicitly within the final version of [A.V. Dicey's] *Law of the Constitution*, is a theory of the rule of law that is based not upon the supremacy of ordinary law as such but on the supremacy of the *ordinary interpretive process* or the *ordinary legal method* that is a distinctive part of legal discourse generally."[34] Another proponent of this approach to the continuity of public law and common law is T.R.S. Allan, who concisely summarizes his view as follows: "Beneath and beyond our various constitutional enactments, including our modern charters and bills of rights, lies a *common law constitution* – a set of ideas and assumptions about the nature and conditions of legality, which, in turn, define the character of legitimate government."[35] Allan

30 John Finnis, *Natural Law and Natural Rights* (Oxford: Clarendon Press, 1980).

31 Ronald Dworkin, *Law's Empire* (Cambridge, MA: Harvard University Press, 1986) at 228–57; for a description of his approach, see Mark D Walters, "Public Law and Ordinary Legal Method: Revisiting Dicey's Approach to *Droit Administratif*" (2016) 66:1 UTLJ 53 at 78; see also Dyzenhaus, *supra* note 3.

32 Dyzenhaus, *supra* note 3 at 74.

33 Walters, *supra* note 31.

34 *Ibid* at 57, 77. Walters' characterization of Dicey is more complex than this because he teases out of Dicey's work a tendency to regard general principles as emerging through the process of interpreting and applying law. He says that Dicey "edged toward an interpretivist theory of law and legality" (*ibid* at 78).

35 TRS Allan, "The Moral Unity of Public Law" (2017) 67 UTLJ 1 at 1.

identifies a particular process of legal reasoning derived from his notion of common law constitutionalism. He writes:

> If common law adjudication provides a model of legal reasoning about individual rights, we may draw an analogy with Rawlsian reflective equilibrium. We move between abstract statements of fundamental rights, on the one hand, and the specific illustrations of them provided by judicial precedent, on the other, seeking harmony between the two. The constitutional principles we invoke must justify the precedents we take to be correctly decided, supplying cogent moral reasons; and the precedents must have plausibility as examples of legitimate decision making, consonant with our convictions about the general character of a just legal order.[36]

Allan explains that common law reasoning involves, first, the identification in precedent-setting cases of an abstract principle that provides a normative justification for the decisions, followed by the second step: a verification of whether this principle is consistent with our current view of a just legal order.

However, there are more steps to common law reasoning than the two identified by Allan. In the famous tort law case of *Home Office v Dorset Yacht Co Ltd*,[37] Lord Diplock describes the process as involving three stages:

1 Identification of a principle through "analytical and inductive" reasoning. The judge examines past authoritative cases and extracts a common principle or argument that explains the decisions arrived at in each. This stage involves "inductive reasoning" because it requires generalizing from a set of actual cases.[38]
2 Determining whether the case confronting the judge is one to which the principle applies. This stage is "deductive and analytical" because it involves applying the general principle or argument identified at the first step.
3 Where a case does not clearly fit the principle, the judge makes a policy decision as to whether the principle should be altered so that the novel case can be classed with the other authoritative ones under the reinterpreted rule. Lord Diplock emphasizes that the policy

---

36 *Ibid* at 5–6.

37 *Dorset Yacht*, *supra* note 4.

38 This inductive step is also part of the common law method as described by John Gardner in "Some Types of Law" in D Edlin, ed, *Common Law Theory* (New York: Cambridge University Press, 2007) 51 at 75–6.

> decision should not develop the common law too far; rather, the modified principle must be "influenced by the same general conception of what ought to give rise [to a particular legal rule] as was used in [the old cases]."[39]

While Allan uses "the general character of a just legal order" – i.e., political values – as a touchstone for deciding whether to extend and apply a principle to a new case, Lord Diplock emphasizes that the normative source is not political but legal: it is to be found in past cases (in the case of a common law decision), and the extension of the principle to include a new factual situation should be of the "same general conception" as the old principle.

While the origins of much of Canadian criminal law is in the common law, statutes dominate today, and judges' powers are diminished: judges cannot create new offences, but they can continue to develop defences and other criminal law rules and principles that are not inconsistent with the *Criminal Code*.[40] As we will see, the common law method can be applied even in areas that are primarily regulated by statute, such as criminal law. The only difference between public and private law is that the process of determining the principles that underlie a statutory provision does not involve induction (generalization from a series of cases), as is the case with the common law contained in judicial decisions, but rather the application of the principles of statutory interpretation to legislative provisions by judges over time in an iterative process.[41] On this view, statutes and common law are unified into a coherent legal system by respect for certain basic norms such as the rule of law.[42] As Allan explains, the purpose of the "various canons of interpretation that guide the construction of statutes in common law practice play an important role in the reconciliation of legislative policy and basic justice."[43] The rules of statutory interpretation are thus "the means of seeking an accommodation between statutory objective and constitutional principle."[44] The other steps of the method are the same: a court must deduce if a particular statutory provision applies, and, as social circumstances change, the court may reinterpret the law

39 *Dorset Yacht*, *supra* note 4 at 1140.

40 See the combined effects of sections 8 and 9 of the *Criminal Code*, RSC 1985, c C-46.

41 Gardner, *supra* note 38 at 55 and 57.

42 Allan, *supra* note 35 at 4.

43 *Ibid* at 5.

44 *Ibid*.

to cover new cases, either by reinterpreting principles or reformulating them.[45]

As we have seen, the common law approach requires identifying a principle by induction from past cases or by interpreting a statute and ensuring that the principle evolves in an appropriate way. Allan suggests that this be done by using political values as a touchstone. In contrast, as we have seen, Lord Diplock proposes that the touchstone be the old principle itself. In all cases, changes to the governing principle must be incremental: indeed, it is this requirement of *incrementalism* that is a defining characteristic of Chief Justice McLachlin's criminal law judgments during the 1990s. Another defining feature is something that Allan and Lord Diplock tacitly acknowledge: the law should evolve in a way that adapts it to a modern social and political context. This context is defined by the factual matrix of the specific case to be decided (case-specific context), contemporary social and political conditions (socio-political context), and the temporal continuity of the present with the past (historical context).

As we will see in the next section, Chief Justice McLachlin's public law judgments deploy this common law approach: in them, she identifies an applicable general principle and then determines if a case can be decided by simple application of the principle. If not, which turns out to more often be the case, the principle must be modified or extended. Finally, where modification is required, it is the *context of judgment* accompanied by the limits of incrementalism that determine how much the old principle should be adapted to the new context. One final point: sometimes, judges must interpret a new legal rule – for instance, when the *Criminal Code* is amended, as is the case with the fraud provision at issue in *R v Théroux*, which will be discussed in the next section. In this situation, ancient cases may not be available from which a principle can be distilled through inductive reasoning based on precedent. Nonetheless, a judge who adopts the common law approach must search for

45 A good example of this is the reinterpretation of the kinds of fraud that vitiate consent in the meaning of section 265(3)(c) of the *Criminal Code*, *supra* note 40, as applied to those who are HIV-positive and fail to disclose this to a sexual partner. While *Cuerrier* had decided that consent to sex is vitiated if the accused exposed the complainant to a "significant risk of serious bodily harm" (for which vaginal sex while the accused was knowingly HIV-positive met the test), in *Mabior*, changing scientific knowledge about the transmissibility of HIV and changes in medical science in regard to treatment reinterpreted the word "fraud" in section 265(3)(c) to require disclosure of HIV status only when there is "a realistic possibility of transmission of HIV" (*R v Cuerrier*, [1998] 2 SCR 371 [*Cuerrier*]; *R v Mabior*, 2012 SCC 47 [*Mabior*]).

a principle on which to base their interpretation of the rule. Here, the decisions of other courts (lower courts or courts in other jurisdictions) can be used to identify the underlying principle. Context can then be used as a touchstone for tweaking the principle and determining its application to a particular situation.

III. Key Criminal Law Judgments from the 1990s

In this section, I analyse key criminal law judgments rendered by Chief Justice McLachlin. As we will see, they provide ample evidence for her use of the common law approach to public law.

a. R v Théroux *(1993)*

Chief Justice McLachlin wrote the majority reasons in *R v Théroux*,[46] which involved the interpretation of fraud provisions in section 380(1) of the *Criminal Code*.[47] It is an instructive case because she clearly describes the method of reasoning she uses. While the interpretation of the fraud provisions of the *Criminal Code* involves a classic public law issue – how law regulates the relationship between the state and an individual – it is noteworthy that the principles McLachlin J uses in *Théroux* to determine the boundaries of commercial fraud are drawn purely from case law.[48] The decision is thus an excellent example of how the common law method is deployed in a public law context.

McLachlin J began her reasons by identifying the general criminal law principles used to identify the mental element of an offence and any principles specific to the interpretation of section 380(1). While many of the general principles that McLachlin J identified, such as the prohibition on punishing the morally innocent, have been constitutionalized, they

46 *R v Théroux*, [1993] 2 SCR 5 [*Théroux*].

47 *Criminal Code*, *supra* note 40.

48 J Douglas Ewart makes this point in his description of the history of the fraud provisions in the *Crimimal Code*. He writes, "As can be seen, the amendments to the fraud provisions of the Criminal Code since 1892 have been few and minor. There is no evidence of a conscious legislative design to turn the fraud section into the major criminal law instrument for the promotion of honesty in commercial matters. And yet, year by year, case by case, the legal complexities and technicalities which have bedeviled other property offences have been peeled away by the judiciary to reveal the simple proposition which lies at the core of the offence of fraud: commercial affairs are to be conducted honestly" (*Criminal Fraud* (Toronto: Carswell, 1986) at 9); see also David Debenham, *The Law of Fraud and the Forensic Investigator*, 5th ed (Toronto: Thomson Reuters, 2016) at 32.

have their origin in the common law.[49] The second step involved determining whether the principles could be applied without modification to the facts of the case, or whether it was necessary to modify general principles of criminal fault in order to settle the issue at the heart of the case – namely, the fault element of fraud. Justice McLachlin concluded that, while existing principles were sound, they could not be easily applied to the facts because the behaviour of Théroux came very close to negligent misrepresentation, which, though tortious, is not criminal. In consequence, the judge moved on to the third step of the method I outlined above based on Lord Diplock's description in *Dorset Yacht*: the consideration of the policy issues relevant to interpreting the section. However, she was quick to point out the limited scope for such consideration: change in the common law must be incremental, and this sets strict limits to the extent of the policy debate in which a court can engage.

In practical terms, the limits on the policy debate are set by past cases, from which McLachlin J identified two policy goals: ensuring that business dealings are honest, while allowing sufficient leeway for sharp business practice that is generally considered permissible in the business world (regardless of whether it might seem improper to the general public). In *Théroux,* McLachlin J thus recognized that, while the common law can develop, it must do so in accordance with modern business mores tolerated by the law: in methodological terms, she assumes that any changes to the law are to be incremental, with more wide-ranging changes left to Parliament. Let us examine the decision in greater detail to see how the methodology was applied in context.

Robert Théroux had accepted deposits from prospective purchasers on homes that were being built in Laprairie and Sainte-Catherine, Quebec. He assured buyers that the deposits were insured by the Fédération de construction du Québec, although this was not true. The construction company went bankrupt, and most of the depositors lost their money. Théroux was charged with fraud as a result. In his defence, the accused argued he did not have the necessary *mens rea* because, while he told purchasers that their deposits were insured, knowing that they were not, he honestly believed that the houses would be built and that no one would lose their money.

To search for principles established in previous cases, McLachlin J began with *R v Olan,*[50] in which the Supreme Court of Canada had

49 *Re BC Motor Vehicle Act,* [1985] 2 SCR 486 [*Re Motor Vehicle Act*] at para 69.

50 *R v Olan,* [1978] 2 SCR 1175 [*Olan*]. In this case, Dickson J, writing for the Court, drew on the previous offence of conspiracy to defraud in order to identify the

determined that the *actus reus* of the offence of fraud had two elements: (1) proof that the accused had acted dishonestly, and proof that this dishonesty had caused (2) financial deprivation to the victim.[51] The case also held that such a deprivation could be proven by demonstration of prejudice or risk of prejudice to the financial interests of the victim: the risk did not have to materialize in actual financial loss.[52] *Théroux* addressed the *mens rea* element of the offence, which had not been settled in *Olan*. This required settling two questions. The first was whether there is a *mens rea* element corresponding to each element of the *actus reus:* the companion case to *R v Théroux, R v Zlatic*, turned in part on the question of whether the Crown was obliged to prove both that the accused intended to act dishonestly and that he knew that his dishonesty would deprive the victim of a financial interest.[53] The second question was whether the *mens rea* required proof of subjective dishonesty, i.e., proof that the accused subjectively believed that what he said was dishonest. The latter was the key point in the *Théroux* case because the accused maintained that he honestly believed the houses would be built, and so he did not think that the failure to disclose the lack of insurance for the deposits was wrong.

McLachlin J first identified two sets of principles: principles relating to the purpose of section 380(1) of the *Criminal Code*, and general common law principles relating to the determination of *mens rea* for criminal offences. Her analysis involved the common law method, even though section 380(1) had been introduced into the *Criminal Code* only in 1948 and therefore was not a codification of the old common law offence of conspiracy to commit fraud.[54] The fact that McLachlin J drew on common law principles demonstrates her recognition that, even in

---

elements of the offence. This offence was a codification of the common law offence (Andrew Ashworth, *Principles of Criminal Law*, 4th ed (Oxford: Oxford University Press, 2003) at 406).

51 *Olan, supra* note 50 at 1182.

52 *Ibid.*

53 In the Quebec Court of Appeal, the judges dealt solely with the issue of whether gambling away the money that could have been used to pay business creditors was evidence of an intent to commit an act of dishonesty. However, as Sopinka J points out in his dissent at the Supreme Court of Canada, neither the trial judge nor the appeal court judges considered that there was evidence that the accused did not intend to deprive the victim of a pecuniary interest, because, when the accused signed the contracts for purchase of goods from the victims, he fully intended to pay for them (*R v Zlatic*, [1993] 2 SCR 29 at 31 [*Zlatic* (SCC)]).

54 The interpretation of section 380(1) by the courts is an interesting example of the blurry line between statute and common law in Canadian criminal law. As Ewart points out, while cases interpreting that section "demonstrated a willingness [on the

the *Charter* era, the principles that underlie public law are continuous with those established by the common law.

McLachlin J noted that the principle underlying the offence of fraud is that "commercial affairs are to be conducted honestly."[55] The general principles relating to the determination of the *mens rea* of a criminal offence included the following:

a the principle that there is generally a mental element for every *actus reus* element;[56]
b the principle that *mens rea* is required in order to ensure that the morally innocent are not convicted;[57]
c the principle that a criminal offence presumptively requires proof of subjective *mens rea*;[58] and
d the principle that subjective *mens rea* can be assumed without proof of the subjective state of mind of the accused at the time of committing the offence, "barring some explanation casting doubt on such inference."[59]

Applying the principle to interpreting section 380(1) of the *Criminal Code*, McLachlin J determined that the *mens rea* elements of the offence must correspond with the two elements of the *actus reus* confirmed in *Olan*. This yielded the following elements:[60]

---

part of judges] to interpret the words of the *Criminal Code* apart from earlier common law preconceptions about the law of fraud" (*supra* note 48 at 26), he also notes that the law developed into a tool for ensuring that "commercial affairs are to be conducted honestly," despite the fact that "[t]here is no evidence [in the *Criminal Code* provisions] of a conscious legislative design to turn the fraud section into the major criminal law instrument for the promotion" of this principle (at 9). For an appreciation of the complex relationship between common law and statute, see Chapter 17 of Ruth Sullivan, *Sullivan on the Construction of Statutes*, 6th ed (Toronto: LexisNexis 2014).

55 *Théroux*, *supra* note 46 at 15, quoting Ewart, *supra* note 48 at 9.

56 This point is implicit in McLachlin J's reasoning in *Théroux*, *supra* note 46 at 17 and 19–20. On the limits of this principle, see *R v Creighton*, [1993] 3 SCR 3 at 54 [*Creighton*].

57 *Théroux*, *supra* note 46 at 17.

58 *Ibid* at 18.

59 *Ibid*. McLachlin J wrote, "the Crown need not, in every case, show precisely what thought was in the accused's mind at the time of the criminal act. In certain cases, subjective awareness of the consequences can be inferred from the act itself, barring some explanation casting doubt on such inference. The fact that such an inference is made does not detract from the subjectivity of the test" (*ibid*). The age-old presumption that a person intends the natural consequences of their acts is rebuttable.

60 *Ibid* at 20.

actus reus: the accused committed an act of dishonesty;
actus reus: the act of dishonesty resulted in a (financial) deprivation of the victim (or risk of deprivation);
mens rea: the accused knowingly committed the act of dishonesty; and
mens rea: the accused knew that committing the dishonest act would result in financial deprivation (or potential financial deprivation).

Having identified the relevant principles underlying section 380(1), the first step in the common law method is complete. As we recall from Lord Diplock's explanation of the method in *Dorset Yacht*, the next step is to determine whether the facts of a particular case fall within the principle. In the case of *Théroux*, this meant determining if Théroux's failure to disclose the lack of proper insurance was objectively dishonest, and whether his belief that he had done nothing wrong in failing to make this disclosure meant that he did not have the *mens rea* necessary for conviction. As McLachlin J pointed out, Théroux's behaviour was arguably quite close to the kind of misrepresentation that, while negligent, is not necessarily criminal.[61] Thus, the case could not be decided simply by the application of existing principles. In consequence, McLachlin J moved on to the third and final step of the common law analysis, which involves deciding whether to extend the principle underlying the criminalization of fraud to encompass Théroux's non-disclosure.[62]

The third phase of the common law method requires engaging in policy arguments. However, contrary to what Ronald Dworkin or T.R.S. Allan might suggest, political norms and values are not invoked to determine whether or not to extend liability in this case. Justice McLachlin did not inquire whether there was a social consensus that the kind of behaviour in which Théroux engaged warrants imprisonment; instead, she looked for policy arguments in the case law and limited an expansive interpretation of section 380(1) by the application of the principle of common law incrementalism. McLachlin J expressed the policy issue thus:

61 See Sopinka J's discussion of the case in *Théroux*, *ibid* at 10.

62 The potential breadth of the combined decisions in *Olan* and *Théroux* can be appreciated in this way. In *Olan*, the Court held that the test of dishonesty is objective: this opens the door to criminalization of conduct that a reasonable person would consider dishonest although the accused subjectively did not. When the objective test is combined with the *mens rea* identified in *Théroux*, which requires proof only that the accused knowingly committed the objectively dishonest *actus reus*, the potential breadth of the offence becomes clear, because accused cannot defend themselves by saying that they did not think what they had done was dishonest.

> The question arises whether the definition of *mens rea* for fraud which I have proposed may catch conduct which does not warrant criminalization. I refer to the fear, reflected in the appellate decisions adopting a narrower definition of the required *mens rea*, that the reach of the offence of fraud may be extended beyond criminal dishonesty to catch sharp or improvident business practices which, although not to be encouraged, do not merit the stigma and loss of liberty that attends the criminal sanction. The concern is that any misrepresentation or practice which induces an incorrect understanding or belief in the minds of customers, or which causes deprivation, will become criminal.

The debate in which McLachlin J engaged about the proper scope of criminal fraud was limited to responding to the concerns raised by judges of the provincial courts of appeal – for instance, in the *Mugford* case, which she cited in her reasons.[63] She did not engage with public policy debates outside the judicial sphere but limited herself to ascertaining the policy underlying the courts' interpretation of the offence.[64]

Accepting that the Court ought not to broaden the scope of section 380(1) to capture all forms of dishonest business practice, McLachlin J implicitly relied on the principle of incrementalism. An incremental change to the law is permissible, but she pointed to no social science evidence or government studies to justify where she drew the limit to the liability for commercial fraud; instead, she relied on the policy identified by previous courts. The boundaries McLachlin J drew for commercial fraud, on behalf of the majority of the Supreme Court, are circumscribed by the requirement that, to be guilty under section 380(1), the Crown must prove that the accused's failure to disclose the lack of insurance for deposits was "objectively dishonest" and that the accused subjectively believed that the non-disclosure could put homebuyers' deposits at risk. Proof of these elements is sufficient to ensure that only truly criminal behaviour, and not mere negligence or sharp business practice, is captured by the Court's interpretation of the offence.

---

63 *R v Mugford* (1990), 58 CCC (3d) 172 (NL CA) at 175–6.

64 *Théroux*, *supra* note 46 at 24; see also Ewart, *supra* note 48 at 9; see also Debenham, *supra* note 48 at 32. Engaging political or social norms would have required the courts to consider whether it was necessary to criminalize negligent conduct in order to ensure that the financial interests of the public were sufficiently protected. It might also require consideration of whether a lay person (rather than a lawyer) would consider negligent misrepresentation of what McLachlin J calls "sharp or improvident business practices" to be fraudulent (*Théroux*, *supra* note 46 at 25).

McLachlin J did not explicitly use the term "incrementalism."[65] However, it is clear that she did not engage in a broad policy debate about the proper scope of fraud: her policy discussion was not an exposé of fraudulent activity in the business world or even in the restricted domain of retail home sales.[66] The limits she placed on the debate are more evident in her reasons in the companion case to *R v Théroux*, *R v Zlatic*,[67] decided on the same date. While Sopinka J, in his dissenting judgment, is clearly concerned with the broad interpretation McLachlin J gives to section 380(1) in *Théroux*, McLachlin J did not rebut the points he raised with policy arguments drawn from social science or government policy papers; instead, she refered exclusively to the policy evident in past fraud cases – i.e., the policy of the common law as it has evolved incrementally over time.

The facts in *Zlatic* were as follows. Zlatic, who operated a retail clothing business, had gambled away money that he had earned from sales of clothes, instead of paying creditors for goods worth $375,000 that he had obtained in return for post-dated cheques or on credit. The trial judge accepted that Zlatic honestly believed that he would win enough through his gambling to make the payments.[68] This evidence, Sopinka J wrote, raised a reasonable doubt about whether the accused intended to put the financial interests of his creditors at risk.[69] In regard to the *actus reus*, the dissent argued that, although Zlatic owed money to his creditors, the money, at the time he gambled, was his, not the creditors, and so he did not put any financial interest of the latter at risk.[70] Sopinka J began his reasons by proclaiming the policy issue he thought should be addressed: "While we are not asked to overrule any specific decision, I am concerned in this case that we might criminalize

65 The idea that judges have the authority to make small changes to the common law is a long-standing one. It appears that the first judge to label this "incrementalism" was Iacobucci J in *R v Salituro*, [1991] 3 SCR 654. He points to a number of Supreme Court cases that illustrate the principle, including *Ares v Venner*, [1970] SCR 608; *Watkins v Olafson*, [1989] 2 SCR 750; *R v Khan*, [1990] 2 SCR 531; and *R v Seaboyer*, [1991] 2 SCR 577.

66 For an example of such an exposé, see the *Globe and Mail*'s investigation of how little Canadian securities regulators are able to collect of fines imposed for securities fraud (Grant Robertson & Tom Cardoso, "Canada's $1.1-Billion Problem: Regulators Dish Out Big Fines but Only Collect a Fraction," *Globe and Mail* (22 December 2017), online: <https://www.theglobeandmail.com/news/investigations/billion-dollars-unpaid-fines-white-collar-crime/article37416140/>).

67 *Zlatic* (SCC), *supra* note 53.

68 *Ibid* at 38.

69 *Ibid* at 38–9.

70 *Ibid* at 34–5.

non-payment of debts because we disapprove of the way in which the debtor spent his money. This is a concept that has been disapproved of in our jurisprudence since the abolition of debtor prisons."[71] Sopinka J disapproved of broadening liability for fraud on the facts in *Zlatic* because he was concerned that section 380(1) would confuse a petit bourgeois disapproval of debt with a criminal act.[72] Recall that, according to the majority, criminal fraud would be made out if the Crown could prove that a reasonable person would find the accused's acts to be dishonest and that the accused knowingly committed that act. But, while the average person might consider gambling with business profits to be immoral, these profits, as Sopinka J pointed out, belonged to Zlatic, not his creditors, and it would therefore be unjust to bridge the gap between improvident and criminal business practices by social prejudice. Indeed, the testimony of Zlatic was that he gambled his business profits precisely because he thought this would enable him to solve his financial woes.[73]

Sopinka J's mode of reasoning is a classic "public law" approach that involves stating the principle upfront rather than deriving it through inference from past cases and then interpreting section 380(1) in a way that gives effect to the principle. What differentiates this approach from that of McLachlin J, as we will see below, is that it requires more than an incremental adjustment of the rule to deal with the facts in *Théroux* and *Zlatic*; instead, Sopinka J's approach begins with an abstract principle – such as the importance of not criminalizing debt – which is then used to interpret the offence of fraud without regard to whether the proposed change in the law is, to use the words of Lord Diplock in *Dorset Yacht*, "influenced by the same general conception of what ought to give rise [to a particular legal rule] as was used in [the old cases]."[74]

In her judgment in *Zlatic*, McLachlin J prefered to first settle the policy issue raised by Sopinka J by applying the common law method,

71 *Ibid* at 34.

72 This common opinion is referred to in the judgment of the Court of Appeal (*R c Zlatic* (1991), 65 CCC (3d) 86, 1991 CanLII 3555 (QC CA), for instance at 9–10 (CanLII), where Justice Proulx quotes the trial judge:

> En somme, à part la contestation de la défense sur des points secondaires, l'affaire qui fait l'objet de l'accusation est dans les faits relativement simple: *l'accusé a dreiné le plus gros et le plus clair de l'actif de ses opérations, représenté par les paiements de ses acheteurs pour s'adonner au jeu et entreprendre des périples qui n'avaient aucun lien avec le commerce exploité.* Il est évident qu'à partir de la mi-novembre, l'accusé n'a eu aucun souci, n'a éprouvé aucun désir de payer les marchandises que ses fournisseurs continuaient de lui livrer. Cette préoccupation était inexistante. [emphasis added]

73 *Zlatic* (SCC), *supra* note 53 at 38.

74 *Dorset Yacht*, *supra* note 4.

which emphasizes the identification of a principle underlying past cases and restricting any modifications to incremental changes consistent with "the same general conception" of fraud in those cases.[75] She acknowledged that, while the principle that business affairs ought to be conducted honestly is potentially very broad, it should not be applied so broadly as to criminalize conduct that neither past cases nor present practice would consider criminal. Surveying old cases, McLachlin J noted that they make a distinction between diverting funds from a business for "personal ends" from transactions that do so for "*bona fides* [*sic*] business ends." She thus refered to old cases and to the jurisprudence of lower courts interpreting section 380(1) to limit an overly broad interpretation and application of the principle that "commercial affairs are to be conducted honestly." As applied to the facts of the case, McLachlin J acknowledged that, although Zlatic had a right to the money that he earned through his business, it had to be used for *bona fide* business ends. She concluded:

> The appellant did not … have an unrestricted right to use these funds as he pleased. In accepting these goods with no concern for payment and in diverting the funds to a non-business, notoriously risky enterprise, he put these funds to a wrongful use. I am satisfied that a reasonable person would regard as dishonest a scheme involving the acceptance of merchandise for resale without concern for repayment and the diversion of the proceeds to a reckless gambling adventure. The distinction is the same as the distinction between a corporate officer using corporate funds for unwise business purposes, which is not fraud, and the diversion of corporate funds to private purposes having nothing to do with business. Unwise business practices are not fraudulent. The wrongful use of money in which others have a pecuniary interest for purposes that have nothing to do with business, may however, in appropriate circumstances, constitute fraud.[76]

Both *Théroux* and *Zlatic* are clear illustrations of the common law method applied in a typical public law context. McLachlin J searched past cases for the principles that underlie commercial fraud, and even the policy considerations against which she tested the scope of the offence that she interpreted are found in the common law. What is missing is an explicit acknowledgment of the principle of incremental change essential

75 *Zlatic* (SCC), *supra* note 53 at 45–7.
76 *Ibid* at 48.

to common law reasoning. In the next subsection, we will review *R v Cuerrier*, in which McLachlin J described more clearly the incremental approach that restricts a wide-ranging consideration of policy when interpreting the *Criminal Code*.

b. R v Cuerrier *(1998)*

The criminalization of the non-disclosure of HIV-positive status to sexual partners in *R v Cuerrier*[77] remains controversial.[78] We will not examine the public policy aspects of the decision; instead, we will focus on the common law method employed by McLachlin J. The case, which involves determining when consent to sexual activity is negated by fraud on the part of the accused, provides a good example of this method because the reasoning she used in her concurring minority reasons is so different from that employed by Cory J, writing for the majority, or by L'Heureux-Dubé J in her separate concurring reasons.

Henry Cuerrier, the accused in the case, knew that he was HIV-positive, and he had been warned by a public health nurse that he must use a condom when having sexual intercourse and that he must inform all of his sexual partners of his HIV status before engaging in sex with them. Cuerrier ignored the advice and had sex with two women without disclosing to them that he had been diagnosed with HIV. Section 265(3) of the *Criminal Code* states that there is no consent to sexual touching where that consent is obtained by means of fraud, which the Crown in this case argued was made out by Cuerrier's deliberate non-disclosure of his HIV status. In *Cuerrier*, the Supreme Court interpreted the meaning of "fraud" for the first time in this context. While the origins of section 265(3) could arguably have been traced to the common law, the relevant cases narrowed the situations in which deceit vitiated consent to those in which the accused had deceived the complainant about the identity of the person with whom she was to have sex or deceived him or her as to the "nature and quality of the act" in which the two would be engaged. Moreover, the "nature and quality of the act" had been interpreted narrowly in *R v Clarence*,[79] so that the accused's failure to

---

77 *Cuerrier*, *supra* note 45.

78 For an indication of the controversy, see André Picard, "Countries, Including Canada, Are Prosecuting People with HIV because They Misunderstand Science, Leading Researchers Say," *Globe and Mail* (27 July 2018), online <https://www.theglobeandmail.com/canada/article-countries-including-canada-are-prosecuting-people-with-hiv-because/>; see generally Kyle Kirkup, "Releasing Stigma: Police, Journalists and Crimes of HIV Non-Disclosure" (2015) 46:1 Ottawa L Rev 129.

79 *R v Clarence* (1888), 22 QBD 23 [*Clarence*].

disclose a sexually transmitted infection did not meet the definition, and therefore such non-disclosure did not vitiate consent.[80] It is clear from reading the reasons of Cory, L'Heureux-Dubé, and McLachlin JJ that all judges accepted that section 265(3)(c) had to be interpreted in such a way as to impose criminal liability for failure to disclose the accused's HIV-positive status to sexual partners. However, each judge used a different form of reasoning to achieve this goal.

Justice Cory, writing for the plurality, grafted the test for fraud from section 380(1) of the *Criminal Code* (interpreted in *R v Théroux*) onto the law of assault, thus applying a test for fraud developed in the commercial context to determine when consent to sexual touching is vitiated by fraud under section 265(3)(c) of the *Criminal Code*. To achieve the public policy effect that the plurality sought – i.e., to broaden the situations in which consent is vitiated by fraud to encompass non-disclosure of HIV status – Cory J essentially rewrote the statute, a far cry from the incremental approach used by McLachlin J.

L'Heureux-Dubé J, too, used quite radical (as opposed to incremental) means for interpreting section 265(3), drawing on general political norms of equality and autonomy to justify her interpretation of these sections. Like the interpretation of section 265(3) by Cory J, L'Heureux-Dubé J's interpretation of the section had no internal limits – it was entirely up to the Court to decide, when interpreting section 265(3)(c), how far women's autonomy and dignity ought to be protected. Thus, like Cory J, she considered policy issues that went far beyond the consensus established in the common law.

In contrast, Justice McLachlin's reasons in this case are a classic example of her application of common law reasoning in a public law context in which she recognizes the continuity of public and private law. Her interpretation of section 265(3)(c) takes as its starting point the traditional common law approach to fraud in cases dealing specifically with sexual assault (rather than the concept of fraud in commercial contexts), and it extends the common law rule incrementally in a way that is consistent with the general principle underlying past cases. She identifies the principle or "internal morality" of the common law rules about when consent is vitiated by fraud and then incrementally updates them to deal with the contemporary social context.

Both the majority reasons written by Cory J and the concurring reasons of L'Heureux-Dubé J begin from the assumption that the 1983 reform to the assault provisions was intended to eradicate the common law rules limiting consent in cases of fraud. This starting point is

80 *Ibid* at 44.

emblematic of the approach of those who see a discontinuity between public and private law: they are quick to presume that legislation ousts common law rules rather than being a codification or modification of them.[81] Having considered the slate to have been cleaned, the majority used the commercial definition of "fraud" in section 380(1) of the *Code* to interpret the meaning of "fraud" in section 265(3)(c), concluding that, where an accused has committed an objectively dishonest act, such as failure to disclose positive HIV status, and the resulting sex causes the complainant to be "deprived" in some way, her actual consent to the activity will be vitiated. In the context of sex with an HIV-positive person, "deprivation" was defined to include any activity that results in "a significant risk of serious bodily harm" to the complainant.[82]

In her concurring reasons, L'Heureux-Dubé J did not resort to the commercial fraud provisions to interpret section 265(3)(c), because, in comparison to the majority, she regarded the assault provisions as providing a much broader protection of the autonomy of women to consent to sexual touching.[83] Thus, in her view, deception of any kind that causes the complainant to consent to the touching will negative consent, regardless of whether it exposed them to a risk of bodily harm.[84] Her interpretation of section 265(3)(c) is arguably most consistent with the broad protection of equality in the *Charter*.[85] But it was also a sweeping change to the law of consent.

In contrast to her colleagues, McLachlin J adopted the same common law methodology she employed in *Théroux*, despite the fact that she sympathized with the goal of both Cory and L'Heureux-Dubé JJ to "criminalize dishonestly obtained sex."[86] In her view, the sweeping changes they advocate "are too broad, falling outside the power of the courts to make incremental changes to the common law."[87] She instead proposed to modify the common law rule incrementally. In

81 For a discussion of the proper policy context within which the 1983 revisions ought to be considered, see e.g. Christine Boyle, "Sexual Assault and the Feminist Judge" (1985) 1 CJWL 93 at 97.

82 *Cuerrier, supra* note 45 at para 128; see also *R v Ewanchuk*, [1999] 1 SCR 330 at para 69, L'Heureux-Dubé J.

83 *Cuerrier, supra* note 45 at paras 12, 15, and 18.

84 *Ibid* at paras 19–20.

85 For a comparison of the various judgments in *Cuerrier*, see Allison Symington, "HIV Exposure as Assault: Progressive Development or Misplaced Focus?" in Elizabeth A Sheehy, ed, *Sexual Assault in Canada: Law, Legal Practice, and Women's Activism* (Ottawa: University of Ottawa Press, 2012) 635; see also Martha Shaffer, "Sex, Lies, and HIV: *Mabior* and the Concept of Sexual Fraud" (2013) 63:3 UTLJ 466.

86 *Cuerrier, supra* note 45 at para 26.

87 *Ibid* at para 26.

consequence, the interpretation of section 265(3)(c) must begin from the fact that the common law vitiated consent only if the accused had deceived the complainant about the identity of their sexual partner or deceived them about the "nature and quality" of the sexual acts in which they would engage. While Cory and L'Heureux-Dubé JJ had wiped the slate clean, interpreting section 265(3)(c) purely on the basis of policy without regard to the common law, McLachlin J took the same approach to the relationship between the common law and the *Criminal Code* as the Supreme Court of Canada had taken in *R v Jobidon*, in which Gonthier J wrote for the majority that the list of vitiating factors in section 265(3) "merely concretized, and made more explicit, basic limits on the legal effectiveness of consent which had for centuries formed part of the criminal law in England and in Canada."[88]

Unlike the fraud provisions interpreted in *Théroux*, the common law was very clear: only deception as to the identity of the person with whom the complainant would engage in sexual touching or deception as to the "nature and quality of the act" to be engaged in would vitiate consent. Until 1888, English courts had accepted that deception as to whether the accused had a venereal disease constituted deception as to the "nature and quality of the act." But in *R v Clarence*,[89] the English court of Queen's Bench rejected this view, restricting deception as to the "nature and quality of the act" to deception about whether the touching the complainant and accused engaged in was sexual or non-sexual. Thus, if the complainant had consented to a gynaecological examination (a non-sexual act), and it turned out that the person performing the examination was obtaining sexual gratification from conducting it and had not alerted the patient to this fact, the latter's consent to the examination would be vitiated and the accused could be convicted.[90] As McLachlin J pointed out, such a restrictive interpretation of when consent would be vitiated by fraud is not consistent with contemporary Canadian values.[91]

In order to determine what the proper scope of section 265(3)(c) should be, McLachlin J turned to the common law method, which

88 *R v Jobidon*, [1991] 2 SCR 714 at 739, quoted in *Cuerrier*, *ibid* at para 39. For criticism of Gonthier J's interpretation of the relationship between the common law and the *Criminal Code*, see Kent Roach, *Criminal Law*, 6th ed (Toronto: Irwin Law, 2015) at 111 and the judgment of Sopinka J in *Jobidon*, *supra* note 88 itself.

89 *Clarence*, *supra* note 79.

90 Examples include *R v Case* (1850), 1 Den 580, 169 ER 281, and *R v Flattery* (1877), 2 QBD 410.

91 *Cuerrier*, *supra* note 45 at para 66.

requires identification of the principle that animated the common law. While L'Heureux-Dubé J had defined the relevant principle broadly as the protection of women's dignity and autonomy,[92] the principle that McLachlin J identified is much narrower. To overcome the very restrictive interpretation of "nature and quality of the act" in *Clarence*, McLachlin J first examined the reason for the narrowness of the rule. The judges in *Clarence* and cases that supported its reasoning objected that widening "nature and quality of the act" to go beyond the distinction between sexual and non-sexual acts would result in an unprincipled approach and allow consent to be vitiated on the basis of trifling deceptions, such as whether the accused had promised a fur coat to his sexual partner.[93] However, McLachlin J deprecated such an assessment of the pre-*Clarence* cases. In her view, the older cases did rest on a principled distinction that allowed deception as to a venereal disease to vitiate consent.

What was the principle underlying the pre-*Clarence* cases? The old cases, she wrote, intended to protect a person's autonomy by allowing them to control their body in regard to the exchange of bodily fluids. The cases recognized that exposure to infected fluids could be "a potential sentence of disease or death." Such exposure violated the notion that sexual touching was intended to be for the purpose of "pleasure, pain or pregnancy."[94] In other words, the old cases were based on a notion of autonomy that required disclosure of information necessary for a person to determine whether sex would endanger their life.

Having identified a principled basis for the pre-*Clarence* cases, McLachlin J then considered whether the Court could legitimately return to the notion of autonomy expounded in them, despite the later restriction of this principle in *Clarence*. To justify this move, McLachlin J deployed the third element of the common law methodology – incremental change should be made to bring the law into line with current social values.[95] McLachlin J's approach to incrementalism exactly reflects that described by Diplock J in *Dorset Yacht*: the application of the old principle can be modified as long as it is "influenced by the same general conception of what ought to give rise [to a particular legal rule] as was used in [the old cases]."[96] She explained this principle of incrementalism as follows:

92 *Ibid* at paras 12 and 19.
93 *Ibid* at para 68.
94 *Ibid* at para 72.
95 *Ibid* at paras 59 and 66.
96 *Dorset Yacht, supra* note 4 at 1140.

> From a theoretical point of view, the proposed change follows the time-honoured methodology of making changes to the common law on an incremental basis. This, however, is not enough. The addition of a new common law category should reflect some underlying principle that ties it to the logic and policy underlying the existing rule and permits future developments, if any, to proceed on a reasoned, principled basis. If the underlying principle is so broad that it admits of extension into debateable or undesirable areas, then the proposed change should not be made.[97]

A review of policy arguments presented by the parties and intervenors in the case affirms that McLachlin J's narrower interpretation of section 265(3)(c) of the *Criminal Code* was more in line with contemporary social and political context. Public interest intervenors had argued that public health initiatives are more effective than criminalization for preventing the spread of HIV, since criminalization makes it less likely that populations at risk of contracting and communicating the disease will seek treatment.[98] According to the interveners and public health advocates, the definition of "fraud" in section 265(3)(c) should be sufficiently narrow so as to minimize the types of sexual behaviour that are subject to criminal penalty and support public health initiatives by ensuring that positive HIV status is not unduly stigmatized.[99] Justice Cory was unwilling to accept the public health approach to preventing the transmission of HIV, stating that the behaviour of Cuerrier demonstrated the "ineffectiveness of the health scheme."[100] Justice McLachlin's reasons tried to find a middle ground between a pure public health approach and a simple criminalization by minimizing the situations in which non-disclosure of HIV would be criminalized while still allowing Parliament the leeway to use the criminal law to reinforce public health initiatives.

As I mentioned at the outset of this review of *Cuerrier*, the case also demonstrates McLachlin J's prescience: her criticism that the majority's position could create uncertainty because it employs a vague concept of "significant risk" of harm[101] has been borne out by confusion in lower courts, requiring the Supreme Court to provide a gloss on the *Cuerrier*

97 *Cuerrier*, *supra* note 45 at para 71.

98 *Ibid* at para 55.

99 For a useful analysis of *Cuerrier* and subsequent HIV-criminalization cases from a queer perspective, see Kirkup, *supra* note 78.

100 *Cuerrier*, *supra* note 45 at para 141.

101 *Ibid* at para 48.

definition in *R v Mabior.*[102] In *Cuerrier,* McLachlin J criticized the approach of the majority as being unprincipled, writing,

> The problem with [the majority's approach to when consent is vitiated by fraud] ... is that failure to disclose virtually any known risk of harm would potentially be capable of vitiating consent to sexual intercourse. The commercial fraud theory of consent offers no principled rationale for allowing some risks to vitiate consent to sex but excluding others. For example, pregnancy may be regarded as a deprivation in some circumstances, as may be the obligation to support a child. It follows that lying about sterility or the effectiveness of birth control may constitute fraud vitiating consent. To take another example, lies about the prospect of marriage or false declarations of affection inducing consent, carry the risk of psychological suffering, depression and other consequences readily characterized as deprivation. The proposed rule thus has the potential to criminalize a vast array of sexual conduct. Deceptions, small and sometimes large, have from time immemorial been the by-product of romance and sexual encounters. They often carry the risk of harm to the deceived party. Thus far in the history of civilization, these deceptions, however sad, have been left to the domain of song, verse and social censure. Now, if the Crown's theory is accepted, they become crimes.
>
> Cory J, recognizing the overbreadth of the theory upon which he founds his reasons, attempts to limit it by introducing an ad hoc qualifier: there must be a "significant risk of serious bodily harm" before consent is vitiated. This limitation, far from solving the problem, introduces new difficulties. First, it contradicts the general theory that deception coupled with risk of deprivation suffices to vitiate consent. A new theory is required to explain why some, but not all kinds of fraud, convert consensual sex into assault. Yet none is offered. Second, it introduces uncertainty. When is a risk significant enough to qualify conduct as criminal? In whose eyes is "significance" to be determined – the victim's, the accused's or the judge's? What is the ambit of "serious bodily harm"? Can a bright line be drawn between psychological harm and bodily harm, when the former may lead to depression, self-destructive behaviour and in extreme cases suicide?[103]

In *R v Mabior,* the Supreme Court of Canada was forced to further define what constitutes a "significant risk of serious bodily harm" in the

102 *Mabior, supra* note 45.
103 *Cuerrier,* supra note 45 at paras 47–8.

case of a person with HIV but who had a low viral load and was unlikely to infect others.

In *Cuerrier*, McLachlin J not only deployed the common law method of reasoning in a public law case, but she also explained the proper boundaries for the extension of the common law. The common law can be extended if doing so is consistent with the principle that underlies past cases. Such incremental change has the benefit of reflecting conflicting policy considerations – in this case, those of a pure public health approach versus simple criminalization of HIV status. What some might consider the inherent conservatism of the incremental common law approach can also preserve a domain of policy flexibility for legislators.

Neither *Cuerrier* nor *Théroux* involved the application of the *Charter*. In the next subsection, we will turn to a constitutional law case to demonstrate how the common law method can be applied even in the most "public" of public law situations – the interpretation and application of the Constitution.

c. R v Creighton *(1993)*

R v Creighton,[104] a case on the constitutionally required level of fault for manslaughter, provides an excellent opportunity to contrast two methods of public law reasoning: the incremental common law method employed by the majority, written by McLachlin J, and the approach of Lamer CJ, who based his judgment on a public law principle not derived from common law – the "stigma" principle. Arguably, *Creighton* is the last gasp for this principle, demonstrating the triumph of common law incrementalism over the abstract approach used by Lamer CJ.[105]

In *Creighton*, Chief Justice Lamer provided his most thorough interpretation of the principle of "stigma," initially articulated in *R v Vaillancourt*[106] and introduced to determine the constitutionally required *mens*

104 *Creighton*, *supra* note 56.

105 There are a few exceptions. Stigma is mentioned in *R v Finta*, [1994] 1 SCR 701 [*Finta*] and *R v Greyeyes*, [1997] 2 SCR 825. It is also briefly mentioned in *R v ADH*, 2013 SCC 28, although without invocation of the *Charter*. As Kent Roach points out, the stigma analysis was not a robust analytical tool because the Supreme Court has increasingly accepted that objective fault is acceptable in Canadian criminal law (Kent Roach, "Mind the Gap: Canada's Different Criminal and Constitutional Standards of Fault" (2011) 61 UTLJ 545). He cites Don Stuart's criticism, echoing Stuart's view that the reasoning in these cases is "shallow and conclusory" (at 558; citing Don Stuart, *Charter Justice in Canadian Criminal Law*, 4th ed (Toronto: Carswell, 2005) at 80).

106 *R v Vaillancourt*, [1987] 2 SCR 636. It was developed further in *R v Martineau*, [1990] 2 SCR 633.

rea for murder. Where a particular offence criminalizes behaviour that "is of sufficient gravity to import significant moral opprobrium on the individual found guilty of engaging in such conduct,"[107] the accused charged with that offence can be convicted only if their mental state at the time of committing the offence warrants such stigmatization.[108] It is clear that the stigma analysis introduces into criminal law a principle that had never previously been articulated – indeed, neither in *Creighton* nor in *Vaillancourt* did Lamer CJ refer to past cases that apply it. This approach implicitly separates public law reasoning from common law reasoning – in the former, it is permissible to use general political principles in constitutional cases, whereas in the latter, the court must first identify a common law principle developed over a long period of time as the starting point for considering incremental change.

In *Creighton,* McLachlin J again employed the common law methodology, but this time to settle a constitutional issue: the constitutionally required level of fault for manslaughter. She implicitly rejected the stigma principle, writing that "[t]he most important feature of the stigma of manslaughter is the stigma which is *not* attached to it."[109] What principle does underlie the criminalization of manslaughter? It is the principle of proportionality between punishment and moral responsibility: "the seriousness of the offence must not be disproportionate to the degree of moral fault." [110] In the view of McLachlin J, this principle is satisfied by requiring the Crown to prove that a reasonable person in the position of the accused would have foreseen the likelihood that non-trivial bodily harm would result from their conduct. And while there was some confusion about whether the Crown also had to prove that the accused's acts were inherently dangerous, this issue was resolved in *R v Javanmardi,* where Justice Abella confirmed that "[t]here is no independent requirement of objective dangerousness."[111] However, where the underlying offence is one of strict liability, she underlined, the Crown must also prove that the accused's behaviour was a "marked departure" from the standard of care of a reasonable person.[112] The principle of proportionality is implicit in a variety of other long-standing principles articulated in previous cases. These include the following:

107 *Creighton, supra* note 56 at 19.

108 *Ibid* at 19.

109 *Ibid* at 47.

110 *Ibid* at 53 and 59.

111 *R v Javanmardi,* 2019 SCC 54 at para 30.

112 *Ibid* at para 31.

1 *Mens rea* must reflect the nature of the crime.[113]
2 People who intentionally harm others should be punished more severely than those who harm others unintentionally.[114]
3 There should generally be symmetry between the *actus reus* and the *mens rea* of an offence.[115]

Having identified applicable common law principles, the second step in the common law method involves determining if the principles can be applied to the facts of the case without modification (Diplock J's second step in *Dorset Yacht*). In the case of *Creighton*, the answer was "no": it was not obvious whether the principle of proportionality required that the Crown prove subjective foresight of death to ensure that the punishment for manslaughter was proportionate to the level of wrongdoing involved when Creighton administered cocaine to the victim without first determining its quality or potency.[116] Thus, McLachlin J quickly passed to the final step in the common law analysis, which is to determine if the current social situation requires incremental modification of the principle: does proportionality between punishment and moral fault in the case of manslaughter require that the Crown prove foresight of death? In this case, McLachlin J decided that it was acceptable to depart from the principle that there should be symmetry between the *actus reus* and the *mens rea*. She wrote:

> It would shock the public's conscience to think that a person could be convicted of manslaughter absent any moral fault based on foreseeability of harm. Conversely, it might well shock the public's conscience to convict a person who has killed another only of aggravated assault – the result of requiring foreseeability of death – on the sole basis that the risk of death was not reasonably foreseeable. The terrible consequence of death demands more.[117]

Pragmatism and the need to take into account contemporary social values dictate departure from the strict application of a well-established common law principle. As McLachlin J noted, "It is important to distinguish between criminal law theory, which seeks the ideal of absolute symmetry between actus reus and mens rea, and the constitutional

113 *Creighton, supra* note 56 at 55, 57.
114 *Ibid* at 49.
115 *Ibid* at 49–55.
116 *Ibid* at 12–13.
117 *Ibid* at 48.

requirements of the Charter. As the Chief Justice has stated several times, 'the Constitution does not always guarantee the 'ideal.'"[118] She goes on to appeal to popular morality: "Just as it would offend fundamental justice to punish a person who did not intend to kill for murder, so it would equally offend common notions of justice to acquit a person who has killed another of manslaughter and find him guilty instead of aggravated assault on the ground that death, as opposed to harm, was not foreseeable."[119]

In this case, departing from the ideal, without undermining it entirely, was justified because of the existence of the thin-skull rule, which effectively eliminates "the disparity ... between the *mens rea* of the offence [of manslaughter] and its consequence."[120] Moreover, the common law has long acknowledged that multiple offences can be distinguished purely on the basis of the *actus reus* while retaining the identical *mens rea*.[121] Thus, McLachlin J proposed to limit the general principle requiring symmetry between the *actus reus* and *mens rea* because it was possible to do so while remaining consistent with the principle that the punishment fit the crime. McLachlin J thus concluded that the *mens rea* for manslaughter can be directed toward foreseeability of bodily harm even though the *actus reus* relates to death.

As we can see, McLachlin J's approach to interpreting the principles of fundamental justice in *Creighton* was in stark contrast to that of Chief Justice Lamer, who had relied on a new concept, "stigma," as a principle of fundamental justice. In contrast, McLachlin J relied on various well-established rules of the common law in order to give meaning to the principles of fundamental justice protected under section 7.[122] Her incremental approach is surely more in line with the Court's insistence in *Re BC Motor Vehicle Act*,[123] and later in *Malmo-Levine*,[124] that the

---

118 *Ibid* at 53.

119 *Ibid* at 54.

120 *Ibid* at 52.

121 *Ibid* at 54. McLachlin J cites the example of attempts, for which the *mens rea* is identical with the completed offence although the *actus reus* differs.

122 She underscores the value of the common law at the very beginning of her judgment, where she writes "I respectfully disagree with the Chief Justice on two points. The first is his conclusion that the common law offence of manslaughter is unconstitutional because it does not require foreseeability of death ... In my view, the offence of unlawful act manslaughter, as defined by our courts and those in other jurisdictions for many centuries, is entirely consistent with the principles of fundamental justice. There is no need to read up its requirements; as it stands, it conforms to the *Charter*" (*ibid* at 40–1).

123 *Re Motor Vehicle Act*, *supra* note 49.

124 *R v Malmo-Levine; R v Caine*, 2003 SCC 74.

Court recognize as principles of fundamental justice only rules that are well-established "basic tenets" of our legal system supported by a social consensus about their importance. Indeed, in subsequent constitutional cases, the Supreme Court has rarely returned to the stigma principle.[125]

We have now examined McLachlin J's common law approach to public law in two cases involving the interpretation of the *Criminal Code* (*R v Théroux* and *R v Cuerrier*) outside the constitutional context, and one involving the interpretation and application of the *Charter*. All three are examples of cases in which McLachlin J either advocated for a change in the law or determined the law in a situation of uncertainty. To avoid the charge that I have selected only those cases that support my thesis, the next subsection will briefly examine a case in which she used the common law method to argue against changing the law.

d. R v McIntosh *(1995)*

The last case we will consider, *R v McIntosh*,[126] highlights McLachlin J's use of the common law approach in a situation in which she advocates *not* changing the law. In this regard, it differs from cases like *Cuerrier* and *Théroux*, in which she advocated incremental change. As we will see, her judgment in *McIntosh* confirms her adherence to the common law method and demonstrates the importance of incrementalism to it: in this case, using the common law method puts a brake on change because the existing interpretation of the self-defence provisions is in line with the long history of these defences.[127] Any radical reinterpretation of the law would require Parliamentary intervention. Indeed, such intervention occurred almost twenty years later with the replacement of the old self-defence provisions with new ones in 2012.[128] What this case demonstrates is that Chief Justice McLachlin used the common law method faithfully, adhering to the principles and values that underlie the method: she did not employ common law reasoning simply for utilitarian reasons to reach a particular outcome.

---

125 While the principle was used in *R v Finta*, *supra* note 106, to determine the *mens rea* for the offences of committing war crimes and crimes against humanity, it notably does not appear in the Court's reinterpretation of those offences in *Mugesera v Canada (Minister of Citizenship and Immigration)*, 2005 SCC 40. For a criticism of the stigma analysis, see Rosemary Cairns Way, "Constitutionalizing Subjectivism: Another View" (1990) 79 CR (3d) 260.

126 *R v McIntosh*, [1995] 1 SCR 686 [*McIntosh*].

127 *Ibid* at paras 76–8 and 82.

128 *Citizen's Arrest and Self-defence Act*, SC 2012, c 9.

The *McIntosh* case involved the interpretation of the notoriously confusing sections 34 and 35 of the *Criminal Code* (the precursors to the current provisions), which codified the rules applicable to the law of self-defence. The accused, McIntosh, had given sound equipment to a friend to repair. The friend never returned it. McIntosh was told that the friend, the eventual victim, was in the neighbourhood, and so McIntosh went out to confront him, bringing with him a kitchen knife. Provoked by McIntosh, an argument broke out, in the course of which the accused was attacked by the victim, whom he then stabbed and killed. The issue was whether self-defence was available to McIntosh in these circumstances, because he was the initial aggressor. The majority interpreted the self-defence provisions to allow the defence to apply even if the accused was the initial aggressor. One of the principal arguments was that, because the self-defence provisions were confusing, they should be interpreted in a way that favoured the accused. This was thought to be more in line with the liberalization of the criminal law that had occurred since the introduction of the *Charter*.[129]

McLachlin J, writing for the dissent, returned to the common law to determine if a person who has provoked an assault can plead self-defence when he kills the assaulter. While the majority's interpretation of the defence was motivated by a desire to expand its availability – a political principle not clearly invoked by the self-defence provisions[130] – the dissenting judges, led by McLachlin J, applied a principle derived from the common law, which was codified in sections 34 and 35. While the majority easily found the sections to be illogical, thus giving them an excuse to apply principles favouring the defence, McLachlin J criticized this approach by pointing out that "courts should not quickly make the assumption that [Parliament] intends to [legislate illogically]."[131] McLachlin J's view clearly placed the search for principle first – only

---

129 Many scholars have noted that the majority's interpretation of the self-defence provisions in *McIntosh* departed from previous case law (see e.g. Gerry Ferguson, "Self-Defence: Selecting the Applicable Provisions" (2000) 5 Can Crim L Rev 179 at 185–93). I am suggesting in this chapter that the reason was the Lamer Court's liberalism in criminal matters, which tended to favour the accused (see CL Ostberg, Matthew E Wetstein & Craig R Ducat, "Attitudinal Dimensions of Supreme Court Decision Making in Canada: The Lamer Court, 1991–1995" (2002) 55:1 Political Research Quarterly 235).

130 The majority's approach contrasts with the traditional view that penal statutes are to be interpreted liberally only where they contain an ambiguity (see McLachlin J's comments on this in *McIntosh, supra* note 127 at para 60; see also Ruth Sullivan, *Sullivan on the Construction of Statutes*, 5th ed (Toronto: LexisNexis, 2008) at 470).

131 *McIntosh, supra* note 126 at para 81.

where the principle underlying the common law cannot be found should a court have recourse to political values not clearly invoked by the legislator. In McLachlin J's approach is an implicit criticism of the public law method employed by the majority, which is premised on the separation of the common law and public law.

What principle did McLachlin J identify as underlying the common law rules (and therefore the codification of these rules in sections 34 and 35 of the *Criminal Code*)? At common law, a distinction was drawn between "justifiable homicide" and "excusable homicide." A justifiable homicide involved a situation in which the accused kills the victim because the victim attacked him without provocation: in such a case, social values dictated that an accused was justified in holding their ground when attacked.[132] In contrast, when the accused provoked the victim into an attack, the death might be excusable, but it was not justified. Because excuses, which are concessions to human frailty (in this case, presumably the human tendency to defend oneself when attacked even if one is in the wrong), do not automatically lead to acquittal, self-defence as a justification could be invoked only if the accused retreated.[133] McLachlin J ended by noting that because section 34 codified "justifiable homicide" and section 35 "excusable homicide,"[134] it was likely that Parliament did not mean for a person who was the aggressor to be able to claim the much broader defence of self-defence in section 34.

Having articulated the principle underlying these sections of the *Criminal Code,* McLachlin J then turned to the second and third steps of the common law method: it was clear that McIntosh's case does not clearly fall within the scope of self-defence in sections 34 and 35 as interpreted in her dissent. The question thus arises as to whether the principle underlying the common law ought to be modified to conform to modern social and political norms, to the extent that they support a more liberal approach to criminal law that provides greater scope for the accused to defend themself. In this case, unlike in others discussed in this chapter, McLachlin J acceped that the policy underlying the common law rules was still as relevant today as it was prior to the enactment of the first *Criminal Code* of 1892. She wrote:

> Not only is the result McIntosh argues for anomalous; to my mind it is unwise and unjust. The common law has for centuries insisted that the

132 *Ibid* at para 63.

133 *Ibid.*

134 *Ibid* at paras 67–73.

> person who provokes an assault and subsequently kills the person he attacks when that person responds to the assault must retreat if he wishes to plead self-defence. Otherwise, a person who wished to kill another and escape punishment might deliberately provoke an attack so that he might respond with a death blow. People who provoke attacks must know that a response, even if it is life-threatening, will not entitle them to stand their ground and kill. Rather, they must retreat. The obligation to retreat from provoked assault has stood the test of time. It should not lightly be discarded. Life is precious; the justification for taking it must be defined with care and circumspection.[135]

McLachlin J here had recourse to the policy underlying the self-defence provisions. She did not refer to social science research, public opinion, or government reports; instead, she pointed to the policy that has motivated the common law courts for centuries. In her view, the value placed on life has changed little in the modern age: its preservation is the greatest duty of humans, however far we may stray from the ideal in practice. People who provoke attacks are wrong to do so, especially when a response to the provocation is likely and the resulting altercation will cause harm and, potentially, death.

In *McIntosh*, as in *Cuerrier*, *Creighton*, and *Théroux*, Chief Justice McLachlin is sensitive to the need for incremental, rather than radical, change that brings the criminal law into alignment with contemporary social and political context. Where there are indications that mainstream social views have not swung as far away from traditional victim-centred values toward values more favourable to the defence, McLachlin J's common law method dictates restraint.

IV. Chief Justice McLachlin's Common Law Approach to Public Law

The common law approach is a *method* of public law reasoning; it is not a self-conscious attempt to deploy particular norms and values. Of course, the common law method, like any legal methodology, has a history that associates it with the social and political values of the time; in consequence, using a common law method has a tendency to promote certain liberal democratic values that underlie the Canadian and British common law systems. Chief Justice McLachlin's criminal law judgments during the 1990s deployed the common law method, with

135 *Ibid* at para 82.

the result that these cases generally promote traditional liberal democratic principles, updated incrementally to conform to modern social and political context.

Why was this method appealing to the Chief Justice? There are no doubt personal reasons related to her educational background, especially her philosophical and legal training, and her experience in practice and on the bench in British Columbia. But just as judges determine legislative intent when interpreting statutes by studying the statute itself rather than placing too much weight on contextual documents such as Hansard, committee minutes, and so on, I propose to make a few comments about Justice McLachlin's purpose in using the common law method, based purely on what can be gleaned from the text of her decisions rather than resorting to extrinsic biographical evidence.

One explanation for the appeal of applying the common law approach in public law cases may have something to do with McLachlin CJ's ideological position on the Supreme Court in the 1990s and the methods adopted by other judges. As we have seen, both Chief Justice Lamer and Justice Cory, who wrote many of the criminal law judgments during this period, tended to use the other dominant public law approach that involves identifying an abstract political principle (such as the "stigma principle" in *Creighton*) or else a policy goal to be achieved (more characteristic of Cory J's judgments) and then interpreting the *Criminal Code* in a way consistent with the desired principle or policy. McLachlin J's judgments often sought to update the law in a more incremental, restrained way, and the common law method reflects this ideological goal.

As well, using the common law method has the advantage of linking the change the Court is proposing to the past and to certain fundamental values that have long been the foundation of our legal system, thereby cloaking the new in the accrued authority of the old. The first step of the common law method requires analysing past judgments and extracting a principle from them, and the process of doing so enables the modern judge to invoke the authority of past jurists and scholars.[136] Also, when judges focus on a method of reasoning rather than on policy arguments, the judgment tends to have a coherence and cogency that can make it more persuasive, especially to readers with a philosophical

---

136 Or in the case of statutes, as I indicated above, the first step is to use the principles of statutory interpretation to determine the legislators' intention. Of course, inherent in these principles of construction is the need for statutes to be interpreted in ways that conform to the basic principles of justice inherent in our written and unwritten (common law) constitution (see Allan, *supra* note 42).

bent who appreciate informal logic. More analysis of the Chief Justice's judgments from the 1990s would have to be done to discern patterns in the judges and scholars to whom she referred. Such research would allow us to draw a more certain conclusion about the value of linking present judgments to the past.

The recent biography of Justice L'Heureux-Dubé by Constance Backhouse[137] documents in a detailed way what has long been known anecdotally about the conflict among the judges of the Supreme Court during the 1990s. Another possible explanation for McLachlin J's preference for the common law method in public law adjudication may be the rhetorical benefit that it conferred in the context of the fractious Lamer Court: when judgments are based on sound reasoning and an analysis of historical precedent, this can lend them objectivity, which may have been a useful rhetorical counterpoint to the more ideological and overtly political debates between other judges on the Court. Here too, more analysis is required in order to substantiate this argument.

Another future study that could be undertaken would involve comparing Chief Justice McLachlin's criminal law judgments after she was appointed Chief Justice with those during the tenure of Chief Justice Lamer. Such a study would also help scholars determine the role that the divisions on the Court in the 1990s played in Chief Justice McLachlin's preference for the common law approach in public law cases. A cursory examination of the Chief Justice's judgments in recent cases such as *R v Nur* (minimum sentences),[138] *R v Cairney* (provocation defence),[139] *Canada (Attorney General) v Bedford* (constitutionality of prostitution offences),[140] and *R v Mabior* (consent vitiated by fraud) indicate a shift in her style of judgment. The decision that adheres most closely to the 1990s cases using the common law approach to public law is, not surprisingly, *Mabior*,[141] which, like the *Cuerrier* case discussed in Part II of this chapter, involved the interpretation of section 265(3)(c) of the *Criminal Code*. However, even in *Mabior*, while McLachlin CJ's reasons review in detail the common law cases relating to the vitiation of consent by fraud, the reset in *Cuerrier* that extensively updated the values underlying sexual assault law[142] meant that she applied *Charter* values such as "equality, autonomy, liberty, privacy and human dignity" in the

137 Constance Backhouse, *Claire L'Heureux-Dubé: A Life* (Vancouver: UBC Press, 2017).

138 *R v Nur*, 2015 SCC 15.

139 *R v Cairney*, 2013 SCC 55.

140 *Canada (Attorney General) v Bedford*, 2013 SCC 72.

141 *Mabior*, *supra* note 45.

142 *Ibid* at para 43.

style of a classic public law judgment without the contextual interpretation and incrementalism characteristic of her earlier decisions. This may suggest that the Court has entered into a new phase of interpreting and applying the *Charter* in which the continuity with past common law principles was less important because most of the applicable *Charter* rights had been interpreted since 1982, making the common law less pertinent.

Another possibility is that the difference between styles of reasoning among judges depends on a judge's legal training in civil versus common law. Perhaps the penchant of civilian judges such as Lamer CJ and L'Heureux-Dubé J to begin with the statement of a general principle rather than an examination of the case law is a result of the unique mode of reasoning in civil law systems. As Eva Steiner explains, "[t]he French Cartesian propensity for conceptual thinking, whereby particulars are subsumed under universals by an act of categorization, explains why the deductive method, when applied in a legal context, is considered in France to be best able to settle legal issues conclusively."[143] This deductive method depends on the articulation of the general principle, and it contrasts markedly from the first step of the common law method as articulated by Diplock J in *Dorset Yacht*, which involves inductive reasoning to identify the unifying principle behind disparate cases, a principle that was generally not identified by individual judges.

A final consideration may be that the Chief Justice changed her style of judgment as a result of her new leadership role at the Court. To the extent that the Supreme Court is now characterized by greater unity and consensus than during the 1990s under Chief Justice Lamer, perhaps the Chief Justice found that a value-based approach focusing on policy arguments was conducive to creating and sustaining consensus. Further research is required to determine why this might be the case. One can speculate that judges drafting reasons encounter less resistance from their colleagues if they remain on the level of general policy or abstract values than would be the case if they undertook a detailed analysis of past cases. Relying on old cases and academic interpretations of them invites disagreement about their meaning and a consequent loss of consensus in regard to the outcome of the decision and applicable policy arguments. Each judge may have a different assessment of the

143 Eva Steiner, *French Law: A Comparative Approach* (Oxford: Oxford University Press, 2018) at 112.

value of a decision by Lord Denning, and this may detract from the consensus about a policy issue.

To conclude, there is much to be learned by studying Chief Justice McLachlin's general approach to public law cases. To take up the metaphor with which I began this chapter, some framework is necessary to give structure to the chaotic legal universe: during the 1990s, McLachlin CJ seems to have relied on a method that sought continuity between the novelty of the *Charter* and well-established legal values. This method was responsive to the social and political context of the present while also providing an inherent, salutary limit on innovation. Relying on a method or style of judgment to provide this order rather than relying on abstract political values appears to have helped anchor the Chief Justice's public law judgments firmly to the liberal democratic values that have long animated our legal system. The method also lends her judgments the authority, coherence, and persuasiveness that have caused them to endure as examples of good judgment for law students, lawyers, and judges.

9 Less Is More: Chief Justice McLachlin and Criminal Law Minimalism

MATTHEW R. GOURLAY

I. Introduction

In *Reference re Assisted Human Reproduction Act*, Chief Justice McLachlin wrote: "Every generation faces unique moral issues. And historically, every generation has turned to the criminal law to address them."[1] While the existence of this societal impulse is clear, jurists and scholars continue to wrestle with the question of how much leeway it should be given. How quick should we be to invoke the criminal law when attempting to discourage unfavoured conduct? What role, if any, do the courts have in limiting the circumstances in which Parliament may legitimately invoke the criminal law to address perceived social ills?

The orthodox response is: Parliament can criminalize pretty much whatever it wants to, and courts will be loath to second-guess such decisions.[2] But popular and scholarly attitudes toward the efficacy of criminal law as a solution to social problems have evolved. "Overcriminalization" is a concept that has generated intense academic interest in recent years, principally but not exclusively from American criminal law scholars.[3] The late Harvard law professor William Stuntz

1 *Reference re Assisted Human Reproduction Act*, 2010 SCC 61 at para 1.

2 After all, for the purposes of section 91(27) of the *Constitution Act, 1867*, 30 & 31 Vict, c 3 (UK), a valid criminal law need only contain a prohibition backed by a penalty and be in furtherance of a "legitimate public purpose," broadly defined: *Reference re Validity of Section 5(a) of the Dairy Industry Act*, [1949] SCR 1.

3 See e.g. William J. Stuntz, "The Pathological Politics of Criminal Law" (2001) 100:3 Mich L Rev 100; Douglas Husak, *Overcriminalization: The Limits of the Criminal Law* (New York: Oxford University Press, 2008); Stephen F. Smith, "Overcoming Overcriminalization" (2012) 102:3 J Crim L & Criminology 537; Erik Luna, "The Overcriminalization Phenomenon" (2005) 54:3 Am UL Rev 703.

memorably described overcriminalization as "the rule of *too much* law."[4] The American focus of much of the work in this area is understandable, given the well-known crisis of mass incarceration that has plagued that country.[5] But Canada is not immune to the phenomenon. To take a highly unscientific measure, the 2018 edition of *Martin's Criminal Code* is 1,806 pages long.[6] This is about double the length of the same volume a quarter-century ago. Although a significant portion of this bulk is taken up with procedural provisions, the unmistakable truth is that Canada has a lot of criminal offences. In Canada, as elsewhere, criminal laws are much more frequently – and more easily – enacted than they are repealed.[7] That means that the volume of criminal law tends to expand with time, regardless of whether anyone thinks it is necessary.

I think that the Supreme Court of Canada under Chief Justice McLachlin's leadership has taken important but admittedly inconsistent steps toward addressing the overcriminalization phenomenon from a judicial perspective. Contrary to what might be inferred from the sweeping language in the *Assisted Reproduction Reference*, I believe that an important theme in Chief Justice McLachlin's criminal law jurisprudence is her healthy scepticism of the criminal law as a cure for social ills. Her contribution usefully can be seen through the lens of what has been called "criminal law minimalism."[8] In her early civil libertarian

---

4 This is the title of the Introduction to William J Stuntz's great work *The Collapse of American Criminal Justice* (Cambridge, MA: Harvard University Press, 2011).

5 See, generally, *ibid*; Michelle Alexander, *The New Jim Crow: Mass Incarceration in the Age of Colorblindness* (New York: New Press, 2010); John F. Pfaff, *Locked In: The True Causes of Mass Incarceration and How to Achieve Real Reform* (New York: Basic Books, 2017). While the damage wrought by the extreme post-1960s incarceration boom has obviously lent moral and political urgency to the critique of overcriminalization, the two phenomena are not necessarily coterminous. Naturally, a system can criminalize too broadly without giving rise to the kind of mass incarceration that has characterized the modern American justice system. Notably, back in 1968, the distinguished criminal law scholar Sanford Kadish was already warning of a "crisis" of overcriminalization in that country: "The Crisis of Overcriminalization" (1967) 374 Annals of the American Academy of Political and Social Science 157. In fact, America's incarceration rate would undergo four decades of astronomical growth before entering a modest decline in recent years.

6 I include here just the annotated *Criminal Code* itself (RSC 1985, c C-46); the related statutes such as the *Controlled Drugs and Substances Act* (SC 1996, c 19) add another few hundred pages.

7 Douglas Husak, "The Criminal Law as a Last Resort" (2004) 24:2 Oxford J Leg Studies 207.

8 Douglas Husak, *The Philosophy of Criminal Law: Selected Essays* (Oxford: Oxford University Press, 2010) at 413, citing Andrew Ashworth, *Principles of Criminal Law*, 4th ed (Oxford: Clarendon, 2003) at 32–7.

judgments – most famously, her dissent in *Keegstra* and her majority reasons in *Zundel* – McLachlin J rejected the proposition that criminal law should police hate speech, at least beyond narrow limits.[9] In her *Rodriguez* dissent, she rejected the criminalization of assisted suicide.[10] These judgments, all dating from the early 1990s, can be seen to evince a philosophically libertarian scepticism about the over-extension of criminal law to the realm of morality.

Chief Justice McLachlin's later landmark rulings de-emphasize the philosophical dimension of criminal law minimalism in favour of an ostensibly more neutral, evidence-based approach. Having declined to join her colleague Arbour J in enshrining the Millian "harm principle" as a principle of fundamental justice in *Malmo-Levine* (upholding the marijuana prohibition),[11] McLachlin CJ's later judgments ask a different question: Does the impugned law, viewed in context, actually do more harm than good? In *Bedford*, McLachlin CJ re-tooled the section 7 principles of overbreadth and gross proportionality to address a package of laws that, while grounded in traditional "moral" concerns, could no longer be justified on the evidence.[12] In *Carter*,[13] McLachlin CJ's *Rodriguez* dissent effectively morphed into a *per curiam* decision striking down the assisted suicide ban – again, on the grounds that its detrimental impact on those affected by it could not be empirically justified. These decisions, I think, reflect the extent to which Chief Justice McLachlin has always been a realist and pragmatist more than a proponent of any judicial ideology.

No doubt owing to her pragmatic judicial outlook, Chief Justice McLachlin never articulated or embraced a minimalist outlook in any systematic fashion. Indeed, some of the Court's judgments under her leadership can be seen as expansionist in orientation and effect: the *Assisted Human Reproduction* reference for one, but also *R v Creighton* (holding that objective foreseeability of a risk of death is not an essential element of unlawful act manslaughter);[14] *R v Mabior* (maintaining an overly broad approach to the criminalization of HIV non-disclosure);[15] and *R v JA* (elaborating a stringent and arguably paternalistic definition of what counts as consent for the purposes of sexual assault).[16] Such

9 *R v Keegstra*, [1990] 3 SCR 697; *R v Zundel*, [1992] 2 SCR 731.

10 *Rodriguez v British Columbia (Attorney General)*, [1993] 3 SCR 519 [*Rodriguez*].

11 *R v Malmo-Levine; R v Caine*, 2003 SCC 74 [*Malmo-Levine*].

12 *Canada (Attorney General) v Bedford*, 2013 SCC 72 [*Bedford*].

13 *Carter v Canada (Attorney General)*, 2015 SCC 5 [*Carter*].

14 *R v Creighton*, [1993] 3 SCR 3.

15 *R v Mabior*, 2012 SCC 47 [*Mabior*].

16 *R v JA*, 2011 SCC 28.

cases tend to be statutory rather than constitutional cases and, in my view, provide support for the contention, advanced toward the end of this chapter, that the McLachlin Court's most significant shortcoming in this area is its failure to consistently bring its *Charter*-derived minimalist ethos to the statutory realm – an area of the law where (in the guise of strict construction) minimalism actually has a venerable doctrinal lineage.[17] (More on that below.)

It is in the constitutional realm that, in my view, a sceptical approach to the breadth of criminalization has made the most significant contributions, which remain ripe for further development. While neither the Court nor McLachlin CJ has ever held that "harm to others" is a constitutional requirement for criminalization, I believe the result of the trajectory described above appears to be a general consensus around something functionally similar. It is striking that both *Bedford* and *Carter*, despite the divisive nature of the underlying issues, featured a unanimous Court under the leadership of the Chief Justice. Canadian law appears to have arrived at something resembling a minimalist principle as a constitutional prerequisite: namely, that a criminal law must not do more harm than good, seen from the perspective of *both* those whom it targets and those whom it is seeks to protect. In this chapter, I trace the development of this consensus and consider its implications.

After discussing criminal law minimalism in general, I want to consider three possible kinds of overcriminalization and what the Court under McLachlin CJ has done about them. They are:

- criminalization of conduct that harms no one other than the putative offender (i.e., purely paternalistic offences);
- criminalization of conduct that does cause harm to others, but not of a nature or magnitude sufficient to justify a specifically criminal law response; and
- overly broad or overly flexible interpretations of generally valid offences.

These are by no means watertight categories, but I think they usefully illustrate different ways in which the criminal law can go too far. I think the Court has made important strides with respect to the first two. The Court has not done enough with respect to the latter, in my opinion.

17 See e.g. *R v McLaughlin*, [1980] 2 SCR 331 at 335 per Laskin CJC.

First, I want to sketch out the terms of criminal law "minimalism," which I see emerging, albeit inconsistently, in the Court's recent jurisprudence and particularly that of Chief Justice McLachlin.

II. Criminal Law Minimalism

While the Chief Justice in the *Assisted Reproduction Reference* spoke of each generation having recourse to the criminal law as a forum for adjudicating emerging moral issues, many jurists and scholars now see criminal law as something of a "last resort" for conduct that cannot be otherwise addressed.[18] In other words, the mere fact that a certain type of conduct is, in some way, socially undesirable doesn't lead automatically to the conclusion that it ought to be criminalized. Back in 1991, Justice Doherty expressed a similar sentiment when he opined that "[t]he criminal law is essentially a means whereby society seeks to prevent, and, failing that, punish blameworthy conduct which strikes at the fundamental values of the community. The criminal law is, however, a weapon of last resort intended for use only in cases where the conduct is so inconsistent with the shared morality of society so as to warrant public condemnation and punishment."[19]

I am not here engaging with the deeper philosophical debate between rights-based and utilitarian theories of prohibition and punishment, because I don't think consensus on those questions is either realistic or necessary. Both, I think, involve a balancing exercise that plays out in roughly similar ways. For instance, one can posit an individual *right* not to be punished,[20] which can be overcome only with compelling state justification. Or one can go straight to the utilitarian balancing of interests for and against criminalization. Either way, I think any civilized system needs to grapple with this question: Is this particular conduct of a kind that merits the imposition of *punishment by the state*?

Criminal prosecutions and penalties are costly in a number of ways. Because of the severe consequences of a criminal conviction, a criminal charge comes with a broad array of procedural protections, many of which have been entrenched in the *Charter*: the right to a jury trial; the right to challenge the constitutionality of evidence gathering; the right to be presumed innocent, and to be found not guilty unless proven

---

18 See Husak, *supra* note 7, in which the author articulates a version of the "last resort" principle but ultimately concludes that it has limited potential as a means of turning back the tide of overcriminalization.

19 *R v Greenwood* (1991), 5 OR (3d) 71 (Ont CA) [*Greenwood*].

20 Husak, *supra* note 3 at 92–103.

guilty beyond a reasonable doubt. All of these are costly for society to put into effect – and justifiably so, given the potential consequences for the accused. Quite apart from the more intangible damage to the social fabric that flows from over-policing and over-incarceration, these direct financial costs suggest that society has an interest in using the criminal law sparingly.

But criminal prosecutions are also usually costly for the accused. This is often given short shrift as an objection to criminalization, given the natural antipathy for an offender who (absent a mental disorder) presumably could have refrained from committing the crime in the first place.

In a real sense, however, criminal laws exist *because* we know people will break them. Conduct that nobody actually commits doesn't generally require specific criminal prohibition. The legal philosopher Douglas Husak points out that, while criminal laws naturally *aspire* to eradicate the targeted conduct altogether, perfect compliance and perfect deterrence are both practically impossible.[21] This has important implications for what qualifies as appropriate subject matter for criminal laws. Consider: if passing a criminal law against some modestly undesirable activity actually stopped people from engaging in it, then such laws may well be justifiable, provided that the right to engage in the activity in question is not particularly important. A criminal law against spitting on the street would be justifiable on the grounds that the conduct is disgusting and the salutary effect of the law is to get rid of it.[22] Because everyone obeyed, we would never need to ask the question of whether it is a proper use of resources to prosecute a person for spitting, or whether it is appropriate to stigmatize and punish the spitter as a criminal.

Professor Husak gives the example of criminalizing consumption of doughnuts in order to promote health.[23] There being no fundamental right to eat doughnuts, this may seem unobjectionable, if we assume that everyone will actually comply. No doughnuts will be consumed, and, overall, people will be healthier. But if we recognize that some people will eat doughnuts anyway, then we need to face up to the question of whether it's justifiable to criminally stigmatize and punish people for a basically innocuous (even if unhealthy) activity. Most people

21 *Ibid* at 78.

22 Naturally, perfect obedience to a draconian criminal law might reveal and perpetuate other social pathologies that might make the law undesirable even if no one were ever punished for breaking it. But that's a different question and not necessary for the point I'm trying to make here.

23 Husak, *supra* note 3 at 124–5.

would say: obviously not. Criminal laws motivated exclusively by paternalism will normally fail this test, Husak observes, because the harm caused to the person who engages in the activity will almost always be exceeded by the harm caused by leveling a criminal penalty against that person: "Almost no conduct that sane adults are voluntarily inclined to perform is so destructive of their welfare that they are better off in jail than free to continue to engage in it."[24]

Seen through this lens, purely paternalistic criminal laws are difficult to justify. If we're concerned about the potential offender's own wrongdoing, it will very rarely be better to subject an individual to criminal prosecution than to allow them to engage in the targeted conduct or find other, less severe means of behaviour modification. By contrast, Mill's harm principle elevates the rejection of paternalism to a categorical proscription. *Even if* the conduct in question is worse for the accused than prosecution and jail, the orthodox Millian would say, this is the individual's problem, not the state's.[25] But, either way, a serious consideration of the prospective *accused*'s own welfare will make purely paternalist laws always or almost always objectionable.

What about prohibitions that *do* involve real or apprehended harm or offence to others? The more serious the apprehended harm or offence, presumably, the easier it will be to justify the imposition of criminal conviction and punishment.

Here, the example of spitting on the street is relevant, since such conduct does impinge on the interests of people other than the spitter, if only minimally. Because the harm to others is minimal, it's unlikely that the costs of criminal conviction *to the offender* would be outweighed by the social good that would flow from criminalization. In this sense, the kind of minimalism I am endorsing asks, first, whether the conduct at issue poses a risk of more than trivial harm to others, and, if so, only then whether criminal law is the best way to go about addressing it. Knowing that total prevention is an illusory goal, we need to face up to the fact that some people will break the law. And then we need to ask whether the criminal law is the fairest and most appropriate way in which to deal with the people who do. This kind of scrutiny is characteristic of what I am calling criminal law minimalism.

---

24 *Ibid* at 152.

25 JS Mill, *On Liberty* (1859), ed Geraint Williams (London: JM Dent & Sons, 1993) at 78: "The only part of the conduct of any one, for which he is amenable to society, is that which concerns others. In the part which merely concerns himself, his independence is, of right, absolute. Over himself, over his own body and mind, the individual is sovereign."

To be sure, minimalism has never been accepted as anything like official doctrine by the Canadian judiciary. Justice Doherty expressed the dominant view when he wrote:[26]

> [M]any argue that the criminal sanction should be a last resort employed only if other forms of governmental action cannot adequately address the harm flowing from the conduct. This minimalist approach to criminal law may well be sound criminal law policy. However, it hardly reflects the historical reality of the scope of the criminal law so as to be properly described as a principle of fundamental justice. Any attempt to apply minimalist doctrine to a specific piece of legislation would raise complex questions of social policy which would defy effective resolution in the context of the adversarial criminal law process.

Although this is probably still true in general terms, I think the Supreme Court under Chief Justice McLachlin has taken strides toward implementing a certain kind of minimalist approach, primarily under the aegis of section 7 of the *Charter*.[27] While this is far from a plenary review of all criminal laws to ensure they meet the kind of "last resort" criterion referred to by Justice Doherty, it has nonetheless entailed closer judicial scrutiny of the state's choice of *what* and *how* to criminalize, particular as those choices impact already marginalized populations.

III. Judicial Recourse against Overcriminalization

Constitutional review in Canadian criminal law under the *Charter* is largely about process, not substance – in other words, *how* the state can go about investigating and prosecuting crime, not what it can criminalize in the first place. This is hardly surprising, since the *Charter*'s legal rights guarantees in sections 7 through 13 are almost all about process – the right to counsel, the right to a jury trial, and so on.

In the early *Charter* landmark *Re BC Motor Vehicle Act*, however, a majority of the Court held that the "principles of fundamental justice" in section 7 are substantive as well as procedural.[28] Writing for the majority,

26 *R v Murdock* (2003), 11 CR (6th) 43 (Ont CA) at para 33.

27 I think that McLachlin CJ's judgments striking down Harper-era mandatory minimum sentences – *R v Lloyd*, 2016 SCC 13; *R v Nur*, 2015 SCC 15 [*Nur*] – evince a properly sceptical attitude toward over-punishment that shares much in common with what I am calling her minimalist approach to criminalization. I don't address the punishment side in this chapter, however.

28 *Re BC Motor Vehicle Act*, [1985] 2 SCR 486.

Lamer J. (as he then was) rejected the very premise of a neat divide between process and substance, deeming it to be an Americanism better avoided in the elaboration of a distinctively Canadian jurisprudence.[29] Justice Lamer emphasized the venerable tradition of Canadian courts placing *substantive* constraints on the criminal law through the development of the common law, giving examples such as the *Kienapple* rule against multiple convictions, the prohibition of retrospective offences, the presumptions against diluting the burden of proof, and the entrapment doctrine.[30] Recognizing the validity of concerns that the Court not become a "super-legislature" enacting its own policy preferences under the guise of constitutional adjudication, Justice Lamer held that the principles of fundamental justice "are to be found in the basic tenets and principles not only of our judicial process but also of the other components of our legal system."[31] In other words, judges do not invent the principles of fundamental justice; the principles are there, already embedded in the fabric of our system, waiting to be identified and given constitutional force.[32] As can be seen from the examples provided by Lamer J, the common law itself contained a number of mechanisms by which the judiciary was able to temper the severity and breadth of the criminal law. (Another example that could have been given was the principle of strict construction of criminal offences, a topic to which I will return below.)

In any event, this crucial rejection of a purely procedural role for section 7 gave some basis for believing that the courts could make substantive inroads against overcriminalization under the auspices of fundamental justice.[33] This hope was encouraged by early decisions like *Morgentaler*, striking down the abortion law,[34] and *Vaillancourt*, striking down the offence of constructive murder.[35]

---

29 *Ibid* at 498.

30 *Ibid* at 499.

31 *Ibid* at 512.

32 For an insightful insider's view of the challenges involved in giving meaning to section 7's promise while staying within the Court's proper institutional role, see Frank Iacobucci, "Some Reflections on Re BC Motor Vehicle Act" (2011) 42:3 Ottawa L Rev 305.

33 In *The Collapse of American Criminal Justice*, William J. Stuntz laments the eclipse of substance by process as a crucial missed opportunity that ended up being one of the causal factors driving the conservative backlash against the Warren Court – which in turn resulted in the contemporary crisis of mass incarceration. *Supra* note 4 at 209–12.

34 *R v Morgentaler*, [1988] 1 SCR 30. Notably, despite the expansive scope of *Re BC Motor Vehicle Act*, four of the five judges in the majority decided the case on fairly traditional procedural grounds that did not engage the substantive question of a constitutional right to abortion.

35 *R v Vaillancourt*, [1987] 2 SCR 636.

While it's true that most purely *subject matter–based* challenges to criminal law have failed,[36] the substantive principles of fundamental justice have, under Chief Justice McLachlin's leadership, increasingly been mobilized to draw boundaries around the scope of permissible criminalization. Most importantly, the concepts of overbreadth and gross disproportionality have, as articulated most forcefully by McLachlin CJ, developed into meaningful bulwarks against overcriminalization – and have allowed the Court to accomplish this in a way that does not overtly commit it to any philosophical or political program, even one as well-pedigreed as Mill's "harm" principle. These are, after all, ostensibly content-neutral principles whose application does not depend on one's *ex ante* view of the appropriateness of criminalizing any particular conduct. Rather, they take the legislative objective on its own terms and try to assess, on the basis of evidence, whether Parliament has gone further than necessary to achieve its desired ends.

With that background in mind, I want to move on to consider the three specific kinds of overcriminalization mentioned above to see how the Court's embrace of this form of minimalism has (and hasn't) affected how specific criminal offences have been judged.

a. Criminalizing Harmless or Socially Valuable Conduct

This is, to my mind, the most obvious form of overcriminalization – but it is one that the Supreme Court has declined the opportunity to expressly proscribe. Nonetheless, as I will explain, I think that the Court's increasingly rigourous approach to section 7 has gone hand in hand with a heightened scepticism of morality-based justifications for imposing the criminal sanction and, in effect, a narrowing of the state's scope for criminalizing generally harmless conduct.

At the outset, it needs to be recognized that the Court has rejected "harm to others" as a general requirement of any valid criminal law. In *Malmo-Levine*, the Court heard several linked appeals challenging the then-existing marijuana prohibition. Although there were several bases for the challenge, the main one was grounded in Mill's harm principle: that the state may validly punish a person *only* for conduct that causes harm (or poses a risk of harm) to someone other than the perpetrator.[37]

---

36 See e.g. *R v Sharpe*, 2001 SCC 2 (child pornography); *R v Butler*, [1992] 1 SCR 452 (obscenity); *Malmo-Levine*, *supra* note 11 (marijuana).

37 The actual force of this principle, even if accepted as a constitutional constraint, would naturally depend on the stringency with which it was applied. The majority of the BC Court of Appeal in *Malmo-Levine* accepted it as a principle of fundamental

Five justices wrote reasons; somewhat surprisingly, McLachlin CJ was not among them. The Chief Justice signed on to the majority opinion penned by Justices Gonthier and Binnie, rejecting the contention that the harm principle amounts to a *Charter* constraint on criminal lawmaking, and maintaining the traditional view that Parliament may properly invoke the criminal law to reflect *moral* standards even with respect to conduct that does not necessarily produce tangible harm to people other than the accused. Criminal laws against bestiality and adult incest were cited as examples supporting this view. While the majority acknowledged that the harm principle is a "description of an important state interest" *justifying* criminalization in many instances, it denied that there was sufficient consensus in Canadian law for considering it to be a *prerequisite* for criminalization in all cases.

In dissent, Arbour J embraced the harm principle as an enforceable constraint on the criminal law power, holding that the state may threaten people with jail only where the conduct in question poses a risk of demonstrable harm to others. Importantly, she forcefully rejected the majority's implicit claim that a risk of harm to vulnerable people like drug users could justify threatening *those very people* with imprisonment.[38]

The result of *Malmo-Levine* may indicate that Canadian law continues to tolerate the criminalization of harmless conduct. However, I think that, in the years since that case was decided, the Court has taken strides toward the decriminalization of harmless conduct in a manner broadly consistent with the Arbour dissent. Let me briefly discuss just a couple of examples.

One example of this movement is *Labaye*, the "swingers" case.[39] There, the accused had been charged and convicted with public indecency for operating a club in Montreal where people engaged in group sex.[40] When the case reached the Supreme Court, Chief Justice McLachlin (for

---

justice but nonetheless upheld the marijuana law. And in *Murdock*, writing just prior to the Supreme Court's decision in *Malmo-Levine*, Doherty JA accepted the harm principle as a principle of fundamental justice, but strictly limited its ambit. Under this formulation, the court's role is to determine only whether the criminal prohibition responds to a reasoned apprehension of harm; if so, the requirements of the principle are satisfied. The court does not go on to weigh the costs and benefits of criminalization. As discussed below, I think the Supreme Court has subsequently adopted a more interventionist approach, albeit under the rubric of overbreadth and gross disproportionality rather than the harm principle per se.

38 *Malmo-Levine, supra* note 11 at para 257.

39 *R v Labaye*, 2005 SCC 80 [*Labaye*].

40 To be exact, the accused was charged with keeping a "common bawdy-house" for the "practice of acts of indecency" under section 210(1) of the *Code*.

the majority) took the opportunity to jettison the last remnants of the old "community standard of tolerance" test for indecency and obscenity, replacing it with a test calibrated around three different types of *harm*.[41] This move was designed to "[bring] this area of the law into step with the vast majority of criminal offences, which are based on the need to protect society from harm."[42] In other words, even if "harm" is not a constitutional deal-breaker, where the elements of an offence are ambiguous, criminal legislation will be interpreted to require a showing of harm. Further, even where the Crown is able to prove that one or more of these contemplated harms flow from the allegedly indecent conduct, in order to obtain a conviction it must still go on to prove that the *degree* of harm thereby caused is "incompatible with the proper functioning of society."[43] This qualitative dimension is meant to ensure that the heavy hand of the criminal law is applied only where really necessary – in effect, something like a "last resort" criterion, although the Court does not use this language.

The impact of *Labaye* itself has been relatively modest, given that it deals with an arcane and seldom-charged offence.[44] But I think its approach of prioritizing demonstrated harm over abstract social values can be seen as informing the Court's approach to more consequential cases. Most notably, in *Carter*, the Court overruled its prior holding in *Rodriguez* and struck down the *Criminal Code* prohibition of assisted suicide.[45]

The Court did *not* directly hold that there is a constitutional right to end one's own life. It did not need to do so, given that suicide itself is not illegal. Rather, the objective of the law, according to the Court, was "protecting vulnerable people from being induced to commit suicide at a moment of weakness."[46] This is a permissible objective – indeed,

41 These were: (1) harm to those whose autonomy and liberty may be restricted by being confronted with inappropriate conduct; (2) harm to society by predisposing others to anti-social conduct; and (3) harm to individuals participating in the conduct: *Labaye, supra* note 39 at para 36.

42 *Ibid* at para 24.

43 *Ibid* at para 52.

44 However, in *R v Katigbak*, 2011 SCC 48, the Court applied a version of the *Labaye* significant harm/incompatibility test to its interpretation of the "public good" and "artistic merit" defences to child pornography offences, rejecting an approach that would focus on the moral views of the community.

45 *Rodriguez, supra* note 10. McLachlin J, in dissent, would have struck down the law as infringing personal autonomy in an arbitrary manner, given that an able-bodied person is entitled to end their life but the law forbids disabled people from obtaining assistance to do so.

46 *Carter, supra* note 13 at para 86.

a "pressing and substantial" one, in the jargon of *Oakes*. The constitutional defect is that the prohibition of assisted suicide pursues this valid objective in a manner that is overbroad, because it also applies to those who make a competent, fully informed decision to end their lives and require physician assistance to do so. Criminalizing the conduct of the physician renders such assistance practically unobtainable, thereby breaching the *Charter* rights of those who wish to seek it out.

I place this case in the "harmless conduct" category because the wrongfulness of assisted death, if any, can be grounded only in religion or other abstract morality. The government did not claim, nor could it, that an individual's considered decision to end their life in the face of a grave medical condition, or the physician's decision to assist them, causes harm to others. Rather, the government's justification of the law was essentially paternalistic: the prohibition was necessary to protect vulnerable people who may not be in a position to make a truly autonomous choice. The government rightly faced a heavy burden of demonstrating that protecting such vulnerable people could be achieved only by imposing extreme suffering on the non-vulnerable for whom physician assistance in dying would not actually occasion any harm.

b. Harmful Conduct Unsuitable for Criminalization

Although some kind of "harm" principle is probably a sensible restriction on what *can* be criminalized, it doesn't necessarily help in determining what *ought* to be criminalized. Plenty of modestly harmful conduct is widely accepted as being better dealt with by non-criminal regulation or merely by way of social disapprobation.

Even conduct posing a risk of significant harm may not be suitable for criminalization if there are countervailing interests at stake. Sometimes those countervailing interests take the form of constitutional entitlements in their own right. To this end, early in her tenure, Justice McLachlin staked out a civil libertarian position sceptical of the wisdom, efficacy, and constitutional permissibility of using the criminal law to mark off the bounds of acceptable speech.

In *Keegstra*, a majority of the Court held that the hate speech provision of the *Criminal Code* was a reasonable and demonstrably justified infringement of freedom of expression. In dissent, McLachlin J would have struck down the law. While her reasons certainty emphasized the fundamental status of free expression as a constitutional principle, she was at least as concerned with the pragmatic effects of criminalization. When it came to the *Oakes* proportionality analysis, McLachlin J acknowledged that the social harms of hate speech were substantial, but she concluded that the costs of a specifically *criminal law* response to them exceeded the benefits. She observed that it was "far from clear that the legislation does not promote the cause of hate-mongering extremists and hinder the possibility of voluntary amendment of conduct more than it discourages the spread of hate propaganda."[47]

Of course, *Keegstra* and *Zundel* are, in one sense, "easy" cases, because the criminalized conduct was actually *Charter*-protected speech. The question was whether harm to the rights of potential victims was sufficient to justify such a draconian impingement on free expression. Cases are more difficult from the standpoint of judicial intervention when the criminalized conduct is something that people would otherwise have the *liberty*, but not the constitutional *right*, to engage in. In such cases, the only potential counterbalance to the state's broad prerogative to criminalize is the individual's section 7 right not to be imprisoned except in accordance with the principles of fundamental justice. And it is here that Chief Justice McLachlin's work in giving substantive "teeth" to those principles has had the most profound impact on the Canadian state's entitlement to criminalize.

The *PHS Community Services Society* and *Bedford* cases mark a crucial development in that they concern activities that – unlike political speech – are far afield from the core of traditionally protected activities: illicit drug use and prostitution, respectively.[48] Both of them deal with core elements of the criminal law that have deep roots in the criminal law's traditional morality-based concerns. Both prostitution and illicit drug use allegedly result in social harm, although the nature and extent of those harms are obviously very much the subject of debate.

Yet in both cases, the Court, led by the Chief Justice, scrutinized the actual impacts of the challenged laws and found that they did more harm than good to the law-breakers themselves. In neither of these cases did the finding rest on any kind of deeper *right* to engage in the targeted conduct, as was claimed unsuccessfully in *Malmo-Levine* and successfully in *Carter*. Again, such cases are easier in the sense that the right to engage in a constitutionally protected (or beneficial) activity can very well win out over the state's right to criminalize, even on a traditional understanding of the criminal law power.

Rather, the *PHS* and *Bedford* cases can be understood as imposing on the state a functional burden of justifying – usually with evidence –

47 *Keegstra*, *supra* note 9 at 864.

48 *Canada (Attorney General) v PHS Community Services Society*, 2011 SCC 44; *Bedford*, *supra* note 12.

the imposition of the criminal sanction where there is a plausible argument that criminalization itself may cause harm. The *PHS* case was a challenge to the refusal of the federal Minister of Health to renew a *Controlled Drugs and Substances Act*[49] (*CDSA*) exemption previously granted to Insite, a supervised injection site in Vancouver's Downtown East Side. The lack of an exemption raised the prospect that both users and staff could be prosecuted for drug offences under the *CDSA*, notwithstanding the evidence at trial that Insite saved lives by providing drug users with a safe and supervised environment in which they could inject drugs with clean equipment. McLachlin CJ held that the Minister's refusal of the exemption was constitutionally impermissible, because the effect of criminalization on the health and safety of the facility's users was grossly disproportionate to any positive health and safety results and could be expected to flow from the refusal.[50]

Bedford, of course, concerned a challenge to a group of prostitution-related offences, with the claimants arguing that the *Criminal Code* regime compromised their safety by preventing them from (for instance) hiring security and screening potential clients. Writing for the Court, McLachlin CJ held that the negative impact of the bawdy-house and public solicitation prohibitions on the personal security of sex workers was grossly disproportionate to the relatively modest public nuisance concerns that were said to justify them. And the criminalization of "living on the avails" was overbroad because it targeted work that was protective, not just exploitative, of sex workers. All of these conclusions were grounded in the extensive factual findings made by the trial judge about the harms occasioned by the law. Abstract considerations of public morality potentially justifying the laws, and considerations of personal autonomy arguably undermining their validity, were alike given strikingly little attention. The Chief Justice's focus was all on real-world impact: do these criminal laws do more harm than good? On the trial judge's factual findings, the answer was relatively clear.

Clearly, a significant feature of the *Bedford* case was that the impugned provisions criminalized aspects of an otherwise legal practice. Indeed, the very first line of the Chief Justice's reasons observed that "[i]t is not a crime in Canada to sell sex for money."[51] And the Chief Justice went on to state that the case is *not* about whether or not prostitution should

49 *Controlled Drugs and Substances Act*, SC 1996, c 19, s 56.

50 The failure to extend Insite's exemption was also found to offend the principle against arbitrariness.

51 *Bedford*, *supra* note 12.

be legal. She focused her section 7 analysis on security of the person rather than liberty, even though liberty was clearly engaged because these were all jailable offences.[52] This focus was, at least in part, because the thrust of the complainants' argument was that *complying* with the law compromised their safety – and only derivatively that imprisonment for non-compliance would be offensive to fundamental justice.[53]

Nonetheless, while the legality of prostitution was important to demonstrating the unjustness of the government's position, I think it's open to question whether it was actually crucial to the result. In answer to the government's contention that sex workers bring the risks upon themselves by engaging in a risky activity, the Chief Justice emphasizes the extent to which many sex workers are members of vulnerable populations who may enjoy no other realistic means of sustenance.[54] This emphasis picks up an aspect of Justice Arbour's dissent in *Malmo-Levine*: namely, the illogic of purporting to help vulnerable people by criminalizing them.

In my view, the logic of *PHS*, *Bedford*, and *Carter* takes us close to recognition of a general right not to be punished – or at least not to be imprisoned – for conduct that causes no significant harm to society, or causes harm that is outweighed by that occasioned by the criminal prohibition itself.[55] This is an important and welcome development, in my view, because it brings us closer to the entrenchment of criminal law minimalism as an enforceable constitutional entitlement.

c. Conduct at the Margins of Otherwise Valid Offences

In this category I put conduct about which there can be reasonable debate on whether it falls within the scope of an otherwise valid criminal offence. In essence, it is a question of how broadly or narrowly to construe offence-creating provisions and what to do in cases of plausible ambiguity.

The "strict construction" principle used to be a widely accepted part of criminal law doctrine, arising in a former era where death was the

52 The "living off the avails" offence would likely not have engaged any of the claimants' liberty interests, however, as McLachlin CJ observed in the footnote to para 58, *ibid*.

53 See McLachlin CJ's footnote to para 58, *ibid*.

54 *Ibid* at para 86.

55 Alana Klein has argued persuasively that *PHS* and *Bedford* involve a judicial embrace of the public health "harm reduction" approach, with its characteristic concern for evidence-based solutions over prohibitionist ideology: "Criminal Law and the Counter-Hegemonic Potential of Harm Reduction" (2015) 38:2 Dalhousie LJ 447.

presumptive punishment across a wide array of offences.[56] It has been formulated as the principle that "[w]here an equivocal word or ambiguous sentence leaves a reasonable doubt of its meaning which the canons of interpretation fail to solve, the benefit of the doubt should be given to the subject and against the Legislature which has failed to explain itself."[57] Strict construction originally arose as a kind of judicial stopgap designed to avoid inappropriate executions and other unduly harsh punishments.[58] Although the Court affirmed the "continued vitality of the doctrine" as late as 1987, it seems to have generally fallen into desuetude as "purposive" and "remedial" interpretation has increasingly held sway.[59]

Purposive interpretation has always seemed to me to be more an aspiration than a methodology and, as such, is difficult to gainsay. But if we really believe that criminal law is a blunt implement to be sparingly invoked, only conduct that unambiguously falls within the scope of a criminal provision should be caught. Unfortunately, purposive interpretation of criminal statutes often ends up assuming that what Parliament wanted to do was criminalize as much conduct as possible.[60]

For instance, in *Maddeaux*, the Ontario Court of Appeal had to decide what counts as "wilfully interfering with the lawful use, enjoyment or operation of property" for the offence of mischief.[61] The accused was charged with mischief after a neighbour complained that he was making too much noise in his apartment. Some earlier cases had read "enjoyment" narrowly in the technical sense (drawn from real property

---

56 *R v Paré*, [1987] 2 SCR 618 [*Paré*] at 630, per Wilson J, citing Stephen Kloepfer, "The Status of Strict Construction in Canadian Criminal Law" (1983) 15:3 Ottawa LR 553. In the United States, a similar idea generally goes under the name of the "rule of lenity": see e.g. *Yates v United States*, 574 US 528 (2015) [*Yates*], per Ginsburg J.

57 *Bélanger v The Queen*, [1970] SCR 567, at 573, per Cartwright CJC (dissenting), quoting GFL Bridgman, *Maxwell on Interpretation of Statutes*, 7th ed. (London: Sweet & Maxwell, 1929) at 244.

58 *Paré, supra* note 56 at 630, per Wilson J.

59 See e.g. *R v Hasselwander*, [1993] 2 SCR 398 at 411–15, per Cory J; *R v JA, supra* note 16 at para 32, per McLachlin CJ.

60 A useful corrective to this tendency was offered by Lord Bridge in *R v Charles*, [1976] 1 WLR 248 (CA) at 256: "[I]t is right, we think, to shun the temptation, which sometimes presses on the mind of the judiciary, to suppose that because a particular course of conduct, as was this course of conduct, was anti-social and undesirable, it can necessarily be fitted into some convenient criminal pigeon-hole." This passage is quoted with approval in Glanville Williams and Dennis Baker, *Textbook of Criminal Law*, 3rd ed (London: Sweet & Maxwell, 2012), noting that, in the result, Lord Bridge was overturned by the House of Lords: *R v Charles*, [1977] AC 177.

61 *R v Maddeaux* (1997), 33 OR (3d) 378 (Ont CA) [*Maddeaux*].

law) of "entitlement or exercise of a right." This was the reading preferred by Fish JA in (as he then was) in *Drapeau*, where, on explicitly minimalist grounds, he declined to "make of a crime in relation to property an offence against feelings and tastes."[62] In *Maddeaux*, by contrast, the court opted for an expansive, colloquial reading of "enjoyment" that caught the accused's noise-making because it was irritating to his neighbour. The court found that the meaning of "enjoyment" admitted of no reasonable doubt, rendering resort to strict construction inappropriate. Nowhere did it consider whether Parliament could really have intended to make criminal offences out of everyday neighbourly annoyances.[63] The fact that the punishment for mischief is not particularly severe should not, in my view, detract from the undesirability of casting the net of criminalization so broadly when other interpretive options are available.

In the United States, objections to overcriminalization have been advanced by activists, lawyers, and academics since the dawn of that country's crisis of mass incarceration.[64] (Only very recently have appreciable numbers of politicians joined the chorus.) The causes of that country's crisis are multifaceted and disputed – but, on any account, largely socio-political rather than judicial in origin.[65] That said, judicial attitudes and methodologies can plausibly be understood to have a modest but significant impact on the scope of what is deemed criminal – and, therefore, on what gets investigated and prosecuted in the first place.

For example, Professor William Stuntz has persuasively argued that an increasingly relaxed judicial attitude toward *mens rea* requirements – together with a legislative trend toward enacting offences of general intent – has been one of the driving forces behind the crisis of overcriminalization in the United States. He gives the example of two American

62 *R v Drapeau* (1995), 37 CR (4th) 180 (QC CA). The court in *R v Phoenix* (1991), 64 CCC (3d) 252 (BC Prov Ct), likewise took a minimalist approach to narrowing the scope of this potentially very broad offence. However, in *R v Nicol*, 2002 MBCA 151, the court adopted the reasoning of *Maddeaux*.

63 Morris Manning & Peter Sankoff, *Manning, Mewett & Sankoff — Criminal Law*, 5th ed. (Markham: LexisNexis, 2015) at 1283, considers the *Maddeaux* approach to be a "highly disappointing development, and one that provides police officers with an extremely broad charging discretion in situations where restraint might be better suited."

64 See e.g. Kadish, "The Crisis of Overcriminalization" (1968) 7:1 American Criminal LQ 17.

65 Most influentially, Michelle Alexander has argued that mass incarceration, particularly by way of the "war on drugs," has operated as a means of perpetuating racial subjugation of African Americans (*supra* note 5). More recently, John Pfaff has argued for unchecked prosecutorial power as the operative factor (*supra* note 5).

decisions, decided in the early 1950s and mid-1990s, respectively, illustrating the courts' increasing willingness to interpret the intent requirement in criminal statutes almost out of existence. In the first case, *Morissette v United States*,[66] Justice Robert Jackson overturned a conviction for theft of government property on the grounds that the accused – who had collected spent bomb casings from government land and sold them for scrap – lacked "wrongful" intent. Jackson reached this result despite the absence of any explicit "wrongful" intent requirement in the statute.

In the second example given by Stuntz, *People v Stark*, a general contractor on the verge of insolvency used payments from a new client to pay off debts owed to subcontractors on a previous project. There was no evidence he was planning to stiff any of his creditors and thus no evidence of wrongful intent, yet the appellate court upheld the conviction for "willful diversion of construction funds" by construing this as a general intent offence.[67] Stuntz opines that decisions like this mean that the law of intent is no longer a "means of ensuring that only those who understand that they are engaged in serious misconduct can be criminally punished."[68] This and other interpretive means of diluting the burden of proof have the effect of placing undesirably broad discretion – and, therefore, dangerously enhanced bargaining power – in the hands of prosecutors.[69]

In Canada, Professor Michael Plaxton has recently written about what he calls a "principle of restraint" running through the Court's interpretive approach to criminal laws.[70] While bearing some resemblance to the old principle of strict construction, this approach speaks the language of purposive interpretation. On this view, Parliament

66 *Morissette v United States*, 342 US 246 (1952).

67 *People v Stark*, 26 Cal App 4th 1179 (1994).

68 Stuntz, *supra* note 4 at 262.

69 There has been some pushback against this trend in the US Supreme Court. In the Enron-related case of *Skilling v United States*, 561 US 358 (2010), the Court read down the notoriously unwieldy offence of "honest services" fraud to include only bribes and kickbacks. And in *Yates*, *supra* note 56, the Court held that the crime of destroying or concealing "any record, document, or tangible object" – an aspect of a post-Enron law meant to promote corporate accountability – did not apply to a fisherman who threw undersized fish overboard in the face of an inspection. Although a fish is indisputedly a "tangible object," this was simply not the sort of thing the law was meant to address. At least according to the majority, literalism works real mischief where the criminal law is concerned. In dissent, Justice Kagan hewed to a literalist reading of the provision but acknowledged that the "real issue" in the case was "overcriminalization and excessive punishment in the U.S. Code" (at 18).

70 Michael Plaxton, *Sovereignty, Restraint, and Guidance: Canadian Criminal Law in the 21st Century* (Toronto: Irwin Law, 2019), 196–234.

cannot have intended to criminalize innocent conduct or trivial misconduct; thus, the elements of the statute should be interpreted to exclude such marginal cases. Among the examples given by Plaxton is *R v Hinchey*,[71] where the Court tried to interpret the public corruption offence in section 121(1)(c) to avoid criminalizing the receipt of trivial benefits by government employees, and *R v Hutchinson*,[72] where the Court took a relatively restrained approach to the circumstances in which deceit with respect to contraception will vitiate consent to sex. In the latter case, the majority was explicit in its concern to avoid the overcriminalization of myriad ways in which people may obtain sex through deceit, echoing the concerns that animated McLachlin J's reasons in *R v Cuerrier*.[73]

I agree that this line of reasoning is evident in a number of significant decisions, but I think the Court has too often failed to apply it. I will give two examples, both involving core, frequently charged offences. In both cases the majority reasons were penned by (Chief) Justice McLachlin, the first near the beginning of her tenure on the Court and the latter toward the end.

The first has to do with fraud. In the linked appeals of *R v Théroux* and *R v Zlatic*,[74] the Court (*per* McLachlin J) confirmed a broad approach to the elements of fraud, under which the accused need not subjectively appreciate the dishonesty of his acts.[75] While the majority was right to hold that an accused's delusional belief in their own honesty should not provide a defence to fraud, it should have accepted Sopinka J's insistence that subjective belief in *facts* that would render the conduct non-culpable should result in an acquittal. Thus, in *Zlatic*, the majority upheld the conviction of a businessman who gambled away a large amount of money, eventually resulting in his bankruptcy and his creditors being out of pocket for the squandered funds. While this behaviour was irresponsible, I think the dissent was right to hold that it was not criminal if the accused actually believed his gambling "system" was

71 *R v Hinchey*, [1996] 3 SCR 1128.

72 *R v Hutchinson*, 2014 SCC 19.

73 There, a majority of the Court broadly interpreted the circumstances in which non-disclosure of a sexually transmitted disease may vitiate consent to sex. In her concurring reasons, Justice McLachlin expressed concern about over-extending the concept of fraud so as to criminalize a range of undesirable but relatively common forms of deception in sexual matters. *R v Cuerrier*, [1998] 2 SCR 371 [*Cuerrier*].

74 *R v Théroux*, [1993] 2 SCR 5 [*Théroux*]; *R v Zlatic*, [1993] 2 SCR 29 [*Zlatic*].

75 As noted by Justice McLachlin, the broader modern approach to the elements of fraud was actually inaugurated by Dickson J (as he then was) in *R v Olan*, [1978] 2 SCR 1175.

so reliable that the risk of loss was small.[76] This is the difference, in my view, between foolish profligacy and real criminality. The worry is that an elastic definition of the offence that includes too much borderline conduct has the effect (as Stuntz explains) of placing undesirably broad discretion in the hands of police and prosecutors. Where economic disputes are concerned, a minimalist conception of the criminal law would leave it to the civil courts to assign liability where the high bar of properly criminal *mens rea* has not been surmounted.

The second example of overly broad offence-definition concerns sexual assault. In *JA*, the Court had to determine whether a person is capable in law of consenting *in advance* to sexual activity expected to take place while the person is asleep or unconscious.[77] Chief Justice McLachlin, writing for the majority, answered this question with a categorical "no." Focusing on the wording of the consent-related provisions of the *Criminal Code*, the Chief Justice portrayed this as a straightforward exercise in statutory interpretation, arguing that those provisions enact a definition of consent that is active and ongoing and must be capable of being revoked at any time. Because a person cannot revoke consent while unconscious, unconsciousness and consent cannot co-exist.

In reaching that result, the Chief Justice had to dismiss the significance of a number of counterfactuals put before the Court of innocuous conduct that the Crown's proposed approach would end up criminalizing. Primary among these was the example of one spouse kissing his or her sleeping partner. Could it really be that every such act constitutes, in law, a sexual assault?

The Chief Justice's reasons for being unconcerned about this absurd extension of criminal liability were, in my view, unconvincing. First, she observed that the notion of "advance consent" would provide a defence only in the event that the sleeping partner actually turned their mind to the question of consent prior to falling asleep. Since that was unlikely, the accused in this scenario would still be committing sexual assault even if advance consent were accepted as a possibility. But this just begs the question, assuming as correct an interpretation of advance consent that doesn't actually solve the problem the hypothetical seeks to illuminate. The real point was that any formulation of consent that criminalized an obviously innocuous

---

76 I also think Justice Sopinka was right to be concerned "that we might criminalize non-payment of debts because we disapprove of the way in which the debtor spent his money": *Zlatic, supra* note 74 at 34.

77 *R v JA, supra* note 16.

activity was overly broad. Instead of engaging meaningfully with this problem, the Chief Justice went on to discuss a number of practical and doctrinal problems said to arise from any notion of advance consent. She ended, a little anticlimactically, with the candid admission that the interpretation of consent allegedly mandated by Parliament "may seem unrealistic" in some instances, while maintaining that it "produces just results in the vast majority of cases."[78] Perhaps cognizant of the way in which this justification would seem to clash with her strong formulation of overbreadth,[79] the Chief Justice noted that *absent a constitutional challenge*, it was for Parliament to determine the scope of the offence.[80]

In dissent, Justice Fish rejected the majority's contention that (as he put it), "the complainant's *yes in fact* means *no in law*."[81] He convincingly demonstrated that Parliament cannot reasonably have intended to criminalize broad swaths of everyday private conduct such as kissing or caressing a sleeping partner. That being so, there was something fundamentally wrong with the interpretation that mandated such a conclusion. The values of personal freedom and sexual autonomy, which purportedly animated the majority, actually militated in favour of an interpretation whereby consenting adults retain the freedom to choose their own sexual practices provided no bodily harm is intended. And the potential for prosecutorial discretion to weed out truly marginal cases provided no justification for an overly broad construction of an offence – a position elsewhere strongly embraced by the Chief Justice.[82]

Fundamentally, the dissent made a powerful case for a minimalist approach to construing the criminal law, even (perhaps especially) with respect to highly stigmatized offences like sexual assault. In my view, the majority's failure to deal with the unruly reach of its broad interpretation runs up against Doherty JA's sage admonition in *Greenwood* that "[t]here must be at least a rough equivalence between what judges say is criminal and what the community regards as morally blameworthy. Judicial interpretation of statutory language so as to

78 *Ibid* at para 65.

79 In *Bedford, supra* note 12 at para 127, McLachlin CJ made clear that a law's arbitrary, overbroad, or grossly disproportionate effect on even a single person will suffice to establish a section 7 breach, which would then potentially be subject to section 1 justification.

80 *R v JA*, supra note 16 at para 65.

81 *Ibid* at para 71 [emphasis in original].

82 *R v Nur, supra* note 27 at paras 91–8.

declare conduct criminal which members of the community view as innocent or morally neutral does a disservice to the overall operation of the criminal law."[83]

These cases on fraud and sexual assault are just two examples. There are others.[84] And they are counterbalanced, to some extent, by the examples of "restraint" cited by Plaxton as well as cases like *Labaye*, discussed above, where the Court has interpreted old offences with a modern, harm-based perspective.[85] My point is this: the same values and insights that motivate the Court's section 7 scrutiny of criminal laws for compliance with the principles of fundamental justice should inform the Court's *interpretive* approach to defining the elements of constitutionally valid offences. After all, it is with respect to these bread-and-butter crimes whose core validity few would question that the vast majority of day-to-day criminal practice is conducted.

As Chief Justice McLachlin has so ably demonstrated in the landmark cases discussed above, the criminal law is often not the only or the best method of preventing or redressing socially deleterious conduct. This is a lesson that successive federal governments, including the present one, have stubbornly failed to grasp, whatever their reformist pretensions to the contrary. Enacting a new criminal law is often a politically expedient solution to a perceived social problem. Repealing a criminal law almost never promises any political mileage. Accordingly, the limited efficacy of the criminal law as a means of

---

83 *Greenwood, supra* note 19.

84 On this list I would include *Mabior, supra* note 15, where the Court maintained the approach to fraud vitiating consent established in *R v Cuerrier, supra* note 73, under which having unprotected sex while HIV-positive can still result in a conviction for aggravated sexual assault even where the risk of transmission is exceedingly small. This ruling has been strongly criticized for criminalizing nearly harmless conduct and for failing to recognize the real harms caused by criminalization itself: see e.g. Alison Symington, "Injustice Amplified by HIV Non-Disclosure Ruling" (2013) 63:3 UTLJ 485. Surprisingly, Chief Justice McLachlin's judgment for a unanimous Court in *Mabior* paid little heed to the minimalist-oriented objections she had earlier raised in her *Cuerrier* concurrence. Also see the Wagner Court's broad formulation of the voyeurism offence in *R v Jarvis*, 2019 SCC 10.

85 In *R v DLW*, 2016 SCC 22, the Court (quite properly in my view) refused to expand the offence of bestiality by applying it to non-penetrative sexual acts not contemplated by the original enactment. The majority, per Cromwell J, relied in part on the hallowed rule from *Frey v Fedoruk*, [1950] SCR 517, that only Parliament, not the courts, can expand the scope of criminal liability. This is another important common law protection that militates in favour of minimalism.

social improvement is a reality upon which lawyers and judges must continue to insist.

Fortunately, the jurisprudence just described suggests that, where the government chooses criminalization over other options, it will need to show that the choice is defensible, not just on some abstract moral basis, but in terms of real-world consequences. I think this is one of Chief Justice McLachlin's most important contributions to the criminal and constitutional jurisprudence of this country, and one that gives those of us in the system much to work with in the years to come as we continue to advocate for a more sensible, humane, and limited criminal law.

10 Controversies in the Common Law of Judicial Review: Tracing the Contributions of Chief Justice McLachlin

ADAM GOLDENBERG

I. Introduction

Canadian judges are never household names. Beverley McLachlin came as close as anyone ever has. Aside from the historic length of her tenure and the fact that she was the first woman to be the country's top jurist, Chief Justice McLachlin made headlines for defending the Supreme Court of Canada, and the judiciary more broadly, as an institution.[1]

Yet, in the area of law most intimately concerned with the relationship between the executive and the judiciary, Chief Justice McLachlin's institutional leadership produced paradoxical results. Despite striving for consensus and clarity in the standard of review analysis in administrative law, the McLachlin Court's achievements proved to be self-defeating during Chief Justice McLachlin's tenure.

Not long after her retirement, however, the Court released a pair of 2019 judgments in which it sought to preserve the virtues of Chief Justice McLachlin's approach while stripping away features of the doctrine that had made it next to unworkable: *Canada (Minister of Citizenship and Immigration) v Vavilov* and *Bell Canada v Canada (Attorney General)*.[2]

1 See e.g. "The PM's Losing Case in Harper v. McLachlin," Editorial, *Globe and Mail* (5 May 2014), online <https://www.theglobeandmail.com/opinion/editorials/the-pms-losing-case-in-harper-v-mclachlin/article18471879/>; and T MacCharles, "Stephen Harper Urged to Apologize for Spat with Chief Justice Beverley McLachlin," *Toronto Star* (25 July 2014), online: <https://www.thestar.com/news/canada/2014/07/25/chief_justice_cleared_in_spat_with_stephen_harper_government.html>. See also E Thompson, "Trudeau Avoids IT Showdown with Top Courts," (18 January 2016), online: <https://ipolitics.ca/2016/01/18/trudeau-avoids-it-showdown-with-top-courts/>.

2 *Canada (Minister of Citizenship and Immigration) v Vavilov*, 2019 SCC 65 [*Vavilov*]; *Bell Canada v Canada (Attorney General)*, 2019 SCC 66 [*Bell Canada*].

Though it is too soon to assess the success of that effort, it reflects a concerted attempt to complete the McLachlin Court's unfinished business. *Vavilov* and *Bell Canada* are, in this way, the final components of Chief Justice McLachlin's contribution to administrative law, even though she took no part in either judgment.

Before *Vavilov* and *Bell Canada*, the state of the standard of review jurisprudence upon Chief Justice McLachlin's retirement was an unintended consequence of her approach to common law adjudication, and to her role as Chief Justice. This chapter traces the causal relationship between Chief Justice McLachlin's recognized virtues as a common lawyer and as an institutional leader and the confusion in administrative law that prevailed at the end of her chief justiceship. In doing so, this chapter identifies patterns in the Court's approach to judicial review that feature prominently in *Vavilov* and *Bell Canada* – and that presumably will continue to shape the law of judicial review in the post-McLachlin era.

Part II considers Chief Justice McLachlin's approach to collegial adjudication in the common law tradition and her view of the Supreme Court of Canada's role in the judicial hierarchy. Part III sketches the evolution of the standard of review jurisprudence between Justice McLachlin's appointment as Chief Justice in 2000 and her final judgments in 2018, and examines the extent to which that evolution reflects Chief Justice McLachlin's approach to Supreme Court judging. Part IV identifies two "process failures" that emerge out of Chief Justice McLachlin's approach, and that proved to be persistent stumbling blocks as the Court has struggled with the standard of review. Part V considers *Vavilov* and *Bell Canada*, and the extent to which they may fairly be considered part of Chief Justice McLachlin's legacy in administrative law.

II. Consensus and Clarity

The McLachlin Court was remarkable for its collegial harmony. Jurisprudentially, this is reflected in the unanimity of its judgments; in every year in which Beverley McLachlin served as Chief Justice, the Court decided most appeals unanimously. As Figure 10.1 illustrates, in only one year of Chief Justice McLachlin's tenure (2017, her last) was the Court unanimous in less than 60 per cent of the appeals it decided.

Note, however, that the Court's own definition of unanimity, which Figure 10.1 reflects, is not necessarily consistent with most lawyers' understanding of the term. A judgment is coded as "unanimous" if every judge agreed in the disposition of the appeal – not, as one might expect,

Figure 10.1. The McLachlin Court's unanimity, by year

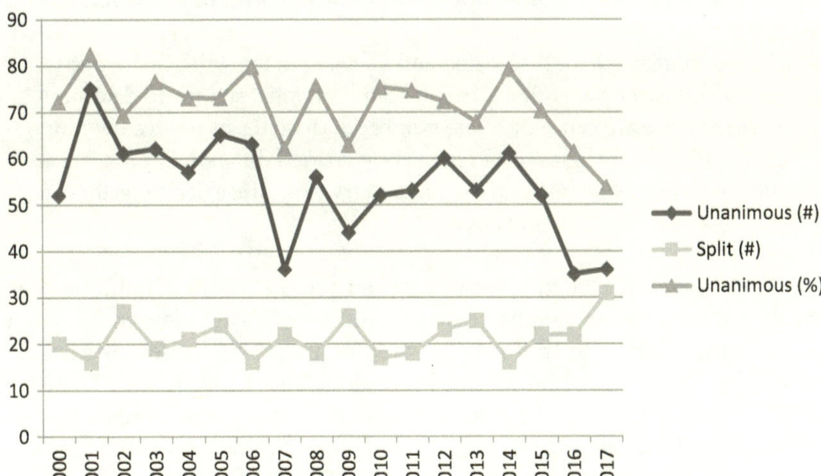

Source: Supreme Court of Canada, "Statistics 2000–2010" (Bulletin of Proceedings, Special Edition, 2011) at 9, online: <http://publications.gc.ca/collections/collection_2018/csc-scc/JU7-3-2010-eng.pdf>; and Supreme Court of Canada, "Statistics, 2007–2017" (2018) at 11, online: <https://scc-csc.ca/case-dossier/stat/pdf/doc-eng.pdf>.

if every judge signed on to a single opinion.[3] Still, Chief Justice McLachlin's elevation also coincided with a significant diminution in the number of cases in which members of the Court issued concurring opinions.[4]

This was no accident: it was Chief Justice McLachlin's stated aim.[5] She set out to build consensus and, thus, clarity. She would seek, in her words, "to minimise our differences as much as possible, [and] cut out things that would unnecessarily create differences."[6] The purpose of "ironing out differences, insofar as this [could] be done, [was] to better fulfill [the Court's] primary function – settling the legal questions of public importance that Canadian society brings up."[7]

3 See P McCormick, "The Choral Court: Separate Concurrence and the McLachlin Court, 2000–2004" (2005) 37:1 Ottawa L Rev 1 at 4–5.

4 *Ibid* at 10.

5 See C Schmitz, "Communication, Consensus among McLachlin's Targets," *Lawyers' Weekly* (19 November 1999); S Harada, "The McLachlin Group," *Walrus* (12 May 2009), online: <https://thewalrus.ca/the-mclachlin-group/>.

6 TAQ Angie, "Interview with the Right Honourable Chief Justice of Canada, Beverley McLachlin, PC" (2010) 28 Sing L Rev 153 at 161.

7 *Ibid.*

Her colleagues confirmed the difference she had made. Justice Bastarache, in a 2001 interview, noted that, under Chief Justice McLachlin:

> There is more place for discussion and dialogue in the sense that we strive more to discover each other's reasons and opinions, and try to determine ways in which we can reduce the number of dissents, or reduce the number of published reasons in a case … [W]e've tried different approaches to reduce the number of written reasons and try to produce decisions that are more useful to the courts of appeal.[8]

Chief Justice McLachlin also practised what she preached. She was chief justice for nearly eight years before, in 2007, she released her own concurring reasons in that role for the first time.[9] As Professor McCormick has observed, Chief Justice McLachlin, like Chief Justice Dickson and *un*like Chief Justice Lamer, authored or joined minority reasons less often after she assumed her office than before.[10] This, Professor McCormick writes, "suggests a moderating influence on [her] colleagues."[11]

To the extent that Chief Justice McLachlin's leadership effected a shift in the Court's culture toward consensus,[12] it can be viewed as part of a long-term trend. It was not until the late 1920s that the Court, under Chief Justice Anglin's leadership, decisively departed from the English tradition of *seriatim* opinions in favour of drafting a single majority opinion whenever one could be agreed upon.[13] It has since moved toward what Professor McCormick describes as the "American model," in which "there is a decision of the court, typically attributed to a single author, which is often signed by (or concurred in) by other members of the panel."[14] This shift was compounded in the 1960s, when Chief Justice Cartwright introduced the practice of conferencing after hearings.[15]

---

8 C Schmitz, "The Bastarache Interview: 'Overall, This Is Not a Frustrating Job'," *Lawyers' Weekly* (2 February 2001).

9 See R Haigh and V Peter, "The Supreme Court by Numbers 2: The McLachlin Years," *The Court.ca* (26 July 2016), online: <http://www.thecourt.ca/supreme-court-numbers-2-mclachlin-years/>.

10 P McCormick, "Blocs, Swarms, and Outliers: Conceptualizing Disagreement on the Modern Supreme Court of Canada" (2004) 42 Osgoode Hall LJ 99 at 135.

11 *Ibid.*

12 See E Macfarlane, "Consensus and Unanimity at the Supreme Court of Canada" (2010) 52 SCLR 379 at 387.

13 PW Hogg and R Amarnath, "Why Judges Should Dissent" (2017) 67:2 UTLJ 126 at 128.

14 McCormick, *supra* note 3 at 8.

15 *Ibid* at 9; Hogg and Amarnath, *supra* note 13 at 128.

Consensus peaked in the early 1980s, under Chief Justice Laskin.[16] In coaxing her colleagues toward unanimity and away from a profusion of separate reasons, Chief Justice McLachlin did not break new ground.

She did, however, couple her push for common ground with the specific purpose of providing clear guidance. In many areas of law, she succeeded – the tests for causation in tort and for the exclusion of evidence under section 24(2) of the *Canadian Charter of Rights and Freedoms* were essentially settled in majority opinions that the Chief Justice authored during her tenure, as was the content of the Crown's duty to consult and accommodate Aboriginal rights holders under section 35 of the *Constitution Act, 1982*.[17] There are other examples, each furthering Chief Justice McLachlin's stated desire to "[express] our result in a way that makes it possible to apply the law without too much difficulty and that furthers respect for the law."[18]

In this way, as other contributions to this volume illustrate, Chief Justice McLachlin aspired to the core ideals of common law adjudication. She sought to lead the Court to embrace clear statements of principle, which would allow for both flexibility of application and the measured evolution of doctrine to match social change. Though her judgments collectively speak to an overriding commitment to incrementalism – to seeking simplicity, ensuring stability, and promoting certainty in resolving legal disputes[19] – both she and the Court under her leadership broke new ground in leaving space for precedent to be unbound by changing circumstances.[20] Still, as some of the McLachlin Court's final pronouncements on *stare decisis* make plain, this limited wiggle room was not intended to be an invitation to question the correctness of judicial reasoning in past cases; unless the law had evolved, society had changed,[21] or experience demanded departing from settled

16 McCormick, *supra* note 3 at 9.

17 *Constitution Act, 1982*, Schedule B to the *Canada Act 1982 (UK)*, 1982, c 111. See *Clements v Clements*, 2012 SCC 32 at para 46; *R v Grant*, 2009 SCC 32 at para 71; *Haida Nation v British Columbia (Minister of Forests)*, 2004 SCC 73.

18 J Tibbetts, "Building Consensus," *Canadian Lawyer* (2 July 2013), online: <http://www.canadianlawyermag.com/article/building-consensus-2100/>.

19 See J Hughes, V MacDonnell & K Pearlston, "Equality and Incrementalism: The Role of Common Law Reasoning in Constitutional Rights Cases" (2013) 44:3 Ottawa L Rev 467 at 473.

20 See *Carter v Canada (Attorney General)*, 2015 SCC 5 [*Carter*] at para 44; *Canada (Attorney General) v Bedford*, 2013 SCC 72 [*Bedford*] at para 42; see also D Parkes, "Precedent Revisited: *Carter v Canada (AG)* and the Contemporary Practice of Precedent" (2016) 10:1 McGill JL & Health S123 at S158. But see *R v Comeau*, 2018 SCC 15 at para 34.

21 See *Carter*, *supra* note 20 at para 44; *Bedford*, *supra* note 20 at para 42.

precedent,[22] the need for legal clarity and doctrinal stability had to remain paramount.[23]

So it was with the Court's approach to administrative law. Under Chief Justice McLachlin's leadership, the Court attempted to bring clarity and consensus to the common law governing curial review of delegated decision making. Superficially, it succeeded: the Court's majority judgment in *Dunsmuir v New Brunswick*,[24] in 2007, attempted to restate and simplify the Canadian approach to determining whether to accord deference to a decision under review. As the next section will show, however, the McLachlin Court's success in achieving clarity in this area ultimately proved to be its undoing.

III. The Standard of Review Analysis, 2000–2018

The two decades of the McLachlin Court's standard of review jurisprudence are not easily summarized. Here, and worth quoting at length, is Chief Justice McLachlin's own attempt at encapsulating the developments in this area of the law during her first decade in the Court's top job:

> Beginning in the late '90s the Supreme Court in a series of cases struggled with how to achieve deference within the rule of law. In 1988 in *Bibeault*, under the consolidating pen of Justice Beetz, the Court announced the "pragmatic and functional approach" to the standard of review. In cases such as *Pezim*, the Court spoke of a "spectrum of deference" depending on various factors. All very contextual. All very loose. And, said the critics, all highly uncertain.
>
> Eventually, in the 1997 case of *Southam*, the Court came to recognize three standards of review – correctness, reasonableness and patent unreasonableness: in ordinary language, strict, deferential and very deferential. Uncertainty continued as to when to apply each standard.
>
> In 2008, after a decade of struggle to find the right formulation, the Court sought to simplify and consolidate in *Dunsmuir*. Reasonableness

---

22 See *Teva Canada Ltd v TD Canada Trust*, 2017 SCC 51 at paras 141–2, Côté and Rowe JJ, dissenting.

23 See A Goldenberg, "Beer, *Bedford*, and Beyond: The Supreme Court of Canada and the Limits of Precedent in *R. v. Comeau*," *Canadian Appeals Monitor* (25 April 2018), online: <https://www.mccarthy.ca/en/insights/blogs/canadian-appeals-monitor/beer-bedford-and-beyond-supreme-court-canada-and-limits-precedent-r-v-comeau>.

24 *Dunsmuir v New Brunswick*, 2008 SCC 9 [*Dunsmuir*].

> and patent unreasonableness were rolled into simple reasonableness, which has come to be the standard applicable to the vast majority of tribunal decisions. Correctness was still the standard for general questions of law and perhaps jurisdiction, but the latter category became less and less applied. *Dunsmuir* maintained the multi-factored contextual test for what standard applied. But it also sought to introduce predictability by stating that once a standard of review has been identified as applicable to a particular type of decision, it was unnecessary to go through all the factors in each decision …
>
> It is probably not an exaggeration to say that by the time *Dunsmuir* came around in 2008, administrative lawyers, academics and judges were suffering from collective standard of review fatigue. The passion that marked the early contretemps between the courts and the tribunals had given way to a weary wish that the problem would just go away. Difficulties remained to be sure. But there was a felt need to take a break from the endless theorizing, to settle down and apply *Dunsmuir* and its progeny and see if what we had, with tweaking here and there as necessary, could be made to work.[25]

It became a matter of consensus, certainly among commentators, that *Dunsmuir* and its progeny were not, in fact, made to work.[26] As Justice David Stratas of the Federal Court of Appeal put it in extrajudicial commentary published before *Vavilov* and *Bell Canada*, "an overwhelming number of leading Canadian commentators find much of the jurisprudence confused, incoherent and troubling."[27]

By this measure, where administrative law is concerned, the McLachlin Court did not live up to its leader's expectations. The attempt "to simplify and consolidate" and "to introduce consistency" in *Dunsmuir* misfired, leaving open judicial exasperation in its wake.[28] As argued

---

25 B McLachlin, "Administrative Tribunals and the Courts: An Evolutionary Relationship" (Remarks to the 6th Annual Conference of the Council of Canadian Administrative Tribunals, Toronto, 27 May 2013) [footnotes omitted].

26 See the thoughtful and illuminating contributions to the "*Dunsmuir* Decade" online symposium organized by Professor Paul Daly in the lead-up to *Dunsmuir*'s tenth anniversary in March 2018: P Daly, "Revisiting Dunsmuir: Food for Thought" (11 May 2018), online (blog): *Administrative Law Matters*, <http://www.administrativelawmatters.com/blog/2018/05/11/revisiting-dunsmuir-food-for-thought/>.

27 DW Stratas, "A Decade of *Dunsmuir*: Please No More" (8 March 2018), online (blog): *Administrative Law Matters* <http://www.administrativelawmatters.com/blog/2018/03/08/a-decade-of-dunsmuir-please-no-more-hon-david-w-stratas/>.

28 See e.g. *West Fraser Mills Ltd v British Columbia (Workers' Compensation Appeal Tribunal)*, 2018 SCC 22 at paras 123–4, Brown J, concurring; *Edmonton (City) v Edmonton*

below, this outcome reflects twin process failures that stemmed from the same desire to achieve clarity and consistency of doctrine that was such a virtue in other areas of the law. Here, it was a vice. The following traces the development of the standard of review analysis during the McLachlin years, and how the Court, under Chief Justice McLachlin's leadership, walked a road paved with the best of intentions, but to an unfortunate destination.

One additional observation merits mention at the outset. As Chief Justice McLachlin's comments, excerpted above, suggest, the Court's preoccupation during her tenure was arguably less with the methodology of deference – i.e., the work of applying a standard of review – than with what the Court came to describe as the "standard of review analysis"[29] – i.e., the work of identifying the standard of review. Put differently, the Court's jurisprudence tended to focus on *whether* (or *how much*) to defer, not *how* to do so. This attracted scholarly and judicial criticism.[30]

Still, and as highlighted below, the McLachlin Court's approach to selecting the standard is a useful lens through which to view its broader approach to the common law of curial review. This is because the question of whether, and how much, a reviewing court should defer to an executive decision maker can have only a limited number of answers in any particular case. Thus, the standard of review analysis offered an obvious opportunity to pursue Chief Justice McLachlin's objective of achieving clarity and consensus; here was a confused area of doctrine whose goal was to produce one of two or three possible outcomes – surely this could be streamlined. And so it was, albeit not with the results for which Chief

---

East (Capilano) Shopping Centres Ltd, 2016 SCC 47 [*Edmonton East*] at para 89, Côté and Brown JJ, dissenting; *Wilson v Atomic Energy of Canada Ltd*, 2016 SCC 29 [*Wilson*] at paras 24–7, per Abella J, concurring, and at para 72, per Cromwell J, concurring; *Kanthasamy v Canada (Citizenship and Immigration)*, 2015 SCC 61 at para 112, Moldaver and Wagner JJ, dissenting; *Canadian Broadcasting Corp v SODRAC 2003 Inc*, 2015 SCC 57 at para 185, Abella J, dissenting; *Tervita Corp v Canada (Commissioner of Competition)*, 2015 SCC 3 [*Tervita*] at para 170, Abella J, concurring; *Canada (Public Safety and Emergency Preparedness) v Tran*, 2015 FCA 237 at para 45.

29 *Dunsmuir*, *supra* note 24 at para 63.

30 See e.g. *Wilson*, *supra* note 28 at para 24, Abella J, concurring; M Lewans, "Deference and Reasonableness since *Dunsmuir*" (2012) 38:1 Queen's LJ 59 at 74; P Daly, "Struggling towards Coherence in Canadian Administrative Law? Recent Cases on Standard of Review and Reasonableness" (2016) 62:2 McGill LJ 527 at 558–9; L Sossin, "The Complexity of Coherence: Justice LeBel's Administrative Law" (2015) 70 SCLR (2d) 145 at 160–1; Y-M Morissette, "What Is a 'Reasonable Decision'?" (2018) 31:3 Can J Admin L & Prac 225 at 227; LJ Wihak, "Whither the Correctness Standard of Review? *Dunsmuir*, Six Years Later" (2014) 27:2 Can J Admin L & Prac 173 at 203.

Justice McLachlin and her colleagues might have hoped before the end of her judicial service.

This chapter accordingly focuses on the evolution of the standard of review analysis, rather than on the actual practice of deference, during Chief Justice McLachlin's tenure. This is not to deny that the two are deeply interrelated.[31] Rather, it reflects the fact that the former was the focus of the Court's efforts to clarify and simplify, in keeping with Chief Justice McLachlin's approach to common law adjudication in administrative law.

a. Neither Pragmatic nor Functional

Chief Justice McLachlin assumed the Court's top job at a moment when, as Professor Mullan recalls, "[t]here was a sense that controversies over the appropriate standard of review to be applied in particular situations would be minimized and the courts freed to deal with the merits of applications for judicial review (and statutory appeals) on the basis of what would, in most instances, be an obvious standard of scrutiny."[32] This optimism was grounded in what were then two of the Court's most recent forays into the standard of review "thicket":[33] *Canada (Director of Investigation and Research) v Southam*[34] and, in particular, *Pushpanathan v Canada (Minister of Citizenship and Immigration)*.[35] In *Southam*, decided in 1997, the Court introduced a third standard of review, "reasonableness *simpliciter*," between "correctness" and "patent unreasonableness." *Pushpanathan*, decided in 1998, was a decennial reformulation of the "pragmatic and functional approach" announced in *UES, Local 298 v Bibeault* in 1988.[36]

---

31 See GP Heckman, "Substantive Review in Appellate Courts since *Dunsmuir*" (2009) 47:4 Osgoode Hall LJ 751 at 776.

32 D Mullan, "The McLachlin Court and the Public Law Standard of Review: A Major Irritant Soothed or a Significant Ongoing Problem?" (paper delivered at the Canadian Bar Association, 2009) online: <http://www.cba.org/cba/cle/PDF/Constit09_Mullan_paper.pdf>.

33 See B McLachlin, "'Administrative Law Is Not for Sissies': Finding a Path through the Thicket" (2016) 29:2 Can J Admin L & Prac 127.

34 *Canada (Director of Investigation and Research) v Southam Inc*, [1997] 1 SCR 748 [*Southam*].

35 *Pushpanathan v Canada (Minister of Citizenship and Immigration)*, [1998] 1 SCR 982 [*Pushpanathan*].

36 *UES, Local 298 v Bibeault*, [1988] 2 SCR 1048 [*Bibeault*]. *Bibeault*, in turn, came nearly a decade after the Court had narrowed the scope of jurisdictional review in *CUPE v NB Liquor Corporation*, [1979] 2 SCR 227 [*CUPE v NB*], while *Pushpanathan* predated *Dunsmuir* by approximately the same length of time. See P Daly, "The Scope and Meaning of Reasonableness Review" (2015) 52:4 Alta L Rev 799 at 827. *Vavilov*, *supra* note 2, fits the roughly ten-year cycle.

As Professor Macklin has noted, *Southam* and its three standards of review emerged from a shift in the Court's focus in the 1990s.[37] Three years earlier, in *Pezim*,[38] the Court had signalled that it was moving away from using the presence or absence of a privative clause as the determining factor in the standard of review analysis, and would instead prefer to investigate the tribunal's relative expertise as the dispositive basis for deference. "[E]ven where there is no privative clause and where there is a statutory right of appeal," Justice Iacobucci stated, "the concept of the specialization of duties requires that deference be shown to decisions of specialized tribunals on matters which fall squarely within the tribunal's expertise."[39]

Southam went further. It concerned an appeal from a decision of the Competition Tribunal concerning the concentration of newspaper ownership in the Lower Mainland of British Columbia. The Tribunal found that Southam's acquisitions had substantially lessened competition. It ordered the company to divest itself of one of two community papers. Both Southam and the director of investigation and research appealed to the Federal Court of Appeal, pursuant to the statutory appeal provision in the *Competition Tribunal Act*.[40] Southam then appealed to the Supreme Court of Canada.

Again writing for the Court, Justice Iacobucci reduced the function of the statutory right of appeal to conferring jurisdiction on the appellate court:

> An appellate court must consider the factors with a view to determining the approach that it should take as a court sitting in appeal of the decision of the tribunal. There is no privative clause, and so jurisdiction is not at issue. The tribunal enjoys jurisdiction by virtue of its constating statute and the appellate court enjoys jurisdiction by virtue of a statutory right of appeal. The legislative intent is clear. The question is what limits an appellate court should observe in the exercise of its statutorily mandated appellate function.
>
> I wish to emphasize that in cases like the instant appeal no question arises about the extent of the tribunal's jurisdiction. *Where the statute confers a right of appeal, an appellate court need not look to see whether the tribunal*

37 See A Macklin, "Standard of Review: Back to the Future?" in CM Flood and L Sossin, eds, *Administrative Law in Context*, 2nd ed (Toronto: Emond Montgomery, 2013) at 291.

38 *Pezim v British Columbia (Superintendent of Brokers)*, [1994] 2 SCR 557.

39 *Ibid* at 593.

40 *Competition Tribunal Act*, RSC 1985, c 19 (2nd Supp).

has exceeded its jurisdiction by breaching the rules of natural justice or by rendering a decision that is patently unreasonable. The manner and standard of review will be determined in the way that appellate courts generally determine the posture they will take with respect to the decisions of courts below. In particular, *appellate courts must have regard to the nature of the problem, to the applicable law properly interpreted in the light of its purpose, and to the expertise of the tribunal.*[41]

Justice Iacobucci acknowledged that the presence of "a broad, even unfettered right of appeal, as if from a judgment of a trial court," may suggest that the reviewing court ought to accord less deference to decisions of the Tribunal than in the absence of such a provision. But he minimized the role of the statutory appeal right by comparison to the relative unimportance, in the Court's standard of review jurisprudence, of a privative clause; since a privative clause "does not settle the question" of deference, Justice Iacobucci suggested, neither could an appeal right.[42] As discussed below, the logic behind this conclusion, coupled as it was with *Southam*'s instruction that a decision maker's expertise "is the most important of the factors that a court must consider in settling on a standard of review,"[43] is somewhat dubious, and would cause problems for the Court decades later.

Weighing up all the factors, Justice Iacobucci considered that some deference, but not too much, was appropriate, and that this required the recognition of an intermediate standard of review, between correctness (no deference) and patent unreasonableness (maximum deference). This he called "reasonableness *simpliciter*," and observed that it was "the same standard that was applied" – albeit not expressly – "in *Pezim*."[44] In both cases, Justice Iacobucci noted, contextual signals that deference was *not* indicated were offset by a pragmatic concern with according proper respect to an administrative decision maker's expertise: "[T]he standard of reasonableness simply instructs reviewing courts to accord considerable weight to the views of tribunals about matters with respect to which they have significant expertise," Justice Iacobucci concluded.[45] The most deferential standard, patent unreasonableness, would henceforth be reserved for cases in which there were

41 *Southam, supra* note 34 at paras 31–2 [emphasis added].

42 *Ibid* at para 46.

43 *Ibid* at para 50.

44 *Ibid* at para 58.

45 *Ibid* at para 62.

no statutory signals favouring less deference – such as a statutory appeal provision – and thus where only a defect that was obvious "on the face of the tribunal's reasons" would justify curial intervention, on the basis that the error had rendered the decision a nullity and outside the decision maker's jurisdiction.[46]

Pushpanathan then picked up where *Southam* left off. In that case, as Professor Sossin has observed, the Court "attempted to reconcile the pragmatic and functional approach" to calibrating deference, as articulated in *Bibeault* and refined in the decade since, "with the court's earlier focus on 'jurisdictional error.'"[47] *Southam* (perhaps unintentionally) highlights the tension between these two bodies of jurisprudence. In that case, Justice Iacobucci appeared to reduce jurisdictional error to the kind that would justify intervention on the patent unreasonableness standard. But what about cases where, unlike in *Southam* or *Pezim*, the authority of the administrative decision maker to make the impugned decision was itself in controversy? It remained for the Court to square Justice Iacobucci's treatment of jurisdiction in *Southam* with the typology relied upon by Justice Beetz in *Bibeault*:

> It is, I think, possible to summarize in two propositions the circumstances in which an administrative tribunal will exceed its jurisdiction because of error:
>
> 1. *if the question of law at issue is within the tribunal's jurisdiction, it will only exceed its jurisdiction if it errs in a patently unreasonable manner*; a tribunal which is competent to answer a question may make errors in so doing without being subject to judicial review;
>
> 2. *if however the question at issue concerns a legislative provision limiting the tribunal's powers, a mere error will cause it to lose jurisdiction* and subject the tribunal to judicial review.[48]

Southam accommodated the first proposition. In *Pushpanathan*, the Court left space for the second. Writing for the majority, Justice Bastarache put the matter this way:

> [I]t is still appropriate and helpful to speak of "jurisdictional questions" which must be answered correctly by the tribunal in order to be acting

46 *Ibid* at paras 55 and 57.

47 L Sossin, "Empty Ritual, Mechanical Exercise or the Discipline of Deference? Revisiting the Standard of Review in Administrative Law" (2003) 27:4 Adv Q 478 at 480.

48 *Bibeault*, *supra* note 36 at 1086 [emphasis added].

> *intra vires*. But it should be understood that *a question which "goes to jurisdiction" is simply descriptive of a provision for which the proper standard of review is correctness, based upon the outcome of the pragmatic and functional analysis*. In other words, "jurisdictional error" is simply an error on an issue with respect to which, according to the outcome of the pragmatic and functional analysis, the tribunal must make a correct interpretation and to which no deference will be shown.[49]

Justice Beetz's two propositions with respect to jurisdictional error were thus reformulated in line with the Court's move away from categorizing questions as either jurisdictional or not, and toward the use of pragmatic and contextual factors to determine the appropriate degree of deference to be accorded to a particular administrative decision. Though Justice Bastarache, in *Pushpanathan*, acknowledged that questions of *vires* were jurisdictional, he also branded as jurisdictional any other questions that, according to the pragmatic and functional analysis, the decision maker was required to answer correctly.

Taken together, then, *Southam* and *Pushpanathan* affirmed Justice Beetz's first category of jurisdictional error and broadened his second. A decision maker commits a jurisdictional error, according to *Southam* and *Pushpanathan*, respectively: (1) when the decision maker acts within the scope of its statutory authority but errs in a patently unreasonable way; *or* (2) when the decision maker errs *at all* on a question in respect of which it is not entitled to deference, according to the pragmatic and functional anaylsis – including, but not limited to, questions of *vires*. As we will see, the McLachlin Court would later build on these restatements to all but eliminate the concept of jurisdictional error from the standard of review analysis.

Pushpanathan arose out of an application for judicial review of the Immigration and Refugee Board's determination that Mr Pushpanathan was not a refugee under the United Nations *Convention Relating to the Status of Refugees*. The Convention provides, in Article 1F(c), that refugee protections are not available to "any person with respect to whom there are serious reasons for considering that … he has been guilty of acts contrary to the purposes and principles of the United Nations."[50] Mr Pushpanathan had been convicted of conspiracy to traffic in narcotics, which the Board concluded made him ineligible for refugee status by operation of the exclusion clause in Article 1F(c). Mr Pushpanathan

49 *Pushpanathan*, *supra* note 35 at para 28 [emphasis added].

50 *Convention relating to the Status of Refugees*, 28 July 1951, 189 UNTS 137 (entered into force 22 April 1954).

sought judicial review in the Federal Court, which dismissed his application but certified "that a serious question of general importance [was] involved" in the application, which afforded Mr Pushpanathan a right of appeal to the Federal Court of Appeal under section 83(1) of the *Immigration Act*.[51] After the Federal Court of Appeal dismissed Mr Pushpanathan's appeal, he brought his case to the Supreme Court of Canada.

The Court allowed Mr Pushpanathan's appeal. Writing for the majority, Justice Bastarache determined that the applicable standard of review was correctness, and that he was thus obliged to interpret Article 1F(c) *de novo*.[52] He reached this conclusion as to the standard of review by applying the pragmatic and contextual factors introduced in *Bibeault*. The purpose of the inquiry, he stated, was to identify: "[T]he *legislative intent of the statute creating the tribunal* whose decision is being reviewed. More specifically, the reviewing court must ask: '[W]as the question which the provision raises one that was intended by the legislators to be left to the exclusive decision of the Board?'"[53] This "more nuanced approach in determining legislative intent" produced a more nuanced "range of possible standards of review" – i.e., the three standards endorsed in *Southam*.[54] The inquiry about what the legislator intended centred around four factors: (1) the presence or absence of a privative clause,[55] or a statutory appeal provision;[56] (2) the decision maker's expertise relative to that of the reviewing court;[57] (3) the purpose of the legislation, and of the provision at issue in particular;[58] and (4) the nature of the question, whether of law, of fact, or of mixed fact and law.[59] *Pushpanathan*'s insight was that, by applying these four factors, a court could determine whether, and how much, deference to an administrative decision maker was consistent with the intent of the legislature. A majority of the Court – of which Justice McLachlin was a member – instructed that, rather than be distracted by the question of whether or not a particular error could be branded as "jurisdictional," a reviewing court should seek to give effect to legislative

---

51 *Immigration Act*, RSC, 1985, c. I-2.

52 *Pushpanathan, supra* note 35 at paras 50 and 51 *et seq.*

53 *Ibid* at para 26, quoting *Pasiechnyk v Saskatchewan (Workers' Compensation Board)*, [1997] 2 SCR 890, 1997 CanLII 316 at para 18, Sopinka J [emphasis added].

54 *Pushpanathan, supra* note 35 at para 27.

55 *Ibid* at paras 30–1.

56 *Ibid* at paras 43–4.

57 *Ibid* at paras 32–5.

58 *Ibid* at para 36.

59 *Ibid* at paras 37–8.

intent, as discerned pragmatically and contextually. This, it was hoped, would provide a stable, doctrinally sound basis on which to conduct the standard of review analysis.

So it was when Justice McLachlin became Chief Justice McLachlin in January 2000. As Professor Mullan has put it, "[l]ife under the new Chief Justice looked as though it would commence with one of the major irritants of the previous twenty years of the Court's history effectively marginalized."[60] If only wishing made it so.

b. A Universal Approach?

Dr Q v College of Physicians and Surgeons of British Columbia was Chief Justice McLachlin's first significant foray into the standard of review jurisprudence.[61] The case arose out of an application for judicial review of a decision of an Inquiry Committee of the BC College of Physicians and Surgeons, which had suspended Dr Q's licence to practice for eighteen months after finding that he had taken physical and emotional advantage of one of his patients. The reviewing judge granted the application, and the Court of Appeal for British Columbia dismissed the College's appeal. The College then appealed successfully to the Supreme Court of Canada.

For a unanimous Court, Chief Justice McLachlin restated and affirmed the pragmatic and functional approach to determining the standard of review. Notably, she addressed persistent uncertainty about the scope of the pragmatic and functional approach's application across the full range of administrative decision making:

> In a case of judicial review such as this, the Court applies the pragmatic and functional approach that was established by this Court in [*Bibeault*], and gained ascendancy in [*Southam*] and [*Pushpanathan*]. The term "judicial review" embraces review of administrative decisions by way of both application for judicial review and statutory rights of appeal. In every case where a statute delegates power to an administrative decision-maker, the reviewing judge must begin by determining the standard of review on the pragmatic and functional approach. In *Pushpanathan*, this Court unequivocally accepted the primacy of the pragmatic and functional approach to determining the standard of judicial review of administrative decisions. Bastarache J. affirmed that "[t]he central inquiry in determining the standard of review exercisable by a court of law is the legislative intent of the

60 Mullan, *supra* note 32 at 4.

61 *Dr Q v College of Physicians and Surgeons of British Columbia*, 2003 SCC 19 [*Dr Q*].

statute creating the tribunal whose decision is being reviewed" (para. 26). However, this approach also gives due regard to "the consequences that flow from a grant of powers" (*Bibeault*, at p. 1089) and, while safeguarding "[t]he role of the superior courts in maintaining the rule of law" (p. 1090), reinforces that this reviewing power should not be employed unnecessarily. In this way, the pragmatic and functional approach inquires into legislative intent, but does so against the backdrop of the courts' constitutional duty to protect the rule of law …

Much as the principled approach to hearsay … eclipsed the traditional categorical exceptions to the hearsay rule … , the pragmatic and functional approach represents a principled conceptual model which the Court has used consistently in judicial review …

The pragmatic and functional approach demands a more nuanced analysis based on consideration of a number of factors. *This approach applies whenever a court reviews the decision of an administrative body*. As Professor D.J. Mullan states … , with the pragmatic and functional approach, "the Court has provided an overarching or unifying theory for review of the substantive decisions of all manner of statutory and prerogative decision makers." Review of the conclusions of an administrative decision-maker must begin by applying the pragmatic and functional approach.[62]

In hindsight, this veneration of the pragmatic and functional approach as "principled," "overarching," and "unifying" is ironic; in less than five years, the Court would jettison the very phrase "pragmatic and functional" as all but taboo.[63] Still, Chief Justice McLachlin's motivations are plain; her express purpose was "to re-articulate the focus of the factors involved" in the pragmatic and functional analysis, and to "update the considerations relevant to each" – an exercise that she felt was necessary because she "f[ound] the approach taken in the courts below problematic."[64]

This is textbook McLachlin. Faced with an area of common law jurisprudence that had proven difficult for lower courts to apply, the Chief Justice sought clarity and consensus through consolidation and synthesis. As Professor Sossin (as he then was) observed at the time, *Dr Q* and the Court's companion judgment in *Law Society of New Brunswick v*

62 *Ibid* at paras 21, 23, and 25 [emphasis added]. The quotation from Professor Mullan's work is DJ Mullan, *Administrative Law: Essential of Canadian Law* (Toronto: Irwin Law, 2001) at 108.

63 See Mullan, *supra* note 32 at 23.

64 *Dr Q, supra* note 61 at para 26.

Ryan[65] "represent attempts at synthesis in the articulation of administrative law doctrines and principles" and "present a portrait of standard of review that is concise, accessible and authoritative."[66] In the wake of these decisions, Professor Sossin predicted that "the pragmatic and functional approach will become even more standardized and entrenched as the framework for determining the standard of review."[67] One hopes he did not find someone to take that bet.

Because all was not quite well. Six months after *Dr Q* and *Ryan*, the Court released its judgment in *Toronto (City) v CUPE, Local 79*.[68] That decision is notable for two reasons: (1) it represents the Court's authoritative statement of the doctrine of abuse of process; and (2) it includes a lengthy concurrence by Justice LeBel, in which Justice Deschamps joined, lamenting the state of administrative law and what Justice LeBel saw as persistent shortcomings of the pragmatic and functional approach. To the extent that Chief Justice McLachlin may have hoped that the debate over the standard of review analysis would be settled after her reasons in *Dr Q* and Justice Iacobucci's companion reasons in *Ryan*, Justice LeBel's concurring reasons in *CUPE* made plain that those hopes had been mislaid.

Broadly, Justice LeBel voiced two concerns. First, he was not convinced that it was appropriate to "[treat] the pragmatic and functional methodology as an overarching analytical framework for substantive judicial review that must be applied, without variation, in *all* administrative law contexts, including those involving non-adjudicative decision makers."[69] Second, he had misgivings about the sustainability of an approach that embraced three allegedly distinct standards of review, two of which (reasonableness *simpliciter* and patent unreasonableness) courts had found difficult to distinguish. Indeed, Justice LeBel queried "whether, in the end, the theoretical efforts necessary to do so are productive."[70] This was because:

> Obviously any decision that fails the test of patent unreasonableness must also fall on a standard of reasonableness *simpliciter*, but it seems hard to imagine situations where the converse is not also true: if a decision is not

65 *Law Society of New Brunswick v Ryan*, 2003 SCC 20.

66 Sossin, *supra* note 47 at 489.

67 *Ibid* at 489; see also P Bryden, "Understanding the Standard of Review in Administrative Law" (2005) 54 UNBLJ 75 at 78–9.

68 *Toronto (City) v CUPE, Local 79*, 2003 SCC 63 [*CUPE*].

69 *Ibid* at para 61, LeBel J, concurring [emphasis in original].

70 *Ibid* at para 121, LeBel J, concurring.

> supported by a tenable explanation (and is thus unreasonable) … , how likely is it that it could be sustained on "any reasonable interpretation of the facts or of the law" (and thus not be patently unreasonable) … ?[71]

Justice LeBel noted that "[a]cademic commentators and practitioners have raised some serious questions as to whether the conceptual basis for each of the existing standards has been delineated with sufficient clarity by this Court," while "[r]eviewing courts too, have occasionally expressed frustration over a perceived lack of clarity in this area."[72] This, he argued, demanded action, even in the absence of submissions on the issue, of which there were none in *CUPE*: "The Court cannot remain unresponsive to sustained concerns or criticism coming from the legal community in relation to the state of Canadian jurisprudence in this important part of the law," Justice LeBel wrote.[73] Concluding, he asked, "[s]hould courts move to a two standard system of judicial review, correctness and a revised unified standard of reasonableness?"

It would take nearly five more years for Justice LeBel's colleagues to vindicate his "*cri de coeur*."[74] When the Court finally did so, it answered his question in the affirmative. Three standards of review became two, as the McLachlin Court made what would prove to be its last major push for lasting clarity and consensus in administrative law.

c. Standards, Restated

Plenty of ink has been spilled on *Dunsmuir*. As Professor Daly has noted, it was, after a decade, "by some distance … the most cited decision of any Canadian court."[75] Despite having doubled down on the pragmatic and functional approach in *Dr Q* and *Ryan*, a majority of the Court, Chief Justice McLachlin among them, concluded that "the phrase 'pragmatic and functional approach' may have misguided courts in the past," and so replaced it with what it simply dubbed the "standard of review analysis."[76] The recalibration of the law of judicial

---

71 *Ibid*, LeBel J, concurring [citations omitted].

72 *Ibid* at para 63, LeBel J, concurring [citations omitted].

73 *Ibid* at para 64, LeBel J, concurring.

74 Macklin, *supra* note 38 at 301.

75 P Daly, "The *Dunsmuir* Decade/10 ans de *Dunsmuir*" (11 January 2018), online (blog): *Administrative Law Matters* <http://www.administrativelawmatters.com/blog/2018/01/11/the-dunsmuir-decade10-ans-de-dunsmuir/>; see also Daly, *supra* note 30 at 529.

76 *Dunsmuir*, *supra* note 24 at para 63.

review was intended, in the finest tradition of the McLachlin Court, to make matters more straightforward and thus more clear and consistent. As Justices Bastarache and LeBel stated for the majority:

> Despite the clear, stable constitutional foundations of the system of judicial review, the operation of judicial review in Canada has been in a constant state of evolution over the years, as courts have attempted to devise approaches to judicial review that are both theoretically sound and effective in practice. *Despite efforts to refine and clarify it, the present system has proven to be difficult to implement*. The time has arrived to re-examine the Canadian approach to judicial review of administrative decisions and develop a principled framework that is more coherent and workable....
>
> The Court has moved from a highly formalistic, artificial "jurisdiction" test that could easily be manipulated, to a highly contextual "functional" test that provides great flexibility but little real on-the-ground guidance, and offers too many standards of review. *What is needed is a test that offers guidance, is not formalistic or artificial, and permits review where justice requires it, but not otherwise. A simpler test is needed.*[77]

In concurring reasons, Justice Binnie took the same view:

> There is afoot in the legal profession a desire for clearer guidance than is provided by lists of principles, factors and spectrums ...
>
> *[T]he law of judicial review should be pruned of some of its unduly subtle, unproductive, or esoteric features.*[78]

As did Justice Deschamps, in concurring reasons in which Justices Charron and Rothstein both joined: "The law of judicial review of administrative action not only requires repairs, it needs to be *cleared of superfluous discussions and processes*," Justice Deschamps wrote.[79]

To accomplish this, the majority took its cue from Justice LeBel's concurring reasons in *CUPE*, collapsing "the two variants of reasonableness review ... into a single form of 'reasonableness' review. The result is a system of judicial review comprising two standards – correctness and reasonableness."[80] To choose between these two standards, the majority proposed a two-step process: "First, courts ascertain *whether the jurisprudence*

77 *Ibid* at paras 32 and 43 [emphasis added].

78 *Ibid* at paras 132–3, Binnie J, concurring.

79 *Ibid* at para 158, Deschamps J, concurring [emphasis added].

80 *Ibid* at para 45.

has already determined in a satisfactory manner the degree of deference to be accorded with regard to a particular category of question. Second, where the first inquiry proves unfruitful, courts must proceed to *an analysis of the factors making it possible to identify the proper standard of review.*"[81]

The new first step, a determination as to whether the applicable standard of review could be determined by reference to precedent, represented a departure from Chief Justice McLachlin's instruction, in *Dr Q*, that, "[i]n every case where a statute delegates power to an administrative decision-maker, the reviewing judge must begin by determining the standard of review on the pragmatic and functional approach."[82] As Professor Mullan has observed, this development "provided welcome relief to lower court judges to the extent that [*Dunsmuir*] excused them from a full standard of review analysis" where precedent was available.[83]

Yet, rather than interpreting *Dunsmuir*'s embrace of precedent as a repudiation of Chief Justice McLachlin's approach in *Dr Q*, one may view the two decisions as complementary, yet mutually exclusive, efforts to advance a single set of common law objectives, namely, to promote consistency in the law and to ensure that lower courts are in a position to apply the law faithfully as prescribed by the Supreme Court of Canada. *Dr Q* attempted to do this by requiring courts to apply the same contextual approach to determining the standard of review in every case. When that effort produced paradoxically inconsistent results and revealed difficulties in application, the Court – with Chief Justice McLachlin's concurrence – switched gears, and instead preferred the practice of precedent as an alternative means of achieving consistency. The McLachlinite goal of providing clear guidance was the same in both cases. With the benefit of experience, however, the majority in *Dunsmuir* decided to pursue that goal differently.

Justices Bastarache and LeBel identified four categories of questions on which precedent had determined correctness to be the appropriate standard of review. These were: (1) "constitutional questions regarding the division of powers between Parliament and the provinces … as well as other constitutional issues";[84] (2) "true questions of jurisdiction or *vires* …. in the narrow sense of whether or not the tribunal had the authority to make the inquiry";[85] (3) "question[s] … of general law 'that

81 *Ibid* at para 62.

82 *Dr Q, supra* note 61 at para 21.

83 D Mullan, "Unresolved Issues on Standard of Review in Canadian Judicial Review of Administrative Action: The Top Fifteen!" (2013) 42:1–2 Adv Q 1 at 4.

84 *Dunsmuir, supra* note 24 at para 58.

85 *Ibid* at para 59.

[are] both of central importance to the legal system as a whole and outside the adjudicator's specialized area of expertise'";[86] and (4) "[q]uestions regarding the jurisdictional lines between two or more competing specialized tribunals."[87] Further, the *Dunsmuir* majority confirmed that reasonableness would likely be the standard of review where the decision maker's enabling statute includes a privative or preclusive clause;[88] "[w]here the question is one of fact, discretion or policy";[89] "where a tribunal is interpreting its own statute or statutes closely connected to its function, with which it will have particular familiarity";[90] and "where an administrative tribunal has developed particular expertise in the application of a general common law or civil law rule in relation to a specific statutory context."[91]

Still, under *Dunsmuir*, this recourse to precedent was not to be the end of the matter. Where the standard of review had not previously been determined, the standard of review analysis required the reviewing court to look to context to determine whether deference was due. As Justices Bastarache and LeBel put it:

> The analysis must be contextual. As mentioned above, it is dependent on the application of a number of relevant factors, including: (1) the presence or absence of a privative clause; (2) the purpose of the tribunal as determined by interpretation of enabling legislation; (3) the nature of the question at issue, and; (4) the expertise of the tribunal.[92]

If these factors look familiar, it is because they are almost *verbatim* the considerations that informed the pragmatic and functional approach of which *Dunsmuir* made short work. Recall Chief Justice McLachlin's restatement of the "four contextual factors" that determined the standard of review in *Dr Q*: "[T]he presence or absence of a privative clause or statutory right of appeal; the expertise of the tribunal relative to that of the reviewing court on the issue in question; the purposes of the legislation and the provision in particular; and, the nature of the question – law, fact, or mixed law and fact."[93] *Dunsmuir* removed the "pragmatic

86 *Ibid* at para 60.
87 *Ibid* at para 61.
88 *Ibid* at para 52.
89 *Ibid* at para 53.
90 *Ibid* at para 54.
91 *Ibid*.
92 *Ibid* at para 64; see also para 55.
93 *Dr Q*, *supra* note 61 at para 26.

and functional" label but retained its component parts, to be considered in the streamlined standard of review analysis once precedent had been found wanting.

Dunsmuir was thus an effort at imposing order and simplicity, and thus clarity, on the framework firmed up in *Southam* and *Pushpanathan* and confirmed in *Dr Q*. But it was not a wholesale departure from what came before. In this respect, the majority opinion in *Dunsmuir*, while not unanimous, reflected the McLachlin Court's operational priorities: *Dunsmuir* represented an incremental effort to provide comprehensible guidance to lower courts without upending binding precedent. That *Dunsmuir* ultimately fell short of this high purpose does not detract from the intentions that led the Chief Justice to agree with a generous finessing of the approach set down in her judgment in *Dr Q*, half a decade prior, in favour of a new model proposed by her colleagues.

But the structure of the majority reasons also bears notice. That Justices Bastarache and LeBel sought to provide a clear roadmap for lower courts is obvious. The discussion of the refreshed standard of review analysis, under the heading "Determining the Appropriate Standard of Review," occupies just fourteen paragraphs, of which the final three are a capsule summary of the previous eleven.[94] As each of the judges who wrote in *Dunsmuir* agreed, the problem with the *status quo ante* was that it had proved impossible to apply consistently and thus had distracted too much attention from the merits of the judicial review applications to which the standard of review ultimately pertains. *Dunsmuir* sought to solve this problem by condensing and simplifying the prescribed approach. It is not to detract from the authors' work on the judgment to suggest that one may detect Chief Justice McLachlin's influence in the manner of its writing.

In striving for simplicity, however, *Dunsmuir* sowed the seeds of its own eventual undoing. Taken at face value, the two-step standard of review analysis that the *Dunsmuir* majority endorsed sought to achieve the clairty and predictability of a formal, categorical approach without compromising the nuance and sensitivity to context that had always been the pragmatic and functional approach's – and, indeed, the common law's – cardinal virtue. But, as Professor Lewans has noted:

> The difficulty is that the reasoning in *Dunsmuir* on the standard of review straddled two conflicting narratives in Canadian administrative law. The first, the formal and conceptual narrative, asserts that judges are entitled to intervene on a correctness basis when the issue under review falls into

94 See *Dunsmuir*, *supra* note 24 at paras 51–64.

> an abstract class or category. The second, the pragmatic and functional narrative, asserts that judges should generally avoid categorizing legal issues that way, and should focus instead on contextual factors which suggest that administrative officials have a legitimate role to play in interpreting relevant legal principles and values.[95]

Recall Justice Bastarache's treatment of "jurisdictional questions" in *Pushpanathan*: "[A] question which 'goes to jurisdiction' is simply descriptive of a provision for which the proper standard of review is correctness."[96] At the time, this represented the Court's attempt to submerge the jurisdiction category within the pragmatic and functional analysis, thus reconciling the Court's historically "formal and conceptual narrative" (in Professor Lewans' words) of administrative law with the more flexible, less Diceyan methodology endorsed in *Bibeault*, *Southam*, and *Pushpanathan* itself. *Dunsmuir* represented the further evolution of this vestigial attraction to form and category, in Justice Bastarache and LeBel's endorsement of precedent. What later came to be known as the "correctness categories"[97] – those questions for which the standard of review had already been determined to be correctness – ultimately ceased to be examples of the role of *stare decisis* in the standard of review analysis, and instead crowded out the contextual approach that, on the face of the majority reasons in *Dunsmuir*, should have remained the ultimate determinant of the standard of review.

This return to form and category haunted the Court after *Dunsmuir*. In the decade following the Court's endorsement of Justices Bastarache and LeBel's two-step, two-standards approach, the fact that categories lend themselves more easily to clear, prescriptive pronouncements – and thus, in theory, to providing useful guidance to lower courts – proved too alluring for the McLachlin Court to resist. Professor Daly has suggested that this reflected a defect in *Dunsmuir* from the very outset:

> At the same time as it purported to establish presumptive categories to which either reasonableness or correctness would be appropriately applied, the Court maintained the four-factor standard of review analysis. It

95 Lewans, *supra* note 30.

96 *Pushpanathan*, *supra* note 35 at para 28.

97 See *Ready v Saskatoon Regional Health Authority*, 2017 SKCA 20 at paras 63, 108–19; *Loewen v Manitoba Teachers' Society*, 2015 MBCA 13 at paras 46, 48, and 69; see also Daly, *supra* note 36 at 809.

> used the words "usually" and "generally" on several occasions. It gave no guidance as to when the presumptions would be rebutted or displaced or what weight the presumptions should be given ... The Court also gave no guidance on the order in which a reviewing court should proceed. Should it consider the presumptions first and then the four factors? Or should it consider the four factors first and then the presumptions?[98]

To a certain extent, this criticism reflected hindsight bias; it looked beyond *Dunsmuir*'s instructions about the order in which to consider what Professor Daly called "presumptive categories" – which, in *Dunsmuir* itself, were really just references to precedent – and the contextual factors that had been part of the analysis since *Bibeault*. Justices Bastarache and LeBel left no doubt that precedent was to be considered first, and context only if precedent proved unavailing. What happened after those marching orders were given, however, was a gradual encroachment of categories, and eventually of an interpretive presumption, onto terrain that *Dunsmuir* itself guarded for contextual analysis. It was in this next chapter of our story that, where administrative law is concerned, Chief Justice McLachlin's signal virtue as a common law jurist and institutional leader helped to push the Court, and the law of judicial review, into a quagmire.

d. A Digression on Common Law Judging

But first, let us briefly pause and return to Beverley McLachlin's approach to common law appellate adjudication. Before her elevation to the chief justiceship, Justice McLachlin's judgments reflected a steadfast commitment to the paradigmatic conception of a common law judge, as one who, in Professor Fuller's words, "foresee[s] that there ... emerge[s] from his treatment of individual cases a body of rules, and that the community ... tend[s] in some degree to adjust itself to those rules."[99] In applying such a rule, the common law appellate judge tests the rule's implications against the policies that justify it, and shapes the evolution of doctrine to better achieve the rule's purpose.[100] The goal is to achieve a consistent commitment to principles that are, at least in

98 P Daly, "The Unfortunate Triumph of Form over Substance in Canadian Administrative Law" (2012) 50:2 Osgoode Hall LJ 317 at 326–7.

99 L Fuller, "Reason and Fiat in Case Law" (1945) 59 Harv L Rev 376 at 378.

100 See RB Cappalli, "At the Point of Decision: Common Law's Advantage over the Civil Law" (1998) 12:1 Temp Intl & Comp LJ 87 at 102.

theory, "capable of infinite application," as Sir Frederick Pollock put it, since "the matter is always changing."[101]

Take *Hall v Hebert*.[102] Justice McLachlin, for the majority, affirmed the doctrine of *ex turpi causa non oritur actio*, which disentitles a plaintiff to damages in tort on the basis of the plaintiff's own immoral or criminal conduct. (Justice Cory, by contrast, would have substituted a judicial power to reject claims "on considerations of public policy.")[103] Justice McLachlin stated the rule and the principles underlying it simply, in a single paragraph, and with such clarity that the United Kingdom Supreme Court would adopt it as a leading statement of the law nearly a quarter century later.[104] In the same judgment, Justice McLachlin expressly eschewed a category-constrained approach to *ex turpi causa*.[105] She acted similarly in a range of other areas of the law during her first decade on the Court, focusing her efforts on the articulation of principles from which jurisprudential categories emerged, rather than emphasizing the categories themselves.[106]

Chief Justice McLachlin, by contrast, seemed comparatively more willing to embrace categories. Writing for the majority with Justice Major in *Cooper v Hobart*, for example, the Chief Justice endorsed a categorical approach to establishing proximity in tort, albeit while allowing the possibility that *prima facie* duties of care may arise in analogous situations.[107] She used categories similarly in the context of defining criminal indecency in *R v Labaye*.[108]

Most strikingly, Chief Justice McLachlin signed on to a string of judgments adopting and then calcifying categories within the standard of review analysis in administrative law. One may posit that she did so, in this area and others, out of a desire to achieve what she once described as the first virtue of "formalism" – namely, that "it is clear

101 F Pollock, *The Genius of the Common Law* (New York: Columbia University Press, 1912) at 112.

102 *Hall v Hebert*, [1993] 2 SCR 159 [*Hall*]. I am indebted to the anonymous reviewer who suggested *Hall* as a basis for comparison with respect to Justice (and later Chief Justice) McLachlin's approach to common law adjudication.

103 *Ibid* at 222, Cory J.

104 *Ibid* at 169; see *Patel v Mirza*, GBR [2016] UKSC 42, [2017] All ER 191 at para 230, Lord Sumption, and paras 100–1, Lord Toulson.

105 See *Hall*, *supra* note 100 at 177–8.

106 See e.g. *Canadian National Railway Co v Norsk Pacific Steamship Co*, [1992] 1 SCR 1021 at 1152–3; *Peter v Beblow*, [1993] 1 SCR 980 at 987 and 993–5; *Soulos v. Korkontzilas*, [1997] 2 SCR 217 at paras 14–15; *Bazley v Curry*, [1999] 2 SCR 534 at para 41.

107 *Cooper v Hobart*, 2001 SCC 79 at para 36.

108 *R v Labaye*, 2005 SCC 80 at para 62.

and predictable. People can readily find the rule and predict what the courts will decide."[109] Producing case law of such clarity was among her standing objectives as Chief Justice, as descibed above. This could explain why her resistence to categories as a puisne justice yielded once she assumed the centre chair. As we shall see, this was ultimately to the Court's, and administrative law's, detriment.

e. Simplicity Triumphs

In retrospect, two of *Dunsmuir*'s features proved most decisive in the evolution of the McLachlin Court's approach to the standard of review. First, the introduction of the "correctness categories," as a representation of precedent, shifted the focus of judicial and academic debate to those categories' scope.[110] This confounded early post-*Dunsmuir* optimism that, by reintroducing categories into the standard of review analysis, the locus of the argument might finally shift away from determining the standard of review to actually applying it.[111] Second, and perhaps more importantly, the *Dunsmuir* majority – Chief Justice McLachlin among them – accepted as a matter of principle that the answer to a decade of judicial hair-tearing over the standard of review was to make simplicity and clarity an unrivalled priority.[112] It was the continuation of this pursuit that caused problems.

The first sign of real trouble came in a series of decisions in 2011, in which the Court consolidated the *Dunsmuir* approach and, in the name of clarity, elevated the categories and presumptions of precedent into increasingly inflexible rules. It subsequently became clear that to apply the rules introduced in this period was to be confronted with their shortcomings, especially their tendency to draw the analysis away from doctrinal coherence and principle.[113] At the time, however, the Court's

---

109 B McLachlin, "The Evolution of the Law of Private Obligation: The Influence of Justice La Forest," in R Johnson and JP McEnvoy, eds, *Gérald V. La Forest at the Supreme Court of Canada, 1985–1997* (Winnipeg: Supreme Court of Canada Historical Society, 2000).

110 See e.g. *McLean v British Columbia (Securities Commission)*, 2013 SCC 67 at para 25; see also M Lewans, "Renovating Judicial Review" (2017) 68 UNBLJ 109 at 122–3; Daly, *supra* note 36 at 810–11.

111 See D Ginn, "New Words for Old Problems: The *Dunsmuir* Era" (2010) 37:3 Adv Q 317 at 326–7.

112 See M Liston, "Governments in Miniature: The Rule of Law in the Administrative State" in Flood and Sossin, *Administrative Law in Context*, *supra* note 37 at 75.

113 See D Stratas, "The Canadian Law of Judicial Review: A Plea for Doctrinal Coherence and Consistency," (2016) 42:1 Queen's LJ 27 at 40 *et seq*.

objective was consistent with Chief Justice McLachlin's broader project of providing useful guidance.

Smith v Alliance Pipeline Ltd was an appeal from a compensation award made by an Arbitration Committee appointed under the *National Energy Board Act*.[114] The underlying dispute concerned the expropriation of farmland for pipeline construction. After two Arbitration Committee hearings and an action in the Court of Queen's Bench, the Arbitration Committee awarded the appellant, whose land had been expropriated, his costs of both arbitrations as well as of the court action. On judicial review, the issue was whether the Arbitration Committee's decision to do so could withstand scrutiny. The Federal Court held that it could, the Federal Court of Appeal that it could not. The Supreme Court of Canada unanimously allowed the appeal, with Justice Deschamps authoring separate concurring reasons.

For the majority, including Chief Justice McLachlin, Justice Fish restated the *Dunsmuir* approach in the crispest – some might say simplest – possible terms:

> The standard of correctness governs: (1) a constitutional issue; (2) a question of general law that is both of central importance to the legal system as a whole and outside the adjudicator's specialized area of expertise ... ; (3) the drawing of jurisdictional lines between two or more competing specialized tribunals; and (4) a "true question of jurisdiction or *vires*" ... On the other hand, reasonableness is normally the governing standard where the question: (1) relates to the interpretation of the tribunal's enabling (or "home") statute or "statutes closely connected to its function, with which it will have particular familiarity" ... ; (2) raises issues of fact, discretion or policy; or (3) involves inextricably intertwined legal and factual issues.[115]

Justice Fish went on to conclude that, since the Arbitration Committee was interpreting its home statute, awards for costs are "invariably fact-sensitive and generally discretionary," and the *Act* at issue evinced a parliamentary intention to leave the issue of costs to the Committee, the applicable standard of review was reasonableness.[116] The merits of that determination aside, the brevity with which the *Smith* majority restated the *Dunsmuir* framework represented an unequivocal step

114 *Smith v Alliance Pipeline Ltd*, 2011 SCC 7 [*Smith*]; *National Energy Board Act*, RSC 1985, c N7.

115 *Smith*, *supra* note 114 at paras 25–6 [citations omitted].

116 *Ibid* at paras 28–33.

toward the clarity of categories, and away from the complexity of context. As Professor Daly put it:

> [T]he message of *Alliance Pipeline* and its confrères is clear: Reviewing courts should approach the task of judicial review by reference to a categorical approach. The first, and usually decisive, step will be to categorize the question at issue. Categorization, rather than a four-factor analysis, will determine the applicable standard of review. If it once were possible to say that *Dunsmuir* is "*Pushpanathan* in a party dress," it is no longer the case.[117]

For many, this categorical turn was suspect.[118] But it also struck an unequivocal blow for simplicity. *Smith* made the selection of the standard of review seem blissfully straightfoward, almost formulaic. For a Court that, under Chief Justice McLachlin, had come to measure its success by the user-friendliness of its judgments, who could ask for anything more?

Justice Deschamps could, for one. In concurring reasons in *Smith*, she took exception to the majority's staccato restatement of *Dunsmuir*. "It is important that the Court's elaboration of categories of question should not be turned into a blind and formalistic application of words rather than principles," she wrote. "The parties to any adjudication must be able to understand why deference is given to the decision of the administrative body considering their case."[119] By embracing a "broad 'home' statute category of question," Justice Deschamps warned, the standard of review jurisprudence was drifting away from the *Dunsmuir* framework's underlying rationale. This required sensitivity to whether the matter interpreted was related to the decision maker's specialized expertise, not mere association with the decision maker's organic legislation.[120] She concluded that, "[i]f the standard of review is to be resolved in favour of reasonableness on the basis of a category of question without the need for a contextual standard of review analysis, the category must be firmly grounded in a clear rationale for deference."[121]

---

117 Daly, *supra* note 98 at 329, quoting H Janisch, "Something Old, Something New" (2010) 23:3 Can J Admin L & Prac 219.

118 See e.g. P Daly, "*Dunsmuir*'s Flaws Exposed: Recent Decisions on Standard of Review" (2012) 58:2 McGill LJ 483 [Daly, "*Dunsmuir*'s Flaws,"]; Daly, *supra* note 98; *cf* A Green, "Can There Be Too Much Context in Administrative Law? Setting the Standard of Review in Canadian Administrative Law" (2014) 47:2 UBC L Rev 443.

119 *Smith, supra* note 114 at para 83, Deschamps J, concurring.

120 *Ibid* at para 91, Deschamps J, concurring.

121 *Ibid* at para 106, Deschamps J, concurring.

If Justice Deschamps hoped to persuade her colleagues to abandon the trend toward clarity at all costs, she failed. The proof came later in 2011, in the Court's judgment in *Alberta (Information and Privacy Commissioner) v Alberta Teachers' Association.*[122] Alberta's *Personal Information Protection Act*[123] gave the province's Information and Privacy Commissioner ninety days from the date on which a complaint was received to complete an inquiry, unless the Commissioner notified the parties in writing that he was extending the deadline. The Commissioner received complaints regarding the Alberta Teachers' Association. Twenty-two months later, the Commissioner notified the parties that he was extending the time period in which he would conclude his inquiry. He ultimately found that the Association had contravened the *Act*. The Association brought an application for judicial review. It argued that the Commissioner had lost jurisdiction when he failed to extend the time period for the inquiry within the first ninety days after receiving the complaint. The chambers judge agreed. So did a majority of the Court of Appeal.

The Supreme Court of Canada unanimously allowed the appeal, but split 6–2–1 on the appropriate application of the *Dunsmuir* framework. The majority, speaking through Justice Rothstein, doubled down on the categorical approach endorsed in *Smith*. Where the administrative decision maker is interpreting its home statute, Justice Rothstein held, the standard of review would be reasonableness "unless the interpretation of the home statute *falls into one of the categories* of questions to which the correctness standard continues to apply."[124]

Having set up a default of deference for questions involving the interpretation of a delegate's home statute, Justice Rothstein next had to avoid the correctness category of "true questions of jurisdiction or *vires*."[125] This he did by defining that category almost out of existence, before questioning whether "the time ha[d] come to reconsider whether, for purposes of judicial review, the category of true questions of jurisdiction exists and is necessary to identifying the appropriate standard of review."[126]

This, then, was the Court's effort to bolt a clear, categorial approach to the standard of review analysis into place, without allowing the

122 *Alberta (Information and Privacy Commissioner) v Alberta Teachers' Association*, 2011 SCC 61 [*Alberta Teachers*].

123 *Personal Information Protection Act*, SA 2003, c P-6.5.

124 *Alberta Teachers, supra* note 122 at para 30 [emphasis added].

125 *Dunsmuir, supra* note 24 at para 59.

126 *Alberta Teachers, supra* note 122 at paras 33–4 [citations omitted].

Dunsmuir framework to slide toward the sort of jurisdiction-obsessed formalism that dominated the administrative law jurisprudence before *CUPE, Local 963 v NB Liquor Corp* in 1979.[127] Providing useful guidance meant avoiding what would otherwise be obvious overlap between a correctness category and a presumption in favour of reasonableness.[128] The answer, for the majority, was to define the former so narrowly as to render the intersection all but theoretical.

Justice Rothstein left no mystery as to why the Court went in this direction. He referred to "the uncertainty and confusion that has plagued standard of review analysis for many years," which he called "the animating reason for this Court's decision in *Dunsmuir*." He noted that "the 'true questions of jurisdiction' category has caused confusion to counsel and judges alike and has unnecessarily increased costs to clients before getting to the actual substance of the case." Creating a presumption that an administrative decision maker's interpretation of its home statute would be reviewed for reasonableness was, he said, "a natural extension of the approach to simplification set out in *Dunsmuir* and follows directly from [*Smith*]."[129]

The majority's candid admission that its goal was "simplification" – and had been in *Dunsmuir* and *Smith* – was striking.[130] It also provoked vigorous disagreement from Justice Binnie (with whom Justice Deschamps concurred) and Justice Cromwell. Justice Binnie observed that the presumption of deference to a decision maker's interpretation of its home statute was a development in the common law of judicial review. In his view, this development risked eliminating a reviewing court's residual discretion to intervene when the interpretation at issue was outside the decision maker's expertise or raised issues of general legal importance.[131]

Justice Cromwell, meanwhile, took an even stronger line. The majority, he argued, had been too attentive to the call of simplicity, and not attentive enough to judicial review's principled foundations: He maintained that "[t]he proposition that provisions of a 'home statute' are generally reviewable on a reasonableness standard does not trump a

---

127 *CUPE v NB*, *supra* note 36; see also Lewans, *supra* note 110 at 113; L Sossin & CM Flood, "The Contextual Turn: Iacobucci's Legacy and the Standard of Review in Administrative Law" (2007) 57:2 UTLJ 581 at 584–5.

128 See Daly, "*Dunsmuir*'s Flaws," *supra* note 118 at 491; see also Lewans, *supra* note 110 at 123.

129 *Alberta Teachers*, *supra* note 122 at paras 36–9.

130 See also *Wilson*, *supra* note 28 at para 25, Abella J.

131 *Alberta Teachers*, *supra* note 122 at paras 82–3, Binnie J, concurring, citing *Canada (Canadian Human Rights Commission) v Canada (Attorney General)*, 2011 SCC 53.

more thorough examination of legislative intent when a plausible argument is advanced that a tribunal must interpret a particular provision correctly."[132] Moreover, Justice Cromwell warned, the majority's approach would ultimately prove self-defeating, since "[c]reating a presumption without providing guidance on how one could tell whether it has been rebutted does not … provide any assistance to reviewing courts."[133] As described below, he would eventually be proven right.

f. Vanishing Correctness

As the Court continued its drive to simplify the standard of review analysis in the opening years of Beverley McLachlin's second decade as Chief Justice, the resonableness standard became an ever-stronger default. The pragmatic justification for this progression was that it supposedly encouraged parties to move more swiftly to the merits of the matter, rather than engage in "law office metaphysics" concerning the applicable standard of review.[134]

There is no more striking example than the evolution of the Court's approach to reviewing administrative decisions that implicate the *Charter*. In 2012, Chief Justice McLachlin joined Justice Abella's unanimous opinion in *Doré v Barreau du Québec*.[135] It immediately became the Court's leading case on this question – and, as we will see, the source of considerable consternation and subsequent dissent.

Gilles Doré was a criminal defence lawyer. He appeared before Justice Boilard of the Superior Court of Quebec. Justice Boilard made disparaging comments about Mr Doré's advocacy, first during Mr Doré's submissions, then subsequently in written reasons denying the relief Mr Doré had sought on his client's behalf.

Mr Doré responded. First, he wrote a private letter to Justice Boilard. Mr Doré accused His Honour of "arrogance" and of "hid[ing] behind your status like a coward," described him as "loathsome" and "fundamentally unjust," and mocked his "chronic inability to master any social skills" and "essentially non-existent listening skills," among other invective. He then wrote to the Chief Justice of the Superior Court, requesting that he not be required to appear before Justice Boilard in the future. Finally, he filed a complaint against Justice Boilard with the

132 *Alberta Teachers, supra* note 122 at para 99, Cromwell J, concurring.

133 *Ibid* at para 92, Cromwell J, concurring.

134 *Dunsmuir, supra* note 24 at para 122, Binnie J, concurring; see also *Wilson, supra* note 28 at paras 20 and 25, Abella J, concurring.

135 *Doré v Barreau du Québec*, 2012 SCC 12 [*Doré*].

Canadian Judicial Council. A month after he did so, the Chief Justice of the Superior Court sent the Syndic du Barreau – the professional disciplinary body for Quebec's lawyers – a copy of Mr Doré's initial letter to Justice Boilard.

The Canadian Judicial Council reprimanded Justice Boilard. The Disciplinary Council of the Barreau du Québec suspended Mr Doré from the practice of law for twenty-one days. Mr Doré's appeal to the Tribunal des professions, his judicial review application to the Superior Court, and his appeal to the Quebec Court of Appeal were all unsuccessful. His case reached the Supreme Court of Canada.[136] The Court dismissed his appeal.[137]

The issue was whether the Barreau's decision to discipline Mr Doré violated his right to freedom of expression, as guaranteed by section 2(b) of the *Charter*. One might have expected this to be a "constitutional [issue]" that, according to *Dunsmuir*, was "necessarily subject to correctness review because of the unique role of s. 96 courts as interpreters of the Constitution."[138]

One would have been wrong. The Court unanimously applied the reasonableness standard. Justice Abella reasoned – and Chief Justice McLachlin agreed – that, "[w]hen *Charter* values are applied to an individual administrative decision, they are being applied in relation to a particular set of facts. *Dunsmuir* tells us this should attract deference."[139]

The Court took the view that deference is warranted, even when the *Charter* is implicated, when an administrative decision maker has exercised its discretion within the scope of its expertise.[140] The alternative, Justice Abella warned, would entail reviewing courts' "'retrying' a range of administrative decisions that would otherwise be subjected to a reasonableness standard."[141] Instead, where "the decision-maker has properly balanced the relevant *Charter* value with the statutory objectives, the decision will be found to be reasonable."[142]

Doré was another incremental step in the McLachlin Court's attempt to simplify the standard of review analysis. Two years before *Dunsmuir*,

136 *Ibid* at paras 9–21.

137 *Ibid* at para 72.

138 *Dunsmuir, supra* note 24 at para 58; see also CD Bredt and E Krajewska, "*Doré*: All That Glitters Is Not Gold" (2014) SCLR (2d) 340 at 355.

139 *Doré, supra* note 135 at para 36.

140 *Ibid* at paras 45 and 47.

141 *Ibid* at para 51, quoting D Mullan, "Administrative Tribunals and Judicial Review of Charter Issues after *Multani*" (2006) 21 NJCL 127 at 145.

142 *Doré, supra* note 135 at para 58.

in *Multani v Commission scolaire Marguerite-Bourgeoys*,[143] a majority of the Court (over Justice Abella's dissent) had asserted that "the fact that an issue relating to constitutional rights is raised in an administrative context does not mean that the constitutional law standards must be dissolved into the administrative law standards."[144] When the Court departed from that conclusion in *Doré*, it did so in the name of "coherence" and "integrati[on]."[145] No longer would *Charter* considerations warrant the bifurcation of the review exercise into "a constitutional law component and an administrative law component."[146] Rather, the *Charter*'s function would henceforth be to serve as "a reminder," within the reasonableness exercise, "that some values are clearly fundamental and ... cannot be violated lightly."[147]

Fault lines soon appeared. It was evident in *Doré* itself that the Court could not both reach a unanimous decision and depart entirely from *Multani*'s deployment of the section 1 analysis in administrative review. Though *Doré* confirmed that courts were not to engage in *de novo* review whenever a *Charter* right was implicated in an administrative decision,[148] it also recognized that "there is ... conceptual harmony between a reasonableness review and the [section 1] framework, since both contemplate giving a 'margin of appreciation,' or deference, to administrative and legislative bodies."[149] As Professor Kong observed, "[e]ither the two approaches are inconsistent because the *Oakes* test results in a more stringent standard of review, or they are in harmony because they accord similar degrees of deference to state action. They cannot be both."[150]

Compounding this tension in *Doré* was the Court's judgment, issued three months earlier, in *Newfoundland and Labrador Nurses' Union*

143 *Multani v Commission scolaire Marguerite-Bourgeoys*, 2006 SCC 6 [*Multani*].

144 *Ibid* at para 16.

145 *Doré, supra* note 135 at para 34, quoting SL Gratton and L Sossin, "In Search of Coherence: The *Charter* and Administrative Law under the McLachlin Court," in DA Wright and AM Dodek, eds., *Public Law at the McLachlin Court: The First Decade* (Toronto: Irwin Law, 2011) at 161.

146 *Multani, supra* note 143 at para 17.

147 *Doré, supra* note 135 at para 35, quoting G Cartier, "The *Baker* Effect: A New Interface between the *Canadian Charter of Rights and Freedoms* and Administrative Law – The Case of Discretion," in D Dyzenhaus, ed, *The Unity of Public Law* (Portland, OR: Hart, 2004) at 86.

148 *Doré, supra* note 135 at para 51, quoting Mullan, *supra* note 141 at 145.

149 *Doré, supra* note 135 at para 57.

150 HL Kong, "*Doré*, Proportionality and the Virtues of Judicial Craft" (2013) 63 SCLR (2d) 501 at 509, citing *R v Oakes*, [1986] 1 SCR 103.

v Newfoundland and Labrador (Treasury Board).[151] There, Justice Abella, also for a unanimous Court – and also with Chief Justice McLachlin's concurrence – rejected "the proposition that the adequacy of reasons is a stand-alone basis for quashing a decision."[152] Rather, the Court held, "courts must show 'respect for the decision-making process of adjudicative bodies with regard to both the facts and the law'" by engaging in an "organic exercise" of "assessing whether the decision is reasonable in light of the outcome and the reasons."[153]

Newfoundland Nurses thus endorsed reasonableness review in its most deferential form. It placed a burden on the reviewing court to seek to make sense of the decision maker's reasoning.[154] *Doré* suggested that the same reasonableness standard applied to discretionary decisions that implicated *Charter* guarantees. These decisions tell a story of analytical unity, layered atop the doctrinal simplicity that *Smith* and *Alberta Teachers* each sanctioned. Yet, this meta-trend toward integration under the rubric of reasonableness laid the groundwork for its own undoing. In Chief Justice McLachlin's final years on the bench, previously submerged normative disagreements between the McLachlin Court's members began to rise to the surface.

g. Paradise Lost

Doré's consensus ended in 2015. In *Loyola High School v Quebec (Attorney General)*,[155] the Court split 4–3 on the application of the framework it had unanimously endorsed just three years earlier.

Loyola arose out of the refusal of Quebec's Minister of Education, Recreation and Sports to exempt a Catholic high school from the province's "Ethics and Religious Culture" program. The school proposed an alternative curriculum, to be taught from a Catholic perspective. The Minister considered this not to be "equivalent" and so denied the request. The school sought judicial review. It lost at first instance, but succeeded in the Court of Appeal of Quebec and again in the Supreme Court of Canada.[156]

151 *Newfoundland and Labrador Nurses' Union v Newfoundland and Labrador (Treasury Board)*, 2011 SCC 62 [*Newfoundland Nurses*].

152 *Ibid* at para 14.

153 *Ibid* at paras 14–15, quoting *Dunsmuir*, *supra* note 24 at para 48.

154 See *Williams Lake Indian Band v Canada (Aboriginal Affairs and Northern Development)*, 2018 SCC 4 [*Williams Lake*] at para 37.

155 *Loyola High School v Quebec (Attorney General)*, 2015 SCC 12 [*Loyola*].

156 *Ibid* at paras 7–31 and 81.

Justice Abella, for the majority, appeared to double down on *Doré*. The Court had, in her words, "eschew[ed] a literal s. 1 approach in favour of a *robust* proportionality analysis consistent with administrative law principles."[157] Notice the word "robust," which Justice Abella herself emphasized. She went further: "A *Doré* proportionality analysis finds *analytical harmony with the final stages of the Oakes framework* used to assess the reasonableness of a limit on a *Charter* right under s. 1: minimal impairment and balancing. *Both [Oakes] and Doré require that Charter protections are affected as little as reasonably possible* in light of the state's particular objectives."[158] Again, one suspects that this deliberate effort to bridge *Doré* and *Oakes* – watering down, as it did, the Court's insistence that section 1 analysis is not appropriate in reviewing administrative decision making – reflected an attempt to reach consensus among the members of the Court. That effort succeeded in *Doré*. It failed in *Loyola*.

Chief Justice McLachlin declined to join Justice Abella's opinion. Writing instead with Justice Moldaver, joined by Justice Rothstein, she took *Doré*'s (and the *Loyola* majority's) concessions to *Oakes* to their logical conclusion. The Chief Justice held that the distinction between the frameworks was one without a difference: "However one describes the precise analytic approach taken, the essential question is this: did the Minister's decision limit Loyola's right to freedom of religion proportionately – that is, no more than was reasonably necessary?"[159] This methodology did not accord deference to a decision maker on the constitutional issue of whether the infringement of a *Charter* right was lawful. The consensus in favour of default deference was beginning to recede. Indeed, even the *Loyola* majority's approach, which entailed a stricter minimal impairment inquiry than *Doré* countenanced, left little margin of appreciation for the executive.[160]

The next significant rupture came over the presumption that, when an administrative decision maker has interpreted its home statute, its interpretation should be reviewed on a standard of reasonableness. This presumption, endorsed in *Alberta Teachers*, had nudged the Court's post-*Dunsmuir* approach in a still-more-categorical direction. But Justice Cromwell's question in *Alberta Teachers* lingered: If there is such a presumption, then how may it be rebutted?

157 *Ibid* at para 3 [emphasis in original].
158 *Ibid* at para 40 [emphasis added].
159 *Ibid* at para 114, per McLachlin CJ and Moldaver J, concurring in the result.
160 See J Safayeni, "The *Doré* Framework: Five Years Later, Four Key Questions (and Some Suggested Answers)" (2018) 31:1 Can J Admin L & Prac 31 at 39–40.

The Court gave its answer in one of the final standard of review appeals in which Chief Justice McLachlin participated: *Edmonton (City) v Edmonton East (Capilano) Shopping Centres Ltd*.[161] The Court's judgment was that, unless a reviewing court found that a "correctness category" applied – as the Court had in *Mouvement laïque québécois v Saguenay (City)*,[162] decided the previous year – the presumption of reasonableness would govern. For Chief Justice McLachlin, this left much to be desired.

The underlying dispute in *Edmonton East* concerned the assessed value of a shopping mall. The City of Edmonton assessed its value in the neighbourhood of $31 million. The owner appealed that assessment to the Assessment Review Board, constituted under Alberta's *Municipal Government Act*.[163] Before the Board, the owner argued for an assessed value of approximately $22 million, while the City sought an *increase* in the mall's assessed value to $41 million. The Board sided with the City.

The owner sought leave to appeal to the Court of Queen's Bench. The *Act* provided for appeals with leave where a judge was "of the opinion that the appeal involves a question of law or jurisdiction of sufficient importance to merit an appeal and has a reasonable chance of success."[164] Leave was granted, and the Board's decision was set aside, on the basis that the Board lacked the power to increase, as opposed to merely decrease or maintain, a property's assessed value on an appeal brought by a taxpayer. The Court of Appeal dismissed the City's appeal.

The Supreme Court of Canada split 5–4, with Chief Justice McLachlin in the minority. Writing for the majority, Justice Karakatsanis began by ruling out the application of the two correctness categories that the courts below had, in turn, held to apply. First, Justice Karakatsanis made short work of the chambers judge's conclusion that the case presented a true question of jurisdiction.[165] Relying on Justice Rothstein's

---

161 *Edmonton East, supra* note 28.

162 *Mouvement laïque québécois v Saguenay (City)*, 2015 SCC 16 at para 49. Justice Abella dissented from the majority's view that one legal question – here, the scope of the statute's duty of religious neutrality – could be hived off and reviewed for correctness, while the rest of the tribunal's decision would remain reviewable for reasonableness. She evoked her own reasons in *Newfoundland Nurses* and argued that "the reasons of a specialized tribunal must be read as a whole to determine whether the result is reasonable" (at para 165). Notably, she rested her argument on a pragmatic concern for "coheren[ce] and "simplifi[cation]," which she said had motivated the Court's efforts in *Dunsmuir* (at para 166).

163 *Municipal Government Act*, RSA 2000, c M-26.

164 *Edmonton East, supra* note 28 at para 75, Côté and Brown JJ, dissenting.

165 See *Edmonton East (Capilano) Shopping Centres Limited v Edmonton*, 2013 ABQB 526, 570 AR 208 at para 18.

determination, in *Alberta Teachers*, that "[t]his category is narrow and these questions, assuming they indeed exist, are rare,"[166] Justice Karakatsanis simply stated that "[i]t is clear here that the Board may hear a complaint about a municipal assessment. The issue is simply one of interpreting the Board's home statute in the course of carrying out its mandate of hearing and deciding assessment complaints. No true question of jurisdiction arises."[167] She then dispensed with the Court of Appeal's holding that "[t]he presence of a statutory right of appeal may not invariably signal a correctness standard of review, but it is clearly enough to displace any presumption that reasonableness applies."[168] Justice Karakatsanis took aim at a claim that the Court of Appeal did not actually make, namely, that "issues arising on statutory appeals [are] a new category to which the correctness standard applies."[169] She noted that "[a]t least six recent decisions of this Court" – including *Smith* – "have applied a reasonableness standard on a statutory appeal from a decision of an administrative tribunal,"[170] and emphasized that administrative law principles govern curial review of a decision by an administrative tribunal, whether that decision comes before the court on an application for judicial review or a statutory appeal.[171]

With the correctness categories behind her – there was no suggestion that any of the others identified in *Dunsmuir* applied – Justice Karakatsanis proceeded to a section of her reasons headed "Contextual Analysis." Yet, in the paragraphs that followed, Justice Karakatsanis concluded that, in the case at bar, contextual analysis had no role to play. Instead, it was preempted by the most significant categorical distinction of them all – that, except in extraordinary cases, an administrative decision maker's interpretation of its home statute was entitled to deference and thus to review on the reasonableness standard. In Justice Karakatsanis's words:

> As discussed, this Court has often applied a reasonableness standard on a statutory appeal from an administrative tribunal, even when the appeal clause contained a leave requirement and limited appeals to questions of law … , or to questions of law or jurisdiction … In light of this strong

166 *Edmonton East, supra* note 28 at para 26.

167 *Ibid.*

168 *Edmonton East (Capilano) Shopping Centres Limited v Edmonton (City)*, 2015 ABCA 85, 599 AR 210 at para 24.

169 *Edmonton East, supra* note 28 at para 28.

170 *Ibid* at para 29.

171 *Ibid* at para 30.

> line of jurisprudence – combined with the absence of unusual statutory language like that at issue in *Tervita* – there was no need for the Court of Appeal to engage in a long and detailed contextual analysis. Inevitably, the result would have been the same as in those cases. The presumption of reasonableness is not rebutted.[172]

Though Justice Karakatsanis acknowledged that "[t]he presumption of reasonableness may be rebutted if the context indicates the legislature intended the standard of review to be correctness,"[173] and though she went so far as to invite legislative intervention to displace the common law and specify the standard of review,[174] she declined to consider the statutory appeal right as a marker of legislative intent in the case before her. There was nothing sufficiently special about this statutory appeal provision to displace the "presumption of reasonabless" recognized in *Alberta Teachers*. The übercategory of deference to home statute interpretation won the day.

The minority, Chief Justice McLachlin among them, were not persuaded. Writing on their behalf, Justices Côté and Brown excoriated the majority for what, in retrospect, seems like the inevitable consequence of the shift toward superficial clarity and simplicity – and thus categorical formalism – in the selection of the standard of review:

> We agree that a statutory right of appeal is not a new "category" of correctness review. However, the ostensibly contextual standard of review analysis should not be confined to deciding whether new categories have been established. An approach to the standard of review analysis that relies exclusively on categories and eschews any role for context risks introducing the vice of formalism into the law of judicial review …
>
> Because context always matters, we do not agree that the existence of a statutory right of appeal cannot, in combination with other factors, lead to a conclusion that the proper standard of review is correctness. A statutory right of appeal, like a privative clause, "is an important indicator of legislative intent" and, depending on its wording, it "may be at ease with [judicial intervention]" … In our view, the wording of this statutory appeal clause, in combination with the legislative scheme, points to the

172 *Edmonton East*, *supra* note 28 at para 34. In *Tervita*, *supra* note 28, the Court applied the correctness standard where the statutory appeal clause stated that a decision of the tribunal was appealable "as if it were a judgment of the Federal Court": at para 38, citing the *Competition Tribunal Act*, RSC 1985, c 19 (2nd Supp), s 13(1).

173 *Edmonton East*, *supra* note 28 at para 32.

174 *Ibid* at para 35.

conclusion that the legislature intended that a more exacting standard of review be applied to questions appealed to the Court of Queen's Bench.[175]

The specifics of the exercise in statutory interpretation that the *Edmonton East* minority undertook need not detain us. The important point is that Justices Côté and Brown undertook it at all – they asserted that, notwithstanding the categorical turn in the Court's standard of review jurisprudence, contextual analysis in the service of effectuating legislative intent was still the end and aim of the inquiry. They earned Chief Justice McLachlin's vote in doing so. Moreover, as we shall see, the members of the Court who lost the battle in *Edmonton East* subsequently won the war in *Vavilov* and *Bell Canada*. In *Edmonton East*, however, the majority of the Court was satisfied to stiffen the "presumption of reasonableness," even as the minority could not accept an approach to determining the standard of review that was so resolutely mechanical. As Justice Côté put it subsequently, this time in a lone dissent in support of the correctness standard: "[T]he presumption in favour of the reasonableness standard must not be sanctified to such an extent that we lose sight of the fact that it is rebuttable."[176]

h. Game Over

More cracks soon appeared. In three judgments in 2018, Chief Justice McLachlin lent her vote to reasons that cut against the ever-hardening, category-based consensus on the standard of review analysis that the Court had achieved in the preceding decade.

The first was *Groia v Law Society of Upper Canada*,[177] a case about the limits of the Law Society's authority to discipline a lawyer for "uncivil behaviour" as a form of professional misconduct. Chief Justice McLachlin joined Justice Moldaver's reasons for the majority. He acknowledged that the presumption in favour of the reasonableness standard had been "firmly entrenched" in the Court's "post-*Dunsmuir* jurisprudence," including *Edmonton East*,[178] and that "*Dunsmuir* identifies four narrow categories for which correctness review is appropriate."[179] However,

175 *Edmonton East*, *supra* note 28 at paras 70 and 73, Côté and Brown JJ, dissenting [emphasis added; citation omitted], quoting *Canada (Citizenship and Immigration) v Khosa*, 2009 SCC 12 at para 55.

176 *Barreau du Québec v Quebec (Attorney General)*, 2017 SCC 56 at para 66, Côté J, dissenting.

177 *Groia v Law Society of Upper Canada*, 2018 SCC 27 [*Groia*].

178 *Ibid* at para 46.

179 *Ibid* at para 49.

he also left space for contextual analysis and legislative intent, each of which the *Edmonton East* majority had eschewed in favour of framework simplicity: "Even where the question under review does not fit neatly into one of the four *Dunsmuir* correctness categories, a contextual analysis that reveals a legislative intent not to defer to a tribunal's decision may nonetheless rebut the presumption of reasonableness."[180]

Next were two companion cases, *Law Society of British Columbia v Trinity Western University* and *Trinity Western University v Law Society of Upper Canada*.[181] Both considered the legality of the law societies' decisions not to accredit Trinity Western University's then-proposed law school on account of the university's mandatory "community covenant," which required students to agree to abstain from sexual intimacy outside of heterosexual marriage. The university and a graduate of its undergraduate program challenged the law societies' decisions on the basis that they violated their rights to freedom of religion under section 2(a) of the *Charter*. A majority of the Court deferred to, and ultimately sided with, the law societies.[182]

In separate, solo concurring reasons, the Chief Justice departed from the majority's application of the *Doré/Loyola* framework for reviewing discretionary administrative decisions that engage the *Charter*. The majority held that, "[u]nder … *Doré* and *Loyola*," the court considers whether "[t]he extent of the impact on the *Charter* protection" – which it defined as including "both rights *and values*" – is "proportionate in light of the statutory objectives."[183] Chief Justice McLachlin insisted that, "to adequately protect the right, the initial focus must be on whether the claimant's constitutional right has been infringed. *Charter* values may play a role in defining the scope of rights; it is the right itself, however, that receives protection under the *Charter*."[184] And, while the majority maintained *Loyola*'s line on reasonableness review – namely, that "[w]hen a decision enages the *Charter*, reasonableness and proportionality become synonymous"[185] – the Chief Justice suggested that "relying on the language of 'deference' and 'reasonableness' … may be

180 *Ibid* at para 53.

181 *Law Society of British Columbia v Trinity Western University*, 2018 SCC 32 [*Trinity Western (BC)*]; *Trinity Western University v Law Society of Upper Canada*, 2018 SCC 33 [*Trinity Western (Ont)*].

182 *Trinity Western (BC)*, *supra* note 181 at paras 1–3; *Trinity Western (Ont)*, *supra* note 181 at paras 1–3.

183 *Trinity Western (BC)*, *supra* note 181 at para 58 [emphasis added].

184 *Trinity Western (BC)*, *supra* note 181 at para 115, McLachlin CJ, concurring; *Trinity Western (Ont)*, *supra* note 181 at para 46, McLachlin CJ, concurring.

185 *Trinity Western (BC)*, *supra* note 181 at para 80; *Trinity Western (Ont)*, *supra* note 181 at para 35.

unhelpful. Quite simply, where an administrative decision-maker renders a decision that has an unjustified and disproportionate impact on a Charter right, it will always be unreasonable."[186]

One way to read Chief Justice McLachlin's reasons in the *Trinity Western* appeals is as the continuation of the approach she and Justice Moldaver took in *Loyola*. In both cases, the Chief Justice avoided the majority's unequivocal commitment to "robust" deference in a judicial review application in which *Charter* rights were implicated.[187] However, such a limited reading risks missing a broader jurisprudential trend in the final years of the McLachlin Court's administrative law jurisprudence – the fracturing of the consensus that favoured a unified, streamlined approach that the Court had pursued in the first half-decade after *Dunsmuir*. That the Chief Justice herself participated in this withdrawal from clarity and simplicity is remarkable. While she had determinedly pursued simplicity in the name of clarity in this area of the law, as in others, she seemed to be conceding, in her final years on the Court, that administrative law did not lend itself quite so readily to that goal.

In this regard, Chief Justice McLachlin's final months on the Court also saw her endorse a retreat from broadly deferential reasonableness review as endorsed in *Newfoundland Nurses*. First, in *Delta Air Lines Inc v Lukács*,[188] the Chief Justice (for the majority) rejected the proposition that a reviewing court must consider not only the reasons actually given, but the reasons that could be given, in support of an administrative decision under review for reasonableness. "Supplementing reasons *may* be appropriate in cases where the reasons are either non-existent or insufficient," the Chief Justice wrote. Yet, "[t]he requirement that respectful attention be paid to the reasons offered, or the reasons that could be offered, does not empower a reviewing court to ignore the reasons altogether and substitute its own."[189]

Commentators took this as a rejection of, or at least a response to, Justice Karakatsanis's approach to reasons and reasonableness in *Edmonton East*.[190] There, for the majority, Justice Karakatsanis had reviewed

186 *Trinity Western (BC), supra* note 181 at para 118, McLachlin CJ, concurring; *Trinity Western (Ont), supra* note 181 at para 46, McLachlin CJ, concurring.

187 *Trinity Western (BC), supra* note 181 at paras 79–80; *Trinity Western (Ont), supra* note 181 at para 30; *Loyola, supra* note 155 at para 3.

188 *Delta Air Lines Inc v Lukács*, 2018 SCC 2 [*Delta Air Lines*].

189 *Ibid* at paras 23–4.

190 See e.g. P Daly, "Reasons and Reasonableness in Administrative Law: *Delta Air Lines Inc v Lukács*" (2018) 31:2 Can J Admin L & Prac 209 at 214; JT Robertson, "Administrative Deference: The Canadian Doctrine That Continues to Disappoint" (10 May 2018) at 58–9, online: <https:// ssrn.com/ABSTRACT=3165083>.

the Board's determination – for which the Board itself had not provided reasons – that it had jurisdiction to increase the tax assessment at issue "in light of the reasons which *could be* offered in support of it."[191] Justice Karakatsanis did not join Chief Justice McLachlin's majority reasons in *Delta Air Lines*, in which the Chief Justice ruled out deference to reasons other than those that the decision maker has given, and suggested that deference may not be appropriate where the decision maker has given no reasons at all.

She continued along these lines, albeit in dissent, in *Williams Lake Indian Band v Canada (Aboriginal Affairs and Northern Development)*. This was an appeal from the judicial review of a decision of the statutory Specific Claims Tribunal, which adjudicates claims by First Nations against the Crown.[192] The majority, led by Justice Wagner (as he then was), stuck with the approach endorsed in *Newfoundland Nurses*, upholding the decision under review as reasonable despite tribunal reasons that the majority acknowledged to be "conclusory" and "sparse."[193] This was because, "to fulfil the timeliness aspect of its mandate, the [Specific Claims] Tribunal must be able to rely on reviewing courts to endeavour to make sense of its reasons by looking to the authorities on which it relied, the submissions of the parties to which it responded and the materials before it." As John Evans, formerly of the Federal Court and the Federal Court of Appeal, has noted, "[t]he take-away for decision makers is that their reasons need merely hint at the basis of the interpretation; if necessary, reasons can be elaborated and patched up on judicial review."[194]

Chief Justice McLachlin joined Justice Brown's dissent, in which he rejected this view. The Tribunal's "bare assertion[s]," "unstated implication[s]," questions it had "yet to answer," "[incongruous] conclu[sions]," and "unclear" reasoning with respect to Canada's liability under section 14(2) of the *Specific Claims Tribunal Act* added up, in Justice Brown's view, to an unreasonable determination of the First Nation's claim.[195] As Justice Brown put it, "the Tribunal's treatment in its reasons of s. 14(2) lacks each of the principal hallmarks of a reasonable

191 *Edmonton East*, *supra* note 28 at para 40 [emphasis in original].

192 *Williams Lake*, *supra* note 154.

193 *Ibid* at paras 37 and 107.

194 JM Evans, "*Dunsmuir*: Reflections of a Recovering Judge" (1 March 2018), online (blog): *Administrative Law Matters*, <https://www.administrativelawmatters.com/blog/2018/03/01/dunsmuir-reflections-of-a-recovering-judge-hon-john-m-evans/>.

195 *Williams Lake*, *supra* note 154 at paras 168, 173, 175, 186, and 187, Brown J, dissenting in part; see also *Specific Claims Tribunal Act*, SC 2008, c 22, s 14(2).

decision: justification, transparency, and intelligibility."[196] Relying on the Chief Justice's reasons in *Delta Air Lines*, Justice Brown concluded that "[j]udicial review is not artificial resuscitation" and that "[t]he Tribunal's reasons for finding that Canada is liable … are just not amenable to judicial supplementing, and this Court should not strain to do so by insisting that, if we just look hard enough, we will be able to see what really isn't there."[197]

The Chief Justice's votes in these cases speak to a significant change in direction, for her personally and for the Court, at the end of her tenure. Since she assumed the chief justiceship, the trend – from *Dr Q* through *Edmonton East* – had been in favour of crisper statements of the law, crystallized into categories and category-like presumptions, all in the interest of clarity, and all superimposed on a reasonableness standard described in highly deferential terms. Yet, even if the standard of review analysis in any particular judgment was presented as uncomplicated, this area of the law as a whole could not be said to have become clearer.

It was only as Chief Justice McLachlin's retirement loomed that normative disagreements about curial review, long submerged, began to emerge into public view in nearly every significant administrative law case the Court decided. Her voting record suggests that the Chief Justice, who had long laboured for unanimity behind the scenes, came to accept the reality of this discord.

Finally, a month before Chief Justice McLachlin signed her final judgments, the Court announced that it would "consider the nature and scope of judicial review of administrative action, as addressed in *Dunsmuir* … and subsequent cases."[198] The message, to scholars and practitioners, was that it might soon be open season on the McLachlin Court's entire adminstrative law corpus. As discussed below, *Vavilov* and *Bell Canada* ultimately vindicated (or at least reflected) the shift in Chief Justice McLachlin's own approach to the standard of review in administrative law at the end of her time on the bench.

The next part describes how Chief Justice McLachlin's approach to common law judging helped to produce two process failures in the area of administrative law. These process failures combined to lead the Court to the unsatisfying spot from which the Court sought to extricate itself in *Vavilov* and *Bell Canada* after Chief Justice McLachlin's retirement.

---

196 *Williams Lake, supra* note 154 at para 195, Brown J, dissenting in part.

197 *Ibid* at paras 206–7, Brown J, dissenting in part.

198 *National Football League, et al v Attorney General of Canada*, 2018 CanLII 40806 (SCC); *Bell Canada, et al v Attorney General of Canada*, 2018 CanLII 40808 (SCC); *Minister of Citizenship and Immigration v Alexander Vavilov*, 2018 CanLII 40807 (SCC).

IV. What Went Wrong? Common Law Virtue as Administrative Law Vice

Five months before *Edmonton East* was argued, in a speech in Vancouver, Chief Justice McLachlin offered a sort of *mea culpa* for the confused state of the standard of review analysis. Acknowledging that "[l]awyers and judges ... are finely attuned to the power of words and their propensity to take on a life of their own," the Chief Justice cautioned that

> [judicial review] provides no shortage of vague terms that lawyers and judges must somehow use to make sense of concrete problems ... This vagueness may prompt lawyers and judges to lose sight of the goal at hand and start down winding paths that lead nowhere ...
>
> The hard reality is that, as lawyers and judges, our method of communication, as imperfect as it might be, is language. What are we to do? The answer, it seems to me, lies in accepting that imprecision is in the nature of things, while resolving firmly to keep our eyes focused on the purpose of our endeavor. Yes, lawyers will be lawyers, but this does not mean that the vagueness of language should be an invitation to obfuscate or to mislead.
>
> While formal legal categories are not clear in and of themselves, they do take their concrete meaning in specific situations. To determine their meaning, we need to think about what we are really trying to do, in the clearest and most honest fashion possible. Put another way, judges and lawyers should approach legal rules and terms with a clear understanding of the underlying legal principles, and with a focus on the substantive questions that underpin them. In a nutshell: what is this rule for?
>
> [J]udicial review of administrative action is a fundamentally normative task, where the questions to be answered are not simply "Is this decision reasonable?" or "Is this process unfair?" They are, also, "Should this decision be reviewed?" and "What process should this claimant be entitled to?" A focus on the normative questions rather than the purely descriptive language also amounts to privileging substance over form – a sure recipe for achieving justice in a given case.[199]

These comments foreshadowed Chief Justice McLachlin's vote in *Edmonton East* – the case in which the Court's categorical approach to the standard of review analysis finally crossed the threshold of the

199 McLachlin, *supra* note 33 at 131–2.

Chief Justice's tolerance. They reflect what subsequently became the slow-motion breakdown of the *Dunsmuir* consensus, as the normative disagreements that had previously been submerged by an agreed-upon vocabulary were forced back to the surface. This, in turn, prompted the doctrinal recalibration that the Court undertook in *Vavilov* and *Bell Canada*.

The underlying points of dispute may be viewed through the lens of two complementary process failures in the McLachlin Court's approach to judicial review of administrative action. The first was an over-reliance on categorical presumptions, rooted in a well-intentioned desire to make the standard of review analysis more straightforward to apply, but culminating in a near total disassociation of the Court's approach from the principles that ought to have underlain it. The second was the emergence of deference as a default, as opposed to as the result of a principled reasoning process as to the legislative intent to which a reviewing court must give effect.

The first process failure was practical. The second was substantive. Each of them was rooted in Chief Justice McLachlin's virtuous approach to her role as Chief Justice of a common law apex court, with its focus on clarity and simplicity of guidance. Yet, each was responsible for the confused state of the law, a decade after *Dunsmuir* – and, as discussed in the next part, both appear to have been within the Court's contemplation when it decided *Vavilov* and *Bell Canada*.

a. Process Failure 1: Categorical Presumptions

Amendments to the *Supreme Court Act* in 1974 enhanced the Court's power to control its own docket and decisively entrenched its role in the judicial hierarchy as one of supervision rather than error correction. Since then, the Court has measured its success by the quality of leadership it provides to the judges it oversees.[200] Nowhere has this been more self-consciously true than in the development of the standard of review jurisprudence, particularly during Beverley McLachlin's years as chief justice.

Dunsmuir itself was the Court's attempt to achieve clarity and predictability in the common law of judicial review, after the apparent consensus achieved in *Southam* and *Pushpanathan* and restated in *Dr Q* and *Ryan* proved unsustainable.[201] As noted above, *Dunsmuir*'s most

200 See *R v Henry*, 2005 SCC 76 at para 53; see also PJ Monahan, "The Supreme Court of Canada in the 21st Century" (2001) 80 Can Bar Rev 374 at 377–8.

201 *Dunsmuir*, *supra* note 24 at para 32; see also A Woolley and S Fluker, "What Has *Dunsmuir* Taught?" (2010) 47:4 Alta L Rev 1017 at 1021.

important innovation – aside from the fusion of the previous "patent unreasonableness" and "reasonableness *simpliciter*" standards – was the introduction of precedential, as opposed to merely contextual, reasoning in determining the degree of deference to be accorded to an administrative decision. Henceforth, courts were to skip the analysis and rely on case law where "the jurisprudence has already determined in a satisfactory manner the degree of deference to be accorded with regard to a particular category of question."[202]

As a matter of common law reasoning, this approach was next to unimpeachable. But it also represented a fateful bite of the apple – a gateway to the expediency of relying on categories to do the work where the alternative (contextual analysis) is more complicated. As Professor Daly put it, "[f]rom the perspective of an overworked judge struggling to clear a docket, the categorical approach has an appeal that [contextual] analysis cannot hope to match."[203]

And so it did not. Ten years after *Dunsmuir*, the majority of the Court in *Edmonton East* effectively sidelined what remained of the role of context in determining the standard of review. The presumption that the standard of review is reasonableness when reviewing an administrative decision maker's interpretation of its own home statute proved impossible to overcome, despite clear signals that the legislature did not intend for courts to defer on sufficiently important questions of law or jurisdiction. Justice Cromwell's concerns in *Alberta Teachers* proved prescient, and Chief Justice McLachlin – who had been in the majority in *Dunsmuir*, *Smith*, and *Alberta Teachers* – shifted her vote to the dissent.

This, then, was the first process failure in the McLachlin Court's approach to administrative law. In seeking simplicity, the Court bound itself and lower courts to spend more time debating the parameters of categories and category-like presumptions than the merits of the decisions under review. This was precisely the opposite of what the ever-more-categorical post-*Dunsmuir* approach was meant to accomplish.[204] But when the outcome of the exercise was made to depend almost entirely on whether a particular decision fit within a particular category, it should have been no wonder that the categories, rather than the decision, became the focal point of the analysis. So it was in *Edmonton East*. The *Groia* majority's subsequent references to contextual analysis and legislative intent suggested that the Court itself may quickly

202 *Dunsmuir*, *supra* note 24 at para 62.

203 Daly, *supra* note 98 at 356.

204 See *Wilson*, *supra* note 28 at para 25.

have recognized that, in *Edmonton East*, it had gone too far. *Vavilov* and *Bell Canada* confirmed as much; the Court overruled *Edmonton East* just three years after it was decided.

In furthering its own embrace of categories in the decade after *Dunsmuir*, the McLachlin Court turned one of the great virtues of Chief Justice McLachlin's approach to chief justiceship – the deliberate pursuit of clarity – into a vice. Rather than make the determination of the standard of review simpler by reference to precedent, and rather than emphasize broad, if contestable, statements of principle of the sort that *Justice* McLachlin so skilfully developed and deployed in other areas of the law, the Court's turn to categories created a growing number of "debating points" that distracted from the real work of determining how much deference a particular decision was due.[205] As Chief Justice McLachlin herself put it, some two years before her retirement: "Jurists who appreciate the limits of language in administrative law will think more clearly about doctrine and will not be distracted from the real issue – is the court justified in reversing the particular administrative decision at issue?"[206]

b. Process Failure 2: Deference as Default

A further distraction from what Chief Justice McLachlin described as "the real issue" in judicial review is what became a strong default in favour of deference to administrative decision-makers. This, too, reflected the McLachlin Court's efforts over the span of nearly two decades to quell consistent sources of controversy in administrative law. And it is another way in which the Court's efforts had precisely the opposite effect from that intended.

In historical terms, the emergence of deference as default represented a striking reversal, one that had been the focus of considerable scholarly attention.[207] But, since *Dunsmuir*, the Court's instructions – if not always, perhaps, its own actions[208] – consistently trended toward an ever-stronger presumption that administrative decision makers should be afforded considerable latitude within their domains.

This makes practical sense: the more quickly the reviewing court can resolve the question of whether to defer to the administrative decision

205 See Stratas, *supra* note 113 at 49.

206 McLachlin, *supra* note 33 at 133.

207 See e.g. G van Harten, G Heckman & D Mullan, eds, *Administrative Law*, 6th ed. (Toronto: Emond Montgomery, 2010) at 797–9 and 804–7; Lewans, *supra* note 20 at 65–9.

208 See Stratas, *supra* note 113 at 35.

maker, the more quickly it can turn to the question of whether the decision under review is correct (if deference is not due) or reasonable (if deference is due). The narrower the range of questions in respect of which correctness review is available, the more efficiently the reviewing court can move on to the merits. Hence, Justice Abella's suggestion, in *Wilson v Atomic Energy of Canada Ltd*, that "it would, I think, ... be beneficial if the template so compellingly developed in *Dunsmuir*, were adhered to, including by applying the residual 'correctness' standard only in those four circumstances *Dunsmuir* articulated."[209] To do so would not, in fact, have been in keeping with *Dunsmuir*. Justices Bastarache and LeBel offered their four correctness categories not as a means of excluding the possibility of correctness review in other circumstances, but to provide examples of questions in respect of which the case law had already appropriately established that deference should not be accorded.[210] Still, even if Justice Abella's reasoning in *Wilson* was not in keeping with *Dunsmuir* itself, it was consistent with the Court's subsequent trajectory. In *Edmonton East*, that trajectory culminated with Justice Abella's joining a majority of the Court in holding that, where a tribunal is interpreting its home statute, no amount of contextual analysis would push the needle back toward correctness, absent extraordinary, *Tervita*-like circumstances.[211] The message to lower courts was plain: stop trying to make correctness happen; it's not going to happen.

Measured against Chief Justice McLachlin's meta-objective of clarifying the law so as to offer more useful guidance to lower courts, this approach had intuitive appeal. And yet, there was pushback.[212] Why?

---

209 *Wilson, supra* note 28 at para 38.

210 See the discussion of *Dunsmuir, supra* Part III (c).

211 It should be noted that Justice Abella disagreed with the *Tervita* majority on the applicable standard of review. In partially concurring reasons, she argued that:

> [J]udges and lawyers engaging in judicial review proceedings came to believe, rightly and reasonably, that the jurisprudence of this Court had developed into a presumption that regardless of the presence or absence of either a right of appeal or a privative clause – that is notwithstanding legislative wording – when a tribunal is interpreting its home statute, reasonableness applies. I am at a loss to see why we would chip away – again – at this precedential certainty. It seems to me that what we should be doing instead is confirming, not undermining, the reasonableness presumption and our jurisprudence that statutory language alone is not determinative of the applicable standard of review. (*Tervita, supra* note 28 at para 170 [footnote omitted])

212 See e.g. D Ginn, "Some Initial Thoughts on *Wilson v Atomic Energy of Canada Ltd and Edmonton (City) v Edmonton East (Capilano) Shopping Centres Ltd*" (2017) 68 UNBLJ 285 at 295–300; JT Robertson, "Identifying the Review Standard: Administrative Difference in a Nutshell" (2017) 68 UNBLJ 145.

Dunsmuir achieved *linguistic* consensus. A majority of the Court agreed on the language that courts should use in discussing whether to defer to an administrative decision maker. But there was not, and never subsequently was, an underlying *normative* consensus as to how that language ought to be used. It was one thing for Justice Abella and other members of the Court – or even a majority, as in *Edmonton East* – to say that deference ought to be a strong default so as not to require undue attention to be devoted to the selection of the standard of review, thus distracting from the merits of the matter. Yet, even if that assertion were accepted as true,[213] it did not resolve the underlying normative question of whether a particular decision maker *should* receive deference in a particular set of circumstances. As Justices Côté and Brown put it in their *Edmonton East* dissent, with Chief Justice McLachlin's concurrence, "In every case, a court must determine what the appropriate standard of review is for *this* question decided by *this* decision maker."[214]

Some judges had had no difficulty following the Supreme Court of Canada's instructions to defer in all but exceptional cases outside the four *Dunsmuir* correctness categories. But many others – including, in *Edmonton East*, four members of the Court itself – struggled or found it impossible to do so where there were good reasons to conclude that the legislature did not intend judicial deference in the circumstances. In this way, normative disagreement frayed *Dunsmuir*'s linguistic consensus to the point of incoherence.

By making deference a strong default, the McLachlin Court achieved a jurisprudential outcome that, from a common law adjudication standpoint, was entirely defensible. Instead of requiring courts to undertake a contextual analysis, or even a review of precedent followed by a contextual analysis, a majority of the Court said that deference (reasonableness review) was the assumed default, with non-deference (correctness review) as a comparably rare, category-specific exception. That should have been simpler and clearer. Yet, in practice, it was anything but.

V. *Vavilov* and *Bell Canada*: The McLachlin Court's Final Judgments

A decade after *CUPE v NB Liquor Corporation* came *Bibeault*. A decade later came *Pushpanathan*. A decade after that was *Dunsmuir*. Another

213 And it proved a debatable proposition in practice: see Ginn, *supra* note 212 at 298–300.

214 *Edmonton East*, *supra* note 28 at para 71, Côté and Brown JJ, dissenting [emphasis in original].

decade brought *Vavilov* and *Bell Canada* – the Supreme Court of Canada's latest efforts to consolidate, clarify, and recalibrate the governing framework for judicial review.

By the time the Court heard the appeals in *Vavilov* and *Bell Canada*, Chief Justice McLachlin had retired. Still, the Court's judgments bear the residual imprint of her leadership, not only in the substance of how the Court reformulated its approach to the standard of review, but also in the form of the seven-justice majority's guidance to litigants, lawyers, and lower courts. *Vavilov* and *Bell Canada* are properly understood not only as the start of a new decade in Canadian administrative law, but also as the culmination of the two decades of jurisprudence that preceded them. They are, in this respect, the McLachlin Court's final judgments on the standard of review.

Vavilov maintains the presumption that the standard of review of an administrative decision will be reasonableness. Importantly, however, the Court confirmed that this presumption is one of legislative intent: "[I]t is the *very fact* that the legislature has chosen to delegate authority [to an administrative decision maker] which justifies a default position for reasonableness review."[215] It follows that, when the legislator has indicated that the reviewing court should not defer to an administrative decision maker, either by prescribing the standard of review[216] or by "provid[ing] for an appeal from an administrative decision to a court,"[217] the presumption is rebutted. The Court also preserved three of the four former "correctness categories" – namely, "constitutional questions, general questions of law of central importance to the legal system as a whole, and questions regarding jurisdictional boundaries between administrative bodies" – as "situations in which a derogation from the presumption of reasonableness review is warranted ... because correctness review is required by the rule of law."[218]

In this way, the Court attempted to align the linguistic consensus achieved in *Dunsmuir* (and solidified in *Smith* and *Alberta Teachers*) about when courts *must* defer to administrative decision makers with normative consensus about *why* they should do so. The Court did this by using the language of legislative intent to articulate the reason for which the presumption of reasonableness is warranted:

---

215 *Vavilov, supra* note 2 at para 30 [emphasis in original].

216 *Ibid* at para 35.

217 *Ibid* at para 37; see also *Bell Canada, supra* note 2 at paras 4 and 34.

218 *Vavilov, supra* note 2 at para 69.

> Where a legislature has created an administrative decision maker for the specific purpose of administering a statutory scheme, it must be presumed that the legislature also intended that decision maker to be able to fulfill its mandate and interpret the law as applicable to all issues that come before it. Where a legislature has not explicitly prescribed that a court is to have a role in reviewing the decisions of that decision maker, it can safely be assumed that the legislature intended the administrative decision maker to function with a minimum of judicial interference.[219]

Similarly, even as it modified the linguistic consensus about when courts cannot defer to administrative decision makers – i.e., when one of the (remaining) correctness categories applies – the Court also suffused the categories with normative content: they are "types of legal questions" for which "respect for the rule of law requires courts to apply the standard of correctness," regardless of legislative intent.[220] This explanation, like the Court's explanation for the presumption of reasonableness, sought to make the *Vavilov* framework more durable than its predecessors by finding common ground not just on the doctrine's features, but also on its substantive justification.

In this way, the Court responded to the second process failure described above: the insistence on deference as a strong default, with little apparent normative justification other than making the standard of review analysis simpler to apply. Rather than continue to try (and fail) to advance the cause of clarity by maintaining an essentially un-rebuttable presumption of reasonableness and circumscribed correctness categories as ends in themselves, the *Vavilov* Court reframed the presumption and the categories as means of, respectively, effectuating legislative intent and upholding the rule of law. This allowed the *Vavilov* Court to side with the dissenters in *Edmonton East*, Chief Justice McLachlin among them, in recognizing that a statutory appeal provision rebuts the presumption that a legislature intends courts to defer to a particular administrative decision maker.[221]

By keeping the correctness categories – and by jettisoning the "contextual analysis" that had been falling out of favour since *Dunsmuir* – the *Vavilov* Court endorsed and advanced the McLachlin Court's long-standing goal of achieving clarity through simplicity. Indeed, the *Vavilov* Court described the McLachlin Court's "simplification of the standard

219 *Ibid* at para 24.
220 *Ibid* at para 53.
221 *Ibid* at paras 38 and 40; see also *Edmonton East*, *supra* note 28 at paras 88–9, Côté and Brown JJ, dissenting.

of review analysis" by "shift[ing] from a contextual analysis to an approach more focused on categories" as "laudable."[222] Still, the *Vavilov* Court married its further simplification, and particularly the elimination of the former "jurisdictional questions" correctness category, with a more robust approach to reasonableness review. It notably endorsed Chief Justice McLachlin's majority judgment in *Delta Air Lines* and confirmed the necessity of reviewing an administrative decision maker's reasoning process, not just its outcome.[223] It also held that

> [r]easonableness review does not give administrative decision makers free rein in interpreting their enabling statutes, and therefore does not give them licence to enlarge their powers beyond what the legislature intended. Instead, it confirms that the governing statutory scheme will always operate as a constraint on administrative decision makers and as a limit on their authority. Even where the reasonableness standard is applied in reviewing a decision maker's interpretation of its authority, precise or narrow statutory language will necessarily limit the number of reasonable interpretations open to the decision maker – perhaps limiting it [to] one. Conversely, where the legislature has afforded a decision maker broad powers in general terms – and has provided no right of appeal to a court – the legislature's intention that the decision maker have greater leeway in interpreting its enabling statute should be given effect.[224]

This aims to address the first process failure described above. Though the Court kept the correctness categories – indeed, it reduced them in number from four to three – its recasting of reasonableness review, coupled with its better-late-than-never embrace of statutory appeal provisions as markers of legislative intent, arguably makes the consequences of not conforming to a correctness category less stark. In other words, by lowering the stakes of failing to fit within a correctness category, the Court sought to preserve the principal benefit of the categorical approach (its clarity and simplicity) while avoiding its principal detriment (encouraging disputes about the categories themselves).

Time will tell whether *Vavilov* will succeed in shifting the focus of litigants and lower courts away from disagreements about whether one of the correctness categories applies and toward arguments about whether a particular administrative decision was reasonable. What bears notice,

---

222 *Vavilov, supra* note 2 at para 43.

223 See *ibid* at para 87.

224 *Ibid* at para 68.

for present purposes, is the Court's continued commitment to the common law virtues of Chief Justice McLachlin's approach to the standard of review in administrative law, as well as its vindication of the buyer's remorse that characterized her final votes and opinions in administrative law cases. *Vavilov* and *Bell Canada* reflect the Wagner Court's desire to succeed where the McLachlin Court failed: by achieving consensus and providing clear guidance on how the standard of review analysis is to be conducted, while avoiding the process failures that became *Dunsmuir*'s undoing. This, together with the *Vavilov* majority's endorsement of Chief Justice McLachlin's pre-retirement reservations about what *Dunsmuir* had wrought, make *Vavilov* and *Bell Canada* the final destination of the McLachlin Court's standard of review jurisprudence. History teaches that they are unlikely to be the last word on the subject. But the next chapter will be the Wagner Court's to write.

VI. Conclusion

Canada has never produced a finer common law jurist than Beverley McLachlin. In administrative law, however, Chief Justice McLachlin's common law virtues proved to be a vice, as the Court allowed doctrinal disputes to simmer unresolved beneath the surface of linguistic and structural consensus.

The standard of review analysis, as fashioned in *Dunsmuir*, was a signal achievement. But even more important than *Dunsmuir* are the lessons to be drawn from the decade that followed – from how the standard of review framework frayed once maintaining clarity and simplicity became more important than protecting and affirming first principles.

None of this is to detract from the progress made under Chief Justice McLachlin's leadership. As she herself put it, in a speech in 2013:

> One way to look at the last half-century in Canadian judicial review is as a time of tension between administrative decision-makers and the courts, marked by doctrinal uncertainty. Another is to say that over the last fifty years, we have made considerable progress in reconciling the modern administrative state with the rule of law on a theoretical and practical basis. The task we faced was difficult and important, and the journey has not always been smooth. But we have come a long way.[225]

225 McLachlin, *supra* note 25.

Vavilov and *Bell Canada* are in this vein – or seek to be, at least. Even as it reshaped the governing framework for judicial review of administrative decisions, the Court hewed to its former leader's common law approach, while seeking to address the problems it produced in the preceding decade. Cases to come will test the extent of the normative consensus that *Vavilov* and *Bell Canada* appear to have achieved, as the Wagner Court continues to confront controversies that the McLachlin Court could not resolve. A frank assessment of Chief Justice McLachlin's record, spots and all, reveals what those are. The rest is up to us.

11 The McLachlin Court and the Concept of Open Justice

ESZTER BODNÁR

The Supreme Court of Canada is considered to be one of the most open and transparent apex courts in the world. This openness and transparency are the result of an ongoing development process that began in the 1970s and that has accelerated over the past two decades. Legislators abroad take the Court as a model when legislating open justice, and courts in other jurisdictions take note of its practices to find ways to improve their own.

Although the main aspects of the open justice principle are fixed by law, the Court and its judges must nonetheless fill this framework with content and decide on the level of openness appropriate to the institution. Chief Justice Beverley McLachlin emphasized the importance of open justice for cultivating public confidence in the Court, stressing the need for courts to open up and convey the right message about justice. In a series of decisions, articles, public lectures, and interviews, she never missed an opportunity to emphasize the importance of the openness of courts.

Chief Justice McLachlin was a proponent of openness not only in words but also in actions. During her mandate, she made several efforts to enhance the relationship between the media and the Court and to open up the Court as an institution. However, she had to achieve a fair balance among countervailing interests, and she was naturally obliged to consider the fundamental rights, constitutional principles, and practical considerations that might place limitations on the concept of open justice.

This chapter aims to analyse Chief Justice Beverley McLachlin's approach to the concept of open justice as expressed in her writings and speeches, and to demonstrate the development of this field under her leadership. It will also highlight how the Court has responded to the challenges of the twenty-first century.

The research for this chapter was supported by a Hungarian Eötvös Research Grant. I am grateful for the valuable comments of Kathryn Chan, Donna Greschner, Vanessa MacDonnell, and Owen Rees.

Part I sets the scene by providing an overview of the possible definitions, elements, justifications, and limits of open justice from a comparative point of view. This is a necessary introduction, as the term "open justice" can have several different meanings, and it is therefore important to define what the term means when used in this chapter. Based on the theoretical background of Part I, Part II analyses the writings and speeches of Chief Justice McLachlin on the concept of open justice to understand her opinion on the content and limitations of the open courts concept. The Chief Justice gave twenty-five to thirty lectures a year; as most of them have been published. In addition, the texts of several of her speeches are accessible on the website of the Supreme Court of Canada. She also published book chapters and journal articles, and gave regular interviews. Part III assesses how her ideas about the concept of open justice became a reality in the daily practice of the Supreme Court of Canada under her leadership. The section covers the steps that contributed to the opening up of the institution, the enhancement of its relationship with the media, and the fostering of public confidence in the Court. Finally, Part IV examines possible future routes for the Court in the field of open justice. There are lessons to be learned from the McLachlin era that can be helpful for subsequent chief justices, who will face the challenges of this century.

I. Open Justice in Canada and the World

"Open justice" is a basic concept in the common law tradition. It is related to the age-old aphorism, "Justice should not only be done, but should manifestly and undoubtedly be seen to be done,"[1] which is one of the most fundamental rules of common law systems. However, there is no agreement on the exact content and elements of the concept of open justice. This lack of agreement becomes particularly obvious if one examines the issue from a comparative point of view, looking at international human rights documents and the regulations, practices, and legal scholarship in countries from both the common law and civil law traditions. In this section, I give an overview of the possible definitions of the term "open justice" – its content, justifications, and limits – in order to provide the background against which the role of open justice in Canada will be analysed.

The most commonly used definition equates open justice with public hearings or trials, which may be attended by the public and the media,

1 JJ Spigelman, "Seen to Be Done: The Principle of Open Justice – Part I" (2000) 74 Austl LJ 290 at 290.

and the public pronouncement of court decisions.[2] Most international and regional human rights documents use this definition.[3] In other cases, the public trial element is complemented by the principle of public access to court decisions. This latter approach is most often used in the legal scholarship of civil law countries but is also evident in common law countries.[4]

A third, and broader, definition includes access to all information that is connected to the courts, including that related to the court's procedure and institutions. In this sense, open justice means the accessibility of information about courts and their activities.[5] In this chapter, I will adopt this broad approach, positing that open justice is not a single fundamental right or principle but a very complex concept that should be evaluated in its complexity. As we will see, this is also the definition adopted by Chief Justice McLachlin.

Open justice covers a variety of elements, which may be divided into two main parts: procedural openness and institutional-organizational

2 E.g. Rolf Stürner, "Gerichtsöffentlichkeit und Meidenöffentlichkeit in der Informationsgesellschaft. Das Bundesverfassungsgericht zwischen Liberalität und Zensur" (2001) 56:13 JuristenZeitung; Joachim Scherer, *Gerichtsöffentlichkeit als Medienöffentlichkeit* (Hamburg: Athenäum, 1979); Joseph Jaconelli, *Open Justice: A Critique of the Public Trial* (Oxford: Oxford University Press, 2002).

3 According to Article 10 of the *Universal Declaration of Human Rights*, everyone is entitled in full equality to a fair and public hearing by an independent and impartial tribunal, in the determination of their rights and obligations and of any criminal charge against them. Similarly, Article 14 (1) of the *International Covenant on Civil and Political Rights*, GA Res 2200A (XXI), 1966, UNGAOR, *Treaty Series* vol 999, 171, stipulates that, "In the determination of any criminal charge against him, or of his rights and obligations in a suit at law, everyone shall be entitled to a fair and public hearing by a competent, independent and impartial tribunal established by law. Regional human rights documents also contain a similar provision. The *European Convention on Human Rights*, Council of Europe, 4 November 1950, guarantees a fair and public hearing as an element of the right to a fair trial (Article 6, point 1). The *American Convention on Human Rights*, "Pact of San Jose," Organization of American States (OAS), 22 November 1969, prescribes that "[c]riminal proceedings shall be public, except insofar as may be necessary to protect the interests of justice" (Article 8, point 5).

4 E.g. Beverley McLachlin, "Courts, Transparency and Public Confidence: To the Better Administration of Justice" (2003) 8:1 Deakin L Rev 1.

5 There is also a broader concept that embraces the access to justice component. It is derived from the idea that courts should be open to everyone who wishes to enforce their rights, independent of their social status, financial situation, race, gender, age, or any other characteristics. See e.g. Judith Resnik, "A2J/A2K: Access to Justice, Access to Knowledge, and Economic Inequalities in Open Courts and Arbitrations" (2018) 96 NCL Rev 605. However, this approach broadens the topic extensively, so this chapter focuses on the concept of open justice in a narrower sense.

openness. "Procedural openness" refers to the public's ability to access information that relates to a specific judicial procedure. The main tool for procedural transparency (i.e., the institution that realizes such transparency in its most direct form) is the public trial. The presence of the visitors and media and the availability of the transcripts and audio recordings are all potential tools for ensuring openness. Open justice also includes the promotion of full, fair, and accurate reporting on court proceedings. Another basic component of procedural transparency is the accessibility of court documents, including court decisions and case files. The obligation of openness also includes the requirement for the court to present the reasoning behind a decision publicly, not only to the parties.[6] Sometimes the decisions include the results of the votes, and judges, especially at the highest courts, are often allowed to publish dissenting or concurring opinions.[7] This information helps the public understand what happened during the decision-making process and what the opinions of the individual judges are. After making its decision, the court can provide press releases and commentaries about the ruling.[8] The chief justice of the court, or its judges, may explain the decisions in publications and interviews.[9] These elements all ensure that the public, media, and other stakeholders can receive information about the procedures before the court.

On the other hand, "institutional-organizational openness" means that information about institutional issues and the daily operation of the courts should be generally available to the public, independent of interest in a specific case. This part of the concept of open justice includes, among other things, access to information on the administration of courts (openness about the process of appointing judges, transparency of budgets and procurement, access to judges' assets and income disclosure statements, etc.); access to information about the function of the court (statistics, distribution of cases among judges, timing of cases, etc.); and the publishing of internal regulations. Communication

---

6 Spigelman, *supra* note 1 at 294.

7 For a comprehensive overview of judicial dissents in constitutional courts, see Katalin Kelemen, *Judicial Dissent in European Constitutional Courts: A Comparative and Legal Perspective* (London: Routledge, 2018).

8 E.g. the press office of the German Federal Constitutional Court prepares press releases on major decisions.

9 E.g. "Hogy ne kelljen a múltat végképp eltörölni. Lévay Miklós alkotmánybíróval Kazai Viktor Zoltán beszélget," Fundamentum 2016/1. (An interview given by Miklós Lévay, Justice of the Hungarian Constitutional Court in a Hungarian law journal, explaining several finished cases of the court.)

between the court and the media as well as public outreach activities are also elements of institutional-organizational openness.[10]

These two parts of open justice complement each other. Without both, open justice would remain unrealized: for example, if a court holds public trials but keeps the judges' income disclosure statements secret, it is not truly open, for, while the public would be able to monitor the independence of the judge while the court is in session, it cannot ensure the judge's personal independence.

Open justice has multiple justifications: some are fundamental rights or constitutional principles, others are abstract or practical considerations. Some are included in constitutions, others come from statutory requirements or case law. The list of fundamental rights justifying open justice includes the right to a fair trial, access to justice, freedom of expression, freedom of the press, the right to public information, freedom of research, and freedom of science.[11] The constitutional principles that justify open justice include the separation of powers, judicial accountability, judicial independence, the legitimacy of courts, legal certainty, and the unity of law. In addition to these fundamental rights and constitutional principles, other abstract and practical considerations may justify the concept of open justice. Open justice has an important educational function, and it enhances citizens' legal knowledge and confidence in courts. Being public is an important condition of "therapeutic" justice.[12] Open justice is also a means of enhancing the efficient handling of cases[13] and of fighting corruption.[14]

Open justice is not absolute, and, in certain circumstances, it must yield to conflicting rights or principles. Such conflicting rights and principles include privacy, the independence of judges, the right to a fair trial, and

10 For a detailed overview of institutional-organizational openness and its elements, see Alvaro Herrero & Gaspar López, *Access to Information and Transparency in the Judiciary* (Washington: World Bank Institute, 2010).

11 Freedom of research and freedom of science are rights that are usually derived from freedom of expression. See e.g. *Basic Law for the Federal Republic of Germany* (*Grundgesetz für die Bundesrepublik Deutschland*), 23 May 1949, BGBL 1, Article 5 (3): "Arts and sciences, research and teaching shall be free."

12 McLachlin, *supra* note 4 at 8.

13 The idea behind this enhancement of efficiency is that, if information about court procedures is public, individuals will be able to evaluate whether that court is a useful venue for vindicating their rights and settling their disputes, and they will avoid initiating a procedure if that venue is ineffective.

14 Transparency International, "Policy Position, 01/2007: Enhancing Judicial Transparency," online: <https://www.transparency.org/en/publications/policy-position-01-2007-enhancing-judicial-transparency>.

the presumption of innocence. There are also abstract and practical considerations that compete with the open justice concept. International human rights law acknowledges the interests of morality, national security, and public order as limits on open justice.[15] The risk of sensationalism and distortion can also be a legitimate reason to limit open justice.

Courts throughout the world have the difficult task of balancing these justifications and limitations to promote an ideal level of open justice. In some cases, the constitution or the legislature strikes a balance between the countervailing interests. Case law is frequently silent about how to choose between competing objectives when open justice is at stake, and it provides little guidance on what evidence of interference with countervailing interests is required to justify limiting open justice.[16] As a result, it is usually up to each individual judge to do the weighing. This task is made more difficult by the fact that circumstances are constantly changing, and so the balance that was struck in the past may not be appropriate for contemporary conditions.[17]

Few legal scholars have recognized the complexity of open justice. However, as we will see in the rest of this chapter, Chief Justice McLachlin has done so in her speeches, texts, and actions, thereby making a crucial contribution to this area of legal thought.

II. Open Justice in Words: Chief Justice McLachlin's Opinions about the Concept

In this part and the one that follows, I assess how the concept of open justice has been used in the writings of Chief Justice McLachlin and in the practice of the Supreme Court of Canada under her leadership. I will focus on her definition of "open justice" as well as the justifications and limitations on the concept that she has emphasized. I will also examine how she situates open justice among other constitutional concepts.

Open justice is an axiom in Canada, both in law and legal scholarship. The *Canadian Charter of Rights and Freedoms* expressly protects freedom of expression, including through freedom of the press and other means, and the right not to be deprived of life, liberty, and security of

15 *International Covenant of Civil and Political Rights, supra* note 3 at Article 14 (1); *European Convention of Human Rights, supra* note 3 as amended by protocols 11, 14, and 15 and supplemented by protocols 1, 4, 6, 7, 12, 13, and 16 at Article 6 (1).

16 For the Australian experience in this regard, see Emma Cunliffe, "Open Justice: Concepts and Judicial Approaches" (2012) 40 Fed L Rev 385 at 398.

17 For definitions, elements, justifications, and limits of open justice, see Eszter Bodnár, "Transparency and Openness of Courts in the 21st Century: An Issue Worth Researching On" (2016) 18 Iuris Dictio Revista de Derecho 153.

the person, except in accordance with the principles of fundamental justice. These provisions are collectively interpreted as guaranteeing a right to open justice that may be enforced by participants in a court process or evoked by the public in general.[18]

Chief Justice McLachlin gave public lectures and speeches to a wide variety of audiences, including lawyers, law students, and the public at large.[19] These speeches, along with her published writing, frequently addressed the topic of open justice, allowing us to become acquainted with her thoughts on this concept.

While focusing on the usual dual content of open justice (public trials and public documents), it is clear from McLachlin CJ's writings – and, as we will see below, from her actions – that she adopts a broad concept of open justice. Her writings also deal with both the procedural and the institutional-organizational aspects of open justice. She identifies the following important components: the publication of judgments;[20] the need for full, fair, and accurate reporting of court proceedings by the media;[21] the usefulness of public criticism of judicial decisions by lawyers and legal academics;[22] and the need for access to information about the law, legal system, and courts.[23] She encouraged judges to give speeches to community groups and schools,[24] and advocated for courts to open their doors to visitors.[25] She also dealt with the phenomenon of "vanishing trials" and how it influences the concept of open justice.[26] These various

18 Cunliffe, *supra* note 16 at 388.

19 The Executive Legal Officer (ELO) gives advice on which of the many speaking requests to accept and prepares the first drafts of speeches that the Chief Justice will give. Florian Sauvageau, David Schneiderman & David Taras, *The Last Word: Media Coverage of the Supreme Court of Canada* (Vancouver: UBC Press, 2006) at 201.

20 Beverley McLachlin, "Judicial Accountability" (Remarks delivered at the Conference on Law and Parliament in Ottawa, Ontario, 2 November 2006), online: <https://www.scc-csc.ca/judges-juges/spe-dis/bm-2006-11-02-eng.aspx>.

21 McLachlin, *supra* note 4.

22 McLachlin, *supra* note 20.

23 Beverley McLachlin, "Preserving Public Confidence in the Courts and the Legal Profession" (2002) 29 Man LJ 277 at 284.

24 Beverley McLachlin, "The Decline of Democracy and the Rule of Law: How to Preserve the Rule of Law and Judicial Independence" (Remarks delivered at the Saskatchewan and Manitoba Courts of Appeal Joint Meeting in Saskatoon, SK, 28 September 2017), online: <https://www.scc-csc.ca/judges-juges/spe-dis/bm-2017-09-28-eng.aspx>.

25 Beverley McLachlin, "The Supreme Court and the Public Interest" (2001) 64 Sask L Rev 309 at 321.

26 Beverley McLachlin, "Judging the 'Vanishing Trial' in the Construction Industry" (2011) 2:2 Faulkner L Rev 315.

components contribute to an understanding of open justice as a complex concept, one in which each element contributes to the whole, and the absence of any one can seriously weaken the openness of the courts.

From among the many justifications for open justice that I discussed in Part I, McLachlin CJ in her writings highlights three core values that she regards as animating the concept of open justice. The first value is that open justice assists in the search for truth and is essential to the effective exercise of the rights to freedom of expression and freedom of the press. Freedom of expression protects the right of each citizen to publicly comment on, discuss, and critique the operation of the courts and their decisions. As the majority of citizens receive information about the courts only through the press, it is crucial that the press be guaranteed access to the courts in order to gather accurate information. Besides its informational value, open justice also has an educational role: it informs people about their rights and obligations, and about the role of the courts in democratic governance.[27] Courts and judges should therefore accept an open approach toward the public and the media, since to do otherwise would hinder the free exercise of these fundamental rights.

Promoting judicial accountability is a second core value of open justice that is emphasized by Chief Justice McLachlin. Judges are accountable to the Canadian public, and numerous mechanisms are in place that ensure this accountability while respecting the need for judicial independence.[28] Publicity is a deterrent against misconduct by both judges and the state. Judges' knowledge that their activity is under observation, and may be broadly reported, provides a strong motivation to avoid any perception of bias and to ensure that trials are fair.[29] The openness of the courts provides an important assurance that judges are using their power not for their own interest, but in the public interest.[30]

The third core value is what McLachlin CJ calls "therapeutic justice." This refers to a process in which a citizen who is wronged seeks reparation not in private, but in the form of public vindication. The judgment proclaims to the community the correctness or the error of the claimant's claim, expresses the importance of resolving disputes, and reminds us of the importance of moving on.[31] Originally, open trials ensured the enforcement of decisions: each person witnessing the verdict became part

---

27 McLachlin, *supra* note 4 at 6–7.

28 McLachlin, *supra* note 20.

29 McLachlin, *supra* note 4 at 7–8.

30 McLachlin, *supra* note 25 at 320.

31 McLachlin, *supra* note 4 at 8.

of a public control system that made it harder for the responsible party to disrespect or deny the judgment. The public nature of the judgment assured collective acceptance and affirmation of norms of behaviour. It also confirmed the leadership role of judicial powers in determining the rules and regulations according to which communities defined themselves.[32] Although this function of justice may seem to be largely historical, it still applies today; however, the way in which the community participates in the process has changed. While, originally, the community attended trials in person, as either observers or participants in the process, today this participation is realized remotely via the media.

While identifying these three main justifications, McLachlin CJ also adopted a dynamic approach by emphasizing that open justice is justified by the changes that have affected the judiciary in recent times. The duty of judges was historically to resolve disputes, but, as a result of the justiciability of human rights issues and the new social policy role of judges, the scope of their activities has become much broader. These changes have modified the way judges discharge their duties and have altered the public's expectations as well, with the result that judges must be sensitive to a broad range of social concerns; the ivory tower can no longer be the residence of choice for judges. As a consequence, the appointment and governance of judges are also coming under increasing scrutiny. These developments have resulted in a change in the relationship between judges and the public.[33]

While aware of the core values of open justice, Chief Justice McLachlin also identified its limits, which she called the "costs of open justice." From among the possible limits identified in Part I, she emphasized privacy, trial fairness, sensationalism and distortion, and security.

Privacy is the top of her list because, once a matter is submitted to the courts, the parties cannot expect the details of their dispute to remain private. Traditionally, the courts have indicated that the embarrassment that results from having one's affairs subjected to public viewing is an insufficient justification for curtailing the openness of court proceedings. Today, it is no longer so simple, for at least two reasons. First, privacy is recognized as an important human right and an aspect of human dignity. Second, while, in the past, the loss of privacy was limited

32 Barbara Deimling, "The Courtroom: From Church Portal to Town Hall" in Wilfried Hartmann & Kenneth Pennington, eds, *The History of Courts and Procedure in Medieval Canon Law* (Washington, DC: Catholic University of America Press, 2016) 30 at 31.

33 Beverley McLachlin, "The Role of Judges in Modern Society" (Remarks delivered at the Fourth Worldwide Common Law Judiciary Conference in Vancouver, BC, 5 May 2001), online: <https://www.scc-csc.ca/judges-juges/spe-dis/bm-2001-05-05-eng.aspx>.

largely to the courts, today, with the development of new technology, the loss of privacy that can result from having recourse to the justice system is much broader. Trade secrets, the private lives of victims of sexual abuse, the affairs of those involved in a family dispute, and the experience, if not the identity, of juvenile offenders are just a few examples of what can be exposed to public view in court.[34]

While trial fairness is one of the main justifications for open justice, openness can, paradoxically, impair trial fairness in some cases. As an example, openness can make it difficult to select an impartial jury. As the right to trial by an impartial jury is a constitutional requirement and a fundamental pillar of the criminal justice system in the common law tradition, courts must in some cases limit pre-trial publication of information about the case or use other means to restrict openness in order to help ensure impartiality.[35]

Besides privacy and trial fairness, McLachlin CJ also lists sensationalism and distortion as disadvantages of open justice. Both traditional and new media operate in a highly competitive environment that can contribute to sensational or distorted reporting on court procedures.[36] In many cases, the media is unable to communicate the complexity of a case or judgment. Their reports refer only to the high points of a decision, with perhaps a few additional quotes from the lawyers involved in the case or from a law professor. Such reporting "does give the public an idea of what the court did and the general reaction, but it really doesn't give the public any idea about the legal reasoning involved or the doctrines involved or the basis of the decision."[37]

McLachlin CJ also identifies personal attacks on judges as a possible consequence of the concept of open justice. Finally, she adds security concerns as a legitimate reason to limit open justice.[38]

Even if legislators must have a role in establishing a fair balance between the countervailing fundamental rights and constitutional principles in the field of open justice, the most challenging task must be undertaken by the courts and judges. Chief Justice McLachlin suggests that the first step should be the recognition of the tension that exists between the open court concept, on the one hand, and the interests of privacy, justice, security, and the need to avoid sensationalism on the other. The second step is working out the appropriate balance contextually as

34 McLachlin, *supra* note 4 at 3–4.
35 *Ibid* at 4–5.
36 *Ibid* at 5–6.
37 Sauvageau *et al*, *supra* note 19 at 205.
38 McLachlin, *supra* note 4 at 5–6.

issues arise.[39] Yet, she has proposed that the conflicting interests are not as diametrically opposed as we might think. For example, the protection of the privacy of victims is important in a good justice system, but so too is the accused's right to trial by jury and respect for judges. Thus, she recommends that, instead of regarding these factors as opposed, they should simply be considered components of a good justice system. As a result, the task is to find the right balance between them on a contextual and case-by-case basis.[40]

Balancing the countervailing rights and principles in the field of open justice is definitely not an issue that can be resolved once and for all. Chief Justice McLachlin is aware that this area is subject to continuous change. The development of technology has expanded the audience for public trials and enabled online access to court documents. While broadening the scope of open justice, these developments have also made it more difficult not only to find jurors who will decide only on the basis of what they hear in court but also to reconcile concerns for privacy, reputation, and the well-being of individuals engaged in the justice system with the open and public administration of justice.[41]

The main conclusion that McLachlin CJ reaches in her writings about open justice is that the concept is not an end in itself but serves to preserve public confidence in the administration of justice and to maintain the authority of the courts. The principle that justice is rendered in open courts, freely accessible to the public and the media, is crucial for ensuring that justice is manifestly and undoubtedly seen to be done. It also helps to reinforce the belief that the courts administer justice fairly, impartially, independently, and according to law.[42] According to McLachlin CJ, Canadians are entitled to know what kind of people judges are if confidence in the justice system is to be maintained. In order to trust judges, she maintains, "you need to know a little bit about them, where they were educated, what their judicial experience is, how they approach their work."[43]

But public confidence is not an end in itself: it is a means to promote the rule of law. The courts preserve public confidence in the justice system, not egoistically to protect the power of the judiciary, but as a necessary and key tool for maintaining the rule of law. Without

39 *Ibid* at 3.

40 *Ibid* at 10.

41 *Ibid* at 4–5.

42 *Ibid* at 8.

43 Cited in Susan Harada, "The 'Uncomfortable Embrace': The Supreme Court and the Media in Canada" in Richard Davis & David Taras, eds, *Justices and Journalists: The Global Perspective* (Cambridge: Cambridge University Press, 2017) 81 at 90.

public confidence in the judiciary and belief in the legitimacy of their pronouncements, the courts are powerless to maintain the authority of law. Public confidence is a prerequisite for the existence of the rule of law.[44] If members of the public do not respect the courts that administer the law, they will not settle their disputes through the courts, they will not obey court orders, and judgments become mere edicts.[45]

In McLachlin CJ's work, the preservation and enhancement of the rule of law are not only of national concern. According to her, while judges should participate in public outreach activities in Canada to mitigate against the recent global trend away from the rule of law, she also encourages them to participate in judicial education in other countries to strengthen understanding of the importance of the rule of law and judicial independence worldwide.[46]

Chief Justice McLachlin did not only reflect on the importance of open justice as a concept. She provided very practical advice on the steps that the legislature, judges, the courts, and the media should take to maintain and enforce public confidence and enhance the rule of law. Besides appointing competent judges with high ethical standards and ensuring access to justice, these measures include educating youth and the public generally about the justice system and publicizing what judges do.[47]

III. Open Justice in Action: Giving Effect to the Concept in the McLachlin Court

Once the Supreme Court became the final court of appeal for Canada, with the elimination of appeals to the Judicial Committee of the Privy Council of the United Kingdom, it was inevitable that the Court would have to become more open; indeed, this became even more important as it began to adjudicate human rights issues following the adoption of the *Canadian Charter of Rights and Freedoms*.[48] While the swearing in of the first Chief Justice of the Supreme Court of Canada merited only a

---

44 McLachlin, *supra* note 4 at 9.

45 Beverley McLachlin, "The Relationship between the Courts and the Media" (Remarks delivered at Carleton University, Ottawa, 31 January 2012), online: <https://www.scc-csc.ca/judges-juges/spe-dis/bm-2012-01-31-eng.aspx>.

46 McLachlin, *supra* note 24.

47 McLachlin, *supra* note 4.

48 Adam Dodek & Rosemary Cairns Way, "The Supreme Court of Canada and Appointment of Judges in Canada" in Peter Oliver, Patrick Macklem & Nathalie Des Rosiers, eds, *The Oxford Handbook of the Canadian Constitution* (Oxford: Oxford University Press, 2017) 211 at 213.

few lines in newspapers,[49] today, the Court is subject to an increasing amount of media coverage.

The process of "opening up" started slowly in the mid-1970s, when Chief Justice Bora Laskin gave his first interview to the press. Subsequent chief justices all made some efforts to make the court more open and to improve the relationship between the court and the media. Chief Justice Brian Dickson established the post of the Executive Legal Officer (ELO), who has the job of briefing and dealing with journalists. He also began the practice of meeting with newspaper editorial boards, conducting interviews, and releasing texts of speeches in advance.[50] Chief Justice Antonio Lamer opened the Court up to even greater scrutiny when cameras were invited into the courtroom and oral arguments were televised live on the Canadian Parliamentary Affairs Channel.[51]

During the tenure of McLachlin CJ, open justice took on increasing importance. According to one of her writings, a Chief Justice has four principal roles: as a judge, the chief administrator of the Supreme Court, the head of the judiciary, and a judicial ambassador abroad.[52] All of these roles involve different tasks from the standpoint of open justice.

a. The Chief Justice's Role in the Field of Open Justice as a Judge

According to McLachlin CJ, the most important role of the Chief Justice is to be a judge.[53] Her contribution to the enhancement of the open justice principle is therefore best gleaned from the positions she has taken in important judgments, which allow the public to witness her thoughts and her judicial approach.

Dagenais v Canadian Broadcasting Corp[54] was one of the most important cases in the field of open justice, due to its recognition of the need to balance the fundamental principle of open justice against other competing principles.[55] It also recognized that this balance could not be simplistic. Thus, in *Dagenais*, which dealt with a challenge to a publication ban, Justice McLachlin (as she then was) stated that the question was not simply where the balance should be struck between a fair trial and freedom of expression: the right to a fair trial is fundamental and

49 Harada, *supra* note 43 at 82.

50 Sauvageau *et al*, *supra* note 19 at 12.

51 *Ibid* at 13.

52 Beverley McLachlin, "Le Rôle du Juge en Chef" (2002) 32 RGD 403 at 403.

53 *Ibid* at 404.

54 *Dagenais v Canadian Broadcasting Corp*, [1994] 3 SCR 835 [*Dagenais*].

55 See a detailed analysis in Cunliffe, *supra* note 16 at 407.

cannot be sacrificed. What is required is that the judges evalute the risk of an unfair trial after taking full account of the general importance of the free dissemination of ideas and after considering measures that might offset or avoid any feared prejudice. In the given case, the judge who had ordered a ban on a mini-series on the physical and sexual abuse of young boys at training schools in Ontario failed to consider whether the ban was rationally connected to the goal of ensuring a fair trial of Mr Dagenais, and the judge had not explained why the ban represented a minimal impairment of the right to freedom of expression. In consequence, the Court set the ban aside.[56]

In a number of cases, the Court has attempted to ensure proportionality between competing *Charter* values such as freedom of expression, trial fairness, and privacy interests, while promoting the proper administration of justice. In *Canadian Broadcasting Corporation v New Brunswick (AG)*,[57] the Court emphasized that the proper balance between these interests is context-dependent and will vary from case to case. This decision, made with the participation of McLachlin J (as she then was), also includes some basic statements on the open court principle. The Court unanimously upheld the constitutionality of a statutory provision that permitted a sentencing judge to exclude members of the public from proceedings where it was necessary to do so in order to uphold the proper administration of justice. The Court held that the statutory provision enabled a judge to craft orders that achieved proportionality between competing *Charter* values while promoting the proper administration of justice. The Court emphasized that the proper balance between these interests is context-dependent and will vary from case to case.[58]

As a judge, McLachlin CJ very consciously used judicial dissent as a tool to express her opinion. Some of her most important dissents are on the topic of freedom of expression,[59] freedom of the press,[60] and Aboriginal rights.[61] However, it is important to emphasize that, according to empirical analysis, after her appointment as Chief Justice, she became a "social leader," who made an effort to increase the level of consensus in the Court, and, as a result, the number of dissents decreased.[62] This

56 *Dagenais, supra* note 54 at 841–2.

57 *Canadian Broadcasting Corporation v New Brunswick (AG)*, [1996] 3 SCR 480.

58 Cunliffe, *supra* note 16 at 407.

59 *R v Keegstra*, [1990] 3 SCR 697.

60 *Canadian Broadcasting Corp v New Brunswick (AG)*, [1991] 3 SCR 459.

61 *R v Marshall*, [1999] 3 SCR 456.

62 Emmett MacFarlane, *Governing from the Bench: The Supreme Court of Canada and the Judicial Role* (Vancouver: UBC Press, 2013) at 31.

can be regarded as a positive development from an institutional point of view (it ensures a more unified and stronger court). However, it is a step backwards from the point of view of open justice, as the opinions of judges' who disagree with the majority is not public, and this, in turn, hinders the public's understanding of the legal debates in the court.

At the same time, Chief Justice McLachlin's style of reasoning contributed to the enhancement of open justice. Observers have characterized it as a "direct, plain spoken, and logical" reasoning style, and "[as] the product of an incisive analytic mind and a no-nonsense prairie temperament."[63] Her emphasis on plain reasoning was also a part of her effort to make the Court and its decisions more accessible to a broader public, and "to protect the legitimacy of the institution from critics eager to find evidence of hubris lurking in judicial exercises of power."[64]

b. The Chief Justice's Role in the Field of Open Justice as Chief Administrator

The role of the Chief Justice is crucial to ensuring and promoting the principle of open justice in court. The Chief Justice is responsible for ensuring that the court's procedures function well. The individual in that role is the chief administrator of the Supreme Court.[65] This is perhaps the most important role in relation to the enhancement of open justice. According to Lawrence David, Beverley McLachlin reinvented the role of the Chief Justice to enhance public confidence in the Supreme Court of Canada.[66] With respect to her actions in the field of open justice, this statement does not seem excessive.

Some of the steps taken by McLachlin CJ as chief administrator of the Supreme Court aimed to help journalists to report on the Court, while others were intended to open up the Court as an institution.[67] In the McLachlin era, the Court made several efforts to better organize its relationship with the media. Chief Justice McLachlin emphasized that the

63 Eric Adams, "Reflecting a Chief Justice" (4 December 2017), online (blog): *Int'l J Const L* <http://www.iconnectblog.com/2017/12/i-connect-symposium-the-legacy-of-chief-justice-beverley-mclachlin-reflecting-a-chief-justice>.

64 Ibid.

65 McLachlin, *supra* note 52 at 404.

66 Lawrence David, "The Face of an Institution: Beverley McLachlin's Reinvention of the Role of the Chief Justice of Canada" (7 December 2017), online (blog): *Int'l J Const L* <http://www.iconnectblog.com/2017/12/david-on-Chief-Justice-McLachlin>.

67 Harada, *supra* note 43 at 86.

Court and media need each other, locked as they are in a "mutual, if sometimes uncomfortable embrace."[68] As a first step in this direction, she started her mandate with a news conference in which she invited a group of reporters into the justices' private dining room two months before her official swearing in.[69] This unprecedented event made it clear that improved communication would be one of her key priorities for the Court.[70] In another first, her annual addresses at the Canadian Bar Association were followed by a question-and-answer session with the media.[71]

During her tenure, the ELO routinely briefed reporters before a hearing and before important rulings were issued. Journalists and members of the general public can sign up to receive emails with information on press releases, appeals, hearings, and upcoming and newly released judgments.[72]

In 2004, the McLachlin Court became the first in the world to pilot "lockups" for journalists for "certain high-profile, complex cases"; it made the initiative permanent in 2006. The lockups make it possible for journalists to digest the content of judgments prior to reporting them, giving journalists fifteen minutes to read the embargoed judgment, followed by a half-hour briefing by the ELO and a forty-five-minute question-and-answer session.[73] This is a very significant step that journalists in other countries have demanded without success.[74]

The installation of a camera system in the 1990s was another instance in which the Supreme Court of Canada was a global pioneer. Since 2009, the Court has livestreamed and archived every appeal hearing, save those with content subject to a publication ban from a lower court.[75] This initiative was followed by several other high courts throughout the world.[76] However, most courts still either hesitate to allow or explicitly reject the presence of cameras in the courtroom.[77]

68 McLachlin, *supra* note 45.

69 Harada, *supra* note 43 at 85.

70 MacFarlane, *supra* note 62 at 177.

71 David, *supra* note 66.

72 Sauvageau *et al*, *supra* note 19 at 13.

73 Harada, *supra* note 43 at 88–9.

74 E.g. Rachel Spencer, "Communication beyond the Judgments: The Australian High Court, Speaking for Itself, but Not Tweeting" in Davis & Taras, eds, *supra* note 19 at 41; Richard Davis, "Symbiosis: The US Supreme Court and the Journalists Who Cover It" in Davis & Taras, *supra* note 19 at 286.

75 Harada, *supra* note 43 at 87.

76 E.g. the oral hearings of the Constitutional Council of France are transmitted on its website.

77 E.g. the Supreme Court of United States is totally closed to cameras. MC Miller, *Judicial Politics in the United States* (Boulder, CO: Westview, 2015) at 168.

The scope of access to court documents has also increased: appellants' and respondents' factums, interveners' factums, and memoranda of arguments on applications for leave to appeal that were granted are all available online.[78] The Court regularly publishes statistics on its work (e.g., numbers of applications and judgments, breakdown by subject matter, average times taken to deal with the cases).[79] These statistics help the media and legal scholars to assess the operation and performance of the Court and the judges.

The Court also became active in public outreach activities. After her appointment, Chief Justice McLachlin conducted a media tour, giving interviews and accepting a host of speaking invitations. "I did it more than any other chief justice has. These are the people's courts and the people are entitled to know who's been named to that court and who is chief justice responsible for the administration of that court."[80]

Beside the opportunity for the public to attend hearings, the Supreme Court of Canada also offers guided tours to better acquaint citizens with Canada's highest court. In the Mayor's Breakfast Series, Chief Justice McLachlin talked to the public about the history of the Supreme Court building, the jurisdiction of the Court, and the importance of open justice.[81] She hosted an annual open-door celebration at the Supreme Court on Canada Day.[82] On the Court's website, there are free resources such as an educational kit and interactive games to help children understand what judges do.[83] For years, Chief Justice McLachlin, usually in the company of one or more of her colleagues, participated in the Stratford Festival, a prominent theatrical festival in Ontario, in a mock trial of a Shakespearean character.[84]

The Supreme Court has found its way into the world of social media. In 2011, it started a Facebook page (although posting is not very

78 Harada, *supra* note 43 at 86. For comparison, the German Federal Constitutional Court does not make any document in the case file available online; only the decisions are public on the website.

79 McLachlin, *supra* note 45.

80 Sauvageau *et al*, *supra* note 19 at 13.

81 Beverley McLachlin, "The Supreme Court of Canada" (Remarks delivered at the Mayor's Breakfast Series, Ottawa, ON, 25 November 2014), online: <https://www.scc-csc.ca/judges-juges/spe-dis/bm-2014-11-25-eng.aspx>.

82 David, *supra* note 64.

83 "Resources for Teachers" (last modified 12 April 2019), online: *Supreme Court of Canada* <https://www.scc-csc.ca/vis/education/index-eng.aspx>.

84 "Lady and Lord Macbeth on Trial: Guilty or Bewitched?" *CBC* (12 June 2017), online <www.cbc.ca/radio/ideas/lady-and-lord-macbeth-on-trial-guilty-or-bewitched-1.4156488>.

active).[85] Its Twitter account has been in use since 2016, sharing a Bulletin of Proceedings every week, as well as information about judgments, hearings, and statistics.[86] These tools facilitate one-way communication, but they have not opened up a dialogue between the Court and citizens. As Chief Justice McLachlin explained, "a lot of back and forth with the public is not really going to necessarily help us in doing our job."[87] While most of the highest courts in the world use some form of social media, the Supreme Court of Canada does it in a conscious way as part of its very active public outreach activities.

c. The Chief Justice's Role in the Field of Open Justice as Head of the Judiciary

Besides being a judge and the chief administrator of the Supreme Court, in Canada, the Chief Justice also serves as the head of the federal judiciary.[88] At the beginning of one of her speeches, McLachlin CJ admits that "a judge is most often guided by facts and rules that delimit the extent of his or her remarks"; however, most of her public speeches offered her a "much less restricted forum for expression."[89] Being the head of the judiciary is a role that demands much more speaking out than is possible when one is "just" a trial judge.

And, indeed, she spoke out regularly, talking not only about topics closely connected to the activity of the Court, such as judicial impartiality,[90] judicial accountability,[91] judicial independence,[92] the use of foreign law in the Court's practice,[93] judicial education,[94] and access

85 Supreme Court of Canada, "Profile," online: *Facebook* <www.facebook.com/supremecourtofcanada>.

86 Supreme Court of Canada, "Profile," online: *Twitter* <www.twitter.com/scc>.

87 Harada, *supra* note 43 at 94.

88 McLachlin, *supra* note 52 at 405.

89 Beverley McLachlin, "4th Annual Lafontaine-Baldwin Lecture" in Rudyard Griffiths, ed, *Dialogue on Democracy* (Toronto: Penguin Canada, 2006) at 105.

90 Beverley McLachlin, "On Impartiality" in Andrew Stockely & David Rowe, eds, *A Canadian Judgment: The Lectures of Chief Justice Beverley McLachlin in New Zealand, April 2003* (Christchurch: Centre for Commercial and Corporate Law, 2004) 1.

91 McLachlin, *supra* note 20.

92 Beverley McLachlin, "Judicial Independence" (Remarks delivered at the 300th Anniversary of the Act of Settlement Conference in Vancouver, BC, 11 May 2001), online: <https://www.scc-csc.ca/judges-juges/spe-dis/bm-2001-05-11-eng.as>.

93 Beverley McLachlin, "Keynote Address: The Use of Foreign Law – A Comparative View of Canada and the United States" in (2010) 104 *Proceedings of the Annual Meeting (American Society of International Law)* 491.

94 Beverley McLachlin, "Remarks of the Right Honourable Beverley McLachlin, PC" (Remarks to the Second International Conference on the Training of the Judiciary

to justice,[95] but also about several other legal, political, and societal themes. She gave speeches on, and wrote about, the Canadian Constitution and its history,[96] the *Canadian Charter of Rights and Freedoms*,[97] diversity,[98] bilingualism and biculturalism,[99] Indigenous rights and reconciliation,[100] equality issues,[101] the autonomy of Parliament,[102] globalization and identity,[103] unwritten constitutional principles,[104] the legal challenges of mental illness,[105] and the fight against terrorism.[106]

Chief Justice McLachlin did not hesitate to raise controversial or politically sensitive topics. She repeatedly and publicly urged the government to fill the vacancies at the Supreme Court and at other courts, referring to the "perpetual crises of judicial vacancies."[107] On one

---

in Ottawa, ON, 1 November 2004), online: <https://www.scc-csc.ca/judges-juges/spe-dis/bm-2004-11-01-eng.aspx>.

95 Beverley McLachlin, "The Challenges We Face" (2007) 40 UBC L Rev 819.

96 Beverley McLachlin, "Defining Moments: The Canadian Constitution" (Remarks delivered at the Dickson Lecture, Ottawa, ON, 13 February 2014), online: <https://www.scc-csc.ca/judges-juges/spe-dis/bm-2014-02-13-eng.aspx>.

97 Beverley McLachlin, "The Charter 25 Years Later: The Good, the Bad, and the Challenges" (2007) 45 Osgoode Hall LJ 365.

98 McLachlin, *supra* note 87.

99 Beverley McLachlin, "The Impact of the Supreme Court of Canada on Bilingualism and Biculturalism" (Remarks delivered at the Constitutional Law Week Speaker Series at McGill University, Montreal, QC, 6 February 2008), online: <https://www.scc-csc.ca/judges-juges/spe-dis/bm-2008-02-06-eng.aspx>.

100 Beverley McLachlin, "Aboriginal Peoples and Reconciliation" in Stockely & Rowe, *supra* note 88.

101 Beverley McLachlin, "Building a Bridge to Equality: A Duty for Lawyers" in Stockely & Rowe, *supra* note 88.

102 Beverley McLachlin, "Reflections on the Autonomy of Parliament" (2004) 27:1 Can Parliamentary Rev 278.

103 Beverley McLachlin, "Globalization, Identity and Citizenship" (Remarks delivered at the ADM Forum in Ottawa, ON, 26 October 2004), online: <https://www.scc-csc.ca/judges-juges/spe-dis/bm-2004-10-26-eng.aspx>.

104 Beverley McLachlin, "Unwritten Constitutional Principles: What Is Going On?" (Remarks given at the 2005 Lord Cooke Lecture in Wellington, NZ, 1 December 2005), online: <https://www.scc-csc.ca/judges-juges/spe-dis/bm-2005-12-01-eng.aspx>.

105 Beverley McLachlin, "Medicine and the Law: The Challenges of Mental Illness" (Remarks given at the 2004 Honourable Mr Justice Michael O'Byrne/AHFMR at the University of Alberta and University of Calgary, 17–18 February 2005), online: <https://www.scc-csc.ca/judges-juges/spe-dis/bm-2005-02-17-eng.aspx>.

106 Beverley McLachlin, "The Challenge of Fighting Terrorism While Maintaining Our Civil Liberties" (Remarks given at the Ottawa Women's Canadian Club in Ottawa, ON, 22 September 2009), online: <https://www.scc-csc.ca/judges-juges/spe-dis/bm-2009-09-22-eng.aspx>.

107 Beverley McLachlin, "Remarks to the Council of the Canadian Bar Association at the Canadian Legal Conference" (Remarks given at the Council of the Canadian

occasion, she described the Canadian government's treatment of First Nations as "cultural genocide."[108] Some commentators felt that her speech was a "violation of juridical rules."[109] Others cheered, because such a statement could have "real and potential capacity to affect reconciliation and forgiveness between Canada's Indigenous and non-Indigenous peoples."[110] In 2014, in one the most critical moments of her mandate, she had to use her public standing to defend herself against baseless allegations by Prime Minister Harper that she had improperly interfered in the appointment of Justice Marc Nadon, whom the Court held to be ineligible for one of the three Supreme Court seats reserved for Quebec.[111] While Chief Justice McLachlin was applauded by judges in Canada and abroad,[112] this incident marked an unprecedented expansion of the Chief Justice's role in public debate, a role that she had clearly not freely chosen.[113]

Chief Justice McLachlin admits that the appropriate response to the question of whether judges should respond to the new demands of the public, and speak out publicly, is not clear. There is a spectrum of opinion on the issue, but in recent decades, the entire spectrum has shifted in favour of a greater willingness on the part of judges to speak out. "This shift is a reflection of the changing role of the judiciary, and perhaps a reflection of the fact that our democracies are becoming more participatory, with citizens taking a more active interest in the way social policy is made."[114]

Bar Association at the Canadian Legal Conference in Ottawa, ON, 11 August 2016), online: <https://www.scc-csc.ca/judges-juges/spe-dis/bm-2016-08-11-eng.aspx>.

108 Beverley McLachlin, "Reconciling Unity and Diversity in the Modern Era: Tolerance and Intolerance" (Remarks given at the Annual Pluralism Lecture 2015 at the Aga Khan Museum, Toronto, ON), online: <www.pluralism.ca/index.php?option=com_content&view=article&id=284:annual-lecture-series-6&catid=107&Itemid=828&lang=en>.

109 Richard Gwyn, "Did Canada Really Commit 'Cultural Genocide'?" *Toronto Star* (8 June 2015).

110 Jenna Sapiano, "Reconciliation and Recognition after 'Cultural Genocide': Beverley McLachlin's Use of Language" (7 December 2017) online (blog): *Int'l J Const L* <http://www.iconnectblog.com/2017/12/sapiano-on-Chief-Justice-McLachlin>. According to the author, her statement of this harm may be one of her most lasting legacies after McLachlin CJ's retirement.

111 *Reference re Supreme Court Act, ss 5 and 6*, 2014 SCC 21.

112 Harada, *supra* note 43 at 81–2.

113 David, *supra* note 66.

114 McLachlin, *supra* note 33.

d. The Role of the Chief Justice in the Field of Open Justice as Judicial Ambassador Abroad

The fourth role that the Chief Justice plays is that of judicial ambassador. Every year, Chief Justice McLachlin received several delegations of judges from foreign countries. She also received invitations from other countries that wanted to strengthen their ties to the Canadian judiciary. As she writes, "I discovered that the Canadian justice system is much appreciated everywhere in the world. And for many people around the world, the chief justice symbolizes justice."[115] This ambassadorial role can be also regarded as an effort to make the Court more open.

IV. Open Justice and the Future of the Supreme Court of Canada

After acknowledging the efforts that Chief Justice Beverley McLachlin has made in the past to enhance open justice at the Supreme Court of Canada, we should also look to the future and consider what approach subsequent chief justices should take.

The fact is that the Supreme Court of Canada already enjoys a high level of public confidence and trust. Surveys from the early years of the McLachlin Court show that it regularly had higher support than other societal institutions.[116] A decade later, a 2015 Angus Reid poll found that 74 per cent of Canadians had a favourable opinion of the Supreme Court, and that twice as many Canadians had a "great deal" or "quite a lot" of confidence in the Court as had such levels of confidence in the media or in Parliament.[117] Consequently, the question is not how to build public trust in the Supreme Court of Canada, as this already exists – in part due to the efforts of previous leadership. The question is, rather, how to maintain and strengthen public confidence.

Having the confidence and support of the public is essential for the Supreme Court as an institution. From its humble constitutional role at its inception, it has become one of the most powerful institutions in the Canadian constitutional state. More and more, political questions become judicial ones, such that, nowadays, the Court is a political

---

115 McLachlin, *supra* note 52 at 406.

116 E.g. Sauvageau *et al*, *supra* note 19 at 26–7.

117 Angus Reid Institute, "Canadians Have a More Favourable View of Their Supreme Court Than Americans Have of Their Own" (17 August 2015), online: *Angus Reid Institute* <http://angusreid.org/wp-content/uploads/2015/08/2015.08.14-Supreme-Court-final.pdf>.

institution. Supreme Court justices have the power to declare the winners and losers in important societal conflicts, and their judgments uphold and celebrate certain societal values and practices while downplaying or denigrating others. According to Sauvageau, justices have the "power to construct both a real and symbolic universe and to impose that universe on the wider society."[118] At the same time, accountability is not as direct as it is for the two other branches of government, given justices' security of tenure and immobility (both elements of judicial independence).[119] Given these considerations, public scrutiny is one of the most important guarantees of accountability and public confidence in the Court. It also protects the institution's independence in the midst of tension with other stakeholders in the political sphere.

As for methods of maintaining and strengthening public confidence, the primary route is, not surprisingly, to enforce the transparency of the institution. According to Sauvageau, the current system "allows the judges to dwell in a netherworld between remoteness and availability."[120] This assessment meshes with MacFarlane's observation that, despite the recent trend of opening up the Court, it remains a secretive place.[121]

However, if we regard Canada from a comparative point of view, the Supreme Court of Canada is still one of the most open institutions of its kind in the world. Even the supreme courts or constitutional courts of developed democracies are not always able to face the challenges of the twenty-first century. The Supreme Court of the United States (SCOTUS), for example, is absolutely against the introduction of cameras into courtrooms and does not officially recognize those who write for SCOTUSblog – a law blog written by lawyers, law professors, and law students – as journalists, as the blog is not considered part of the traditional media. The German Federal Constitutional Court does not post submitted petitions or any other court documents (except decisions) on the internet, and cameras are allowed only for the opening of the oral hearings, not for the substantial part of the proceedings. The French Constitutional Council does not allow its members to give dissenting opinions, and the reasons in each decision are perfunctory and uninformative.[122] The situation elsewhere is even worse in new democracies:

118 Sauvageau *et al*, *supra* note 19 at 21.

119 Harada, *supra* note 43 at 84.

120 Sauvageau *et al*, *supra* note 19 at 234.

121 MacFarlane, *supra* note 62 at 184.

122 See a detailed comparison of these courts in Eszter Bodnár, "Open Justice in the Digital Age: How Can ICT Enhance the Transparency of Constitutional Courts?" in

the Hungarian Constitutional Court, for example, refuses to hold public hearings, and judges almost never give interviews to the media.[123]

A high level of public confidence and transparency does not mean that the Supreme Court of Canada will necessarily avoid a situation in which countervailing interests will exert stronger pressure to limit the principle of open justice. Security and privacy concerns will continue to present themselves as threats to open courts, and if these concerns are coupled in any way with a judiciary that is not committed to open justice, the result can easily be more closed courts.

Being more open and "visible" depends not only on the justices and the Chief Justice. According to Harada, as an institution, the Court is unlikely to further alter its practices in any fundamental way unless it is forced to do so by the legislature. As an example, she raises the adoption of the *Charter*, which prompted the Court to begin reaching out to Canadians via the news media. In a worst case scenario, the Court may shift toward more openness only in response to a perceived threat to or erosion of the public confidence that underpins its legitimacy.[124]

The media have an enormous responsibility in enhancing the visibility of the courts. Yet, according to empirical research, the media take a limited interest in the Court, in comparison to their coverage of other state institutions; this is especially true of the French-language media.[125] Many judges find that the quantity and quality of coverage are not satisfactory. The media does not report on all cases; provide detailed information on judges' reasoning, including majority and dissenting opinions; or generally present the context of judgments.[126] These lapses reveal a gap between the expectations of judges and the realities of the media market. Court coverage does not offer the same opportunities as much political reporting: there are few exciting visuals, and judges do not leak stories, appear at news conferences, or attack their critics. Indeed, there are few settings that erect as many barriers and pose as many challenges to good reporting as the Supreme Court.[127] Production limitations are also a consideration: judgments are highly complex,

---

Alexander Balthasar *et al*, eds, *Central and Eastern European e | Dem and e | Gov Days 2016: Multi-Level (e)Governance – Is ICT a Means to Enhance Transparency and Democracy?* (Vienna: Austrian Computer Society, 2016) 53.

123 Eszter Bodnár, "Gedanken über die Einführung der öffentlichen Verhandlung am ungarischen Verfassungsgericht" (2017) 63:1 Osteuroparecht 65.

124 Harada, *supra* note 43 at 95.

125 Sauvageau *et al*, *supra* note 19 at 56.

126 Harada, *supra* note 43 at 91.

127 Sauvageau *et al*, *supra* note 19 at 13–14.

containing abstract and subtle arguments that are often difficult to explain in a few paragraphs in a newspaper or a few moments on the nightly news. However, the ability to operate in the digital realm has now made it possible for journalists to provide more detailed coverage. The internet has clearly expanded the ability of journalists to offer context and analysis on a scale previously not possible.[128]

Faced with declining traditional media coverage, on the one hand, and intense public scrutiny under the gaze of interactive and fast-paced new media forums, on the other, the courts have found it necessary to develop strategies of direct community engagement to preserve both open justice and public confidence in the judiciary.[129] The view appears to be that, if the media is no longer able to report on the courts, the courts should take steps to communicate more effectively with the media and the public at large. Even if judges cannot comment on cases before the Court, there is still a need for a more active approach to communication. David A. Sellers, the Public Affairs Officer at the Administrative Office of the US Courts proposes four solutions to this end: increasing the number of Public Information Officers, easier access to court records, developing court websites, and more active use of videos and social media.[130]

Although the Supreme Court of Canada has already taken steps to communicate better, there are certainly areas for improvement. As Chief Justice McLachlin wrote, "[j]ustice is an ongoing process. It is never done, never fully achieved. Each decade, each year, each month, indeed each day, brings new challenges."[131] The new challenges include technical changes and changes in the structure of media, which coincide with changing expectations of the public.

These developments are interrelated: not only is public knowledge improved by active communication by the Court, but the decision to enter the world of media relations, to explain and consciously promote its public role, has also altered the nature and role of the Court.[132] Yet, thoughout these changes, as Chief Justice McLachlin has stated, judges must remain true to their highest calling: being impartial decision

128 Harada, *supra* note 43 at 92.

129 Marilyn Warren, "Open Justice in the Technological Age" (2014) 40 Monash UL Rev 45 at 47.

130 David A. Sellers, "As Today's Tony Lewises Disappear, Courts Fill Void" (2014) 79:7 Mo L Rev 1024.

131 McLachlin, *supra* note 95.

132 Canadian Judicial Council, *The Judicial Role in Public Information* (Canadian Judicial Council, September 1999) at 7.

makers.[133] She continues: "The judges in modern society are not potentates: they are rather servants, servants of the people in the highest and most honourable sense of that term. The judge has a task, a more important task than ever before. It is precisely because of the importance of this task that the judge is expected to perform it well and efficiently, to be responsive and responsible."[134]

Open justice is not a "super weapon" that can solve every problem of the justice system and the judiciary. It should be supplemented by several other measures, including the enforcement of access to justice, judicial education, and a more democratic judicial appointment system. Nonetheless, as Jeremy Bentham wrote, "[p]ublicity is the very soul of justice."[135] Or, rather, as McLachlin CJ, observed, Bentham "would agree that publicity is really … [the] servant" of justice.[136]

133 McLachlin, *supra* note 33.

134 Ibid.

135 Jeremy Bentham, "Bentham's Draught for the Organization of Judicial Establishments, Compared with That of the National Assembly, with a Commentary on the Came" in Jeremy Bentham, *The Works of Jeremy Bentham*, vol 4 (1843) at 494.

136 McLachlin, *supra* note 4 at 11.

Statutes, Cases, and Works Cited

I. Legislation: International

Basic Law for the Federal Republic of Germany (*Grundgesetz für die Bundesrepublik Deutschland*), 23 May 1949, BGBL 1 at 1.

Convention Relating to the Status of Refugees, 1951, 189 UNTS 2545 (entered into force on 22 April 1954).

Council of Europe, ECHR, 4 November 1950, *European Convention of Human Rights*, as amended by protocols 11, 14, and 15 and supplemented by protocols 1, 4, 6, 7, 12, 13, and 16.

International Covenant of Civil and Political Rights, GA Res 2200A (XXI), 1966, UNGAOR, *Treaty Series* vol 999, 171.

OAS, Inter-American Commission on Human Rights, *American Convention on Human Rights*, OR B-32 (1969).

Universal Declaration of Human Rights, GA Res 217A (III), UNGAOR, 3rd Sess, Supp No 13, UN Doc A/810 (1948).

II. Legislation: Federal

Act to amend the Supreme Court Act and to make related amendments to the Federal Court Act, SC 1974–75–76, c 18.

An act to amend the Criminal Code (protection of children and other vulnerable persons) and the Canada Evidence Act, SC 2005, c 32.

Canada Elections Act, RSC 1985, c E-2.

Canada Evidence Act, RSC 1985, c C-5.

Canadian Charter of Rights and Freedoms, Part I of the *Constitution Act 1982*, being Schedule B to the *Canada Act 1982* (UK).

Canadian Human Rights Act, RSC 1985, c H-6.

Citizen's Arrest and Self-defence Act, SC 2012, c 9.

Competition Tribunal Act, RSC 1985, c 19 (2nd Supp.).

Constitution Act, 1982, being Schedule B to the *Canada Act 1982* (UK), 1982, c 11.

Controlled Drugs and Substances Act, RSC 1985, c C-5.
Criminal Code of Canada, RSC 1985, c C-46.
Federal Courts Act, RSC 1985, c F-7.
Immigration Act, RSC 1985, c I-2.
Juvenile Delinquents Act, RSC 1970, c J-3.
Specific Claims Tribunal Act, SC 2008, c 22.

III. Legislation: Provincial

An Act to Secure Adequate Provision for the Maintenance of the Wife and Children of a Testator, SBC 1920, c 94.
Courts of Justice Act, RSO 1990, c C.43.
Family Law Act, 1986, SO 1986, c 4.
Judicial Review Procedure Act, RSO 1990, c J.1.
Mortgage Brokers Act, RSBC 1996, c 313.
Municipal Government Act, RSA 2000, c M-26.
Personal Information Protection Act, SA 2003, c P-6.5.
Police Act, SNB 1977, c P-9.2.
Police Services Act, RSO 1990, c P.15.
Statutory Powers Procedure Act, RSO 1990, c S.22.
Tobacco Damages and Health Care Costs Recovery Act, SBC 2000, c 30.

IV. Jurisprudence: Canadian

1318847 Ontario Ltd v Laval Tool & Mould Ltd, 2015 ONSC 2664.
495793 Ontario Ltd. (Central Auto Parts) v Barclay, 2014 ONSC 3517.
495793 Ontario Ltd. (Central Auto Parts) v Barclay, 2016 ONCA 656.
628356 Saskatchewan Ltd v Water Security Agency, 2018 SKQB 4.
720654 Alberta Ltd v El Hajj, 2011 ABPC 64.
Air Canada v Ontario (Liquor Control Board), [1997] 2 SCR 581.
Alberta (Information and Privacy Commissioner) v Alberta Teachers' Association, 2011 SCC 61.
Ares v Venner, [1970] SCR 608.
Athey v Leonati, [1996] 3 SCR 458.
Attis v Canada (Minister of Health), 2008 ONCA 660.
Attorney General of Quebec v Labrecque and al., [1980] 2 SCR 1057.
Bank of America Canada v Mutual Trust Co, 2002 SCC 43.
Barreau du Québec v Quebec (Attorney General), 2017 SCC 56.
Bazley v Curry, [1999] 2 SCR 534.
Bélanger v The Queen, [1970] SCR 567.
Bell Canada et al v Attorney General of Canada, 2018 CanLII 40808 (SCC).
Bell Canada v Canada (AG), 2019 SCC 66.

Bhasin v Hrynew, 2014 SCC 71.
Blackwater v Plint, 2005 SCC 58.
Boucher v The King, [1951] SCR 265.
Bow Valley Husky (Bermuda) Ltd v Saint John Shipbuilding Ltd, [1997] 3 SCR 1210.
British Columbia (AG) v Christie, 2007 SCC 21.
Cadbury Schweppes Inc v FBI Foods Ltd, [1999] 1 SCR 142.
Calvert v Law Society of Upper Canada (1981), 121 DLR (3d) 169 (Ont HC).
Canada (AG) v Bedford, 2013 SCC 72.
Canada (AG) v PHS Community Services Society, 2011 SCC 44.
Canada (Canadian Human Rights Commission) v Canada (AG), 2011 SCC 53.
Canada (Citizenship and Immigration) v Khosa, 2009 SCC 12.
Canada (Director of Investigation and Research) v Southam Inc, [1997] 1 SCR 748.
Canada (Minister of Citizenship and Immigration) v Vavilov, 2019 SCC 65.
Canada (Prime Minister) v Khadr, [2010] 1 SCR 44.
Canada (Public Safety and Emergency Preparedness) v Tran, 2015 FCA 237.
Canada v Taylor, [1990] 3 SCR 892.
Canadian Broadcasting Corp v New Brunswick (AG), [1991] 3 SCR 459.
Canadian Broadcasting Corp v New Brunswick (AG), [1996] 3 SCR 480.
Canadian Broadcasting Corp v. SODRAC 2003 Inc, 2015 SCC 57.
Canadian National Railway Co v Norsk Pacific Steamship Co, [1992] 1 SCR 1021.
Canadian Pacific Railway Co v Vancouver (City), 2006 SCC 5.
Canson Enterprises Ltd v Boughton & Co, [1991] 3 SCR 534.
Carleton (County) v Ottawa (City), [1965] SCR 663.
Carrington Petroleum & Fertilizers Ltd v Imperial Oil Ltd, 2003 ABQB 545.
Carter v Canada (AG), 2015 SCC 5.
Central Guaranty Trust Co v Dixdale Mortgage Investment Corp, [1994] 24 OR (3d) 506 (CA).
Chaoulli v Quebec (AG), 2005 SCC 35.
Chatfield v Bell Mobility Inc, 2016 SKQB 364.
Chernichan v Chernichan Estate, 2001 ABQB 913.
Childs v Desormeaux, 2006 SCC 18.
Cie Immobilière Viger v L Guiguère Inc, [1977] 2 SCR 67.
Cinar Corp v Robinson, 2013 SCC 73.
Citadel General Assurance Co v Lloyds Bank Canada, [1997] 3 SCR 805.
Clarke v Johnson, 2014 ONCA 237.
Clarkson v McCrossen Estate (1995), 122 DLR (4th) 239 (BC CA).
Clements v Clements, 2012 SCC 32.
Cooper v Hobart, 2001 SCC 79.
Crocker v Sundance Northwest Resorts Ltd, [1988] 1 SCR 1186.
CUPE v NB Liquor Corporation, [1979] 2 SCR 227.
Dagenais v Canadian Broadcasting Corp, [1994] 3 SCR 835.
Davey v Rur Mun Cornwallis, [1931] 2 DLR 80 (MB CA).

Deglman v Guaranty Trust Co of Canada and Constantineau, [1954] SCR 725.
Delgamuukw v British Columbia, [1997] 3 SCR 1010.
Deloitte & Touche v Livent Inc (Receiver of), 2017 SCC 63.
Delta Air Lines Inc v Lukács, 2018 SCC 2.
Demarco v Ungaro (1979), 95 DLR (3d) 385 (Ont HCJ).
Dobson (Litigation Guardian of) v Dobson, [1999] 2 SCR 753.
Donaldson v John Doe, 2009 BCCA 38.
Doré v Barreau du Québec, 2012 SCC 12.
Dr Q v College of Physicians and Surgeons of British Columbia, 2003 SCC 19.
Dube v Labar, [1986] 1 SCR 649.
Dunsmuir v New Brunswick, 2008 SCC 9.
Dutertre Manufacturing Inc v Palliser Regional Park Authority, 2012 SKQB 335.
EB v Order of the Oblates of Mary Immaculate in the Province of British Columbia, 2003 SCC 51.
EDG v Hammer, 2003 SCC 52.
Edmonton (City) v Edmonton East (Capilano) Shopping Centres Ltd, 2016 SCC 47.
Edmonton East (Capilano) Shopping Centres Limited v Edmonton (City), 2015 ABCA 85, 599 AR 210.
Edmonton East (Capilano) Shopping Centres Limited v Edmonton, 2013 ABQB 526, 570 AR 208.
Edwards v Attorney-General for Canada, [1930] AC 124 (PC).
Edwards v Law Society of Upper Canada, 2001 SCC 80.
Eliopoulos v Ontario (Minister of Health and Long Term Care) (2006), 82 OR (3d) 321 (CA).
Ermineskin Indian Band and Nation v Canada (AG), 2009 SCC 9.
Ernst v Alberta Energy Regulator, 2017 SCC 1.
Estok v Heguy (1963), 40 DLR (2d) 88 (BC SC).
Everard v Devereaux, 2004 NLSCTD 158.
Fidler v Sun Life Assurance Co of Canada, 2006 SCC 30.
Forestier SL Inc v Gestion Unibec Inc, 2017 QCCA 998.
Fraser River Pile & Dredge Ltd v Can-Dive Services Ltd, [1999] 3 SCR 108.
Fraser v Westminer Canada Ltd, 2003 NSCA 76.
Frey v Fedoruk, [1950] SCR 517.
Gari Holdings Ltd v Langham Credit Union Ltd, 2005 SKCA 97.
Garland v Consumers' Gas Co, 2004 SCC 25.
Ghanati v Chemist Holdings Ltd, 2017 BCSC 1921.
Gill Tech Framing Ltd v Gill, 2012 BCSC 1913.
Groia v Law Society of Upper Canada, 2018 SCC 27.
Haida Nation v British Columbia (Minister of Forests), 2004 SCC 73.
Hall v Hebert, [1993] 2 SCR 159.
Halvorson v British Columbia (Medical Services Commission), 2001 BCSC 632.
Hamelin v Mousseau, 2018 ONSC 276.

Harrison v Carswell, [1976] 2 SCR 200.
Harvey v New Brunswick (AG), [1996] 2 SCR 876.
Henderson (Trustee of) v Pitters, 2014 ONSC 6227.
Henry v British Columbia (AG), 2015 SCC 24.
Hercules Managements v Ernst & Young, [1997] 2 SCR 165.
Hill v Hamilton-Wentworth Police Services Board, 2007 SCC 41.
Hollis v Dow Corning, [1995] 4 SCR 634.
Holowaychuk v Lopushinsky, 2015 ABQB 63.
Honda Canada Inc v Keays, 2008 SCC 39.
Horch v Horch, 2017 MBCA 97.
Hunter Engineering Co v Syncrude Canada Ltd, [1989] 1 SCR 426.
Hutterian Brethren of Wilson Colony v Alberta, 2009 SCC 37.
Idle-O Apartments Inc v Charlyn Investments Ltd, 2013 BCSC 2158.
Idle-O Apartments Inc v Charlyn Investments Ltd, 2014 BCCA 451.
Indutech Canada Ltd v Gibbs Pipe Distributors Ltd, 2011 ABQB 38.
Ivic v Lakovic, 2017 ONCA 446.
Jacobi v Griffiths, [1999] 2 SCR 570.
Jarrett v Halifax (Regional Municipality), 2014 NSSC 116.
JH v Windsor Police Services Board et al, 2017 ONSC 6507.
Jin v Ren, 2015 ABQB 115.
John Doe v Bennett, 2004 SCC 17.
Just v British Columbia (1985), 64 BCLR 349 (SC).
Just v British Columbia, [1989] 2 SCR 1228.
Kamloops v Neilson, [1984] 2 SCR 2.
Kanthasamy v Canada (Citizenship and Immigration), 2015 SCC 61.
Kerr v Baranow; Vanasse v Seguin, 2011 SCC 10.
Khadr v Canada (Prime Minister), 2009 FCA 246.
Kindler v Canada, [1991] 2 SCR 779.
Kingstreet Investments Ltd v New Brunswick (Department of Finance), 2007 SCC 1.
KLB v British Columbia, 2003 SCC 51.
Lac Minerals Ltd v International Corona Resources Ltd, [1989] 2 SCR 574.
Lakin v Nuttal (1879), 3 SCR 685.
Law Society of British Columbia v Trinity Western University, 2018 SCC 32.
Law Society of New Brunswick v Ryan, 2003 SCC 20.
Leslie v Ball (1863), 22 UCQB 522 (Upper Canada Queen's Bench).
Loewen v Manitoba Teachers' Society, 2015 MBCA 13.
London Drugs Ltd v Kuehne & Nagel International Ltd, [1992] 3 SCR 299.
Loranger v Haines (1921), 50 OLR 268 (CA).
Los Angeles Salad Company v Canadian Food Inspection Agency, 2013 BCCA 34.
Love v Schumacher Estate, 2014 ONSC 4080.
Loyola High School v Quebec (Attorney General), 2015 SCC 12.
MacLellan v Morash, 2006 NSSC 101.

Magical Waters Fountain Ltd v Sarnia (City) (1990), 74 OR (2d) 682 (Ont GD).
Magical Waters Fountain Ltd v Sarnia (City) (1992), 8 OR (3d) 689 (CA).
Malette v Shulman (1987), 47 DLR (4th) 18 (Ont HCJ).
Malik (Estate of) v State Petroleum Corp, 2009 BCCA 505.
Martel Building Ltd v Canada, 2000 SCC 60.
Matheson v Smiley, [1932] 2 DLR 787 (MB CA).
McKay v Toronto Police Services Board, 2011 HRTO 499.
McKeown v Cavalier Yachts Pty Ltd (1988), 13 NSWLR 303 (SC).
McLean v British Columbia (Securities Commission), 2013 SCC 67.
Middlesex Condominium Corp 229 v WMJO Ltd, 2015 ONSC 3879.
Minister of Citizenship and Immigration v Alexander Vavilov, 2018 CanLII 40807 (SCC).
Mitchell v MNR, 2001 SCC 33.
Moncton (City) v Stephen (1956), 5 DLR (2d) 722 (NBSC (AD)).
Moore v Sweet, 2017 ONCA 182.
Mouvement laïque québécois v Saguenay (City), 2015 SCC 16.
Mugesera v Canada (Minister of Citizenship and Immigration), 2005 SCC 40.
Multani v Commission scolaire Marguerite-Bourgeoys, 2006 SCC 6.
Murdoch v Murdoch, [1975] 1 SCR 423.
Murphy v MacDonald, 2009 PESC 30.
Mustapha v Culligan of Canada Ltd, 2008 SCC 27.
Myers v Peel County Board of Education, [1981] 2 SCR 21.
National Football League, et al v Attorney General of Canada, 2018 CanLII 40806 (SCC).
New Brunswick Broadcasting Co v Nova Scotia (Speaker of the House of Assembly), [1993] 1 SCR 319.
Newfoundland and Labrador Nurses' Union v Newfoundland and Labrador (Treasury Board), 2011 SCC 62.
Niles v Lake, [1947] SCR 291.
Non-Marine Underwriters, Lloyd's of London v Scalera, 2000 SCC 24.
Norberg v Wynrib, [1992] 2 SCR 226.
Nunavut Tunngavik Inc v Canada (AG), 2012 NUCJ 11.
Olchowy v McKay, [1996] 1 WWR 36 (Sask QB).
Paradis Honey Ltd v Canada, 2015 FCA 89.
Pasiechnyk v Saskatchewan (Workers' Compensation Board), [1997] 2 SCR 890.
Pearce v Diensthuber (1977), 17 OR (2d) 401 (CA).
Pecore v Pecore, 2007 SCC 17.
Peel (Regional Municipality) v Canada, [1992] 3 SCR 762.
Pembina County Water Resource District v Manitoba, 2008 FC 1390.
Peter v Beblow, [1993] 1 SCR 980.
Pettkus v Becker, [1980] 2 SCR 834.
Pezim v British Columbia (Superintendent of Brokers), [1994] 2 SCR 557.

Porteous v Nuekomm, 2015 BCSC 1171.
Price Waterhouse Coopers v Bank of Montreal, 2017 NLTD(G) 43.
Pushpanathan v Canada (Minister of Citizenship and Immigration), [1998] 1 SCR 982.
Quebec (AG) v A, 2013 SCC 5.
R v ADH, 2013 SCC 28.
R v B(KG), [1993] 1 SCR 740.
R v Baldree, 2013 SCC 35.
R v Barton, 2019 SCC 33.
R v Bradshaw, 2017 SCC 35.
R v Buric, [1997] 1 SCR 535.
R v Butler, [1992] 1 SCR 452.
R v Cairney, 2013 SCC 55.
R v Comeau, 2018 SCC 15.
R v Corbett, [1988] 1 SCR 670.
R v Creighton, [1993] 3 SCR 3.
R v Cuerrier, [1998] 2 SCR 371.
R v DAI, 2012 SCC 5.
R v Darrach, 2000 SCC 46.
R v DLW, 2016 SCC 22.
R v Drapeau (1995), 37 CR (4th) 180 (QC CA).
R v Ewanchuk, [1999] 1 SCR 330.
R v Finta, [1994] 1 SCR 701.
R v Gladue, [1999] 1 SCR 688.
R v Goldfinch, 2019 SCC 38.
R v Grant, 2009 SCC 32.
R v Grant, 2015 SCC 9.
R v Greenwood (1991), 5 OR (3d) 71 (ON CA).
R v Greyeyes, [1997] 2 SCR 825.
R v Handy, 2002 SCC 56.
R v Hart, 2014 SCC 52.
R v Hasselwander, [1993] 2 SCR 398.
R v Henry, 2005 SCC 76.
R v Hinchey, [1996] 3 SCR 1128.
R v Hutchinson, 2014 SCC 19.
R v Imperial Tobacco Canada Ltd, 2011 SCC 42.
R v Ipeelee, 2012 SCC 13.
R v JA, 2011 SCC 28.
R v Javanmardi, 2019 SCC 54.
R v Jobidon, [1991] 2 SCR 714.
R v Katigbak, 2011 SCC 48.
R v Keegstra, [1990] 3 SCR 697.

R v Khan, [1990] 2 SCR 531.
R v Khelawon, 2006 SCC 57
R v Labaye, 2005 SCC 80.
R v Lavallee, [1990] 1 SCR 852.
R v Le, 2019 SCC 34.
R v Lloyd, 2016 SCC 13.
R v Mabior, 2012 SCC 47.
R v Mack, [1988] 2 SCR 903.
R v Maddeaux, 33 OR (3d) 378 (ON CA).
R v Malmo-Levine; R v Caine, 2003 SCC 74.
R v Mapara, 2005 SCC 23.
R v Marshall (1983), 57 NSR (2d) 286 (NS CA).
R v Marshall, [1999] 3 SCR 456.
R v Martineau, [1990] 2 SCR 633.
R v McIntosh, [1995] 1 SCR 686.
R v McLaughlin, [1980] 2 SCR 331.
R v Mezzo, [1986] 1 SCR 802.
R v Mohan, [1994] 2 SCR 9.
R v Morgentaler, [1988] 1 SCR 30.
R v Mugford (1990), 58 CCC (3d) 172 (NL CA).
R v Murdock (2003), 11 CR (6th) 43 (ON CA).
R v Nicol, 2002 MBCA 151.
R v Nur, 2015 SCC 15.
R v Oakes, [1986] 1 SCR 103.
R v Olan, [1978] 2 SCR 1175.
R v Paré, [1987] 2 SCR 618.
R v Parks (1993), 15 OR (3d) 324, 84 CCC (3d) 353 (ON CA).
R v Robinson, 2009 ONCA 205.
R v Ruzic, 2001 SCC 24.
R v Salituro, [1991] 3 SCR 654.
R v Saroya (1992), 36 CR (4th) 253, 76 OAC 25 (ON CA).
R v Saskatchewan Wheat Pool, [1983] 1 SCR 205.
R v Seaboyer; R v Gayme, [1991] 2 SCR 577.
R v Sharpe, 2001 SCC 2.
R v Shearing, 2002 SCC 58.
R v Smith, [1992] 2 SCR 915.
R v Spence, 2005 SCC 71.
R v Starr, 2000 SCC 40.
R v Tener, [1985] 1 SCR 533.
R v Théroux, [1993] 2 SCR 5.
R v Thibert, [1996] 1 SCR 37.
R v Tran, 2010 SCC 58.

R v Vaillancourt, [1987] 2 SCR 636.
R v Van Der Peet, [1996] 2 SCR 507.
R v W(R), [1992] 2 SCR 122.
R v Williams, [1998] 1 SCR 1128.
R c Zlatic (1991), 65 CCC (3d) 86, 1991 CanLII 3555 (QC CA).
R v Zlatic, [1993] 2 SCR 29.
R v Zundel, [1992] 2 SCR 731.
Rankin (Rankin's Garage & Sales) v JJ, 2018 SCC 19.
Rathwell v Rathwell, [1978] 2 SCR 436.
Rawluk v Rawluk, [1990] 1 SCR 70.
Re BC Motor Vehicle Act, [1985] 2 SCR 486.
Re Drummond Wren, [1945] OR 778 (ON SC).
Re Gareau Estate (1995), 9 ETR (2d) 25 (Ont Ct J (Gen Div)).
Re Noble and Wolf, [1948] OR 579 (ON SC).
Ready v Saskatoon Regional Health Authority, 2017 SKCA 20.
Reference re Assisted Human Reproduction Act, 2010 SCC 61.
Reference re Remuneration of Judges of the Provincial Court of Prince Edward Island, [1997] 3 SCR 3.
Reference re Same-Sex Marriage, 2004 SCC 79.
Reference re Supreme Court Act, ss 5 and 6, 2014 SCC 21.
Reference re Validity of Section 5(a) of the Dairy Industry Act, [1949] SCR 1.
Resurfice Corp v Hanke, 2007 SCC 7.
Rio Tinto Alcan Inc v Carrier Sekani Tribal Council, 2010 SCC 43.
RJR-MacDonald Inc v Canada, [1995] 3 SCR 199.
Roda v Toronto Police Services Board, 2016 ONSC 743, aff'd 2017 ONCA 768.
Rodriguez v British Columbia (AG), [1993] 3 SCR 519.
Ross v British Columbia Lottery Corporation, 2014 BCSC 320.
Royal Bank v The King, [1931] 2 DLR 685 (MB QB).
RWDSU v Dolphin Delivery Ltd, [1986] 2 SCR 573.
Saadati v Moorhead, 2017 SCC 28.
Salna v Awad, 2011 ABCA 20.
Sanderson v Campsall, 2000 BCSC 583.
Sauvé v Canada (Chief Electoral Officer), 2002 SCC 68.
Schara Tzedeck v Royal Trust Co, [1953] 1 SCR 31.
Semelhago v Paramadevan, [1996] 2 SCR 415.
Servello v Servello, 2014 ONSC 5035.
Sharwood & Co v Municipal Financial Corp (2001), 53 OR (3d) 470 (CA).
Sherbeth v Sherbeth, 2007 MBQB 50.
Simonin v Simonin Estate, 2010 ONCA 900.
Smith v Alliance Pipeline Ltd., 2011 SCC 7.
Snell v Farrell, [1990] 2 SCR 311.
Sorochan v Sorochan, [1986] 2 SCR 38.

Soulos v Korkontzilas, [1997] 2 SCR 217.
Southcott Estates Inc v Toronto Catholic District School Board, 2012 SCC 51.
Stevested Machinery & Engineering Ltd v Metso Paper Ltd, 2014 BCCA 91.
Stewart v Pettie, [1995] 1 SCR 131.
Sullivan v Lee (1994), 95 BCLR (2d) 195 (SC).
Swinamer v Nova Scotia, [1994] 1 SCR 445.
Syl Apps Secure Treatment Centre v BD, 2007 SCC 38.
Tang v Jarrett (2009), 251 OAC 123 (Ont Sup Ct (Div Ct)).
Tataryn v Tataryn, [1994] 2 SCR 807.
Taylor v Canada (AG), 2012 ONCA 479.
Tercon Contractors Ltd v British Columbia (Transportation and Highways), 2010 SCC 4.
Tervita Corp v Canada (Commissioner of Competition), 2015 SCC 3.
Teva Canada Ltd v TD Canada Trust, 2017 SCC 51.
Toronto (City) v CUPE, Local 79, 2003 SCC 63.
Trial Lawyers Association of British Columbia v British Columbia (AG), 2014 SCC 59.
Trinity Western University v Law Society of Upper Canada, 2018 SCC 33.
Tsilqot'in Nation v British Columbia, 2014 SCC 44.
UES, Local 298 v Bibeault, [1988] 2 SCR 1048.
United States v Burns, 2001 SCC 7.
Vancouver (City) v Ward, 2010 SCC 27.
Wade v Ball (1870), 20 UCCP 302 (Upper Canada Court of Common Pleas).
Walford v Jacuzzi Canada Ltd (2007), 2007 ONCA 729.
Watkins v Olafson, [1989] 2 SCR 750.
Webster v Robbins Parking Service Ltd, 2016 BCSC 1863.
West Fraser Mills Ltd v British Columbia (Workers' Compensation Appeal Tribunal), 2018 SCC 22.
Williams Lake Indian Band v Canada (Aboriginal Affairs and Northern Development), 2018 SCC 4.
Williams v Toronto (City), 2016 ONCA 666.
Wilson v Atomic Energy of Canada Ltd, 2016 SCC 29.
Winnipeg Child and Family Services (Northwest Area) v G (DF), [1997] 3 SCR 925.
Winnipeg Condominium Corp No. 36 v Bird Construction, [1995] 1 SCR 85.

V. Jurisprudence: International

AFLS v Hills Industries Limited & Anor, [2014] HCA 14.
Agip (Africa) Ltd v Jackson, [1990] 1 EWCA Civ 2.
Allen v Flood, [1898] 1 AC 1 (HL).
Anns v Merton LBC, [1977] UKHL 4, [1978] AC 728.
Armes v Nottinghamshire County Council, [2017] UKSC 60.

Bank Mellat v Her Majesty's Treasury, [2013] UKSC 39.
Benedetti v Sawiris, [2013] UKSC 50.
Bookmakers' Afternoon Greyhound Services Ltd v Gilbert, [1994] FSR 723 (Ch).
Brooks v Commissioner of Police for the Metropolis, [2005] UKHL 24.
Chamberlains v Lai, [2006] NZSC 70.
Chief Constable of Greater Manchester Police v Wigan Athletic AFC Ltd, [2008] EWCA 1449.
Cox v Ministry of Justice, [2016] UKSC 10.
Cran v New South Wales (2004), 62 NSWLR 95 (CA).
Craven-Ellis v Canons Ltd, [1936] 2 KB 403 (CA).
David Securities Pty Ltd v Commonwealth Bank of Australia, (1992) 175 CLR 353 (HCA).
de Freitas v Permanent Secretary of the Ministry of Agriculture, Fisheries, Lands and Housing, [1999] 1 AC 69 (PC).
Donoghue v Stevenson, [1932] AC 562 (HL).
Dunlea v Attorney-General, [2000] NZCA 84, [2000] 3 NZLR 136.
Egerton v Brownlow, (1853) 4 HLC 1 (HL).
El Ajou v Dollar Land Holdings plc, [1993] EWCA Civ 4.
Elguzouli-Daf v Commissioner of Police of the Metropolis, [1995] QB 335 (Eng CA).
Escola v Coca Cola Bottling Co of Fresno, 150 P 2d 436 (Cal Sup Ct 1944).
Everett v Griffiths, [1921] 1 AC 631 (HL).
Falcke v Scottish Imperial Insurance Co, (1886) 34 Ch 234 (CA).
Fibrosa Spolka Akcyjna v Fairbairn Lawson Combe Barbour Ltd, [1942] UKHL 4.
Glanzer v Shepard, 135 NE 275 (NY CA 1922).
Greenman v Yuba Power Products, 59 Cal 2d 57 (Sup Ct 1963).
Haley v London Electricity Board, [1964] 3 WLR 479 (EW CA).
Harrison v Madejski, [2014] EWCA Civ 361.
Hill v Chief Constable of West Yorkshire, [1989] 1 AC 53 (HL).
Hills v Snell, 104 Mass 173 (Mass Sup Jud Ct 1870).
Home Office v Dorset Yacht Co Ltd, [1970] AC 1004 (HL).
Hounga v Allen, [2014] UKSC 47, [2014] 1 WLR 2889.
Huang v Secretary of State for the Home Department, [2007] UKHL 11.
Indiana Lumbermans Mutual Insurance Co v Reinsurance Results Inc, 513 F (3d) 652 at 656 (7th Cir Ct 2008).
Investment Trust Companies v Revenue and Customs Commissioners, [2017] UKSC 29.
Jetivia SA v Bilta (UK) Ltd, [2015] UKSC 23.
JS Hall and Co v Simons, [2000] 3 WLR 543 (HL).
Kelly v Solari, (1841) 9 M & W 54, 152 ER 24 (Exch).
Kleinwort Benson Ltd v Lincoln City Council, [1999] 2 AC 349 (HL).
Les Laboratoires Servier v Apotex Inc, [2014] UKSC 55.
Lipkin Gorman (a firm) v Karpnale Ltd, [1988] UKHL 12.

Lister v Hesley Hall, [2001] UKHL 22.
Littlewoods Ltd v HMRC, [2017] UKSC 70.
Lumbers v W Cook Builders Pty Ltd (in liquidation), [2008] HCA 27.
Michael v The Chief Constable of South Wales Police, [2015] UKSC 2.
Mohamud v WM Morrison Supermarkets plc, [2016] UKSC 11.
Moses v Macferlan, (1760) 2 Burr 1005, 97 ER 676 (KB).
Overseas Tankship (UK) Ltd v The Miller SS Co Pty Ltd, [1967] 1 AC 617, (*sub nom Wagon Mound (No 2)*).
Patel v Mirza, [2016] UKSC 42.
People v Stark, 26 Cal App 4th 1179 (Ct App1994).
Prudential Assurance Co Ltd v HMRC, [2018] UKSC 39.
R v A, [2001] UKHL 25.
R v Case (1850), 1 Den 580, 169 ER 281 (EW CA).
R v Charles, [1976] 1 WLR 248.
R v Charles, [1977] AC 177 (UK).
R v Clarence (1888), 22 QBD 23 (UK).
R v Flattery (1877), 2 QBD 410 (UK).
R (C) v Secretary of State for Work and Pensions, [2017] UKSC 72.
R (Lord Carlile of Berriew) v Secretary of State for the Home Department, [2014] UKSC 60.
Robinson v Chief Constable of West Yorkshire Police, [2018] UKSC 4.
Roy v Lagona, [2010] VSC 250.
Royal Brunei Airlines Sdn Bhd v Tan, [1995] UKPC 4.
Sempra Metals Ltd v IRC, [2007] UKHL 34.
Skilling v United States, 561 US 358 (2010).
Smith v Chief Constable of Sussex Police, [2008] UKHL 50.
Stovin v Wise, [1996] AC 923 (HL).
Sutherland Shire Council v Heyman, [1985] 50 ALR 1, 157 CLR 424 (HCA).
Taylor v Laird, (1856) 25 LJ Ex 329.
Thomas v Thomas, (1842) 2 QB 851 (UK).
Tinsley v Milligan, [1993] UKHL 3.
Ultramares Corporation v Touche, 174 NE 441 (NY CA 1932).
Various Claimants v Catholic Child Welfare Society, [2012] UKSC 56.
Various claimants v Giambrone & Law (a firm), [2017] EWCA Civ 1193, [2018] PNLR 2 (CA (Eng & Wales) (Civ Div)).
Whitlock v Moree, [2017] UKPC 44.
Yates v United States, 574 US 528 (2015).

VI. Secondary Materials: Speeches

McLachlin, Beverley. "Administrative Tribunals and the Courts: An Evolutionary Relationship" (Remarks delivered at the 6th Annual

Conference of the Council of Canadian Administrative Tribunals, Toronto, 27 May 2013), online: <https://www.scc-csc.ca/judges-juges/spe-dis/bm-2013-05-27-eng.aspx>.

– "Canada's Legal System at 150: Democracy and the Judiciary" (Speech delivered at the Empire Club of Canada, 3 June 2016), online: <https://www.scc-csc.ca/judges-juges/spe-dis/bm-2016-06-03-eng.aspx>.

– "The Challenge of Fighting Terrorism While Maintaining Our Civil Liberties" (Remarks delivered at the Ottawa Women's Canadian Club, Ottawa, 22 September 2009), online: <https://www.scc-csc.ca/judges-juges/spe-dis/bm-2009-09-22-eng.aspx>.

– "The Decline of Democracy and the Rule of Law: How to Preserve the Rule of Law and Judicial Independence" (Remarks delivered at the Saskatchewan and Manitoba Courts of Appeal Joint Meeting, Saskatoon, 28 September 2017), online: <https://www.scc-csc.ca/judges-juges/spe-dis/bm-2017-09-28-eng.aspx>.

– "Defining Moments: The Canadian Constitution" (Remarks delivered at the Dickson Lecture, Ottawa, 13 February 2014), online: <https://www.scc-csc.ca/judges-juges/spe-dis/bm-2014-02-13-eng.aspx>.

– "Globalization, Identity and Citizenship" (Remarks delivered at the ADM Forum in Ottawa, Ontario, 26 October 2004), online: <https://www.scc-csc.ca/judges-juges/spe-dis/bm-2004-10-26-eng.aspx>.

– "The Impact of the Supreme Court of Canada on Bilingualism and Biculturalism" (Remarks delivered at the Constitutional Law Week Speaker Series, McGill University, 6 February 2008), online: <https://www.scc-csc.ca/judges-juges/spe-dis/bm-2008-02-06-eng.aspx>.

– "Judicial Accountability" (Remarks delivered at the Conference on Law and Parliament in Ottawa, Ontario, 2 November 2006), online: <https://www.scc-csc.ca/judges-juges/spe-dis/bm-2006-11-02-eng.aspx>.

– "Judicial Independence" (Remarks delivered at the 300th Anniversary of the Act of Settlement Conference in Vancouver, 11 May 2001), online: <https://www.scc-csc.ca/judges-juges/spe-dis/bm-2001-05-11-eng.as>.

– "Medicine and the Law: The Challenges of Mental Illness" (Remarks delivered at the 2004 Honourable Mr Justice Michael O'Byrne/AHFMR, University of Alberta and University of Calgary, 17–18 February 2005), online: <https://www.scc-csc.ca/judges-juges/spe-dis/bm-2005-02-17-eng.aspx>.

– "Reconciling Unity and Diversity in the Modern Era: Tolerance and Intolerance" (Remarks delivered at the Annual Pluralism Lecture 2015, Aga Khan Museum), online: <https://www.pluralism.ca/wp-content/uploads/2017/10/APL2015_BeverleyMcLachlin_Lecture.pdf>.

– "The Relationship between the Courts and the Media" (Remarks delivered at Carleton University, 31 January 2012), online: <https://www.scc-csc.ca/judges-juges/spe-dis/bm-2012-01-31-eng.aspx>.

– "Remarks to the Council of the Canadian Bar Association at the Canadian Legal Conference" (Canadian Legal Conference, Ottawa, 11 August 2016), online: <https://www.scc-csc.ca/judges-juges/spe-dis/bm-2016-08-11-eng.aspx>.

– "The Role of Judges in Modern Society" (Remarks delivered at the Fourth Worldwide Common Law Judiciary Conference, Vancouver, 5 May 2001), online: <https://www.scc-csc.ca/judges-juges/spe-dis/bm-2001-05-05-eng.aspx>.

– "Second International Conference on the Training of the Judiciary" (Remarks delivered in Ottawa, 1 November 2004), online: <https://www.scc-csc.ca/judges-juges/spe-dis/bm-2004-11-01-eng.aspx>.

– "The Supreme Court of Canada" (Remarks delivered at the Mayor's Breakfast Series, Ottawa, 25 November 2014), online: <https://www.scc-csc.ca/judges-juges/spe-dis/bm-2014-11-25-eng.aspx>.

– "Unwritten Constitutional Principles: What Is Going On?" (Remarks given at the 2005 Lord Cooke Lecture, Wellington, New Zealand, 1 December 2005), online: <https://www.scc-csc.ca/judges-juges/spe-dis/bm-2005-12-01-eng.aspx>.

VII. Secondary Materials: Books and Book Chapters

Alexander, Michelle. *The New Jim Crow: Mass Incarceration in the Age of Colorblindness* (New York: New Press, 2010).

Allan, TRS. "Constitutional Justice and the Concept of Law" in Grant Huscroft, ed, *Expounding the Constitution: Essays in Constitutional Theory* (Cambridge: Cambridge University Press, 2008) 219.

– "Text, Context, and Constitution: The Common Law as Public Reason" in Douglas E Edlin, ed, *Common Law Theory* (Cambridge: Cambridge University Press, 2007) 185.

American Law Institute. *Restatement of the Law of Restitution: Quasi Contracts and Constructive Trusts* (St Paul: American Law Institute, 1937).

Ashworth, Andrew. *Principles of Criminal Law*, 4th ed (Oxford: Oxford University Press, 2003).

Backhouse, Constance. *Claire L'Heureux-Dubé: A Life* (Vancouver: UBC Press, 2017).

Bagshaw, Roderick. "Tort Law, Concepts and What Really Matters" in Andrew Robertson & Tang Hang Wu, eds, *The Goals of Private Law* (London: Hart Publishing, 2009) 239.

Beever, Allan. *Rediscovering the Law of Negligence* (Oxford: Hart Publishing, 2007).

Bentham, Jeremy. "Bentham's Draught for the Organization of judicial establishments, compared with that of the National Assembly, with a

commentary on the same" in Jeremy Bentham, *The Works of Jeremy Bentham*, vol 4 (1843).
– *Comment on the Commentaries and a Fragment on Government*, ed JH Burns & HLA Hart (London: Athlone Press, 1977).
– *Of Laws in General*, ed HLA Hart (London: Athlone Press, 1970).
Bernstein, R. *Economic Loss* (London: Longman, 1993).
Birks, Peter. "In Defence of Free Acceptance" in AS Burrows, ed, *Essays on the Law of Restitution* (Oxford: Clarendon, 1991) 105.
– *An Introduction to the Law of Restitution* (Oxford: Clarendon, 1985).
Blackstone, William. *Commentaries on the Laws of England*, vol 1 (New York, 1827).
Bodnár, Eszter. "Open Justice in the Digital Age: How Can ICT Enhance the Transparency of Constitutional Courts?" in Alexander Balthasar et al, eds, *Central and Eastern European e | Dem and e | Gov Days 2016. Multi-Level (e) Governance: Is ICT a Means to Enhance Transparency and Democracy?* (Vienna: Austrian Computer Society, 2016).
Bork, Robert H. *Coercing Virtue: The Worldwide Rule of Judges* (Toronto: Vintage, 2002).
Brown, Russell. *Pure Economic Loss in Canadian Negligence Law* (Toronto: LexisNexis, 2011).
Brudner, Alan. *The Unity of the Common Law: Studies in Hegelian Jurisprudence* (Berkeley and Los Angeles: University of California Press, 1995).
Brütt, Lorenz. *Die Kunst der Rechtsanwendung. Zugleich ein Beitrag zur Methodenlehre der Geisteswissenschaften* (Berlin: J. Guttentag, 1907).
Burns, JH & HLA Hart, eds. *Comment on the Commentaries and a Fragment on Government* (London: Athlone Press, 1977).
Canadian Judicial Council. *The Judicial Role in Public Information* (Canadian Judicial Council, September 1999).
Cardozo, Benjamin N. *The Nature of the Judicial Process* (New Haven, CT: Yale University Press, 1949).
Cartier, G. "The *Baker* Effect: A New Interface Between the *Canadian Charter of Rights and Freedoms* and Administrative Law – The Case of Discretion" in David Dyzenhaus, ed, *The Unity of Public Law* (Portland, OR: Hart, 2004) 61.
Chamberlain, Erika. "Negligent Investigation: Tort Law as Police Ombudsman" in Andrew Robertson & Tang Hang Wu, eds, *The Goals of Private Law* (London: Hart Publishing, 2009) 283.
Davis, Richard. "Symbiosis: The US Supreme Court and the Journalists Who Cover It" in Richard Davis & Davis Taras, eds, *Justices and Journalists: The Global Perspective* (Cambridge: Cambridge University Press, 2017).
Debenham, David. *The Law of Fraud and the Forensic Investigator*, 5th ed (Toronto: Thomson Reuters, 2016).
Deimling, Barbara. "The Courtroom: From Church Portal to Town Hall" in Wilfried Hartmann & Kenneth Pennington, eds, *The History of Courts and*

Procedure in Medieval Canon Law (Washington, DC: Catholic University of America Press, 2016).

Deshman, Abby & Nicole Myers. *Set-Up to Fail: Bail and the Revolving Door of Pre-Trial Detention* (Toronto: Canadian Civil Liberties Association, 2014).

Dicey, AV. *The Law of the Constitution*, 10th ed (London: Macmillan, 1959).

Dodek, Adam & Rosemary Cairns Way. "The Supreme Court of Canada and Appointment of Judges in Canada" in Peter Oliver, Patrick Macklem & Nathalie Des Rosiers, eds, *The Oxford Handbook of the Canadian Constitution* (Oxford: Oxford University Press, 2017).

Duff, RA & Stuart Green, eds. *Philosophical Foundations of Criminal Law* (Oxford: Oxford University Press, 2011).

Dworkin, Ronald. *Law's Empire* (Cambridge, MA: Harvard University Press, 1986).

– *Taking Rights Seriously* (Cambridge, MA: Harvard University Press, 1977).

Dyzenhaus, David. "The Incoherence of Constitutional Positivism" in Grant Huscroft, ed, *Expounding the Constitution: Essays in Constitutional Theory* (Cambridge: Cambridge University Press, 2008) 138.

– "The Rule of Law as the Rule of Liberal Principle" in Arthur Ripstein, ed, *Ronald Dworkin* (Cambridge: Cambridge University Press, 2007).

Edlin, Douglas E. "Introduction" in Douglas E Edlin, ed, *Common Law Theory* (Cambridge: Cambridge University Press, 2007).

–, ed. *Common Law Theory* (Cambridge: Cambridge University Press, 2007).

Ewert, J Douglas. *Criminal Fraud* (Toronto: Carswell, 1986).

Feldthusen, Bruce. "Ten Reasons to Reject Unique Public Duties of Care in Negligence" in Margaret Hall, ed, *The Canadian Law of Obligations: Private Law for the 21st Century and Beyond* (Toronto: LexisNexis, 2018) 25.

Finnis, John. *Natural Law and Natural Rights* (Oxford: Clarendon Press, 1980).

Fleming, John G. *The Law of Torts*, 2nd ed (Sydney, AU: Law Book Co, 1957).

Foster, Lorne et al. *Racial Profiling and Human Rights in Canada: The New Legal Landscape* (Toronto: Irwin Law, 2018).

Fridman, GHL. *Canadian Law of Torts*, 3rd ed (Toronto: Lexis Nexis, 2012).

– *The Law of Torts in Canada*, 2nd ed (Toronto: Carswell, 2002).

Fuller, Lon L. *The Morality of* Law (New Haven, CT: Yale University Press, 1969).

Gardner, John. "Some Types of Law" in Douglas E Edlin, ed, *Common Law Theory* (New York: Cambridge University Press, 2007) 51.

Goff, Robert & Gareth H Jones. *The Law of Restitution* (London: Sweet & Maxwell, 1966).

Goldsworthy, Jeffrey. "The Myth of the Common Law Constitution" in Douglas E Edlin, ed, *Common Law Theory* (Cambridge: Cambridge University Press, 2007) 204.

Gratton, SL & L Sossin. "In Search of Coherence: The *Charter* and Administrative Law under the McLachlin Court" in DA Wright & AM Dodek, eds, *Public Law at the McLachlin Court: The First Decade* (Toronto: Irwin Law, 2011).

Guth, DeLloyd J. "Method and Matter in the Gonthier Legacy: Legal History and Judgment Writing, 1989–2003" in Michel Morin et al, eds, *Responsibility, Fraternity and Sustainability in Law: In Memory of the Honourable Charles Doherty Gonthier* (Markham, ON: LexisNexis, 2012) 39.

Harada, Susan. "The 'Uncomfortable Embrace': The Supreme Court and the Media in Canada" in Richard Davis & Davis Taras, eds, *Justices and Journalists: The Global Perspective* (Cambridge: Cambridge University Press, 2017).

Herrero, Alvaro & Gaspar López. *Access to Information and Transparency in the Judiciary* (World Bank Institute Governance Working Paper Series, 2010).

Hill, S Casey, David M Tanovich & Louis P Strezos. eds, *McWilliams' Canadian Criminal Evidence*, 5th ed (Toronto: Thomson Reuters, 2018).

Hobbes, Thomas. *Dialogue between a Philosopher and a Student of the Common Laws of England*, ed Joseph Cropsey (Chicago: University of Chicago Press, 1971).

Hogg, Peter W. "The Duty to Consult and Accommodate Aboriginal Peoples" in Daniel Jutras & Marcus Moore, eds, *Canada's Chief Justice: Beverley McLachlin's Legacy of Law and Leadership* (Toronto: LexisNexis Canada, 2018).

– Patrick J Monahan & Wade K Wright. *Liability of the Crown*, 4th ed (Toronto: Carswell, 2011).

Husak, Douglas. *Overcriminalization: The Limits of the Criminal Law* (Oxford: Oxford University Press, 2008).

– *The Philosophy of Criminal Law: Selected Essays* (Oxford: Oxford University Press, 2010).

Huscroft, Grant, ed. *Expounding the Constitution: Essays in Constitutional Theory* (Cambridge: Cambridge University Press, 2008).

Jaconelli, Joseph. *Open Justice: A Critique of the Public Trial* (Oxford: Oxford University Press, 2002).

Jowell, J. "Administrative Law" in Vernon Bogdanor, ed, *The British Constitution in the Twentieth Century* (Oxford: Oxford University Press, 2003) 373.

Jutras, Daniel & Marcus Moore, eds. *Canada's Chief Justice: Beverley McLachlin's Legacy of Law and Leadership* (Toronto: LexisNexis Canada, 2018).

Kelemen, Katalin. *Judicial Dissent in European Constitutional Courts: A Comparative and Legal Perspective* (London and New York: Routledge, 2018).

L'Heureux-Dubé, Claire. *Claire L'Heureux-Dubé: A Life* (Vancouver: UBC Press, 2017).

Linden, Allen. "Torts Tomorrow: Empowering the Injured" in Nicholas Mullany & Allen Linden, eds, *Torts Tomorrow: A Tribute to John Fleming* (Sydney, AU: LBC Information Services, 1998) 321.

Liston, M. "Governments in Miniature: The Rule of Law in the Administrative State" in CM Flood & L Sossin, eds, *Administrative Law in Context*, 2nd ed (Toronto: Emond Montgomery, 2013).

Llewellyn, Karl N. *The Bramble Bush: On Our Law and Its Study* (New York: Oceana Publications, 1960).

Loughlin, Martin. *The Foundations of Public Law* (Oxford: Oxford University Press, 2010).

– *The Idea of Public Law* (Oxford: Oxford University Press, 2010).

Luntz, Harold. "The Use of Policy in Negligence Cases in the High Court of Australia" in Michael Bryan, ed, *Private Law in Theory and Practice* (London: Routledge-Cavendish, 2006) 55.

MacFarlane, Emmett. *Governing from the Bench: The Supreme Court of Canada and the Judicial Role* (Vancouver: UBC Press, 2013).

Macklin, A. "Standard of Review: Back to the Future?" in CM Flood & L Sossin, eds, *Administrative Law in Context*, 2nd ed (Toronto: Emond Montgomery, 2013).

Madden, M Stuart, ed. *Exploring Tort Law* (Cambridge: Cambridge University Press).

Mandel, M. *The Charter of Rights and the Legalization of Politics in Canada* (Toronto: Wall and Thompson, 1989).

Manfredi, Christopher P. *Judicial Power and the Charter: Canada and the Paradox of Liberal Constitutionalism* (Oxford: Oxford University Press, 2001).

Manning, Morris, Alan Mewett & Peter Sankoff. *Manning, Mewett & Sankoff on Criminal Law*, 5th ed (Markham, ON: LexisNexis, 2015).

Markesinis, BS, Laurie Ackermann, & Jorg Fedtke. *Judicial Recourse to Foreign Law: A New Source of Inspiration* (London: UCL Press, 2006).

Markovits, Daniel. *Contract Law and Legal Methods* (New York: Foundation Press, 2012).

Mayeda, Graham. "Between Principle and Pragmatism: The Decline of Principled Reasoning in the Jurisprudence of the McLachlin Court" in Sanda Rodgers & Sheila McIntyre, eds, *The Supreme Court of Canada and Social Justice: Commitment, Retrenchment or Retreat* (Markham, ON: LexisNexis, 2010) 41.

Mayeda, Graham & Peter Oliver. "Principles and Pragmatism: An Introduction" in Mayeda & Oliver, eds, *Principles and Pragmatism: Essays in Honour of Louise Charron* (Markham, ON: LexisNexis, 2014).

–, eds. *Principles and Pragmatism: Essays in Honour of Louise Charron* (Markham, ON: LexisNexis, 2014).

McInnes, Mitchell. *The Canadian Law of Unjust Enrichment and Restitution* (Markham, ON: LexisNexis, 2014).

McIntyre, Sheila. "The Equality Jurisprudence of the McLachlin Court: Back to the 70s" in Sanda Rodgers and Sheila McIntyre, eds, *The Supreme Court of Canada and Social Justice: Commitment, Retrenchment or Retreat* (Toronto: LexisNexis, 2010) 129.

McLachlin, Beverley. "4th Annual Lafontaine-Baldwin lecture" in Rudyard Griffiths, ed, *Dialogue on Democracy* (Toronto: Penguin Canada, 2006).

– "Aboriginal Peoples and Reconciliation" in Andrew Stockely & David Rowe, eds, *A Canadian Judgment: The Lectures of Chief Justice Beverley McLachlin in New Zealand, April 2003* (Christchurch: Centre for Commercial & Corporate Law, 2004).

– "Building a Bridge to Equality: A Duty for Lawyers" in Andrew Stockely & David Rowe, eds, *A Canadian Judgment: The Lectures of Chief Justice Beverley McLachlin in New Zealand, April 2003* (Christchurch: Centre for Commercial & Corporate Law, 2004).

– "The Evolution of the Law of Private Obligation: The Influence of Justice La Forest" in R Johnson & JP McEvoy, eds, *Gérald V. La Forest at the Supreme Court of Canada, 1985–1997* (Winnipeg: Supreme Court of Canada Historical Society, 2000).

– "On Impartiality" in Andrew Stockely & David Rowe, eds, *A Canadian Judgment: The Lectures of Chief Justice Beverley McLachlin in New Zealand, April 2003* (Christchurch: Centre for Commercial & Corporate Law, 2004).

Mensch, Elizabeth. "The History of Mainstream Legal Thought" in David Kairys, ed, *The Politics of Law: A Progressive Critique*, revised ed (New York: Pantheon Books, 1990).

Mill, JS. *On Liberty*, ed Geraint Williams (London: JM Dent & Sons, 1993).

Miller, MC. *Judicial Politics in the United States* (Boulder, CO: Westview, 2015).

Morin, Michel et al. *Responsibility, Fraternity and Sustainability in Law: In Memory of the Honourable Charles Doherty Gonthier* (Markham, ON: LexisNexis, 2012).

Morton, FL & Rainer Knopff. *The Charter Revolution and the Court Party* (Peterborough, ON: Broadview Pres, 2000).

Mullan, DJ. *Administrative Law* (Toronto: Irwin Law, 2001).

Pfaff, John F. *Locked In: The True Causes of Mass Incarceration and How to Achieve Real Reform* (New York: Basic Books, 2017).

Plunkett, James. *The Duty of Care in Negligence* (Oxford: Hart Publishing, 2018).

Pollock, F. *The Genius of the Common Law* (New York: Columbia University Press, 1912).

Posner, Richard A. *Economic Analysis of Law*, 4th ed (Boston: Little, Brown, 1992).

Postema, Gerald J. "*A Similibus ad Similia:* Analogical Thinking in Law" in Douglas E Edlin, ed, *Common Law Theory* (Cambridge: Cambridge University Press, 2007) 102.
– *The Oxford Handbook of Jurisprudence and Philosophy of Law* (Oxford: Oxford University Press, 2004).
Rawls, John. *A Theory of Justice* (Cambridge, MA: Harvard University Press, 1971).
Roach, Kent. *Criminal Law*, 6th ed (Toronto: Irwin Law, 2015).
– *The Supreme Court on Trial: Judicial Activism or Democratic Dialogue* (Toronto: Irwin Law, 2001).
Robertson, Andrew. "Constraints on Policy-Based Reasoning in Private Law" in Andrew Robertson & Tang Hang Wu, eds, *The Goals of Private Law* (London: Hart Publishing, 2009) 261.
– "Rights, Pluralism, and the Duty of Care" in Donal Nolan & Andrew Robertson, eds, *Rights and Private Law* (Oxford: Hart Publishing, 2012) 435.
Robertson, Andrew & Tang Hang Wu, eds. *The Goals of Private Law* (Oxford: Hart Publishing, 2009).
Rodgers, Sanda & Sheila McIntyre, eds. *The Supreme Court of Canada and Social Justice: Commitment, Retrenchment or Retreat* (Toronto: LexisNexis, 2010) 129.
Sandomierski, David. *Aspiration and Reality in Legal Education* (Toronto: University of Toronto Press, 2020).
Sauvageau, Florian, David Schneiderman & David Taras. *The Last Word: Media Coverage of the Supreme Court of Canada* (Vancouver: UBC Press, 2006).
Scherer, Joachim. *Gerichtsöffentlichkeit als Medienöffentlichkeit* (Hamburg: Athenäum, 1979).
Sharpe, Robert J & Kent Roach. *Brian Dickson: A Judge's Journey* (Toronto: University of Toronto Press, 2003).
Sheehy, Elizabeth A. "Equality and Supreme Court Criminal Jurisprudence: Never the Twain Shall Meet" in Sanda Rodgers and Sheila McIntyre, eds, *The Supreme Court of Canada and Social Justice: Commitment, Retrenchment or Retreat* (Toronto: LexisNexis, 2010) 329.
– *Sexual Assault in Canada: Law, Legal Practice, and Women's Activism* (Ottawa: University of Ottawa Press, 2012).
Spencer, Rachel. "Communication beyond the Judgments: The Australian High Court, Speaking for Itself, but Not Tweeting" in Richard Davis & Davis Taras, eds, *Justices and Journalists: The Global Perspective* (Cambridge: Cambridge University Press, 2017).
Stapleton, Jane. "Duty of Care Factors: A Selection from the Judicial Menus" in Jane Stapleton & Peter Cane, eds, *The Law of Obligations: Essays in Celebration of John Fleming* (Oxford: Clarendon Press, 1998).
Steiner, Eva. *French Law: A Comparative Approach* (Oxford: Oxford University Press, 2018).

Stevens, Robert. *Torts and Rights* (Oxford: Oxford University Press, 2007).
Stoner, James R Jr. "Natural Law, Common Law, and the Constitution" in Douglas E Edlin, ed, *Common Law Theory* (Cambridge: Cambridge University Press, 2007) 171.
Stuart, Don. "Criminal Justice in the McLachlin Court: Many More Kudos than Brickbats" in David A Wright and Adam M Dodek, eds, *Public Law at the McLachlin Court: The First Decade* (Toronto: Irwin Law, 2011) 329.
– *Charter Justice in Canadian Criminal Law*, 4th ed (Toronto: Carswell, 2005).
Stuntz, William J. *The Collapse of American Criminal Justice* (Cambridge, MA: Harvard University Press, 2011.
Sullivan, Ruth. *Sullivan on the Construction of Statutes,* 5th ed (Toronto: LexisNexis, 2008).
– *Sullivan on the Construction of Statutes*, 6th ed (Toronto: LexisNexis 2014).
Sunstein, Cass R. *One Case at a Time: Judicial Minimalism and the Supreme Court* (Cambridge, MA: Harvard University Press, 1999).
Swan, Angela, Nicholas C Bala & Jakub Adamski. *Contracts: Cases, Notes and Materials*, 9th ed (Markham, ON: LexisNexis Canada, 2015).
Symington, Allison. "HIV Exposure as Assault: Progressive Development or Misplaced Focus?" in Elizabeth A Sheehy, ed, *Sexual Assault in Canada: Law, Legal Practice, and Women's Activism* (Ottawa: University of Ottawa Press, 2012) 635.
Tanovich, David M. "Regulating Inductive Reasoning in Sexual Assault Cases" in Benjamin L Berger, Emma Cunliffe & James Stribopoulos, eds, *To Ensure that Justice Is Done: Essays in Memory of Marc Rosenberg* (Toronto: Carswell, 2017) 73.
Thorburn, Malcolm. "Criminal Law as Public Law" in RA Duff & Stuart Green, eds, *Philosophical Foundations of Criminal* Law (Oxford: Oxford University Press, 2011) 21.
van Harten, G, G Heckman & David Mullan. *Administrative Law*, 6th ed (Toronto: Emond Montgomery, 2010).
Waddams, SM. *Principle and Policy in Contract Law: Competing or Complementary Concepts?* (Cambridge: Cambridge University Press, 2011).
Walters, Mark D. "Written Constitutions and Unwritten Constitutionalism" in Grant Huscroft, ed, *Expounding the Constitution: Essays in Constitutional Theory* (Cambridge: Cambridge University Press, 2008) 245.
Waluchow, Wilfrid J. *A Common Law Theory of Judicial Review: The Living Tree* (Cambridge:Cambridge University Press, 2007).
Watson, Alan. *The Digest of Justinian*, vol 1 (Philadelphia: University of Pennsylvania Press, 2009).
Weinrib, Ernest J. "The Disintegration of Duty" in M Stuart Madden, ed, *Exploring Tort Law* (Cambridge: Cambridge University Press) 143.
– *The Idea of Private Law* (Cambridge, MA: Harvard University Press, 1995).

Williams, Glanville & Dennis Baker. *Textbook of Criminal Law*, 3rd ed (London: Sweet & Maxwell, 2012).

Wright, David A & Adam M Dodek, eds. *Public Law at the McLachlin Court: The First Decade* (Toronto: Irwin Law, 2011).

VIII. Secondary Materials: Articles

Adams, Eric. "Reflecting a Chief Justice" (4 December 2017), online (blog): *Intl J Const L* <http://www.iconnectblog.com/2017/12/i-connect-symposium-the-legacy-of-chief-justice-beverley-mclachlin-reflecting-a-chief-justice>.

Alarie, Benjamin & Andrew James Green. "Policy Preference Change and Appointments to the Supreme Court of Canada" (2009) 47:1 Osgoode Hall LJ 1.

Allan, TRS. "The Moral Unity of Public Law" (2017) 67 UTLJ 1.

Bailey, SH & MJ Bowman. "The Policy/Operational Dichotomy: A Cuckoo in the Nest" (1986) 45:3 Cambridge LJ 430.

Beever, Allan. "A Rights-Based Approach to the Recovery of Economic Loss in Negligence" (2004) 4:1 Oxford Commonwealth LJ 25.

Bodnár, Eszter. "Gedanken über die Einführung der öffentlichen Verhandlung am ungarischen Verfassungsgericht" (2017) 63:1 Osteuroparecht.

Borrows, John. "Challenging Historical Frameworks: Aboriginal Rights, the Trickster, and Originalism" (2017) 98:1 Can Historical Rev 114.

Boyle, Christine. "Sexual Assault and the Feminist Judge" (1985) 1 CJWL 93.

Bredt, CD & E Krajewska. "*Doré*: All that Glitters Is Not Gold" (2014) 2d:67 SCLR 339.

Bryden, P. "Understanding the Standard of Review in Administrative Law" (2005) 54 UNBLJ 75.

Cairns Way, Rosemary. "Constitutionalizing Subjectivism: Another View" (1990) 79 CR (3d) 260.

Cappalli, RB. "At the Point of Decision: Common Law's Advantage over the Civil Law" (1998) 12:1 Temp Intl & Comp LJ 87.

Carodine, Montre D. "'The Mis-Characterization of the Negro': A Race Critique of the Prior Conviction Impeachment Rule" (2009) 84:2 Ind LJ 525.

Chamberlain, Erika. "Negligent Investigation: The End of Malicious Prosecution in Canada?" (2008) 124:2 Law Q Rev 205.

– "Negligent Investigation: Faint Hope for the Wrongly Accused?" (2011) 39:2 Adv Q 153.

Chartrand, Larry. "Eagle Soaring on the Emergent Winds of Indigenous Legal Authority" (2013) 18:1 Rev of Const Stud 49.

Cunliffe, Emma. "Open Justice: Concepts and Judicial Approaches" (2012) 40 Fed L Rev at 398.

Daly, P. "The *Dunsmuir* Decade/10 ans de *Dunsmuir*" (11 January 2018), online (blog): *Administrative Law Matters* <http://www.administrativelawmatters.com/blog/2018/01/11/the-dunsmuir-decade10-ans-de-dunsmuir/>.

– "*Dunsmuir*'s Flaws Exposed: Recent Decisions on Standard of Review" (2012) 58:2 McGill LJ 483.
– "Reasons and Reasonableness in Administrative Law: *Delta Air Lines Inc. v. Lukács*" (2018) 31:2 Can J Admin L & Prac 209.
– "Revisiting Dunsmuir: Food for Thought" (11 May 2018), online (blog): *Administrative Law Matters* <http://www.administrativelawmatters.com/blog/2018/05/11/revisiting-dunsmuir-food-for-thought/>.
– "The Scope and Meaning of Reasonableness Review" (2015) 52:4 Alta L Rev 799.
– "Struggling towards Coherence in Canadian Administrative Law? Recent Cases on Standard of Review and Reasonableness" (2016) 62:2 McGill LJ 527.
– "The Unfortunate Triumph of Form over Substance in Canadian Administrative Law" (2012) 50:2 Osgoode Hall LJ 317.
David, Lawrence. "The Face of an Institution: Beverley McLachlin's Reinvention of the Role of the Chief Justice of Canada" (7 December 2017), online (blog): *Intl J Const L* <http://www.iconnectblog.com/2017/12/david-on-Chief-Justice-McLachlin>.
– "Resource Allocation and Judicial Deference on Charter Review: The Price of Rights Protection According to the McLachlin Court" (2015) 73:1 UT Fac L Rev 35.
Dworkin, Ronald. "Law's Ambitions for Itself" (1985) 71:2 Virginia L Rev 176.
Dyzenhaus, David. "Process and Substance as Aspects of the Public Law Form" (2015) 74:2 Cambridge LJ 284.
Evans, JM. "*Dunsmuir*: Reflections of a Recovering Judge" (1 March 2018) online (blog): *Administrative Law Matters* <https://www.administrativelawmatters.com/blog/2018/03/01/dunsmuir-reflections-of-a-recovering-judge-hon-john-m-evans/>.
Feldthusen, Bruce. "Public Authority Immunity from Negligence Liability: Uncertain, Unnecessary, and Unjustified" (2014) 92:2 Can Bar Rev 211.
Ferguson, Gerry. "Self-Defence: Selecting the Applicable Provisions" (2000) 5 Can Crim L Rev 179.
Fine, Sean. "Harper Alleges Supreme Court Chief Justice Broke Key Rule with Phone Call" *Globe and Mail* (1 May 2014), online: <https://www.theglobeandmail.com/news/politics/harper-alleges-supreme-court-chief-justice-broke-key-rule-with-phone-call/article18382971/>.
– "How Beverley McLachlin Found Her Bliss: Where She Came From and What She Leaves Behind" *Globe and Mail* (12 January 2018), online: <https://www.theglobeandmail.com/news/national/beverley-mclachlin-profile/article37588525/>.
Fuller, L "Reason and Fiat in Case Law" (1945) 59 Harv L Rev 376.

– "What the Law Schools Can Contribute to the Making of Lawyers" (1948) 1 J Leg Educ 189.

Fuller, L & William R Perdue Jr. "The Reliance Interest in Contract Damages: 1" (1936) 46:1 Yale LJ 52.

Gautreau, JR Maurice. "When Are Enrichments Unjust?" (May 1989) 10:3 Adv Q 258.

Ginn, D. "New Words for Old Problems: The *Dunsmuir* Era" (2010) 37:3 Adv Q 317.

– "Some Initial Thoughts on *Wilson v. Atomic Energy of Canada Ltd and Edmonton (City) v. Edmonton East (Capilano) Shopping Centres Ltd*" (2017) 68 UNBLJ 285.

Girard, Philip. "The Making of the Canadian Legal Profession: A Hybrid Heritage" (2014) 21:2 Intl J Leg Profession 145.

Green, A. "Can There Be Too Much Context in Administrative Law? Setting the Standard of Review in Canadian Administrative Law" (2014) 47:2 UBC L Rev 469.

Gwyn, Richard. "Did Canada Really Commit 'Cultural Genocide'?" *Toronto Star* (8 June 2015), online: <https://www.thestar.com/opinion/commentary/2015/06/08/did-canada-really-commit-cultural-genocide-gwyn.html>.

Hardcastle, Lorian. "Government Liability for Negligence in the Health Sector: A Critique of the Canadian Jurisprudence" (2012) 37:2 Queen's LJ 525.

Harris, Nikos. "Justice for All: The Implications of *Hart* and *Hay* for *Vetrovec* Witnesses" (2015) 7th:22 Crim Reports 105.

Hart, HLA. "Bentham's *Of Laws in* General" (1971) Cambrian L Rev 24.

Heckman, GP. "Substantive Review in Appellate Courts since *Dunsmuir*" (2009) 47:4 Osgoode Hall LJ 751.

Hogg, PW & R Amarnath. "Why Judges Should Dissent" (2017) 67:2 UTLJ 126.

Holmes, Oliver Wendell. "The Path of the Law" (1997) 110:5 Harv L Rev 991.

Hughes, J, Vanessa MacDonnell & Karen Pearlston. "Equality and Incrementalism: The Role of Common Law Reasoning in Constitutional Rights Cases" (2013) 44:3 Ottawa L Rev 467.

Husak, Douglas. "The Criminal Law as a Last Resort" (2004) 24:2 Oxford J Leg Stud 207.

Iacobucci, Frank. "Some Reflections on *Re BC Motor Vehicle Act*" (2011) 42:3 Ottawa L Rev 305.

Iftene, Adelina. "The 'Hart' of the (Mr) Big Problem" (2016) 63 Crim LQ 178.

Janisch, H. "Something Old, Something New" (2010) 23:3 Can J Admin L & Prac 219.

Kari, Shannon. "SCC May Look at Vicarious Liability Again" *Law Times* (2 October 2017), online: <https://www.lawtimesnews.com/author/shannon-kari/scc-may-look-at-vicarious-liability-again-14736/>.

Kennedy, Duncan. "Form and Substance in Private Law Adjudication" (1976) 89:8 Harv L Rev 1685.

– "Politicizing the Classroom" (1995) 4 Rev L Women's Stud 84.

Kirkup, Kyle. "Releasing Stigma: Police, Journalists and Crimes of HIV Non-Disclosure" (2015) 46:1 Ottawa L Rev 129.

Klar, Lewis. "*R v Imperial Tobacco Ltd*: More Restrictions on Public Authority Tort Liability" (2012) 50:1 Alta L Rev 157.

– "*Syl Apps Secure Treatment Centre v BD:* Looking for Proximity within Statutory Provisions" (2007) 86:3 Can Bar Rev 337.

– "The Tort Liability of the Crown: Back to *Canada v Saskatchewan Wheat Pool*" (2007) 32:3 Adv Q 293.

Klein, Alana. "Criminal Law and the Counter-Hegemonic Potential of Harm Reduction" (2015) 38:2 Dal LJ 447.

Kloepfer, Stephen. "The Status of Strict Construction in Canadian Criminal Law" (1983) 15:3 Ottawa L Rev 553.

Kong, HL. "*Doré*, Proportionality and the Virtues of Judicial Craft" (2013) 2d:63 SCLR 501.

L'Heureux-Dubé, Claire. "The Dissenting Opinion: Voice of the Future?" (2000) 28:3 Osgoode Hall LJ 495.

Lewans, M. "Deference and Reasonableness since *Dunsmuir*" (2012) 38:1 Queen's LJ 59.

– "Renovating Judicial Review" (2017) 68 UNBLJ 109.

Luna, Erik. "The Overcriminalization Phenomenon" (2005) 54:3 Am U L Rev 703.

MacCharles, Tonda. "Stephen Harper Lashes Out at Top Judge on Supreme Court" *Toronto Star* (2 May 2014), online: <https://www.thestar.com/news/canada/2014/05/02/stephen_harper_lashes_out_at_top_judge_on_supreme_court.html>.

Macdonald, Roderick. "Comments" (1980) 58 Can B Rev 185.

Macfarlane, E. "Consensus and Unanimity at the Supreme Court of Canada" (2010) 52 SCLR.

Mayeda, Graham. "Uncommonly Common: The Nature of Common Law Judgment" (2006) 19:1 Can JL & Jur 107.

McBride, Nicholas J & Paul McGrath. "The Nature of Restitution" (1995) 15:1 Ox J Leg Stud 15 33.

McCormick, P. "Blocs, Swarms, and Outliers: Conceptualizing Disagreement on the Modern Supreme Court of Canada" (2004) 42 Osgoode Hall LJ 99.

– "The Choral Court: Separate Concurrence and the McLachlin Court, 2000–2004" (2005) 37:1 Ottawa L Rev 1.

McInnes, Mitchell. "Improvements to Land, Equity, Proprietary Estoppel, and Unjust Enrichment" (2016) 2:2 Can J Comparative & Contemporary L 421.

McLachlin, Beverley. "'Administrative Law Is Not for Sissies': Finding a Path through the Thicket" (June 2016) 29:2 Can J Admin L & Prac 127.

– "The Challenges We Face" (2007) 40 UBC L Rev 819.
– "The Charter 25 Years Later: The Good, the Bad, and the Challenges" (2007) 45 Osgoode Hall LJ 365.
– "Courts, Transparency and Public Confidence: To the Better Administration of Justice" (2003) 8:1 Deakin L Rev.
– "Judging the 'Vanishing Trial' in the Construction Industry" (2011) Spring Faulkner L Rev 2.2.
– "Keynote Address: The Use of Foreign Law – A Comparative View of Canada and the United States" *Proceedings of the Annual Meeting (American Society of International Law): International Law in a Time of Change*, vol 104 (2010)
– "Preserving Public Confidence in the Courts and the Legal Profession" (2002) 29 Man LJ 277.
– "Racism and the Law: The Canadian Experience" (2002) 1 JL & Equality 7.
– "Reflections on the Autonomy of Parliament" (2004) 27:1 Can Parliamentary Rev.
– "Le Rôle du Juge en Chef" (2002) 32 RGD 403.
– "The Supreme Court and the Public Interest" (2001) 64 Sask L Rev 309.

Monahan, PJ. "The Supreme Court of Canada in the 21st Century" (2001) 80 Can Bar Rev 374.

Morissette, YM. "What Is a 'Reasonable Decision'?" (2018) 31:3 Can J Admin L & Prac 225.

Mullan, DJ. "Administrative Tribunals and Judicial Review of Charter Issues after *Multani*" (2006) 21 NJCL 127.
– "The McLachlin Court and the Public Law Standard of Review: A Major Irritant Soothed or a Significant Ongoing Problem?" (2009) online (pdf): *Canadian Bar Association* <http://www.cba.org/cba/cle/PDF/Constit09_Mullan_paper.pdf>.
– "Unresolved Issues on Standard of Review in Canadian Judicial Review of Administrative Action: the Top Fifteen!" (2013) 42 Adv Q 1.

Murphy, John. "Rethinking Tortious Immunity for Judicial Acts." (2013) 33:3 LS 455.
– "Rights, Reductionism and Tort Law" (2008) 28:2 Oxford J Leg Stud 393.

Neyers, Jason W. "*Donoghue v Stevenson* and the Rescue Doctrine: A Public Justification of Recovery in Situations Involving the Negligent Supply of Dangerous Structures" (1999) 49:4 UTLJ 475.

Nova Scotia. *Royal Commission on the Donald Marshall, Jr, Prosecution: Digest of Findings and Recommendations* (Halifax: Canadian Cataloguing in Publication Data, 1989).

Ostberg, CL, Matthew E Wetstein & Craig R Ducat. "Attitudinal Dimensions of Supreme Court Decision Making in Canada: The Lamer Court, 1991–1995" (2002) 55:1 Political Research Q 235.

Pagliaro, Jennifer & Robert Benzie. "Ford Plans to Invoke Notwithstanding Clause for First Time in Province's History and Will Call Back Legislature on Bill 5" *Toronto Star* (10 September 2018), online: <https://www.thestar

.com/news/toronto-election/2018/09/10/superior-court-judge-strikes-down-legislation-cutting-the-size-of-toronto-city-council.html>.

Parkes, D. "Precedent Revisited: *Carter v. Canada (AG)* and the Contemporary Practice of Precedent" (2016) 10:1 McGill JL & Health 123.

Picard, André. "Countries, Including Canada, Are Prosecuting People with HIV Because They Misunderstand Science, Leading Researchers Say" *Globe and Mail* (27 July 2018), online <https://www.theglobeandmail.com/canada/article-countries-including-canada-are-prosecuting-people-with-hiv-because/>.

Resnik, Judith. "Access to Justice, Access to Knowledge, Economic Inequalities and Public Knowledge about Justice in Courts and in Arbitration" (2018) 96 NCL Rev.

Roach, Kent. "Mind the Gap: Canada's Different Criminal and Constitutional Standards of Fault" (2011) 61 UTLJ 545.

Roberts, Anna. "Impeachment by Unreliable Conviction" (2014) 55:2 Boston College L Rev 563.

– "Reclaiming the Importance of the Defendant's Testimony: Prior Conviction Impeachment and the Fight against Implicit Stereotyping" (2016) 83:2 U Chicago L Rev 835.

Robertson, Andrew. "Policy-based Reasoning in Duty of Care Cases" (2013) 33:1 LS 119.

Robertson, Grant & Tom Cardoso. "Canada's $1.1-Billion Problem: Regulators Dish Out Big Fines but Only Collect a Fraction" *Globe and Mail* (22 December 2017), online: <https://www.theglobeandmail.com/news/investigations/billion-dollars-unpaid-fines-white-collar-crime/article37416140/>.

Robertson, JT. "Identifying the Review Standard: Administrative Difference in a Nutshell" (2017) 68 UNBLJ 145.

Rogin, Jillian. "*Gladue* and Bail: The Pre-Trial Sentencing of Aboriginal People in Canada" (2017) 95:2 Can Bar Rev 325.

Russell, Peter H. "The Political Purposes of the Canadian Charter of Rights and Freedoms" (1983) 16:1 *Can Bar Rev* 30.

Sadler, Robert J. "Judicial and Quasi-Judicial Immunities: A Remedy Denied" (1982) 4:4 Melbourne UL Rev 508.

Safayeni, J. "The *Doré* Framework: Five Years Later, Four Key Questions (and Some Suggested Answers)" (2018) 31:1 Can J Admin L & Prac 31.

Sandomierski, David. "Catalytic Agents? Lon Fuller, James Milner, and the Lawyer as Social Architect, 1950–1969" (2021) 71 UTLJ 91.

Sankoff, Peter. "*Corbett*, Crimes of Dishonesty and the Credibility Contest: Challenging the Accepted Wisdom of What Makes a Prior Conviction Probative" (2006) 10:3 Can Crim L Rev 215.

– "*Corbett* Revisited: A Fairer Approach to the Admission of an Accused's Prior Criminal Record in Cross-Examination" (2006) 51:4 Crim LQ 400.

– "*R v Laing*: Two Major Steps Backward on *Corbett* Applications" (2017) 7th:33 Crim Reports 63.

Sapiano, Jenna. "Reconciliation and Recognition after 'Cultural Genocide': Beverley McLachlin's Use of Language" (7 December 2017) online (blog): *Intl J Const L* <http://www.iconnectblog.com/2017/12/sapiano-on-Chief-Justice-McLachlin>.

Schafer, Martha. "*Seaboyer v. R*: A Case Comment" (1992) 5 CJWL 202.

Schneiderman, David. "The Separation of Powers and Constitutional Balance at the McLachlin Court" (2018) 2d:86 SCLR 137.

Schuller, Regina A, & Marc A Klippenstine. "The Impact of Complainant Sexual History Evidence on Jurors' Decisions: Considerations for a Psychological Perspective" (2004) 10:3 Psych Pub Pol & Law 321.

Sellers, David A. "As Today's Tony Lewises Disappear, Courts Fill Void" (2014) 79:7 Mo L Rev 1024.

Shaffer, Martha. "Sex, Lies, and HIV: *Mabior* and the Concept of Sexual Fraud" (2013) 63:3 UTLJ 466.

Simpson, Jeffery. "The Court of No Resort" *Globe and Mail* (22 November 2002) A25.

Singer, Joseph William. "Legal Realism Now" (1988) 76:2 Cal L Rev 465.

Smith, Stephen. "Justifying the Law of Unjust Enrichment" (June 2001) 79:7 Tex L Rev 2083.

Smith, Stephen F. "Overcoming Overcriminalization" (2012) 102:3 J Crim L & Criminology 565.

Sossin, L. "The Complexity of Coherence: Justice LeBel's Administrative Law" (2015) 2d:70 SCLR 145.

– "Empty Ritual, Mechanical Exercise or the Discipline of Deference? Revisiting the Standard of Review in Administrative Law" (2003) 27:4 Adv Q 478.

Sossin, L & CM Flood. "The Contextual Turn: Iacobucci's Legacy and the Standard of Review in Administrative Law" (2007) 57:2 UTLJ 581.

Spigelman, JJ. "Seen to Be Done: The Principle of Open Justice – Part I" (2000) 74 Austl LJ 290.

Stratas, DW. "The Canadian Law of Judicial Review: A Plea for Doctrinal Coherence and Consistency" (2016) 42:1 Queen's LJ 27.

– "A Decade of *Dunsmuir*: Please No More" (8 May 2018), online (blog): *Administrative Law Matters* <http://www.administrativelawmatters.com/blog/2018/03/08/a-decade-of-dunsmuir-please-no-more-hon-david-w-stratas/>.

Strezos, Louis P. "Unreasonable Verdicts and Tainted Eyewitness Identification Evidence: Let's Start Thinking about Probative Value" (2018) 7th:47 Crim Reports 376.

Stribopoulos, James & Moin A Yahya. "Does a Judge's Party of Appointment or Gender Matter to Case Outcomes? An Empirical Study of the Court of Appeal for Ontario" (2007) 45:2 Osgoode Hall LJ 315.

Stuntz, William J. "The Pathological Politics of Criminal Law" (2001) 100:3 Mich L Rev 505.

Stürner, Rolf. "Gerichtsöffentlichkeit und Meidenöffentlichkeit in der Informationsgesellschaft. Das Bundesverfassungsgericht zwischen Liberalität und Zensur" (2001) 56:13 JuristenZeitung 699.

Sykes, Alan O. "The Boundaries of Vicarious Liability: An Economic Analysis of the Scope of Employment Rule and Related Legal Doctrines" (1988) 101:3 Harv LR 563.

Symington, Alison. "Injustice Amplified by HIV Non-Disclosure Ruling" (2013) 63:3 UTLJ 485.

Tamanaha, Brian Z. "The Dark Side of the Relationship between the Rule of Law and Liberalism" (2008) 3:3 NYUJ L & Liberty 516.

Tanovich, David M. "*Angelis*: Inductive Reasoning, Post-Offence Conduct and Intimate Femicide" (2013) 6th:99 Crim Reports 338.

– "*R v Hart*: A Welcome New Emphasis on Reliability and Admissibility" (2014) 7th:12 Crim Reports 298.

– "Safeguarding Trials from Racial Bias" (2 October 2018), online: *Policy Options*, <policyoptions.irpp.org/magazines/october-2018/safeguarding-trials-from-racial-bias/>.

Tofaris, Stelios & Sandy Steel. "Negligence Liability for Omissions and the Police" (2016) 75:1 Cambridge LJ 128.

Valcke, Catherine. "Quebec Civil Law and Canadian Federalism" (1996) 21 Yale J Intl L 67.

van Schouwen, Jasmine. "The King Can Still Do No Wrong: A Critical Perspective on the Crown's Private Law Duty of Care in Canada" (2016) 24 Tort L Rev 159.

Voyvodic, Rose. "Lawyers Meet the Social Context: Understanding Cultural Competence" (2005) 84:3 Can Bar Rev 563.

Waddams, SM. "Unconscionability in Contracts" (1976) 39:4 Mod L Rev 369.

Waldron, Jeremy. "The Core of the Case against Judicial Review" (2006) 115 Yale LJ 1346.

Walters, Mark D. "Public Law and Ordinary Legal Method: Revisiting Dicey's Approach to *Droit Administratif*" (2016) 66:1 UTLJ 53.

Warren, Marilyn. "Open Justice in the Technological Age" (2014) 40 Monash UL Rev 45.

Weinrib, Ernest J. "The Disintegration of Duty" (2006) 31:2 Adv Q 212.

– "The Gains and Losses of Corrective Justice" (November 1994) 44 Duke LJ 277.

Wihak, LJ. "Whither the Correctness Standard of Review? *Dunsmuir*, Six Years Later" (2014) 27:2 Can J Admin L & Prac 173.

Woolf, Harry Kenneth. "Droit Public: English Style" (1995) Public L 57.

Woolley, A & S Fluker. "What Has *Dunsmuir* Taught?" (2010) 47:4 Alta L Rev 1017.

Contributors

Eszter Bodnár is an associate professor in the Faculty of Law of Eötvös Loránd University in Budapest, Hungary. She is an expert on comparative constitutional law and she has written extensively on the judiciary of apex courts. She is also interested in human rights law, having written about the right to free elections and the right to transparent and open courts.

Erika Chamberlain is dean of the Faculty of Law of the University of Western Ontario. Chamberlain has authored numerous articles on tort law, with a particular focus on the tort liability of public authorities. She is the author of *Misfeasance in a Public Office* (2016), co-author of Fridman's *The Law of Torts in Canada*, 3rd ed (2010) and *Cases and Materials on the Law of Torts*, 9th ed (2015), and a co-editor of *Emerging Issues in Tort Law* (2007) and *Tort Law: Challenging Orthodoxy* (2013). She is the General Editor of the *Canadian Cases on the Law of Torts*.

Bruce Feldthusen is the former dean of the Faculty of Law, Common Law Section, of the University of Ottawa. Feldthusen is best known for his book *Economic Negligence*, a sixth edition of which was published in 2011. His analysis of pure economic loss has been adopted by the Supreme Court of Canada and now provides the organizing framework for all negligence actions in that field. He is also an author of the leading text *Canadian Tort Law*, which he co-authored with Justice Linden, and the case book *Canadian Tort Law*, which he co-authored with Justice Linden and Lewis Klar. He was one of the first legal academics in the world to study and write about civil remedies for victims of sexual assault. His multidisciplinary research in this area includes extensive interviewing and publication of how survivors themselves experience the legal compensation processes.

Adam Goldenberg is a partner with McCarthy Tetrault. His litigation practice encompasses trial and appellate advocacy in commercial cases, class actions, and public and administrative law matters, as well as in criminal and regulatory proceedings. He has acted as lead or co-counsel at all levels of court, including in twelve appeals to the Supreme Court of Canada. He also advises corporations, non-profit organizations, and executives on their legal obligations in the political sector, including about ethical compliance, conflicts of interest, election finance, political advertising, and lobbying law. He was a law clerk to Chief Justice Beverley McLachlin at the Supreme Court of Canada.

Matthew R. Gourlay is a partner at Henein Hutchison LLP in Toronto. He practises primarily in criminal and regulatory law, at both the trial and appellate level. He appears regularly in the Ontario Court of Appeal and the Supreme Court of Canada. He is vice-chair of the Pro Bono Inmate Appeal Program, which provides assistance to unrepresented litigants in the Ontario Court of Appeal. He is co-author of *Modern Criminal Evidence* (2021) and *Charter Remedies in Criminal Cases: A Practitioner's Handbook* (2019), and legal editor of *Canadian Criminal Cases*. He served as a law clerk to Chief Justice McLachlin from 2008 to 2009.

Vanessa Gruben is an associate professor in the Faculty of Law of the University of Ottawa. She was a law clerk for Chief Justice Richard of the Federal Court of Appeal and then Justice Bastarache of the Supreme Court of Canada. She joined the Faculty of Law of the University of Ottawa after graduating as a James Kent Scholar from Columbia University's Master of Laws program. Her research focuses on the legal regulation of various aspects of assisted human reproduction, including contractual disputes over frozen embryos, privacy and access to information, gamete donor anonymity, the regulation and funding of assisted reproductive technologies, and the constitutionality of the *Assisted Human Reproduction Act*. Her research also includes health law more generally as well as the protection of language rights in Canada. She is co-author ,with Mary Jane Mossman, Natasha Bakht, and Karen Pearlston, of the third edition of *Families and the Law: Cases and Commentary*.

Brenda Hale, Baroness Hale of Richmond, was President of the Supreme Court of the United Kingdom. She taught law at Manchester University from 1966 to 1984. She was the first woman appointed to the Law Commission of England and Wales, and during that time, she was involved in initiatives that resulted in important legislation such as the *Children Act 1989*, the *Family Law Act 1996*, and the *Mental Capacity Act 2005*. After sitting as a recorder, she was appointed to the High Court in 1994 and to the Court of Appeal in 1999. In 2004, she became the first and only woman appointed as a Law Lord, and, in 2009, the first woman appointed as a Justice of the Supreme Court. She became the President of the Supreme Court in 2017, retiring in January 2020.

Graham Mayeda joined the Faculty of Law at the University of Ottawa in 2005. His current research focuses on international trade and investment law, theories of global justice, law and development, criminal law, and legal philosophy. He is co-author, with Peter Oliver, of *Principles and Pragmatism: Essays in Honour of Louise Charron* (2014), and with J. Anthony Vanduzer and Penelope Simons, he has written *Integrating Sustainable Development into International Investment Agreements* (2013). He has also published two books in philosophy: *Time, Space and Ethics in the Philosophy of Watsuji Tetsurō, Kuki Shūzō and Martin Heidegger* (2006), and *Japanese Cultural and Social Philosophy: Nishida Kitarō, Watsuji Tetsurō and Kuki Shūzō* (2020).

Mitchell McInnes's research focuses on unjust enrichment, restitution, trusts, torts, contracts, and remedies. He is the author of *The Canadian Law of Unjust Enrichment and Restitution* (2014), co-author of *Managing the Law: The Legal Aspects of Doing Business* (2002, 2006, 2010, 2013), *Oosterhoff on Trusts: Text, Commentary and Cases on Trusts* (2004, 2009), *Cases and Materials on the Law of Torts* (2000, 2003, 2007, 2011), and *Cases and Materials on the Law of Restitution* (2004), and editor of *Understanding Unjust Enrichment* (2006) and *Restitution: Developments in Unjust Enrichment* (1996).

Owen Rees is Senior General Counsel with the Department of Justice Canada, where he also served as Deputy Assistant Deputy Attorney General. Previously, he was a partner at Stockwoods LLP and he was the Executive Legal Officer to Chief Justice Beverley McLachlin. Earlier in his career, he was a law clerk to Justice Louis LeBel of the Supreme Court of Canada and was a college lecturer in the University of Oxford. He has taught administrative law at Osgoode Hall Law School and at Queen's University's Faculty of Law.

David Sandomierski joined the Faculty of Law of the University of Western Ontario in 2018 after earning his SJD from the University of

Toronto, where his doctoral dissertation received the Governor General's Academic Gold Medal. He is a former Vanier Scholar, Loran Scholar, and Parliamentary Intern. In 2017–18, he was a Visiting Scholar at Osgoode Hall Law School. He served as law clerk to Chief Justice Beverley McLachlin at the Supreme Court of Canada. At Western Law, he directs the Faculty's Legal Education Seminar Series.

David M. Tanovich is a professor at the Faculty of Law, University of Windsor. He is co-editor of the *Canadian Bar Review*, with Dean Christopher Waters. In 2017, he was inducted as a Fellow of the Royal Society of Canada (Academy of Social Sciences). He teaches and writes in the areas of criminal law, evidence, legal ethics, and racial profiling, and is a nationally recognized expert in these areas. Two of his critically acclaimed works include *The Colour of Justice: Policing Race in Canada* (2006); and "Law's Ambition and the Reconstruction of Role Morality in Canada" (2005) 28 Dalhousie L Rev 267–310.

Index